Arthurian Animation

Arthurian Animation

*A Study of
Cartoon Camelots
on Film and Television*

MICHAEL N. SALDA

McFarland & Company, Inc., Publishers
Jefferson, North Carolina, and London

LIBRARY OF CONGRESS CATALOGUING-IN-PUBLICATION DATA

Salda, Michael Norman, 1957–
Arthurian animation : a study of cartoon Camelots
on film and television / Michael N. Salda.
    p.   cm.
Includes bibliographical references and index.

ISBN 978-0-7864-7468-4
softcover : acid free paper ∞

1. Arthurian romances in motion pictures. 2. Animated films—History and criticism. 3. Arthurian romances—Adaptations—History and criticism. 4. Kings and rulers in motion pictures. 5. Medievalism—History—20th century. 6. Middle Ages in motion pictures. I. Title.
NC1766.5.A78S25 2013   791.43'651—dc23   2013024268

BRITISH LIBRARY CATALOGUING DATA ARE AVAILABLE

© 2013 Michael N. Salda. All rights reserved

*No part of this book may be reproduced or transmitted in any form
or by any means, electronic or mechanical, including photocopying
or recording, or by any information storage and retrieval system,
without permission in writing from the publisher.*

On the cover: Characters from the 1963 animated feature
The Sword in the Stone (Walt Disney Productions/Photofest)

Manufactured in the United States of America

*McFarland & Company, Inc., Publishers
Box 611, Jefferson, North Carolina 28640
www.mcfarlandpub.com*

For Monica, Joel, and Rachel

Table of Contents

Preface   1

Introduction   3

1. The Iris Opens: "Bosko's Knight-Mare"   7
2. The Best Arthurian Cartoon Never Made: Hugh Harman's *King Arthur's Knights*   16
3. "To Ye Jousting Tournament": Arthur's Postwar Rise   36
4. "What's Up, Duke?" Variety in the 1950s and Early 1960s   43
5. *The Sword in the Stone*, a "Full-length Flop," and Arthurianimation's Decline   59
6. The Profane and the Sacred: What Hath Monty Python Wrought?   77
7. Many Returns of the King: The 1980s   85
8. Arthur, Arthur, Everywhere: Short Animation of 1990s   100
9. Four Roads to Camelot: The Feature Film Bumper Crop of 1997–98   131
10. Where Lies Arthur? Arthurianimation Since 2000   151

Coda   175

Chapter Notes   177

Works Cited   189

Index   197

Preface

Seventeen years have passed since Kevin J. Harty (La Salle University), editor of the groundbreaking *Cinema Arthuriana: Essays on Arthurian Film* (1991), casually suggested that I write a study focused on animated works about King Arthur and his court. The present book likely would not exist if not for that first nudge and an invitation to contribute a provisional survey of Arthurian cartoons ("'What's Up, Duke?' A Brief History of Arthurian Animation") to Harty's *King Arthur on Film: New Essays on Arthurian Cinema* (1999). Years of encouragement, introductions, advice, and friendship have followed.

As "Cinema Arthuriana" became increasingly recognized as an area of academic pursuit and Harty followed his first edition with *Cinema Arthuriana: Twenty Essays* (2002), many book-length investigations dedicated in full or in part to Arthurian film began to appear: Rebecca and Samuel Umland's *The Use of Arthurian Legend in Hollywood Film: From Connecticut Yankees to Fisher Kings* (1996), Bert Olton's *Arthurian Legends on Film and Television* (2000), John Aberth's *A Knight at the Movies: Medieval History on Film* (2003), Susan Aronstein's *Hollywood Knights: Arthurian Cinema and the Politics of Nostalgia* (2005), Nickolas Haydock's *Movie Medievalism: The Imaginary Middle Ages* (2008), Kathleen Coyne Kelly and Tyson Pugh's *Queer Movie Medievalisms* (2009), Laurie Finke and Martin Shichtman's *Cinematic Illuminations: The Middle Ages on Film* (2010), Andrew B. R. Elliott's *Remaking the Middle Ages: The Methods of Cinema and History in Portraying the Medieval World* (2011), and more. Scores of essays in collections and journals contributed further insights into Cinema Arthuriana. While animated cartoons were occasionally mentioned in these studies, a comprehensive exploration of Arthurian-themed animation remained to be written. *Arthurian Animation: A Study of Cartoon Camelots on Film and Television* aims to fill this void.

In addition to the debts that all of us owe to Harty's trailblazing efforts, I acknowledge the generous assistance of many others who have also helped along this journey. In 1996, Alan Lupack (University of Rochester) opened his collection of Arthurian cartoons on videotape to me to begin the research. Elizabeth Sklar (emerita of Wayne State University), Bonnie Wheeler (Southern Methodist University), Bert Olton (Palmyra, New York), Michael Torregrossa (Smithfield, Rhode Island), Andrew B. R. Elliott (University of Lincoln), and Stanley Hauer (emeritus of the University of Southern Mississippi) offered invaluable suggestions, materials, wisdom, and ears sympathetic to innumerable trifling matters over the years. Animation historians from across the country—Charles Solomon, Jerry Beck, Steve Stanchfield, Mark Kausler, Michael Barrier,

Preface

and Thad Komorowski—found the time to reply to questions e-mailed from a stranger whom they will likely never meet. Marsha S. Harman (emerita of California State University, Long Beach), daughter-in-law of animator Hugh Harman, and the Harman family graciously allowed me to mine the unpublished materials that form the core of Chapter 2. Nearer home, several chairs, deans, and provosts at the University of Southern Mississippi—most prominently dean of the College of Liberal Arts Glenn T. Harper (emeritus) and chair of the Department of English Michael Mays (now assistant vice chancellor for arts and sciences at Washington State University, Tri-cities)—aided by securing research time and resources to prepare this book for press. Through it all, I've learned that laughing loudly at cartoons with others is much more fun than chuckling quietly alone.

Staff members at the University of Southern Mississippi Libraries also joined in the search for obscure cartoons released long ago. Bridget Reeves and Hugh Donohoe of the Interlibrary Loan unit merit special praise for dogged perseverance. Their diligence located 16mm films and videotapes unlikely to be transferred to digital format at any time in the near future—if ever. This study is the more complete thanks to their efforts.

My family pitched in, too. Son Joel and daughter Rachel grew up watching Dad watch cartoons. Early on they learned to pop a videotape in the VCR quickly when "something Arthurian" seemed to be on the screen. Nickelodeon and Cartoon Network programs have been the topic of many a dinner table conversation. Countless discussions over the years have begun with "Did you see the one where...?" With patience and good humor, my wife Monica has provided unflagging support through her husband's adult-onset juvenescence.

Introduction

In days not so long ago when one could enjoy an animated short cartoon or two before a live-action feature film at the Saturday matinee, theatrical cartoons were widely considered something "extra." They were an extra for the studio that needed to produce them inexpensively in order to maximize profits, extra for the theater manager who wanted to pay the smallest possible fee for the added attractions on the bill, and extra for the patrons who expected to see cartoons but had traveled downtown primarily for the feature. Although the theatrical short[1] has nearly vanished from cineplex screenings today save for rare bounty from deep-pocketed operations such as Disney and Warner Bros. and much of the animation that remains is destined for children's television shows, financial considerations reign as strongly as ever. Cartoons are now frequently designed from the outset to induce young viewers and their parents to purchase both spin-off merchandise (DVDs, toys, costumes, books, and games) and unrelated licensed products (cereal, candy, and fast-food meals) relentlessly hawked during thirty-second television spots. While such commercialism does not necessarily mean that yesterday's or today's animated works lack artistic quality, it does suggest that cartoons have long followed the money.

Animation dealing with Arthurian topics likewise obeys fundamental principles of a market economy. Cartoons with Arthurian characters, motifs, and themes— *Arthurianimation*, for short—debut most often when contemporaneous popular books, films, plays, music, and other cartoons about the legendary king and his court have already paved a path for their arrival. When King Arthur is topical and "in the air," Arthurian cartoons will inevitably be produced. Yet in contrast to many live-action Round Table feature films that trace their roots—as opening title sequences and closing credits commonly albeit usually inaccurately assert—to *medieval* literary classics such as Sir Thomas Malory's *Le Morte Darthur*, cartoons typically boast a pedigree that runs no farther than a fashionable *modern* retelling of the legend. Thus, from one limited perspective, Arthurianimation might be deemed a derivative, coattail-riding phenomenon.

From a broader perspective, however, Arthurianimation provides an important gauge of the modern reception and dissemination of the legend. Arthurian cartoons join a chaotic mass and pop culture panoply that bears witness to the use and abuse of illustrious names and ideas that we typically associate with Camelot. A trip to the local mall, for instance, reveals clothing, shoes, computer software, cleaning products, jewelry, perfume, food, tools, flatware, furniture, dolls, and even bathroom fixtures whose

Introduction

quality and desirability are conveyed via coded (and at times surely ironic) Arthurian associations: Excalibur knives, "Sir Lancelot's Armor" cell phone screen protectors, King Arthur flour, Guinevere bedsheets, Isolde sandals, Merlin welding torches, "Holey Galahad" perforated grinding wheels, and so on.[2] A cursory search of Amazon.com's non-media categories uncovers yet more deals to tempt the consumer: hundreds of products with Arthurian monikers listed under Apparel, Automotive, Baby, Beauty, Cell Phones & Service, Electronics, Gourmet Food, Grocery, Health & Personal Care, Home & Garden, Home Improvement, Industrial & Scientific, Jewelry, Musical Instruments, Office Products, Software, Sports & Outdoors, Toys & Games, Video Games, Watches, and Everything Else.[3]

In this jumble of "Arthurian" products, cartoons hold a unique place. Whether we like it or not, most children today initially encounter the Arthurian kingdom not through the lofty words of Malory or Tennyson but in the antics of Bugs Bunny and SpongeBob SquarePants.[4] This animated introduction to an enduring legend is confused at best. Children learn a fractured narrative, one scattered haphazardly through many animated shorts broadcast 24/7 on network and cable television channels, longer features available at retail outlets and via on-demand video streaming, and excerpts and remixes from both short and long cartoons posted to the Internet by Arthurian enthusiasts. Further, not only is this animated Arthurian legend fragmented and its parts presented with little regard for chronological, historical, or logical order, usually its characters and themes are deployed for overtly comic purposes. As a consequence, young people may well think that a cartoon anvil dropped from the sky deserves a second look — because while it could crush the Road Runner, it might also have Excalibur lodged in it. Animation's playful amalgamation of disparate elements considerably widens the field of expectations and possibilities. These same children then often grow to college age with a rather muddled idea of traditional Arthurian narratives and a grasp of "the facts" — as anyone who has ever taught undergraduates can confirm at the start of any semester — that runs little deeper than "Merlin was a magician," "Morgan le Fey was an evil sorceress," "Launcelot and Guinevere loved each other," and "Mordred was a bad guy."[5] While these rudiments give the class a place to start, there remains a long road of discovery ahead in the next fifteen weeks.

Cartoons did not originally target, however, an audience solely of youngsters. Instead, cartoons aimed to amuse people of all ages as they waited for the day's feature attraction to appear on the theater screen. The juvenilization of cartoons came later.[6] Nor was the Arthurian legend itself composed with children in mind. One does not need to consider the core narratives deeply or for long before the adult topics of lust, incest, adultery, rape, and parricide rise to the surface. In the abstract, creating Arthurianimation from such bristly material may thus seem a nearly impossible task. How might one create funny, family-friendly, animated productions that draw on the legend and simultaneously avoid its taboo landmines? Yet as the existence of well over 170 short cartoons, feature-length cartoons, and animated series amply demonstrates, many writers and animators have tried and more will in years to come. At times the makers of Arthurianimation have run — and often succumbed to — the risks inherent in the

Introduction

enterprise by abridging, bowdlerizing, and dumbing-down the legend almost beyond recognition. At other times, sufficient detail from the old tales remains to make for an entertaining and sometimes even educational romp through touchstones variously acquired in youth.

The present study traces the development of Arthurianimation from its beginning in 1933 to the present.[7] We shall see that the premiere of an Arthurian cartoon regularly relies in large measure on whether the Arthurian legend is in vogue. Animators are openly opportunistic, drawing their inspiration from trends of the day. And given that through the 1950s these cartoons were generally produced to be screened in theaters—a fact often too quickly overlooked in the age of television and the World Wide Web—it should come as small surprise that there exist symbiotic relationships between the live-action feature film and the theatrical cartoon that served as appetizer for the matinee's main course. We shall also witness the legend's remarkable pliability as animators cut, mold, stretch, and twist it far beyond its original contours to serve new needs, messages, politics, mores, and beliefs—just as every generation has remade the Arthurian narrative in its own image since the story was first shared. Arthurianimation represents one of the most recent developments in the legend's ongoing evolution.

Because the earliest cartoons are rarely seen and many of the materials relating to them are in private hands or difficult to obtain, Chapters 1 and 2 rely on critical "thick description" to document and analyze the origins of Arthurianimation in the 1930s and early 1940s. The critical method then shifts for cartoons discussed in subsequent chapters, because postwar cartoons are generally more readily available than earlier ones. Chapter 3 considers the first tentative steps into the Arthurian realm by Bugs Bunny, Popeye, Crusader Rabbit, and others in theatrical shorts made after World War II and in television's early years. The survey continues in Chapter 4 with the introduction of CinemaScope to live-action film in 1953, which brought as many changes to the Arthurian cartoon as it did to the theatrical feature films and television shows inspiring the animators of the day. Chapter 5 examines the first animated feature-length Arthurian film to arrive in theaters, Disney's 1963 *The Sword in the Stone*, followed by a comparatively stagnant period in the production of Arthurian-themed cartoons as the king and his court fell for a time from popular fashion. But then *Monty Python and the Holy Grail* reinvigorated Arthurianimation in the mid–1970s, giving license to a new generation of writers and animators, discussed in Chapter 6, to caricature the realm and its ideals more hilariously than ever before and to express an unprecedented reverence for the legend—sometimes doing both in the very same cartoon. Chapters 7 and 8 investigate the unfettered development of Arthurianimation in the 1980s and 1990s, as cartoons pushed the legend to extremes and explored novel ways both to laugh at the Arthurian kingdom and to honor its continuing relevance. A crescendo could be heard in 1997 and 1998, the subject of Chapter 9, with the near-simultaneous release of no fewer than four Arthurianimation feature films. Chapter 10 explores the present diversity of Arthurian cartoon series, feature films, isolated television episodes, and shorts since 2000—a healthy crop that bodes well for Arthurian-

Introduction

imation's future. With Arthurian cartoons[8] spanning eighty years before us, it is perhaps fitting to recall the words of William Caxton, first publisher of *Le Morte Darthur*, as he inventories and advertises for readers the riches to come: "noble actes, feates of armes of chyualrye, prowesse, hardynesse, humanyte, loue, curtosye, and veray gentylnesse, wyth many wonderful hystoryes and aduentures"—and, let us not forget, anvils.

CHAPTER 1

The Iris Opens: "Bosko's Knight-Mare"

Few today remember Bosko the Talk-Ink Kid, the first bona fide cartoon star from Warner Bros. In part Bosko has quietly faded from memory along with many other animated characters of the early sound era. Who can recall contemporaneous figures such as Cubby Bear, Flip the Frog, or Goopy Geer? But Bosko has also been suppressed because of his racial depiction, which evolved from an intermittently Southern-twanged inkblot character of indeterminate maturity and racial background in his initial years at Warner Bros. from 1930 to 1933 to a clearly defined, fully stereotyped, African American boy in his final years at MGM from 1934 to 1938. Although Nickelodeon in the late 1980s and early 1990s ventured to air in late-night timeslots many of the thirty-nine largely unobjectionable Warner Bros. Bosko shorts and even a few deeply edited portions of the nine MGM Boskos, today a television appearance by Bosko is a rare event. When Bosko does appear, the cartoons have been vigilantly pruned to remove scenes that might offend contemporary audiences.

Among the many mostly forgotten Boskos is Warner's 1933 production of "Bosko's Knight-Mare," a cartoon that holds special significance for followers of the Arthurian legend because it appears to be the first animated cartoon to enter King Arthur's realm. "Bosko's Knight-Mare" employs a range of Arthurian touchstones that an audience of the 1930s would likely have recognized as "Arthurian": a narrative structure borrowed from Mark Twain's *A Connecticut Yankee in King Arthur's Court* (via a highly profitable 1931 film adaptation), a visual nod to a popular Arthurian juvenile book of the day, and musical cues that underscore the idea of chivalric endeavor. King Arthur was "in the air" in the early 1930s and "Bosko's Knight-Mare" aimed to capitalize on his popularity.

Because "Bosko's Knight-Mare" is not commercially available, an extended summary is necessary.[1] The iris opens on a shadowy room illuminated by the glow of a fireplace and candles. Bosko happily rocks in a chair and reads a book. Visible through his parlor window, a storm distorts the nighttime sky. Bosko's dog Bruno naps, wakes long enough to kill a flea, and falls asleep again. While Bruno snores uncaringly, Bosko excitedly reads to him from an illustrated edition of a book entitled *King Arthur's Knights*: "Oh boy! Listen Bruno. 'And then the bold, brave knight....' Oh boy, oh boy, oh boy!" Bruno stirs only for the amount of time it takes to blow a raspberry, clearly unmoved by his master's enthusiasm for Arthuriana.

The camera pans left to reveal a console radio as an announcer loudly reports that it is eight o'clock. Bosko spins the dial in search of something to accompany his reading. He finds it on a station where a booming baritone sings a popular nineteenth-century, round-the-piano ballad: Edwin Thomas and Stephen Adams's "A Warrior Bold," the story of a knight whose pledge to live — or die — in service to his beloved leads ultimately (in the original ballad's second stanza) to the knight's tragic yet triumphant death. The first stanza is just getting underway as Bosko listens, reads, and rocks himself to sleep.

Bosko begins to dream. A cross-fade moves from a 1930s parlor to a forest. A shining-armored and singing Bosko (a tenor) rides a caparisoned white steed modeled after the one he just saw in an illustration to *King Arthur's Knights*.

Bosko reads from *King Arthur's Knights* in "Bosko's Knight-Mare" (Warner Bros., 1933).

Bosko finishes a few lines of "A Warrior Bold," begins to whistle, changes tempo, and launches into "Young and Healthy" from Warner's *42nd Street* (1933) as he prances toward a moated castle. Bruno, accompanying his master into the dream and now armed as well with articulated plate armor on his back and a helmet, cavorts in the rear.

Near the castle, Bosko dismounts by using his lance to pole-vault from the horse, dances a few steps at moat's edge, then calls to the drawbridge with the sound of creaking wood — speaking "drawbridge," it would seem. Down comes the bridge, up rises a portcullis, and gates swing open. Three trumpeters emerge from the castle and strain a sennet until their visors come crashing down on their horns. When they resume playing with their newly abbreviated instruments, they can blow only a weak, reedy version of the greeting. Bosko and Bruno rumba their way across the bridge to the tune of "The Peanut Vendor." Bosko twice cries "Peanuts!" before ending his dance with a snappy "Shave and a Haircut" tap. A hatch opens from the seat of Bosko's armor, allowing him to pop out the rear and run into the main hall.

Eight knights in full armor, visors lowered, sit about a round table. They drink convivially from gallon-sized steins. A black letter–like inscription on the wall reveals that Bosko has come to the home of the "KNIGHTS of the ROUND TABLE." He salutes them with a Cab Calloway–inspired call-and-response "Hi-dee hi!" and "Ho-dee ho!" that rapidly disintegrates into laughter, toasting, and dancing. A reworked stanza of "A Warrior Bold" rises, now as a communal drinking song. Knights raise their visors — or Bosko lifts their helms — to reveal an unexpected congregation of chivalry: the four Marx Brothers, Ed Wynn, Jimmy Durante, Mahatma Gandhi,[2] and Oliver Hardy

1. *The Iris Opens*

(prompting Bosko to transform briefly to Stan Laurel and Hardy to slap him in response). The knights sing a bit more (in the style of Gilbert and Sullivan) about their willingness, as "the captains of the guard," to continue drinking. Then comes Bosko's almost obligatory vaudeville number. This time, Bosko, armed knights, and unoccupied armor tap dance to "42nd Street"—the title melody from *42nd Street*.

With the cartoon more than halfway to its end, the writers must have thought it time to add some conflict to the story. Conflict arrives indeed in the form of a large, hirsute knight in dark armor—a Black Knight, though the cartoon gives him no name. This villain has amorous plans for Honey (Bosko's love interest in other cartoons though not yet introduced here). The Black Knight rides along, singing (as a bass, again à la Gilbert and Sullivan) about his chance of winning Honey's heart. "I know my ways will charm her," he croons confidently. He arrives at the foot of a tower. The camera tilts to a chamber at the top. Honey appears at a window. Her mood quickly darkens to anger when she sees the unwanted suitor below. "Pooh, I don't like that old meanie," she complains. Undeterred, the Black Knight bites the lock off the door, enters the tower, and starts up the stairs. Honey cries, "Woe is me!" and "Help!" Will her boyfriend and protector (Bosko's portrait hangs on Honey's wall) arrive in time?

Still dancing to "42nd Street," Bosko hears Honey's plea. He dashes from the main hall and catches up with the suit of armor that has already started sprinting—without Bosko—toward the tower. An aerial view reveals that the tower adjoins the *same* castle where Bosko has been all this time. Bosko runs the tower stairs. He overtakes the slower Black Knight along the way and confronts his foe at the top of the flight. Bosko's "Stop, you mug!" does nothing to slow the villain. The Black Knight rudely employs the small hero's own armor against him as he uses Bosko's visor to trim the end of a cigar, "clicks" the entire suit of armor as if it were a lighter to ignite his *gigante*, and then blows smoke into the armor before stepping into Honey's room. The villain grabs Honey and leaps out the tower's window, landing so hard that he creates a hole from which his horse must drag him. He gallops off with the shrieking prize tucked under his arm. Bosko follows astride a braying donkey that throws him at the edge of a lake. Bosko's armor morphs to a submarine to bear the hero through the water.

To the accompaniment of Honey's many screams of "Bosko, help!" the pursuit continues into the kidnapper's castle. An anthropomorphized drawbridge (tongue) and castle gate (mouth and teeth) "swallow" Bosko inside. Meanwhile, the Black Knight carries Honey to a cobwebbed bedchamber bestrewn with empty liquor bottles.[3] He tosses his unconscious captive on the bed and secures the door, not realizing that the armorless Bosko[4] has inexplicably passed the villain to the top of the stairs again and already lies hidden within the chamber. From under the bed, the hero empties a machine gun into the villain's backside. The enraged Black Knight turns, rolls up his sleeve (to the sound effect of opening a tin can), and punches Bosko in the face. Bosko sails across the room, his posterior pricked by a row of spears, and smashes head first into the bed with a "Ding!" that rouses Honey. She tries to wake the unconscious, snoring Bosko by stroking his cheek.

A cross-fade returns us from the Middle Ages to the present day and out of the dream. Bosko lies prone in front of his rocker and Bruno licks his face. A serene, moonlit sky outside the window indicates that the storm has passed. Bosko wakes. He realizes that he is being comforted not by his love's touch but by a hound's tongue. Bosko punches Bruno's snout.

Bosko staggers sleepily to the left, beyond the radio and past Honey's portrait on the wall, as the camera pans through the flat. Bosko comes to a suit of armor similar in size, shape, and style to the one worn by the Black Knight in the dream. Bosko seizes the armor's large battle-axe and strikes the empty suit, pulverizing it into a pile of tin cans. A buoyant Bosko now skips, sings "Let's Put Out the Lights and Go to Sleep" (a strain woven into the musical fabric softly at the beginning and now, more distinctly, end of the cartoon), and leaps on a Murphy bed. The bed snaps into the wall to reveal a chamber pot on the floor. As daylight streams through a side window, the iris closes on the chamber pot.[5]

On initial view, little manifestly *Arthurian* appears in this early Arthurian cartoon. Despite the explicit textual indicators provided by Bosko's reading material (*King Arthur's Knights*) and the wall inscription (KNIGHTS of the ROUND TABLE), one might wonder whether without these clumsy pointers anyone would think "Bosko's Knight-Mare" an *Arthurian* cartoon. After all, the short features no King Arthur and none of his usual knights or ladies. Indeed, without the labels that literally *tell* the audience that it has entered Arthur's realm, the cartoon seems to be just another of many shorts in which Bosko proves his love for Honey, this time in a medieval setting.[6]

Yet those textual indicators hold more meaning than might be supposed. Although the inscription is obviously too common a phrase to be traced to any particular source, Bosko's book appears to be modeled after Henry Gilbert's identically titled *King Arthur's Knights* (subtitled *The Tales Re-told for Boys and Girls*) first published by T. C. and E. C. Jack (Edinburgh) in 1911, with sixteen watercolor illustrations by Walter Crane, and then reprinted many times in less expensive editions in the years leading up to "Bosko's Knight-Mare."[7] The frequent reissue of Gilbert's simplified retelling of tales drawn from Malory's *Le Morte Darthur* (and, to a much lesser extent, *The Mabinogion*) was only one sign of a larger Arthurian resurgence in the late 1920s and early 1930s. These years witnessed the burgeoning popularity of the Round Table on several fronts: the publication of Arthurian literary works by Edwin Arlington Robinson (1927), John Masefield (1927), John Erskine (1926, 1932), Charles Williams (1930), and John Cowper Powys (1932); a long-running musical stage adaptation of *A Connecticut Yankee* by Rodgers and Hart (1927–28, 1929); and a film version of *A Connecticut Yankee* (1931). The animators of "Bosko's Knight-Mare" probably had Gilbert's *King Arthur's Knights* in mind if not immediately in hand as they drew the hero's bedtime reading. Both Gilbert's and Bosko's books bear "KING ARTHUR'S KNIGHTS" as the running head on the verso, both are similarly illustrated, and even in such details as shield decorations and the horse's ornamental trappings the animators appear to be taking cues from Crane's watercolors that accompanied Gilbert's text in the 1911 original and some of the more expensive reprint editions of the 1920s and 1930s.[8]

Admittedly, very few in the audience likely recognized an homage to Gilbert and

1. The Iris Opens

"Beaumains Wins the Fight at the Ford," Walter Crane watercolor from Henry Gilbert's *King Arthur's Knights* (1911).

Crane in the few seconds that Bosko's book flashes on the screen. However, any frequent moviegoer of the day would surely have thought "Bosko's Knight-Mare" an *Arthurian* cartoon because of its many parallels to 1931's *A Connecticut Yankee*, a Fox box-office hit starring Will Rogers (the Boss), Myrna Loy (Morgan), and Maureen O'Sullivan (Sandy). What happened to Hank Martin—as the Fox film renames the Boss, whom Twain had pointedly called Hank *Morgan*—plays out again for Bosko in one frame after another, and in nearly the same order. The following elements appear in both the 1931 feature film and 1933 cartoon: a stormy night, a shadowy room, a radio tuned to a program about knights, a suit of armor standing in the room (not seen until the end in the cartoon), the passage of our hero from present to past, a dark-haired and mustached villain, a damsel to be rescued, the hero's use of twentieth-century technology to fight the villain, the hero's return to the present just as he has *lost* the battle, and the intrusion of the dream's medieval elements (the Black Knight's armor and perhaps the chamber pot, too) into reality at the end to make us wonder about the permeable boundaries between sleep and waking, past and present, illusion and reality.

At times the cartoon adopts the same kinds of technological innovations that the 1931 film introduced into Twain's storyline. A machine gun replaces the novel's six-shooter in a contest between the hero from the future and a medieval opponent. A cutting-edge, twentieth-century mechanical lighter replaces Twain's equally cutting-edge, nineteenth-century safety matches—though of "Bosko's Knight-Mare" it must be remarked that Bosko *becomes* the lighter and the technology is then used *against* him.[9] At other times the technological updates logically extend the contemporizing mindset that the Fox film employed. Bosko uses a submarine in pursuit of the Black Knight, a development likely inspired by *A Connecticut Yankee*'s state-of-the-art planes and helicopters that Hank Martin's men bring to their final battle against Sagramore, Merlin, and Morgan.

Even the cartoon's visual layout appears at points influenced by the Fox film, especially in its use of analogous cross-fades to move the audience from dream and the Middle Ages to reality and the present. In Hank Martin's final moments in Camelot, a castle wall falls from the right to bury him. The moment introduces a visual transition back to the present, where we find Hank on the floor, pinned under a suit of armor that has fallen on him from the right. In a similar way, Bosko's transition from dreaming to waking cross-fades from Honey stroking the downed hero's cheek to Bruno licking the face of the weary reader who has tumbled from his rocker to the floor. These narrative and visual similarities suggest that the animators drew much from the familiar well of 1931's *A Connecticut Yankee*, and in doing so counted on their audience to grasp the distinctly referential Arthurian touchstones embedded throughout "Bosko's Knight-Mare."

"Bosko's Knight-Mare" does not, however, slavishly follow the 1931 feature film for all of its Twain-inspired details. For example, Bosko's transition from present to past differs from the way both Twain depicted it in the novel's prefatory "A Word of Explanation"—an account of the argument that ends with a crowbar to Hank Morgan's head—and the 1931 film's accident of storm-blown drapery and a toppling suit of armor

1. The Iris Opens

that knocks Hank Martin to the floor. The cartoon takes yet a third tack by gently effecting the passage with a dream vision induced by the day residue of a radio program (as also in the 1931 film) and the book that Bosko has been reading, *King Arthur's Knights*. Bosko's poring over a text of medieval adventure in the frame story looks back to Twain's original—with the copy of *Le Morte Darthur* that Twain's frame narrator has been reading and the old manuscript that the Yankee stranger gives him. Or possibly the animators reach back to another feature film treatment of Twain's novel, Fox's 1920 *A Connecticut Yankee at King Arthur's Court*, in which the Boss character, there named Martin Cavendish, also has been reading "a book about chivalry" in the frame narrative (Harty, *Reel* 54).[10] Yet one more important example of the cartoon's independence from the 1931 film might be added: "Bosko's Knight-Mare" rejects the 1931 film's love story in which Hank rescues Sandy not for himself but for Clarence, a court page who will initiate a line of descendants that leads ultimately to Hank in the twentieth century. On this point, the cartoon follows the lead of either Twain's novel or the 1920 film in which the hero rescues the distressed maiden for *himself*.

While Warner Bros. assuredly had no interest in promoting a rival studio's films through the release of "Bosko's Knight-Mare," it did employ the cartoon's musical score to advance Warner's own feature productions. In fact Warner animators were contractually obligated to include in their work music owned by the studio.[11] The cartoon's score subliminally—if not brazenly—aimed to remind the audience of Warner's films that used the *same* tunes, thus helping fuel sales of tickets, sheet music, performance licenses, and recordings from subsidiaries controlled by the growing media conglomerate. Bosko dances to "42nd Street" and "Young and Healthy," for instance, not because those songs are intimately tied to the themes of "Bosko's Knight-Mare" but because Warner's *42nd Street* featured those tunes and had been released in February 1933, only a few months before "Bosko's Knight-Mare" premiered.[12] The studio and its ancillaries also owned the sheet music rights to "Let's Put Out the Lights and Go to Sleep," which Rudy Vallee had taken to number 2 on the pop charts in 1932, and Warner Bros. apparently had an interest as well in promoting the number 1 rumba hit from 1931, Don Azpiazu's "The Peanut Vendor." Given that Bosko falls asleep near the start of the cartoon and then jumps into bed at the end, "Let's Put Out the Lights and Go to Sleep" fits the scenario well. "Young and Healthy" is arguably an appropriate (albeit unfocused) tune to accent Bosko's bubbly spirit as he prances toward the castle. Defending the narrative or aesthetic fitness of "42nd Street" and Bosko's "The Peanut Vendor" rumba across the drawbridge, however, may be an impossible task.

"A Warrior Bold," the Thomas/Adams ballad of a knight who fights and dies with his lady foremost in his thoughts, is the sole musical number in "Bosko's Knight-Mare" that directly reinforces the chivalric themes of a cartoon in which Bosko battles a knight to defend his beloved and, in the dream at least, loses to his enemy.[13] Both the original ballad and cartoon's radio program rendition of it open the song identically with four lines about the days when barons governed and bold knights fought and sang of their adventures. In the Thomas/Adams ballad, the knight later dies on the battlefield, yet expires secure in the knowledge that he has kept a pledge to honor his love by fighting valiantly in her name until his last breath. The ballad's second stanza paints the knight's death in bloody detail.

Bosko's upbeat cartoon naturally must eschew this bleak conclusion. As Bosko moves into a second stanza, he shifts to first-person and then begins to scat: "I like to fight, in this armor bright—/ Sing merrily my lay—/ What-dut-ta-dut, to-doot-do-doot-do, buh-buh-buh-bum."[14] Bosko's happy singing thus replaces the ballad's death scene. And yet "A Warrior Bold"—even in Bosko's abridged and elided performance of it—complements the cartoon's medieval subject matter better than do show tunes from *42nd Street*. A corporate link between "A Warrior Bold" and Warner's music holdings remains unclear, though the sheet music was widely printed by many publishers in the early part of the century and perhaps was considered in the public domain by 1933.

I have delayed until now direct discussion of the directors, writers, principal animators, and musical director behind "Bosko's Knight-Mare." Who were these men who first animated the Round Table and its knights? It is difficult topic and mired in red herrings. Let us begin with the screen credits: "Bosko's Knight-Mare" is a "Hugh Harman–Rudolf Ising Production," "Drawn by Bob McKimson [and] Robert Stokes," with "Musical Score by Frank Marsales." Additionally, Leon Schlesinger is listed below Harman and Ising as "Producer" on the title frame. Transparent enough, it would appear. Schlesinger, as producer, held a contract with Warner Bros. to supply the studio with cartoons. He subcontracted the animation work to Harman and Ising. As heads of the animation team, Harman and Ising wrote and directed "Bosko's Knight-Mare," constructed a storyboard, composed dialogue for the voice talent, consulted with musical supervisor Marsales throughout the process to incorporate the songs that Warner Bros. wanted to promote, and drew several dozen to hundreds of illustrations to serve as rough guides for McKimson, Stokes, and lower-ranking in-betweeners who in turn made thousands of intermediate drawings and then inked and painted the cels needed to flesh out Harman and Ising's vision.

Or so it might seem. In a misguided attempt to create a uniform product, Schlesinger imposed a strict system of "rotating credits" on Harman and Ising. The producer mandated that exactly *two* animators' names appear on every cartoon, regardless of how many people or even who in fact worked on it. Sometimes the names listed are accurate; at other times, they are not; often it cannot be precisely determined who did what in a busy studio atmosphere that enjoyed, by all accounts, a hazy division of labor. To cast further doubt on the accuracy of the opening credits, it is even unlikely that Harman and Ising collaborated much (if at all) on "Bosko's Knight-Mare." Around 1932, Harman became the principal writer/director of the Looney Tunes series (of which Bosko was the star property), while Ising turned his attention increasingly to Warner's spin-off Merrie Melodies series. Only two names thus remain uncontested: Marsales, the musical supervisor, and Schlesinger, who had little to do with "Bosko's Knight-Mare" beyond signing paychecks and leaving behind an intractable bibliographic tangle.[15]

"Bosko's Knight-Mare" is an admittedly slight entry in the annals of Arthuriani-

1. The Iris Opens

mation, yet it is the start of something bigger. Bosko's happy medieval adventure reveals nascent patterns that reappear in many Arthurian cartoons to come. Twain's sometimes-comic novel and its invariably comic feature film derivatives provide animators rich materials for further exploitation. The dream vision frame, the hero's reading of a book that leads to a journey through time, and the humorous juxtaposition of past and present will be animated again and again. Some recipes are so successful that they must be reprised.

CHAPTER 2

The Best Arthurian Cartoon Never Made: Hugh Harman's *King Arthur's Knights*

Disagreements with Schlesinger over budgets led Harman, Ising, and many of their crew to abandon the Schlesinger/Warner Bros. arrangement and begin making cartoons for MGM in 1934. In their first cartoon for MGM, "Bosko's Parlor Pranks" (1934), Harman and Ising reused several segments from earlier Warner Bros. cartoons in what amounts to a loosely connected series of stories that Bosko—still an indeterminate inkblot character and not yet an African American boy[1]—introduces to try to entertain a cranky child (Wilbur). Roughly thirty seconds of "Bosko's Parlor Pranks" derives unabashedly from opening scenes of "Bosko's Knight-Mare." In the two-color Technicolor process that MGM's bigger budgets afforded, Harman and Ising recycle scenes that show the book titled *King Arthur's Knights*, Bosko riding through the woods as a knight, and Bruno in armor following behind him. There is no Arthurian story in "Bosko's Parlor Pranks." In fact, there is little story at all. Harman and Ising appear to have included this knight-in-armor segment from "Bosko's Knight-Mare" in "Bosko's Parlor Pranks" to showcase the work of which they were most proud at the time. Of course, they also saved themselves time and money by reusing materials already in hand as they hurried to deliver the first reel to their new employers.

Harman remained with MGM under changing contractual agreements until early 1941 when he decided to launch a new animation studio, Hugh Harman Productions.[2] His partner in the start-up venture was longtime Disney employee Mel Shaw, who had recently left the Disney studio during one of the many Hollywood animators' strikes and lockouts of the day. Harman and Shaw took advantage of the volatile employment environment to raid their established rivals' studios for artists, writers, and technicians with whom they had previously worked. With a small coterie of seasoned veterans[3] and eager, talented up-and-comers, Harman and Shaw set about the task of creating the fledgling studio's first major production, a feature-length animated film about King Arthur.

Using materials gathered in interviews with Shaw and Ising, Charles Solomon in 1994 published the first tantalizing account of this film in *Enchanted Drawings*. According to Solomon, "a feature based on the legend of King Arthur" was begun but never "progressed beyond the storyboard stage" (120, 122). Planning and production were delayed as America entered World War II at the end of 1941 and the entire country—

2. The Best Arthurian Cartoon Never Made

King Arthur (?), by R. G. S., for Harman's *King Arthur's Knights* (detail from a photograph in the author's collection).

Hollywood animators included — turned energies to the war effort. Although Harman Productions attempted to resume work on the project after the war, the film never materialized.[4]

A few years after Solomon's study was published, another brief yet deeply intriguing remark about the unfinished movie appeared in Michael Barrier's 1999 *Hollywood Cartoons*. Barrier quotes from an interview with Harman's colleague Robert Stokes in which he recalled Harman's "intense desire" in the late 1930s to compete with Disney by making a feature-length film on the subject of King Arthur (192). Also in 1999, in an exploratory essay ("'What's Up, Duke?'") that had already gone to press by the time that Barrier's study reached my desk, I referenced Solomon's 1994 account and imagined what "a feature based on the legend of King Arthur" might have been had it come to fruition. I suggested that Harman and Shaw could have been interested in an Arthurian project in the early months of 1941 because Shaw knew that his former employer was planning the June release of *The Reluctant Dragon*, a film whose titular segment touches on medieval and chivalric themes. If Disney's film succeeded, Harman and Shaw might well have reasoned, they could capitalize on his success with their own knights-in-armor fare. But when *The Reluctant Dragon* met with a weak response at the box office,[5] it must have added to reasons that Harman Productions was unable to secure financial support to continue work on the feature. My speculation ended there.

Further inquiry into the nature of the unfinished project itself would require additional evidence, materials of which I was unaware when writing "'What's Up, Duke?'": Harman's working papers for the King Arthur film. Copies of these invaluable documents have since been provided to me by animator/animation historian Mark Kausler, the custodian of Harman's papers.[6] These working papers allow us a glimpse into Harman Productions as the first animated Arthurian feature film began to take shape.

Two different typescripts of a story treatment survive: a sixteen-page "Revised Rough Story Line" dated 11 April 1941 and a 27-page "Second Revised Story Line" dated 17 April 1941. The second typescript is also prefaced by three unnumbered pages (title page, foreword, and cast of characters) and followed by three additional unnumbered pages of "ADDENDA AND RE-REVISIONS" and "SONG SEQUENCES" dated 23 April 1941. Logically, there must have also existed at minimum a still earlier *unrevised* "Rough Story Line," which has not survived, and, as we will see, yet another treatment prepared after the Second Revised Story Line and its addenda.

The Revised Rough Story Line appears to be an in-house document designed for an inner circle at Harman Productions. It lacks a proper title page, formal sequence/scene and paragraph numbers, prefatory materials, and the "copyright registered" notice found in the much more polished Second Revised Story Line. Only the latter would be considered suitable for showing to prospective investors and other interested parties. Yet even the Second Revised Story Line remains very much a work-in-progress. While it outlines the overall narrative flow of the film and divides the action into twenty-two sequences lettered A through V — with each of these sequences containing from two to twenty-two numbered paragraphs — many details remain to be fleshed out. As many tacked-on addenda entries bear witness, scenes continue to be fine-tuned; animators would require significantly more direction than the Second Revised Story Line offers to transform the text into images; and fewer than a dozen brief patches of dialogue were written as of 23 April 1941.

The two treatments also reveal an evolving title for the project. Although originally registered for copyright as "The Knight and the Lady," both typescripts employ a working title of "The Knights of the Round Table." And the title continued to change. Photographs of several sketches prepared sometime later than the two extant April 1941 treatments refer to the production as "King Arthur's Knights." (These photographs will be discussed below.) Of these three potential titles for the film, the copyright registration of "The Knight and the Lady" arguably comes closest to capturing the project's essence; however, "The Knight and the Lady" also lacks the explicit *Arthurian* dimensions offered by either "The Knights of the Round Table" or "King Arthur's Knights." As the production developed, Harman seems to have realized that a title *directly* referencing the Arthurian legend — and then directly *naming* the monarch himself — would make a better marquee draw than the cloudy medieval label under which the story treatment was first registered. Thus the third title, *King Arthur's Knights*, is the one adopted here, because it best represents Harman's final intention to the extent that it can be determined.

Harman and Robert Edmunds share story credit on the title page of the Second Revised Story Line, but the actual composition of both treatments probably fell chiefly to Edmunds, head of the new studio's story department. Traces of Britain-born and -raised Edmunds's writing emerge throughout the documents. These touches range from habitual British spellings such as "favour" and "armour" to English locutions that Harman, reared in Colorado and Missouri, likely would not have employed: a crystal ball is interchangeably called a "crystal" and a "glass"; a knight "kneels in fealty" before the king; a character sings to "the rhythm of the smithies" or "humbles himself" before another or is "besieged with general servility and obsequiousness." Likewise, it seems improbable that an American in 1941 would readily refer to Britain as an "Empire" (as the story treatment does), though it could certainly be expected of a subject of His Majesty George VI. Edmunds is also plausibly the primary hand behind the Second Revised Story Line's conclusion, a diaphanously veiled nationalistic tribute to a country already engaged in war with Germany in April 1941. How else can one explain Merlin's concluding proclamation of victory over invaders from across the Channel with a yet-unwritten speech that the story treatment promises will stress "that it is men such as these courageous Knights who will prove to be the foundation of an even greater England. It [the speech] plays up the theme 'There will always be an England'" (V4)?[7]

The foreword provides a summary introduction for potential sponsors and others coming to the project for the first time:

> In the following original adaptation of the Story of King Arthur and his Knights of the Round Table, care has been taken to retain as much of the authentic Arthurian data as possible.
>
> The characters and incidents are, for the most part, true to the legends, but wherever license has been taken it has been done in order to develop a more attractive and colorful presentation.
>
> This treatment is essentially a cartoon fantasy, embodying all the necessary ingredients for general appeal.
>
> Adventure, charm and broad humor are set in an era when romantic chivalry was in flower.
>
> There is plentiful action and suspense throughout the story, which lends itself naturally to the introduction of musical numbers.
>
> Each character has a strong individual personality which is developed with the progression of the story.

In brief, the implicit goal is a film to rival any Disney picture of the day. Harman and Edmunds occasionally show their intent candidly as they stir recollections of 1937's *Snow White and the Seven Dwarfs* in a note that reminds the production team to "build up the charm" of the female lead's "true character" by "establish[ing] her affinity with the woodland birds and animals, this sequence to be played up whimsically" (I3 addendum). A broader theatrical context rumbles through the Second Revised Story Line in similar telegraphic instructions for animators to portray the hero engaged in a sword fight "à la Fairbanks" (B18) and to depict an old lady-in-waiting as an "Edna Mae Oliver type" (I3), a venerable character actress who had recently played a memorably dour Lady Catherine de Bourgh in *Pride and Prejudice* (1940). Just as "Bosko's Knight-Mare" sought to capitalize on the success of Fox's *A Connecticut Yankee* and non–Arthurian Warner Bros. pictures such as *42nd Street*, so with much more at stake for the young studio, Harman Productions hoped to create a full-length animated Arthurian film actively engaged in a dialogue with many contemporaneous theatrical releases.

According to the foreword, *King Arthur's Knights* explicitly aims both to draw from unspecified sources of "authentic Arthurian data" and, as needed to make "a more attractive and colorful presentation," to depart from that authentic tradition. The one-page cast of characters in the Second Revised Story Line exposes this dual agenda. On the one side, famous names of old:

KING ARTHUR	Just and rightful King of England.
Guinevere	Arthur's Queen.
Gareth	A king's son who works in Arthur's kitchen.
Lynette	Lady-in-waiting to the Queen.
Sir Modred	The Black Knight; traitorous would-be usurper of Arthur's throne.
Merlin	Magician; guardian advisor to Arthur.
Morganna	Evil sorceress; aid to Modred's villainous schemes.
King Ban	Chief of invading army who hopes to overthrow Arthur; in league with Modred and Morganna[.]
Knights of Arthur's Court …	
Sir Launcelot	Grand Steward. Peerless knight and friend to Gareth.
Sir Gawaine	
Sir Tristram	
Sir Bedivere	
etc.	

On the other, new and original characters to make *King Arthur's Knights* a viable animated feature film for a contemporary audience:

The Dwarf	Faithful servant and later squire to Gareth (comedy character).
Oscar	Simple kitchen knave who aspires to become a knight (comedy character).
Head Kitchen Steward	Excitable comedy character.
The Harpy	Evil half human–half beast character in Morganna's power.

2. The Best Arthurian Cartoon Never Made

The Dwarf's Donkey	Whimsical comedy type.
Birds and animals of the woods	for whimsical fantasy sequences.
Knights, Soldiers, Incidental Characters, etc.	

As the roster from Arthurian legend hints, *King Arthur's Knights* derives its spirit primarily from Malory's *Le Morte Darthur* and specifically from his tale of Gareth (Caxton's book VII). However, in the story treatment that follows, the Malorian source becomes almost unrecognizable. It is as if Harman Productions adopts Malory's *characters* but little of his *plot* as Gareth moves to center stage. In the refocused narrative of *King Arthur's Knights*, Malory's larger Arthuriad—from the sword in the stone to the final conflict between Arthur and Mordred—becomes background fodder for Gareth's foreground adventures. And beyond the Arthurian roster, one sees in the

Modred, by R. G. S., for Harman's *King Arthur's Knights* (detail from a photograph in Alan C. Lupack's collection).

script's non–Arthurian elements that Harman Productions is openly challenging Disney on the rival's home turf with a dwarf[8] and woodland creatures who could have stepped out of *Snow White*, a harpy loosed from *Fantasia* (1940), a comedy character (Oscar) intended to exhibit many of Goofy's qualities, and, predictably, no fewer than ten tunes already itemized in the addenda for a film that "lends itself naturally to the introduction of musical numbers."

Before the action proper begins, the story treatment reveals in an unnumbered prefatory note that a montage of "knights and troops of early European nationalities" and "an ancient map of England," both backed by a "stentorian" voiceover, will be used to let the audience know that "many years ago this island was once a group of warring nations which were to provide an agglomerate foundation of that mighty Empire that today is Britain."

The extremely dense narrative of the script's sequence A quickly establishes Arthur's rise to power, his allies, and his enemies. (As we soon realize, this entire segment is mere prologue to the introduction of the film's true hero, Gareth, in sequence B.) In a shot that begins with Merlin gazing into a crystal at an assembly gathered to watch knights attempt to draw the sword from the stone,[9] the audience learns of Morganna's behind-the-scenes scheming to use magic to help Modred win the contest. Modred fails anyway, not once but twice. Morganna's powers are more than offset by Merlin's support for a youth in the crowd, Arthur. The wizard's disembodied voice encourages the surprised lad — it takes Arthur a moment to realize that Merlin's "Now is thine opportunity!" (A7) is meant for him — to draw the sword from the stone and thus become king. Sequence A also establishes Lancelot's[10] leadership as he fosters support for the newly named king. As the first scene ends, Morganna acknowledges to an embarrassed, enraged Modred that Arthur is the "lawful king" because he is Uther Pendragon's son, even though Arthur does not know of his heritage because he was "stolen from his parents as a child and brought up by Merlin" (A20). Regardless of Arthur's right to the throne, Morganna and Modred resolve to overthrow Arthur so that Modred can rule.

For all of the legend that Harman and Edmunds weave into sequence A, it is also telling to note the omission or alteration of many familiar Arthurian narrative threads. The opening of *King Arthur's Knights* conveniently skirts several thorny issues that would arise if it introduced any of Malory's discussion of Igrayne, Arthur's conception, the young king's half-blood relationship to Morgan le Fey, or Mordred's parentage. Such topics lie narrowly beyond the edge of the screen, supplementary storylines for those who may remember their "authentic Arthurian data" from school days. Harman and Edmunds prudently choose not to pursue these threads— or necessarily reject them either. The writers also rework the well-known storyline of Arthur's upbringing in Ector's household by assigning the task instead to Merlin,[11] the wizard to whom Malory's Uther gives the infant in exchange for helping the king satisfy his lust for Igrayne — another difficulty best avoided in a film designed "for general appeal." In yet another departure from the legend as Malory tells it, Arthur in *King Arthur's Knights* is some years younger than Lancelot (the cast of character's "Grand Steward"), who already serves as the de facto general of English chivalry as the story begins. It is this knight who in sequence A champions young Arthur's claim to the throne in the face of Modred's sputtered objections, trumped-up accusations of Arthur's subterfuge in gaining the sword, and insistence that the new king draw the sword from the stone a second time to prove himself.

Two more significant departures from the story as Malory tells it are noteworthy. Given that Arthur and Modred are roughly the same age (teenagers, it seems, in sequence A) in *King Arthur's Knights*, Harman and Edmunds neatly close off another possibility that "authentic Arthurian data" might suggest: Modred cannot be Arthur's *son*. In *Le Morte Darthur*, Mordred is conceived when Arthur unwittingly beds his half-sister Morgause (a character often conflated with Morgan in many modern Arthurian texts and films). By making Arthur and Modred peers, *King Arthur's Knights* departs from a traditional yet vexed narrative that the audience might recall from Malory or a similar source. In a related move, Harman and Edmunds also reject "authentic Arthurian data" that would make Modred and Gareth *brothers* or perhaps *cousins*. In *Le Morte Darthur*, Mordred and Gareth are half-brothers, sons of Morgause by different fathers. Whether the film's Morganna derives straight from Malory's Morgan or combines Malory's Morgause and Morgan, either way, the film's villain Modred and its hero Gareth could conceivably be close kin according to legendary precedent. But Modred's parentage and his precise relationship to Morganna in *King Arthur's Knights* remain obscure — a wise editorial decision that forestalls all such questions. There are no hints of blood ties here between Modred and Gareth.

Ten years have passed as sequence B begins. Camelot has flourished under Arthur's rule. He has already married Guinevere — and again, shrewdly omitted is any mention of many complicating Launcelot-Guinevere strands from the legend. The king, Merlin, Guinevere, her lady-in-waiting Lynette (the last inserted in a B15 addendum to present her on screen earlier than the original sequence D introduction would have allowed), knights, and courtiers observe a tournament's colorful action. This day, an unknown Black Knight is overcoming every adversary. Arthur decides to challenge the mysterious stranger. Merlin stops him, revealing to the king that the Black Knight uses an enchanted spear that will assuredly kill Arthur if they joust. As an embarrassed yet sensible Arthur withdraws his challenge, "a tall, well-built youth with a devil-may-care attitude" (B9) strides in, trailed by a faithful servant dwarf (B4 addendum), and asks — à la *Sir Gawain and the Green Knight*, perhaps, where it is Gawain who similarly offers — to take the king's place in the challenge.

Although the audience will not learn the new arrival's identity until later, a lengthy note appended to the story treatment elaborates how the youth's character is to be developed:

> We plant as much as is necessary of Gareth's background and his reasons for wanting to remain incognito. As in the Arthurian legends, Gareth's mother forbade him to become a knight errant on account of his youth and her fear that he may be killed in combat; hence Gareth's motive in remaining a kitchen boy for a year before asking that his second wish be granted, namely to become a knight on his own merits [B4 addendum].

Arthurian Animation

Arthurian scholars may chuckle at the appeal to authority as it stands "in the Arthurian legends," which is as improbable in this case as it is in Malory's occasional invocation of a nonexistent "Frensshe booke" to bolster his own authority. The writers perhaps unconsciously blend Gareth and Perceval, the latter of whom does indeed have a mother trying to protect her son by raising him in the woods far from chivalric life. In any event, Lancelot objects to the idea of a nameless, untrained, "country lad" (B11) entering the lists. Merlin overrules him: "Sire, methinks in this case the youth's courage doth indeed justify his purpose. And as for his nobility, I trow he will live to prove that" (B12). Arthur agrees to let the unknown fight the Black Knight, "more for the joke of it all than anything else" (B13), and grants the "cocksure" (B14) lad's request for only a horse, sword, and shield before advancing to the field. Meanwhile, having caught sight of Lynette in the stands, Gareth "impishly begs her for a favour, as was the custom" (B15 addendum). The script does not say whether she grants it.[12]

Merlin warns the newcomer to avoid the Black Knight's deadly spear. The caution proves unnecessary, because Gareth has no intention of being struck. As in the Boss's contest against Sagramore in Twain's *Connecticut Yankee*, Gareth's lack of plate armor gives him the advantage. When their horses come together, Gareth "nimbly ducks under the Black Knight's spear and, grasping him around the neck, throws him off his horse" (B17). Both afoot, Gareth proves the superior swordsman, striking the Black Knight's armored wrist so hard that the knight drops his weapon. (The blow creates a bruise that, in sequence D, will reveal that the Black Knight was Modred in disguise, making yet another play for the throne.) Gareth's unchivalric tactics do not allow for his victory to be "accepted officially" (B19), yet the lad becomes an instant favorite of the crowd, "much to the Black Knight's chagrin" (B19).

Arthur offers to reward Gareth. The lad asks for three favors, one now and the other two after a year's time has passed. He then "nonchalantly" asks his first gift: "I crave the privilege of working in thy kitchen, my liege" (B21). The crowd laughs at the bizarre request. Continuing to revel in "the joke of it all," Arthur grants Gareth's wish.

Those familiar with "authentic Arthurian data" recall at this point Malory's related series of events. One Pentecost as Arthur holds a plenary court, a tall, handsome, and preternaturally large-handed youth arrives, accompanied by two dwarves. He asks three gifts, one to be given at once and the other two a year later. Arthur grants the boon. The stranger asks for a year's meat and drink. Arthur deems it a poor first gift and urges the youth to request something better, but the lad insists. When asked his name, the stranger will not reveal it. Arthur assigns Sir Kay, his foster brother and steward, the task of feeding the guest. Kay peevishly complies, though not without nicknaming the incognito stranger Beaumayns ("fayre-handes" as Kay glosses for those with weak French skills) and complaining that the king lavishes good food on one likely to be no better than a knave. Kay adds Beaumayns to the kitchen staff and mocks him relentlessly for the next year.

As Malory continues the tale, Gawain — Beaumayn's older brother, though Gawain does not yet know that they are related — and Launcelot pity the youth, but they cannot

2. The Best Arthurian Cartoon Never Made

appreciably improve his lot under Kay's mean-spirited stewardship. Then one day a damsel arrives with an adventure: to rescue her lady who is oppressed by an evil knight. Beaumayns takes this opportunity to ask for his last two gifts: to take the adventure and be dubbed a knight by Launcelot once he has proven himself during his mission. Arthur grants these requests. But the damsel rides off in a huff from a court that will offer her only kitchen help to save her lady. Beaumayns nonetheless pursues the ungrateful, haughty damsel. He has barely left the castle grounds when he defeats and seriously wounds Kay in a joust. He takes Kay's spear and shield as prizes and gives the knight's horse to a dwarf who has followed Beaumayns out of the castle. He next fights Launcelot to a draw. Beaumayns reveals his true name to Launcelot: he is Gareth, brother to Gawain. Launcelot knights him and they part company.

Gareth pursues and overtakes the proud, scornful damsel. We later learn her name is Lynet. She repeatedly tongue-lashes her companion through one adventure after another on their journey, even as he demonstrates his considerable martial skills and they approach the goal of their quest, Lynet's sister, the lady Lyonesse, in her besieged castle. In the end, Gareth succeeds in the mission, has many more adventures not relevant to our purposes here, and marries Lyonesse. Meanwhile, Lynet marries Gareth's brother Gaheris, as Malory ties up a loose narrative thread.

As Harman and Edmunds strive to develop "a more attractive and colorful presentation," the retelling often bears only incidental relationship to *Le Morte Darthur*. *King Arthur's Knights* takes a largely new direction instead. To be sure, Gareth and Lynette both still find love, but now with each other. Lynette remains a sharp thorn in Gareth's side — and like her Malorian counterpart, eventually relents and accepts the hero — but many more opportu-

Lynette, by R. G. S., for Harman's *King Arthur's Knights* (photograph in the author's collection).

nities for humor arise in *King Arthur's Knights* than in *Le Morte Darthur* as duty and love drive Gareth to press his amorous suit on a damsel who finds him unworthy. Gareth still serves in the king's kitchen under the thumb of a hot-tempered steward and has to prove himself to the girl and the court; however, *King Arthur's Knights* rejects Malory's besieged Lyonesse thread in its entirety in favor of exploits that showcase Gareth's pursuit of Lynette's love and his defense of the kingdom against Arthur's foes. In fine, the writers retool Malory's Gareth tale to make it serve as the focal point of their entire film. Such concentration is achieved by making Modred a five-fold threat: as the disguised Black Knight whom Gareth fights in sequence B, as a rival (and quickly declined) suitor to Lynette, as Morganna's companion, as leader of the anti–Arthur faction in England, and as ally to foreign invaders from across the Channel. Harman and Edmunds have a grand vision, as a summary[13] of the remaining sequences of *King Arthur's Knights* reveals.

C: With a feast to be prepared, Gareth is assigned to the kitchen. His affable, incorrigible ways earn him the friendship of the knaves and the kitchen steward's scorn.

D: At the feast, Gareth clumsily drops a dish, disrupting Lynette's beautiful song: "Lynette stops singing and fiercely turns to see who interrupted her. She strides over to the hapless Gareth and in a fit of temperament, slaps him across the face" (D5). Modred joins in the abuse. Gareth notices Modred's deeply bruised wrist. Later, Gareth secretly witnesses Modred wooing Lynette and her response to his unwanted advances: a slap for him as well. Gareth's attraction to Lynette deepens.

E: Lovelorn Gareth returns to kitchen quarters, where his dwarf jokingly suggests asking Merlin about how to approach the damsel. Failing to get the joke, Gareth accepts the suggestion. Merlin tells Gareth that he knows the boy's concealed backstory (revealed in the B4 addendum material) and would like to help him; however, the best he can offer is "one romantic hour" for Gareth to plead his case before Lynette, during which time she will be "sympathetic to Gareth's romantic protestations" (E9–10). The hour goes well yet expires just as Gareth readies to kiss Lynette. She slaps him so hard that he falls over a balcony and into a pond.

F: The next morning, the Round Table convenes to discuss Merlin's vision of dire days ahead: a conspiracy will arise against the throne, launched by someone at that very table. The camera follows a troubled Modred from the assembly and then outside, where he lashes out at Gareth and orders him to mend his broken spur.

G: Gareth indifferently goes to the armory, jokes with the dwarves working there, and starts singing to the rhythm rising from the beaten anvils. Outside, Modred's impatience builds until he enters, strikes Gareth, and leaves with his spur.

H: Another scullery servant, Oscar, "the Don Quixote (buffoon) character" (H1), who wears armor patched together from old pots and pans, is developed in a playful scene with Gareth and his dwarf. It ends as their supervisor, the angry kitchen steward, chastises all three and sends Gareth to fetch wood for the fires.

I: Lynette's softer side appears as she sings sweetly to the animals in the forest. Gathering wood nearby, an unseen Gareth joins in the melody, leading to a prank in which

2. The Best Arthurian Cartoon Never Made

Lynette temporarily believes it is Gareth's dwarf on the other side of their duet. Gareth reveals himself and recalls for Lynette their previous night's rendezvous. Annoyed once again by his presumption, Lynette rides away. Gareth "resigns himself to his labours with a smile" (I9).

J: Lynette tumbles from her horse and down a bank, landing at the mouth of a cave ("Morganna's Cave") beneath an ancient castle. Within, Modred and Morganna discuss Merlin's vision and the news "that a certain king and his army are ready to invade England to help Modred usurp the throne" (J6). Their discussion is intercut with images of "King Ban and his army massing on the French coast in preparation for the invasion of England, ... awaiting instructions from Modred and Morganna" (J6 addendum). Modred discovers Lynette eavesdropping. He futilely offers to make Arthur's loyal subject his queen once he has taken the throne (J8 addendum). She flees on foot. Modred decides he must kill her to prevent her from revealing what she knows about the coming invasion. As Modred aims his bow at Lynette, Gareth — strolling in the woods and having found Lynette's riderless horse — enters the area unnoticed. Gareth fires his own arrow before Modred can take a shot. Modred's hand is pinned to a tree. The hero mounts Lynette's horse and catches up with her. He dismounts. Without a word to her rescuer, Lynette retrieves her mount and gallops for Camelot. A puzzled Gareth is left behind. Modred frees himself and also takes horse. He pursues Lynette, catches her, and takes her as prisoner to his castle in another county.

K: Gareth returns to Camelot, unaware that Modred has kidnapped Lynette. He forces his way into a closed meeting where the king, Lancelot, and Merlin are busy discussing the threat disclosed by the wizard's vision (sequence F). Gareth reveals Modred's attempt to kill Lynette. Arthur would not believe such treachery possible of a Round Table knight if Merlin's crystal ball did not confirm the fact that Modred has indeed taken Lynette prisoner. Lancelot offers to save Lynette, then relinquishes the adventure to Gareth, who "demands the opportunity" to rescue the maiden and takes this moment to exercise his "second wish" (K7): to become a knight.[14] Merlin supports the petition, "knowing Gareth's true birthright, that he is the son of the King of Orkney and nephew of Arthur himself" (K8). At the lad's request, Lancelot dubs him knight.

L: In full armor, newly invested Sir Gareth enters the kitchen, where the kitchen steward shows the unrecognized knight proper deference and Gareth savors the irony of the steward's turn-about. Gareth announces that the dwarf will accompany him as squire on his adventure. They leave. Having recognized his former scullery companion, Oscar "dons his tin-can suit of armour" (L5) and follows stealthily behind the two, determined not to miss the chance to participate in a noble adventure.

M: Gareth and his dwarf arrive at Modred's castle, though only Gareth succeeds in fighting past the dragons, giants, and other evils that protect the place. The dwarf remains outside. "Morganna is already there, by magic" (M5). Gareth and Modred come to a stand-off over Lynette, with Modred prepared to kill her if Gareth comes closer. But Morganna has a "more subtle scheme" and instead turns Lynette into a red fawn, releases her from the castle, and sets "a pack of vicious dogs" (M13) on her scent. Meanwhile, Gareth falls through a trapdoor into a dungeon that Morganna begins to flood.

N: Oscar arrives at the castle and with some comic struggling manages to come to a window. He spies Modred and Morganna discussing the next stage of their plan: to incapacitate Merlin, Arthur's chief adviser, by using a charmed serpent's bite to turn him to stone. When Modred doubts whether such a plan will work, Morganna demonstrates the serpent's power on her own terrified servant harpy and then reverses the spell with an antidote that she alone possesses. They leave the room. Oscar seizes the chance "to prove himself the hero by frustrating their evil designs" (N13) by stealing the antidote. However, while trying to escape, Oscar falls into the moat, alerting the castle's occupants to his presence. As Oscar continues to flee, Modred fells him with an arrow to the back, apparently killing the would-be hero.

O: Tension builds: Gareth's dungeon fills with water; the dogs pursue the red fawn.

P: The dwarf also comically scrambles about the castle exterior until he comes to an arrow slit through which he can see into Gareth's dungeon and speak to the trapped hero. Gareth explains Lynette's plight. He instructs the dwarf to ignore his master's own peril and focus instead on saving Lynette by rushing to get Merlin's help. The dwarf mounts his donkey and rides away swiftly, passing by the downed yet still barely alive Oscar outside the castle. Oscar ineffectually tries to catch the dwarf's attention as he hurries toward Camelot.

Q: Morganna's harpy flies to Camelot and releases the serpent. It stings Merlin. The harpy gathers up the serpent and departs. As the magician turns to stone, the dwarf arrives. Merlin explains that he cannot cure himself of the venom. He begins to petrify. The dwarf tells the wizard of Lynette's danger. With the last of his strength, Merlin tells the dwarf where to find a silver-tipped arrow that must be shot into the red fawn's heart to return Lynette to human form. As word of Merlin's fate spreads, "great commotion ensues throughout the castle" (Q12). Lancelot enters. The dwarf tells him of the perils threatening Gareth and Lynette. Knights ride to the rescue. As this sequence closes, the action rises to fever pitch with rapid cuts to Gareth in the watery dungeon, Modred and Morganna confidently waiting the harpy's news of their victory over Merlin, Modred donning armor to join the foreign invaders when they make landfall, the dogs poised to savage the red fawn, the knights galloping on a rescue mission toward Modred's castle, and the dwarf bearing the silver-tipped arrow to Gareth.

R: Arthur's knights arrive at Modred's castle and defeat his men. Morganna transforms Modred to a vulture so that he can escape across the Channel. Meanwhile at Morganna's Cave, the dwarf saves Gareth from drowning with but seconds to spare. The dwarf gives Gareth the magic arrow and the two set off to save Lynette. Gareth fires the enchanted arrow at the fawn. Lynette becomes human again. The vicious dogs are killed.[15] "A romantic scene is played between Gareth and Lynette," even though Lynette (like the kitchen steward in sequence L) does not yet recognize Gareth "in his knightly armor" (R10). The confusion amuses lighthearted Gareth. He "teases her about the kitchen boy who is in love with her" (R11). While annoyed by the teasing, Lynette acknowledges "a secret soft spot" for the lad. They ride toward Camelot on one horse, singing happily together, with Lynette telling her unknown rescuer that his voice is "almost as good as that of the kitchen knave." Their conversation continues until she

2. The Best Arthurian Cartoon Never Made

"finds out" (R12) that the kitchen knave and her champion are one and the same. "When they arrive back at the castle Lynette has admitted her true love for Gareth" (R13).

R-S addendum: An inserted sequence that depicts Modred's arrival in France as the invaders prepare to sail for England. An archer among the foreign troops nearly shoots the vulture from the sky, but Modred escapes this fate when the vulture's feet touch ground, Morganna's enchantment ceases, and Modred becomes human again. Modred embarks for England with the invaders' armada.

S: With the enemy landing imminent, "the invasion alarm is broadcast throughout the country by the lighting of beacons and the ringing of bells" (S1 addendum). Arthur marshals his panoply of troops for battle and they march to meet the enemy. Gareth and Lynette arrive at Camelot. Learning that his king has already moved to battle, Gareth and Lynette enjoy a "parting scene" (S2 addendum) in which, from a balcony (the same balcony as in sequence E?), she tosses her love a rose as he and his dwarf depart for war. Gareth joins the troops, taking position next to Lancelot. Meanwhile, the dwarf finds Oscar where he earlier fell outside Modred's castle. Oscar tells the dwarf to fetch a knight. The dwarf returns with Gareth and Lancelot. Oscar reveals what he learned while spying on Morganna and Modred in sequence N. Oscar produces the antidote that can cure Merlin. Lancelot tells him that he will be rewarded for his heroism. Oscar observes that his wound is fatal and that he desires but one reward: for Lancelot to make him a knight before he dies. Lancelot complies. Oscar expires with a smile on his lips. Gareth "has to fight his way through the enemy lines" (S2 addendum) to bring the antidote to Camelot. Merlin is revived. Gareth and Merlin ride to the front. Merlin employs magic stronger than Morganna's spells to harness the elements of nature and help repel the invaders in the final sequences.[16]

T: "The Invasion" (T1). Arthur's knights engage "the invading Saxons on the seashore" (T2). Gareth fights heroically. Modred battles alongside the invaders. "Scene finishes with Modred fatally wounding Arthur" (T5). Gareth kills Modred. The harpy flies to Morganna to report the outcome.

U: At Modred's castle, the harpy plots to "rid himself of his fiendish mistress" (U1) now that Modred can no longer protect her. The harpy turns the serpent on Morganna. She then must watch him gloat, "enjoying the fruition of his long pent-up hate," as with "hopeless terror" (U3) she begins to petrify. The harpy mockingly delivers the news: "Arthur's Knights are victorious! Sir Modred is dead!" (U4). As Morganna uses the last of her power to obliterate the harpy, she realizes "that she is the victim of her own wickedness" (U5) and turns to stone.

One final, brief sequence remains. It appears below in full:

V1: We cut back to the battle.

V2: Arthur dies of his mortal wound and we show the scene of the Sword being thrown back into the Lake, and the Hand coming out of the water to take it.

V3: The Maidens in the barge take away Arthur's body.

V4: Merlin makes a speech, in which he announces that victory is theirs. The invader has been driven off, and that it is men such as these courageous Knights who will prove to be the foundation of an even greater England. It plays up the theme "There will always be an England."

V5: On this note we use an effect such as panning up to the sky from Merlin's words, and see gathered soldiers, knights, etc., passing across the heavens in ghostly form to martial music which swells to a final crescendo as we FADE OUT.

Sequence A establishes Arthur's realm. Sequences B-T trace the career of Gareth, one of the kingdom's exemplary knights. Sequences U-V gather loose ends and conclude the narrative—and look beyond Arthur's time and into England's future where the values upheld by Gareth, Lynette, the king, Lancelot, Merlin, and even the dwarf and Oscar will forever preserve the Empire. Surely the British Edmunds must be primarily responsible for this conclusion. Just as once before the folk of medieval England were able to overcome the "invading Saxons"[17] who crossed the Channel, so in April 1941 their descendants, reeling from the effects of more than eight months of German bombing assaults and fearing an imminent foreign ground invasion, are promised a new victory over modern-day Saxons. The invocation of 1940's morale-boosting wartime ditty "There Will Always Be an England" signals to all reading the final sequence the emotion that *King Arthur's Knights* aims to rouse as the film comes to a close. As in *Le Morte Darthur*, Arthur in the flesh may not come again—*King Arthur's Knights* leaves not even a lingering uncertainty on that score—and yet his example will endure for all time. And every defender of England, past, present, and future, will find a place in a glorious heavenly parade. That Gareth vanishes from the script after killing Modred in sequence T should surprise not at all. He has served his purpose in a larger message that the film intends to deliver.[18]

Harman and Edmunds allusively introduce several time-honored Arthurian motifs into sequence V. Readers of Malory will recall that a young, headstrong Arthur breaks his first sword, the unnamed one that he draws from the stone to become king, and later receives the replacement sword Excalibur from the Lady of the Lake. Popularly, these two swords, from the stone and the lake, are often conflated; Harman and Edmunds are certainly not the first to combine the two into one.[19] Yet "the Sword," "the Lake," and "the Hand" (V2) lend an unmistakable, capitalized, deictic specificity that resonates from chapters of *Le Morte Darthur* untapped until these final moments in *King Arthur's Knights*. One hears Malory's narrative echoing again in "the Maidens"—or as the song list addendum tells us, a hymn to be sung by "Three Black Queens" on a barge—as they ferry away Arthur's body. Malory, however, names *four* who transport the king on his last journey: Nynyue (the chief Lady of the Lake), the Queen of North Galys, the Queen of the Waste Londes, and the king's half-sister, Queen Morgan le Fey (Caxton XXI.6). The petrified Morganna of *King Arthur's Knights* will not, of course, be joining the group that accompanies Arthur's corpse.

Departing further from Malory and loosely following perhaps Disney's *Fantasia* lead instead, Harman and Edmunds envision a climactic (and climatic) clash of mighty magicians in the final scenes as supernatural "storms, fires, winds, etc." (S2 addendum)

2. The Best Arthurian Cartoon Never Made

mirror the frenzied human microcosm on the battlefield below. Indeed, throughout *King Arthur's Knights* magic plays a central role in the action: Merlin's crystal ball, rival magicians, Morganna's ability to transport herself from one location to another, an enchanted arrow, animal metamorphoses, a serpent whose sting can petrify, and so on. Whereas Malory routinely minimizes the use of magic in *Le Morte Darthur*, Harman Productions follows trends of the time by highlighting it. One need hardly scratch the surface of the three Disney feature films that had premiered by April 1941 to find a focus on magic in the Evil Queen of *Snow White*, the Blue Fairy's spell that brings life to a marionette in *Pinocchio*, and Mickey's bumbling use of a wizard's powers in *Fantasia*. Non-Arthurian influences are also likely at work, such as the Wicked Witch's comparable remote-viewing glass in *The Wizard of Oz* (1939). Or, in creating the battling magicians of their film, Harman and Edmunds may have had in mind T. H. White's *The Sword in the Stone* (1939), in which Merlyn and Madame Mim go head-to-head. One could suggest additional proximate sources for the abundant magic in *King Arthur's Knights*, but perhaps it is best to conclude that Harman and Edmunds were simply alert to currents of the times. Magic was "in the air" and thus it needed to be an important force in *King Arthur's Knights*, too.

Harman's working papers from circa 1941–42 provide much more than the two story treatments. We see a projected running time for the film: seventy-two minutes. We learn of estimated production costs and glimpse Harman's intent to build an entire studio around this film: a budget of $530,000, a staff ranging from roughly 28 to 160 employees over the course of production, salaries, square footage required for diverse parts of the business, furnishings and equipment, and even a sketch of a building elevation for new headquarters. There is also a production plan from start to finish: a fifteen-month timeline outlining principal stages of work to be done. In addition, there are two documents among the working papers prepared with an audience of prospective underwriters in mind. The first is a three-page "Summary of production schedule and financial requirements" that explains in layman's terms the steps involved in making an animated film. The second identifies the key members of Harman Productions in a four-page biographical overview of the seven production leads: Hugh Harman (supervising producer and production head), Robert Edmunds (story and assistant supervising producer), James Pabian (animation), Arthur Heineman [*sic*] (art), John Neiendorff (lay-out and backgrounds), Herman (Sid) Ising (technical),[20] and Leigh Harline (music). Missing from the papers, unfortunately, are the drawings or storyboards that Harman's team must have prepared to help promote *King Arthur's Knights*. A few drawings recently surfaced, however, in a most surprising way.

In June 2001 a San Antonio antiques dealer offered on eBay seven lots comprising a total of eleven undated black-and-white photographs (one a duplicate) of ten different charcoal pencil and pen-and-ink sketches.[21] These eleven photographs appear on two paper stocks: a heavy stock with a matte finish and a lighter stock with a glossy finish. A red ink-stamp on the reverse of most reveals that these photographs were once in the offices of "HUGH HARMAN PRODUCTIONS, INC. / 9470 SANTA MONICA BLVD. BEVERLY HILLS, CALIF." Several photographs also bear on the reverse typed blue stickers that tell us that these sketches are for a production entitled "KING ARTHUR'S KNIGHTS." In addition, the stickers provide the *names* of the characters depicted in the sketches: Lynette, Morganna, Modred, Gobbo, a crowned and fully armored figure labeled "Knight in Armor," and another a crowned, jerkin-clad, dignified-looking king — presumably *the* king of the project's title — but without a blue sticker to identify him.[22] All sketches except "Knight in Armor" — in pen-and-ink rather than charcoal pencil and stylistically anomalous in comparison to the others — have been signed "R. G. S."

I believe these initials to be none other than those of Harman's long-time associate Robert Stokes, who first worked with Harman at Warner Bros. in the early 1930s (and on "Bosko's Knight-Mare" no less, if its screen credits are accurate), who followed Harman and Ising to MGM in 1934, whom Mel Shaw would have known from Stokes's years at Disney from 1936 into the early 1940s, and whom Harman Productions perhaps employed as a freelancer about the same time that Stokes apparently left Disney's employ. To uncover Stokes's involvement with *King Arthur's Knights* requires a brief excursus.

Stokes changed jobs often, as did many Hollywood animators in the increasingly anti-labor, anti-union era in the years leading up to World War II. Although no formal biography of Stokes exists,[23] the following account pieces together what we do know. Stokes's name first appeared in screen credits to two 1933 Warner Bros. cartoons, "Bosko's Knight-Mare" and "Bosko the Musketeer." However, as mentioned in chapter 1, these credits cannot be fully trusted because of producer Schlesinger's system of rotating the credits on Harman-Ising cartoons. While Stokes may or may not have been an animator on the two 1933 cartoons that carry his name, it is reasonable to infer at the very least that Stokes *worked* in the Harman-Ising operation for Warner Bros. during roughly the summer and fall of 1933 when cartoons bearing his name were released. The fact that "Bosko's Knight-Mare" and "Bosko the Musketeer" are highly unusual "period" cartoons in the Bosko corpus, set in the past rather than Bosko's usual modern surroundings, suggests that the same animator may be responsible for both; that Stokes's name appears on *both* argues for the accuracy of the screen credits in this instance.

Following these two Bosko cartoons, Stokes vanished from Warner credits. When Harman and Ising left Warner Bros. for MGM in 1934, Stokes went along with them (Maltin 341). Unfortunately, MGM cartoons do not reveal the names of any animators beyond Harman and Ising, so Stokes's work at MGM cannot be tracked precisely. At the same time, perhaps working a second job to make ends meet, Stokes resurfaced at Ub Iwerks's animation studio in 1934, where he was credited as "Robt. G. Stokes" on two Willie Whopper shorts, "Rasslin' Round" (June) and "The Good Scout" (September). As Iwerks reorganized his studio in 1935, many were fired and others quit. It is not possible to say what happened to Stokes in the shake-up. Stokes was next working at the Disney studio in January 1936 (Barrier 197) when Walt Disney, recognizing Stokes's skills and needing another talented character artist to complete work on *Snow White*, tapped him as the fourth and final lead to animate scenes of Snow White and the Evil Queen. David Johnson contends that Stokes's contributions to *Snow White*

2. The Best Arthurian Cartoon Never Made

have often gone underappreciated, even though Stokes was responsible for "perhaps the single most published drawing of the film's heroine: Snow White ready to bite into the apple" and "nearly half" of the Evil Queen's appearances (2). Stokes remained with Disney through at least 1940, where he animated the unforgettable caricature of Katharine Hepburn as Little Bo Peep in 1938's "Mother Goose Goes Hollywood" short (Johnson 2) and was a lead animator on the "Nutcracker Suite" segment of *Fantasia* (Grant 176).

Stokes—if he is our "R. G. S."—seems to turn up next at Harman Productions. Barrier's 1977 interview with Stokes, in which the animator recounted Harman's "intense desire" to make a King Arthur feature film (192), certainly means that Stokes knew of the film his professional colleague and friend was attempting to make at the time. Although nothing definitively links "R. G. S." of the Harman Productions sketches to Robert G. Stokes—the working papers, for instance, do not reveal payments to him or direct responsibilities in the plan to create *King Arthur's Knights*—and the evidence is admittedly circumstantial, I believe the two are one. Stylistic similarities between R. G. S.'s drawings and illustrations conclusively known to be Stokes's work from the early 1940s lend support to the hypothesis. For instance, a side-by-side comparison of Morganna and *Snow White*'s Evil Queen reveals in the appearance of both characters the same dark hair, sinister angularity, frowning sneer, thick eyelids and eyeshadow, heavy lashes, arched and looping eyebrows accented by the shape of the headpiece, and so on. Morganna and the Evil Queen could be sisters.

Irrespective of the identity of R. G. S., the photographs provide additional details about Harman's film. The blue stickers offer a new—perhaps final—title for the project. Neither the accurate yet nonspecific and rather bland *The Knight and the Lady* nor the specific yet commonplace *The Knights of the Round Table* appears. Instead, the stickers offer a title that shows Harman's intent to put the unambiguous *King Arthur's Knights* on the marquee, even if the king himself plays a relatively minor role in the film's action. It is probably not coincidental that this title is identical to the one that appears in the book that Bosko reads in "Bosko's Knight-Mare," a cartoon that Harman and—if the screen credits to "Bosko's Knight-Mare" are correct—Stokes worked on nearly a decade earlier. And just as the creators of "Bosko's Knight-Mare" wanted the audience to associate Bosko's medieval adventure loosely with Gilbert's popular book of the same title in 1933, so in 1941 Harman was again attempting to use name-association to ride the coattails of Gilbert's proven success with a children's book that had been selling well since 1911. However, probably to avoid potential legal entanglements as much as anything else, the Harman-Edmunds script does not rely in any identifiable way on Gilbert's idiosyncratic abridgement of how Arthur becomes king (sequence A), Gareth's tale (sequences B-T), or Arthur's end (sequences U-V). To the very limited degree that it is possible to compare the Second Revised Story Line with both Gilbert's *King Arthur's Knights* and Malory's *Le Morte Darthur*, Malory's public domain text is always the most likely source.

Turning to the sketches themselves, Lynette appears in half of the eBay photographs. Two full-length and three portrait poses depict the heroine. She looks the part of a typical lovely maiden destined for some young man's love,[24] a heroine designed to compete with her peers from Disney films. The single poses for Morganna, Modred, the king, "Knight in Armor," and Gobbo give indications of their dispositions as well. Morganna and Modred, the brains and the muscle behind plots to seize the throne, are suitably dark, heavy, wicked, and menacing. Complementing Morganna's resemblance to the Evil Queen, the caped, scowling Modred is nearly as thickset, densely mustached, and in need of a haircut as the Black Knight of "Bosko's Knight-Mare." The crowned and bearded king bears himself regally, although, as in the story treatment, we see only the surface of an ancillary character on the periphery of Gareth and Lynette's adventures. Yet *King Arthur's Knights* needs a *king*. This one easily fits conventional notions. Sadly, no portrait survives of Gareth — unless it be the crowned "Knight in Armor," a most unlikely possibility for a lad just starting out in life — although one day another auction may bring Gareth to light. The formidable "Knight in Armor" is fully encased in armor. His face cannot be seen. Given that he wears a crown, he may be the King Ban listed in the cast of characters.

"Gobbo" must be the character that the story treatment calls "Oscar"—which further points to a lost version of a script subsequent to the Second Revised Story Line. This lost version must have changed the character's name from Oscar to Gobbo. But why? Gobbo is an unprecedented addition to Arthurian narrative. The name evokes a well-known Shakespearean servant, clown, and fool, the emphatically non–Arthurian yet ironically christened *Launcelot Gobbo* of *The Merchant of Venice*.[25] Although the still-developing script of the Second Revised

Morganna, by R. G. S., for Harman's *King Arthur's Knights* (photograph in Alan C. Lupack's collection).

2. The Best Arthurian Cartoon Never Made

Story Line provides him with no direct dialogue, R. G. S. presents in Gobbo a portrait of consummate goofiness. Indeed, Gobbo looks to be the human equivalent of Disney's comparably almost toothless and similarly named Goofy. The R. G. S. sketch conjures up a Gobbo/Oscar one can readily imagine setting out for quixotic adventures in his "tin-can suit of armour."

King Arthur's Knights could have been an impressive film. Harman and his associates finally failed, however, to find investors for the project. Money was tight during the war, Harman's studio was new and untested, and even the powerful Disney operation was struggling to balance the books as it lost access to European markets. Despite the script's considerable merits, the time and circumstances were not right to venture half a million dollars on Harman's "intense desire." After the war ended, *King Arthur's Knights* remained an impossible sell. The film's conclusion that could be considered deeply patriotic and moving in 1941 rang perhaps of jingoism by 1946. Harman

Gobbo, by R. G. S., for Harman's *King Arthur's Knights* (photograph in Alan C. Lupack's collection).

nonetheless continued to option the screenplay through at least 1955,[26] but the options were not exercised. Plans for *King Arthur's Knights* were eventually relegated to a filing cabinet.

Nevertheless, to Hugh Harman and R. G. S./Robert Stokes we must grant long overdue credit for theatrical animation's initial forays into the Arthurian realm, first with "Bosko's Knight-Mare" and then with the unfinished *King Arthur's Knights*. Others would follow to Camelot shortly: Popeye, Bugs Bunny, Crusader Rabbit, and eventually Disney with the first *completed* feature-length animated Arthurian film, *The Sword in the Stone* (1963). But it all began with Bosko and — almost — Gareth and Lynette.

CHAPTER 3

"To Ye Jousting Tournament": Arthur's Postwar Rise

For whatever combination of reasons, *King Arthur's Knights* was never made. Many causes can be proposed: the lingering economic effects of World War II; Harman's inability to secure sufficient financial backing to support a new studio's first feature film; the increasingly malapropos tone of the screenplay's conclusion as Americans tried to put the war behind them; the industry's long memory of Disney's box-office disappointment with *The Reluctant Dragon*; or simply Harman's waning interest in the project. We will never know with certainty why Harman Productions ceased active development of *King Arthur's Knights*, but cease it did.

Yet by the end of the decade, the time was ripe for others to try their hands at Arthurianimation. With the war's end came a newfound interest in animating the Middle Ages and a desire to do it with greater verisimilitude than ever before. While animators of the 1920s and 1930s had occasionally offered a vague medieval backdrop for the action, the setting was often quite conventional, intended primarily to evoke a "days of yore" atmosphere that could be used to stage such classic fairy tales as *Cinderella*, *Snow White*, and *Little Red Riding Hood*, or to offer brief opportunities for medieval armor and weapons gags. After the war, however, medieval settings began to appear more frequently and were employed as more than decoration in background layouts. And in the foreground of these postwar cartoons, characters from a medieval "history"—broadly understood to include the likes of Robin Hood and King Arthur—came to the animated stage.

Postwar animation's new interest in comparatively more authentic settings and characters can be attributed to a number of trends. First, animators of the late 1940s were relying on a heightened "larger world" awareness on the part of the audience. Many Americans had recently stormed the great castles of Europe firsthand, knew others who had, or had seen troops liberating them in one weekly newsreel after another. The stock cartoon medieval fortress changed as animators began to draw more realistic castles for a public that now knew what castles actually looked like. Second, many Hollywood animators had been occupied throughout the war drawing European fortifications for military purposes.[1] By 1945, these animators had likely for several years been considering—and, one imagines, usually repressing—the joke potential inherent in cartoon castles, moats, drawbridges, turrets, and medieval weapons. War's end allowed the gags to flow freely again. Third, animators had become increasingly accustomed to caricaturing actual headline-making heroes and villains during the 1930s and through the war.[2] It is not a great leap from portraying contemporaries to drawing "real" historical figures from days gone by — even when their likenesses must be fabricated from whole cloth.

Fourth, and perhaps the most important motive for the new postwar interest in animating historical (or pseudohistorical) subjects, was once again bluntly commercial, as animators sought ways to link their cartoons to contemporaneous live-action movies drawing their subject matter from history. Just after the war, the feature-film industries on both sides of the Atlantic launched a number of costume dramas that would be released before decade's end. Among the more well-known films are *The Bandit of Sherwood Forest* (1946), *Caesar and Cleopatra* (1946), *The Unconquered* (1947), *Captain from Castile* (1947), *The Three Musketeers* (1948), *The Black Arrow* (1948), *Oliver Twist* (1948), *Joan of Arc* (1948), *Bonnie Prince Charlie* (1948), *The Prince of Thieves* (1948), and *Prince of Foxes* (1949). Two Arthurian entries also appeared in the mix: *A Connecticut Yankee in King Arthur's Court* (Paramount, 1949) and the fifteen-part serial of *The Adventures of Sir Galahad* (Columbia, 1949). In the late 1940s, history was hot.

Opportunistic animators followed suit in the belief the public must also have acquired a taste for cartoons about the past. Several appeared quickly in the late 1940s. Some of these cartoons debuted in theaters even before the premieres of the features on which they hoped to capitalize, because while a big-budget feature film could take years to bring to the screen, short studio cartoons generally required only eight to ten weeks from conception to release.[3] Disney's masterful "A Knight for a Day" (1945; premiered 8 March 1946), written by Bill Peet and directed by Jack Hannah, was one of the first of the postwar medieval cartoons to come to the screen. While not specifically Arthurian, this cartoon maps territory that later animators would traverse time and again.

"A Knight for a Day" opens on a bustling day of tournament action. An off-camera announcer describes the scene as a radio sports commentator would, taking us back "five hundred years" to "the 123rd running of the Canterbury Tournament at Thunderstone Castle." Two knights prepare for battle. The noble challenger Sir Loinsteak will meet Sir Cumference, a burly, cigar-smoking, battle-hardened warrior. They fight this day for the hand of Princess Esmeralda, who immodestly shouts and whistles from a tower even as the announcer describes her as "the fairest flower in all the kingdom." Loinsteak's slight squire, the eager but clumsy Cedric, helps his master prepare to tourney. Cedric accidentally knocks Loinsteak unconscious, thus paving the way for the squire to take the knight's place in the match.[4]

Throughout the cartoon, the announcer continues his colloquial commentary at breakneck pace. The unfolding action between Cedric and Cumference is compared to modern sporting events that range from baseball, football, and boxing to horse and auto racing. Snack vendors and program hawkers complete the high-spirited scene. Wordplay abounds: "It's a cold knight" (describing an unconscious combatant); "It's a hot knight we have out there this afternoon" (during a knight's rally); "You're in the armor now"; punning names given to the knights themselves; and so on. Medieval weapons are modernized: a lance terminates in a 1940s-era can opener; a shield is an iron-and-brick composite; and Cumference's horse's shoulder is decorated with emblems for every knight that he has conquered, mimicking the practice of World War II pilots who famously tallied their triumphs on the fuselage. Visual and aural gags blend medieval and modern: we *see* a trumpet blown as we *hear* a referee's starting whistle; a sundial worn as a wristwatch measures the passing seconds; a horse charges to the sound of a locomotive; and modern technology intrudes directly when Cumference employs a jackhammer on his opponent. In the end, Cumference defeats himself. He exerts so much energy while attacking Cedric — who decides to take refuge within his protective armor shell rather than continue a battle he cannot possibly win — that the champion collapses from exhaustion. With Cedric the winner, Esmeralda leaps from the tower and ardently kisses her dazed hero. It is not possible to show direct lines of influence from this Disney cartoon to medieval cartoons soon to be produced at other studios; however, many elements from "A Knight for a Day" do reappear in both generally medieval and explicitly Arthurian postwar cartoons.

With Disney pointing the way and Paramount's 1949 vehicle for Bing Crosby, *A Connecticut Yankee in King Arthur's Court*, in production on the studio lot,[5] Paramount's animation unit Famous Studios released two nominally Arthurian cartoons. The first, "Wotta Knight" (1947), directed by Isadore (Izzy) Sparber and written by Carl Meyer and Isadore (Izzy) Klein, brings Popeye from newspaper comics to the realm of animated knights. This energetic short pits Sir Popeye in a joust against Sir Bluto, "the Black Knight from Brooklyn." To the victor goes the privilege of waking Sleeping Beauty (Olive Oyl) with a kiss and then marrying her. The cartoon's opening shot explicitly signals the Arthurian setting with a banner outside a castle: "To Ye Jousting Tournament" (first sequence, in pseudomedieval calligraphy), "Ye Knights of Ye Round Table/NO SQUARES ALLOWED!" (second sequence, first phrase in same script as before, next in modern block capitals and "pasted" on as a billboard announcement would be).

Despite this promising beginning, we soon find ourselves in a cartoon with no recognizable Arthurian characters, themes, or motifs as Popeye (at 500 pounds and riding a goofy white horse) and Bluto (at 1000 pounds and riding a stalwart chestnut mount) duke it out in a tournament reminiscent of the one that Disney had presented in theaters the year before. Of course Popeye eventually wins, defeating his oppo-

Bluto and Popeye share a suit of armor in "Wotta Knight" (King Features/Famous Studios/Paramount, 1947).

3. "To Ye Jousting Tournament"

nent not only in the joust but then again when Bluto tries to prevent the hero from kissing the sleeping damsel. Along the way to victory, many morphing armor and metal weapon jokes arise: a gauntlet becomes a pair of pliers; a lance telescopes and sprouts a studded metal fist at its tip; a suit of armor becomes a coal-fired stove and another collapses into a steam radiator; shields serve as glider wings to help Popeye dive-bomb Bluto and then a tortoise shell to trap the villain; and finally Sleeping Beauty employs a magnet to keep Popeye from fleeing the howling woman whose long slumber and want of a mate have created a most undesirable bride.

Again, as in "A Knight for a Day," writers and animators of "Wotta Knight" compare the medieval tournament to modern sporting events: a vendor sells jousting forms; an announcer provides a radio-style play-by-play; and language and action drawn from arenas of horse racing and boxing suggest parallels between old contests and their modern analogs. The characters speak a blend of modern English and fractured Elizabethan diction, as in Bluto's "Zounds, that scurvy varlet shall see if I'm not calleth the Black Knight for naught," and the like. Yet we never encounter anything beyond the opening banner that makes "Wotta Knight" an explicitly *Arthurian* cartoon. As in "Bosko's Knight-Mare," "Wotta Knight" clumsily asserts its Arthurian dimension with a *label*, the equivalent of a silent film's title card inserted into the action to offer information to orient the audience. But unlike the earlier Bosko cartoon that developed an allusive Arthurian plot derived from Twain via two Fox film adaptations, this Popeye cartoon is Arthurian because it *says* it is. The banner conveys "medieval," little more.

Director Sparber's second Arthurian outing, "The Land of the Lost" (Famous Studios/Paramount, 1948), is another marginally Arthurian excursion, though it is arguably a much better cartoon. Adapted from an excerpt from Isabel Manning Hewson's 1945 children's book of the same title, "The Land of the Lost" tells the story of young Billy's missing multifunction pocket knife. The mislaid item has come to life as the knight-aspirant Jackknife in the Land of the Lost. In this land, Jackknife hopes to prove himself sufficiently "sharp and able"—along with many other puns about "making his point," being "keen," etc.—to join the Knives of the Square Table in King Knife's realm of Table Land. While the king believes the petitioner too "dull" for their company and advises him to return only after he has "carved out a career," when Dirty Dirk kidnaps Princess Butterknife and

The eponymous hero studies chivalric deeds in *Crusader Rabbit* (Television Arts Productions/Jerry Fairbanks, 1950–51).

proposes that she be his "knife," intrepid Jackknife speeds to her rescue. A saw blade, a spring-loaded blade, and fencing skills allow Jackknife to overcome Dirk, save Butterknife from the grinding wheel, and demonstrate talents that the king and his cutlery do not possess. In a final scene, the king dubs the doughty squire Sir Jackknife because he has shown his "mettle." Grateful Butterknife kisses her hero. Billy then leaves the Land of the Lost, happy in the knowledge that his missing knife has found a good home. "The Land of the Lost" flirts with Arthuriana much as "Wotta Knight" does by alluding to the legend without directly engaging it in a meaningful way.

Similarly underdeveloped Arthurian dimensions appear in the first made-for-television cartoon series, the syndicated *Crusader Rabbit* (Television Arts Productions/Jerry Fairbanks, 1949; broadcast on many NBC stations in 1950–51), from creators Jay Ward and Alex Anderson. With 1949's *A Connecticut Yankee in King Arthur's Court* and *The Adventures of Sir Galahad* serial already in theaters, Ward and Anderson sought to cash in on the Arthurian bubble by bringing to the small screen a taste of what was happening on the large one. In the premiere episode, the audience meets the diminutive hero, with his "big, big ideals," who, "when he wasn't out on a crusade, ... was reading about other bold and fearless men." Crusader Rabbit's voice replaces the narrator's as the hero makes his inaugural appearance: seated beneath a mushroom, finishing a book entitled *Sir Galahad*. He reads aloud: "Sir Galahad rescued the fair maiden from the wicked dragon. And they lived happily ever after." He sighs longingly as he identifies with the traditionally chaste knight who, in Crusader Rabbit's book at least, wins a damsel's favor.

The narrator's voice returns to catalog the many ways in which Crusader Rabbit differs from the typical superhero of the day: he cannot stop trains or fly through the air; he lacks X-ray vision and in truth is nearsighted; and his greatest ability lies in his knack for fleeing trouble, a talent that "he developed to the highest degree." Although later episodes reveal that Crusader Rabbit and companion Ragland T. (Rags) Tiger hail from *Galahad* Glen, and although by large stretch of the imagination Crusader Rabbit's quixotic struggles against the forces of evil and oppression could be deemed as distantly derived from Arthurian ideals, this series also merely dabbles with the legend. Yet *Crusader Rabbit*'s ostensibly offhand introduction of a book with *Sir Galahad* on its cover shows the work of savvy animators tapping into the same subject matter that Americans were increasingly finding at the movies in the years after World War II.

The 1949 Arthurian matinee offerings of *A Connecticut Yankee in King Arthur's Court* and *The Adventures of Sir Galahad* also must have provided much of the impetus behind the July release of director Isadore (Friz) Freleng and writer Tedd Pierce's Bugs Bunny short, "Knights Must Fall" (Warner Bros.). "Knights Must Fall" is simultaneously much less and much more Arthurian than "Wotta Knight," "The Land of the Lost," and *Crusader Rabbit*. It is less Arthurian, because it makes no overt Arthurian allusions; yet it is also more, because it concludes with the catastrophic ending of Twain's *Connecticut Yankee* that live-action filmmakers have avoided to the present day.[6]

"Knights Must Fall" evokes a decided postwar atmosphere, down to the patched canvas army surplus tent — supported in part by a pitchfork rather than a regulation

3. "To Ye Jousting Tournament"

tent pole — that serves as Bugs's pavilion. In this short, Bugs plays his usual Everyman (every American, that is) role as the sometimes rude yet nonetheless admirable little guy who beats the odds. Bugs plays a minor courtier. He merrily flouts convention from the very start when he cannot find a place to dispose of his carrot stub and so steps on the spur of a suit of armor — as if opening a trashcan — to cause the seat to open so that Bugs can pitch the butt where it punningly belongs. Bugs's heedless act upsets the armor's occupant, Sir Pantsalot[7] of Dropseat Manor, who challenges Bugs to a joust of honor by striking him with a white glove. Bugs accepts, removing Pantsalot's metal gauntlet to deliver "boiler boy" a considerably more damaging blow.

The joust that follows puts us on medieval sporting turf again: a motormouthed announcer, a football field, references to baseball, boxing, and billiards, and a punning vendor — "Programs! Get your programs! You can't tell a knight from a day without a program!" The audience in the stands cheers champion Pantsalot as, astride a gallant warhorse, he enters the field from a line of splendid pavilions. Jeers then follow Bugs as, atop a tiny yet fierce mule, he emerges from his makeshift tent. Bugs addresses the theater audience in an aside: "You were expecting maybe Errol Flynn?"[8] — one in a series of allusions to the time's films and cartoons, Dick Tracy comics, speakeasies, and World War II bombers. The joust itself is in two parts, with the signature Warner Bros. cartoon kazoo marching band parading at halftime. The first half of the contest brings three passes. Bugs loses each time, cast back to the arena wall on passes one and two and then shivering — chipping away to nothing, actually — his lance on the third. We *see* a hybrid crossbow/revolver fire a bolt to signal the half as we *hear* the sound of a gunshot.

The second half of the joust is a free-for-all as Bugs and Pantsalot employ weapons that materialize out of nowhere. They smash each other with clubs to the tune of "I've Been Working on the Railroad." Bugs uses a jackhammer on Pantsalot, causing the knight to laugh uncontrollably as vibrations ripple through his suit. Pantsalot next tries a mace, which Bugs deflects back to the knight's head with a well-placed spring. Bugs dives into a hole, followed by Pantsalot. When Bugs emerges, he reprises the trashcan gag, now stepping near Pantsalot's head (all that projects from the hole) to make the top of the helm pop open so that Bugs can bash him with a hammer — and so on through several more furious encounters. At one point, Freleng and Pierce borrow a gag that had appeared in "Wotta Knight." In one of their encounters in "Wotta Knight," Bluto hacks away Popeye's armor, piece by piece, until we lose sight of him. Popeye reappears inside Bluto's armor, his head poking through the neck opening next to Bluto's. Popeye drops down inside the armor, using the opportunity to pummel hapless Bluto into submission. In "Knights Must Fall," Pantsalot chops Bugs's armor until nothing remains. When next we see Bugs, he is inside Pantsalot's armor, from which vantage the little challenger can antagonize Pantsalot and make him pound himself silly trying to get at the invader within his suit. Taking the gag a couple of steps further than "Wotta Knight" did, Bugs smooches defenseless Pantsalot and jabs a large needle into his opponent's vulnerable bottom before the sequence ends.

Just as Bugs believes that he has won and crows about his victory — "I guess I'd better go phone Lady Windermere not to expect her spouse home for dinner"—Pantsalot returns to the field with more than a dozen reinforcements. Bugs contacts the striped-shirt referee for a timeout—measured by ticks on a stopwatch sundial—and dashes to "Ye Blacksmith Shoppe" with his mule. They reappear in a contrivance that is half cast iron stove, half aviation gunner's turret. Bugs charges the enemy, ordering the "bombardier" (his mule) to extend the lance from the machine's belly. The camera cuts to the faces of the crowd in the stands to reveal the spectators' horror at the off-screen collision, a Twain-inspired final confrontation between modern American technology and old English ways.

A blackout gag and a moment's silence provide the transition to the next scene: a pile of scrap armor that fills the screen as Freleng and Pierce recall Twain's grotesque "The Battle of the Sand-Belt" (chap. 43) from *Connecticut Yankee* with its mountains of electrocuted yet still-standing dead. A panning shot takes us beyond the rubble to many empty, upright suits of armor with for sale signs on them. A banner announces that we have come to the lot of "THE SMILING RABBIT/DEALER IN/USED ARMOR." For the third time, the trashcan gag: "So it shouldn't be a total loss," Bugs says, as the practical, entrepreneurial Yankee bunny pitches a carrot into Pantsalot's vacant suit of armor.

To the degree that a direct comparison is relevant, we may say that "Knights Must Fall" retains the core of Twain's novel by showing the disastrous consequences of inserting modern American ways into medieval England. In the cartoon's abridgement of *Connecticut Yankee*, no narrative frame explains how Bugs arrives in the Middle Ages[9]; he is simply present as the cartoon begins. Yet Bugs's impact on medieval society proves every bit as calamitous as Hank Morgan's attempts to make Camelot follow his (American) ways. While undeniably amusing, "Knights Must Fall" thus has a very dark side. It is perhaps because of this undercurrent that "Knights Must Fall" remains one of the Bugs Bunny cartoons that Warner Bros. has not released on DVD.[10]

As the 1940s came to a close, on the big screen and small, animated Arthurian plots and themes percolated. King Arthur himself, however, had yet to make an appearance.

CHAPTER 4

"What's Up, Duke?" Variety in the 1950s and Early 1960s

The advent of CinemaScope in 1953 made historical dramas even more popular at the box office than they had been in the 1940s. The panoramic vista seemed to be made for spectacles such as *The Robe* (1953), the first in a long series of historical recreations that in only a few years would include such medieval fare in CinemaScope (and similar widescreen processes) as *The Black Shield of Falworth* (1954), *The Saracen Blade* (1954), *King Richard and the Crusaders* (1954), *The Court Jester* (1955), *Quentin Durward* (1955), *The Conqueror* (1956), *The Vagabond King* (1956), *Richard III* (1956) and *The Vikings* (1958).[1] Major Hollywood studios also released earnest costume dramas focusing on the Arthurian era with *Knights of the Round Table* (MGM, 1953; the studio's first CinemaScope film), *Prince Valiant* (Twentieth Century–Fox, 1954; in CinemaScope), and *The Black Knight* (Columbia, 1954; in the older Academy ratio). In these same years, new productions of *Connecticut Yankee* graced every American television network (CBS in 1952, ABC in 1954, and NBC in 1955), while the United Kingdom's serialized *Adventures of Sir Lancelot* (ITV, 1956) was telecast for audiences eager for weekly installments of Round Table life. Toward the end of the spate, even Hollywood could lampoon the flood of medieval pictures with its own self-parodies in such films as Roger Corman's *The Undead* and *The Saga of the Viking Women and Their Voyage to the Waters of the Great Sea Serpent*, both made at lightning speed for American International Pictures and released in March and December 1957.[2]

One beat behind the release of these features, animators responded to public appetite by creating both generally "medieval" cartoons with jousting knights, fair maidens in distress, and marauding dragons, and explicitly "Arthurian" ones, where these knights and maidens are assigned names, sometimes arbitrarily, from the Arthurian roster. Although some of these cartoons do a better job than others of directly engaging Arthurian themes, deep engagement remains relatively rare. Three Warner Bros. theatrical releases, several made-for-television cartoons, and a short film produced for the education market provide a snapshot of the many ways animators used the matter of the Round Table in the ten years following the debut of Arthurian feature films in CinemaScope.

Bugs Bunny made his second jaunt into Arthurianimation in "Knight-Mare Hare" (Warner Bros., 1955), written by Pierce (who also had written 1949's "Knights Must Fall") and directed by Chuck Jones. Pierce once again adapts Twain's story for Bugs, updating the storyline with elements likely drawn from Paramount's 1949 *Connecticut*

Arthurian Animation

Yankee and perhaps the era's three American network television performances of the novel as well.

"Knight-Mare Hare" reintroduces Twain's time-travel frame narrative that "Knights Must Fall" shunned. As the short begins, we find Bugs reclining under a salon hairdryer—"Just washed my ears and I can't do a thing with 'em," he confides—beneath a tree, in a field with a farm in the distance. Bugs reads aloud a tale of the "Black K-night" and "Sir Launsilliot" from a large red tome purporting to be a certain Burton's *Tales of Knighthood and Gallantry*.[3] As Bugs reaches the point in the tale that the Black Knight strikes Launcelot "such a resounding buffet on the helm that everything went black," Jones and Pierce recall the blow to the head that Twain used to cast Hank Morgan into the past. In Twain's novel, a factory worker employs a crowbar on his overbearing boss to launch the fantasy; in the cartoon, an apple strikes the metal canopy surrounding Bugs's head. Bugs loses consciousness. As the hairdryer continues to resonate like a struck bell, Bugs travels from the present into medieval times. He continues to wear the salon bonnet with its dangling wires—Bugs's "helm" through much of the short.

The cartoon traces Bugs's journey from countryside to court in three movements. In the first, the naive newcomer must defeat "Sir O of K, Earl of Watercress, Sir Osis of the Liver, Knight of the Garter, and Baron of Wooster-cester-shister-shyster-schuster-schuster-shister-shire ... shire,"[4] who holds him at lance-point in a scene drawn from Twain or, more likely, from Paramount's film version of *Connecticut Yankee*. Indeed, a side-by-side comparison of Paramount's 1949 feature and Warner's 1955 cartoon reveals many visual similarities, almost as if the animators were using the film's mise en scène as a guide to establish the cartoon's sequence with Bugs and Sir O.

As in his earlier venture into the Middle Ages in "Knights Must Fall," Bugs once again unintentionally insults the first noble he encounters. Bugs's overcasual "What's up, Duke?" fails to show due obeisance to and proper recognition of the status of his social better. Next Bugs responds to the knight's many royal titles by asking whether the nobleman knows Bugs's equally regal friends from the American jazz scene: "Duke of Ellington, Count of Basie, Earl of Hines, Cab of Calloway, [and] Satchmo of Armstrong." "Upstarts and rogues," replies the knight,

Bugs Bunny confronts Sir O of K in "Knight-Mare Hare" (Warner Bros., 1955).

4. "What's Up, Duke?"

unwilling to admit New World claims to Old World degrees of peerage. Bugs leaps to defend the honor of his pals against the charges of the "pressure cooker," whom he disparages as the medicinal laxative "Sir Rup [Syrup] of Figs." The knight scoffs at the puny challenger: "What? Wouldst tilt with me?" Bugs responds in kind: "Tilt with thee I will and I won't wilt!" Sir O grants Bugs's request for a sword and then rides off to gather steam for a charge. Meanwhile, Bugs discovers that he cannot lift the heavy weapon, so he prepares for death with a blindfold and cigarette as the knight bears down on him sounding like a sack full of tin cans. At the last moment, Bugs steps aside and extends his foot to trip the charging horse, catapulting Sir O into a nearby castle—a medieval structure with contours that recall the modern barn, silos, and farmhouse of the cartoon's opening frames—and eliminating Sir O from the remainder of the storyline.

In the second movement, although pleased that he has defeated the knight, Bugs wonders how he can leave this "booby hatchery"—thus calling to the audience's mind Hank's similar doubts about the sanity of the knight he meets at the beginning of Twain's novel or one of its more recent incarnations on the large or small screen.[5] A fire-breathing dragon—Bugs dismisses it is a big "horny toad"—interrupts the hero's thoughts by trying to cook him. Vaudeville-fashion, Bugs extinguishes the dragon's flames with a seltzer bottle. The dragon whimpers as he disappears over the horizon, tail between his legs. Bugs has vanquished his second adversary.

In the final movement, an Arthurian character at last appears, but it is neither the Black Knight nor Sir Launcelot suggested by the book that Bugs was reading. As our hero walks along, he comes to a tower—Bugs, remembering the farmer's field where this adventure began, mistakes it for a silo—and a mailbox in the foreground that reveals the occupant's identity as "Merlin of Monroe."[6] Bugs crosses a lowered drawbridge and a Peter Lorre–like voice welcomes him inside: "Come right in. How do you do? My name is Merlin. I'm a sorcerer." Jones and Pierce understand that the character's barefaced self-introduction is necessary. While the mailbox informs the audience that Merlin is near, there is little in the depiction of the gnarled, ridiculous figure to confirm his identity for us. Further, Merlin of Monroe's propeller-topped beanie fails to enhance the legendary magician's gravitas in any way as "Knight-Mare Hare" presents a Merlin who runs counter to the sober portrayal of the ancient sage in, for example, MGM's *Knights of the Round Table*. This Merlin has more in common with the wizard of the 1931 *Connecticut Yankee* film.

Bugs begs to see Merlin "sorce." Merlin obliges with magic powder that turns Bugs into a pig. Pig Bugs then unzips his belly and steps out as a rabbit again to challenge the magician. Bugs asks whether Merlin can equal Bugs's skill in striking fire from his thumb—presumably with a matchstick slid from his palm, as Crosby does in the 1949 *Connecticut Yankee*, though the cartoon does not disclose how Bugs manages the trick. Just as Merlin in Paramount's film can next be observed repeatedly flicking the Boss's discarded burnt stick in a futile attempt to generate a flame, so here Merlin of Monroe vainly flicks his thumb again and again to no effect. With Merlin preoccupied trying to replicate the challenger's magic, Bugs has the opportunity to dip into the magic powder. He turns the sorcerer into a beanie-wearing jackass. Yet unlike Bugs, no matter how many times Merlin unzips, a jackass emerges every time.

Thrice victorious, Bugs begins to wonder how to return home. A nearby bowl of fruit gives him an idea: if an apple got him into the Middle Ages, perhaps another can get him out. He tosses an apple into the air and it falls on his head. Once more to the sound of a tolling bell, Bugs returns to the present. He finds himself again under the hairdryer and his book is on the ground.

Bugs is convinced that it has all been just a nightmare — until the sight of a jackass wearing a beanie shakes his confidence. Bugs dismisses the notion: "Nah, impossible. It couldn't be him." He is then shocked into apoplexy as a farmer calls the jackass "Merlin" and the cartoon comes to a close. As at the end of Twain's novel, every feature film version of *Connecticut Yankee*, and "Bosko's Knight-Mare," elements from the dream invade the waking reality. Did the day residue of reading a book and a character's immediate surroundings create the dream or did the protagonist actually travel back in time to the days of Arthur? Hank, Bosko, and Bugs can never know for certain. Deliciously irresolvable ambiguity enriches the narrative and makes us want to see the cartoon again.

Director Freleng teamed with writer Warren Foster to use Bugs once again for an Arthurian tale in "Knighty Knight Bugs" (Warner Bros., 1957; premiered 23 August 1958), winner of the 1958 Oscar for Best Animated Short. The cartoon opens with an unnamed king — presumably Arthur — speaking: "Noble knights of the Round Table[7] [burbling pause], ever since the accursed Black Knight captured our Singing Sword, evil times hath befallen us [more burbling]. One of ye knights must recover the Singing Sword." A tippling Sir Osis of Liver and stocky Sir Loin of Beef (identified by the nameplates before them) object. They fear the "invincible" Black Knight (Yosemite Sam) and the fire-breathing dragon that serves him. "Odds bodkins!" exclaims the king as he castigates his knights' cowardice. Enter Bugs as court jester. He asserts that "only a fool would go after the Singing Sword." The king shrewdly notes that Bugs *is* the fool and thus the task of recovery falls to him. If Bugs should fail, he will suffer torture on the rack, be burned at the stake, and lose his head.

Cut to the Black Knight's castle. The hot-tempered knight and his "idyot" dragon slumber. The dragon occasionally sneezes up a fireball because it has caught a cold. Bugs sneaks into the castle, locates the Singing Sword and — unimpressed by it — wonders aloud why it is called what it is. The audience already knows. Contemporary viewers must have recalled the weapon that Hal Foster had introduced into the storyline of the *Prince Valiant* comic strip in the late 1930s and that Twentieth Century–Fox had recently popularized again in its crowd-pleasing 1954 *Prince Valiant*. As Robert Wagner's Valiant explains in the feature film: "The Singing Sword will only give its power to its rightful owners. It will never sing in the hands of a traitor." And, as if in answer to Bugs's question, the sword in his hands begins to warble, making the sound of a musical saw. The sword has found its rightful owner at last, a moment underscored by the amorous tune it performs for Bugs: the perennial hit "Cuddle Up a Little Closer, Lovey Mine," which Gordon MacRae had sung memorably to Doris Day in a recent Warner Bros. picture, *On Moonlight Bay* (1951).[8] The sword's warbling wakes the knight and dragon.

4. "What's Up, Duke?"

A conventional chase sequence in a medieval setting follows. A drawbridge drops on the Black Knight's head. An imprecisely aimed catapult launches him into a wall. The Black Knight is repeatedly drenched in the moat and scorched by his dragon's involuntary fireballs. Finally, the dragon sneezes inside an anachronistic TNT storeroom to send a castle tower and its two occupants "to the moon." (The moment may have made audiences think of the *Sputnik*, *Explorer*, and *Vanguard* missions of the day.) As a gloating Bugs leaves the castle and sets out for the horizon, the sword begins to sing once more. This time it performs "Aloha 'Oe"—for the Black Knight and dragon bound for space, for Bugs as he heads down the road, and for the audience until the next Bugs Bunny short. The premise that began the action—that Bugs must return the sword to the unimpressive and rather mean-spirited king who presides over the equally unimpressive Round Table—seems to have been forgotten as the iris closes. Or perhaps there is no reason to return to court because the Singing Sword is where it belongs: in the hands of the true hero of this tale, Bugs Bunny.

Five years later, Warner Bros. co-directors Jones—pompously styling himself "Chuck Jones, Esq." in the credits for this transatlantic romp—and Maurice Noble collaborated on "I Was a Teenage Thumb" (1962; premiered 19 January 1963), a version of the Tom Thumb story in which the lilliputian hero finds himself in Arthur's kingdom.[9] The title is significant. It suggests that Warner Bros. veterans thought it more profitable to play for the *I Was a Teenage ...* niche market than to attempt to capture what was by the early 1960s an audience whose interest in films about medieval knights had waned since the heyday of the 1950s.[10] Nevertheless, there are several casual, diffuse, almost nonsensical Arthurian references in "I Was a Teenage Thumb." We meet an itinerant "great and famous magician" named Ralph K. Merlin, Jr.—much the same odd-looking sorcerer from Jones's own 1955 "Knight-Mare Hare"—who changes form every time that he hiccups. Merlin grants Prunhilda Thumb's "reasonable enough" wish for a baby no larger than a thumb. Infant Tom makes his traditional journey via house cat, bird, and fish to Arthur's court. Near the castle, "Sir Mordred of Herringbone Fleet" angles from a rowboat, the "H. M. S. Guinevere."[11] He lands the fish that has swallowed Tom and presents it to King Arthur.

The king thanks the servile "Morty" for the day's catch and is delighted to discover Tom inside the fish. "Well bless my royal liver!" the king exclaims, "It's a boy! And no bigger 'n me thumb. By George, I think I'll shower him with gold and jewels and make him a knight. And I don't want any argument! I'm king around here!" Arthur dubs the little one Sir Thumbus of Thumbatten.[12] As Tom develops into a mouse-riding knight, he fights dragons ("only the smaller varieties, of course") and giants ("only the larger varieties, of course"), then marries a "beautiful yet haughty princess" with whom he begins his line of progressively diminutive descendants, each the size of the father's thumb from the preceding generation. "And they all lived happily ever after," the narrator concludes, save for a quick return to Tom's parents out in the countryside. Prunhilda is again pregnant, craving sardines and strawberry popovers, as she knits a colossal baby booty for her *next* child.

"I Was a Teenage Thumb" lacks the vigor that created earlier Warner Bros. Arthurianimation. The enervated gags take cheap jabs at British life, with the Arthurian references serving as metonyms for that way of life. The cartoon offers a portrait of an uninspiring and insipid royal court over which a petulant monarch presides. Mordred (Arthur's son? nephew?) does not engage in chivalric adventures but spends his days fishing and serving as steward — performing both duties in full armor topped by a straw "boater" hat. Guinevere makes an appearance solely as a name for the dinghy from which Mordred fishes. The king's subjects, as represented by the Thumbs, a "happy, typical British family," arouse neither respect nor laughter. George Ebenezer Thumb (Tom's father) sports stereotypical snaggleteeth, smokes a meerschaum, wears a waistcoat and tie even when going to the barn for milk, and mutters incomprehensibly when not humming "Barbara Ellen" and reading *Tyme* magazine. Mom Prunhilda spends her days dressed in a housecoat and knitting booties. Even the weary-voiced narrator seems tired of the subject as he begins one segment: "Now we all know the rest of the story...." A sense of exhaustion pervades "I Was a Teenage Thumb." Had Arthurianimation run its course?

While Warner Bros. was supplying theatergoers with Arthurianimation, other studios were turning to the growing television market with similar fare. With a story directed and lightly revised by Art Heinemann,[13] UPA (United Productions of America) produced a narratively straightforward, limited-animation adaptation of Heywood Broun's 1919 short story "The Fifty-First Dragon" for CBS's *The Gerald McBoing Boing Show* (1956; broadcast in 1957). The highly stylized, eleven-minute cartoon offers a mildly abridged version of Broun's brief tale of Gawaine le Coeur-Hardy, an unremarkable, timorous student attending Knight School. Only when the headmaster gives Gawaine a magic word of invincibility ("Rumplesnitz") and sets the lad to a vigorous training regimen does Gawaine gain the confidence required to fight dragons. While Broun's more acid satire has been suppressed in Heinemann's adaptation[14] and glossed over as well is the probable *death* of Gawaine in combat against his fifty-first dragon — as he learns that "Rumplesnitz" has no real power — the cartoon nonetheless remains material primarily for mature viewers. (The harp strains of "Ave Maria" as the end credits roll leave little doubt as to Gawaine's fate, but it is a subtle gag for parents rather than their children.) The Arthurian dimension runs no deeper than the name Broun had originally assigned the character, a name that a 1950s audience would associate with other Arthurian stories appearing at the theater and on television at the time.

Hanna-Barbera Productions had less sophisticated viewers in mind when it placed one of its most lucrative television properties, Huckleberry Hound, in medieval surroundings in "Sir Huckleberry Hound" (1958), "Dragon Slayer Huck" (1958), and an explicitly Arthurian kingdom in "Knight School" (1960), produced for CBS's *The Huckleberry Hound Show*. Written by Warren Foster and directed by Alex Lovy, "Knight School" bears some resemblance to UPA's "The Fifty-First Dragon," though Foster's earlier work at Warner Bros. on the award-winning "Knighty Knight Bugs" provides clearer echoes. "Knight School" opens with a narrator:

4. "What's Up, Duke?"

> In the days of King Arthur, the golden age of knighthood was in its finest hour. The famed Round Table was the meeting place of knights whose splendid deeds became legend. Little wonder then that it was every young lad's ambition to become a knight of the Round Table.

Enter Huckleberry Hound, breaking the fourth wall to dispute the narrator's claims and admit that he has in fact been drafted. While Huck's thirty days at Knight School (a labored pun in this cartoon) are difficult, private Huck serendipitously passes the trials set by the drill sergeant at "Ye Boote Camp for Knights" and ultimately, though quite inadvertently, graduates at the top of his class. King Arthur dubs him Sir Huckleberry Hound.

The incongruously small Sir Huck joins his peers at the Round Table. The king addresses them: "Brave knights, the fire-breathing dragon of Shropshire is on the loose again." Inverting the knights' cowardly response that appeared in "Knighty Knight Bugs," the "Knight School" men keenly vie for the opportunity to battle the menace — except for apprehensive Huck, who hesitates to face such a monster. "You can't all go," says Arthur, as he settles on a fair solution to select the knight-adventurer: cutting cards, with the high card to determine who will take the mission. Huck is relieved when he draws a three, until several other knights get twos and Arthur a "one"— not the high-card ace, Arthur explains, but a card with "1" printed on it. Huck raises the suggestion that the king perhaps cheats at cards.

To the accompaniment of the narrator's magisterial description of a novice knight embarking "to do battle for the honor of King Arthur and the glory of the Round Table," Huck modestly sets out for Shropshire. He fusses gently about his ill-fitting "G. I. helmet," a medieval helm with a squeaky, uncooperative visor. When he locates his quarry, Huck makes a couple of clumsy passes at the beast before deciding he must escape the dragon's flames by leaping into a lake. Luckily for Huck, the dragon plunges his head into the water to finish off his adversary. The water douses the dragon's fire, changing "hot stuff" to "just a king-size lizard." As the weeping dragon runs away, Huck observes that extinguished dragons are known to "skedaddle off and hide. No one ever sees 'em again."

Huck returns to court to learn that a new adventure has already come. An ogre needs defeating by a champion yet to be chosen. A wiser Huck is ready this time. He has procured a "0" card. All appears well for Huck's plan until the capricious king announces that today the *low* number will win the right to engage the beast. Huck laments, "No wonder they use a Round Table. Nuthin's on the square around here."

While both children and their parents could conceivably enjoy "Knight School," some cartoons were made just for kids. "Sir Lancelot" (1959), one of 104 limited-animation episodes in the *Mel-o-Toons* (New World Productions) syndicated television series, was evidently created with an audience of second-graders in mind. As was the case with many other *Mel-o-Toons* cartoons, the inspiration for "Sir Lancelot" rose from "preexisting children's records—those little yellow '45 rpm' discs with red labels that were tossed in free with the first record player you ever owned" (Erickson 329).

As the short opens, a smiling boy reclines in bed, engrossed in a book entitled *Knights of Old* on his lap. A mind-numbingly simplistic marching tune plays as the camera turns from the young reader to scenes of Lancelot in the Middle Ages. As the song proceeds, three tales of Lancelot's chivalry unfold: using his Singing Sword to defeat a dragon that eats Arthur's cattle and burns Camelot, fighting and jailing highwaymen, and stepping forward from the Round Table ranks to rescue "fair maid Guinevere" when she has been captured by a "knight in black."

With Lancelot's reputation established, we return to the boy. He has fallen asleep while reading *Knights of Old*. The march begins anew as the camera pans from the sleeping lad to a nearby photograph of the boy (armed with toy sword) and a girl. We move into his dream. The boy imagines himself astride a burro ("his charger") reenacting Lancelot's three adventures, though now in America circa 1959. The dragon that had burned Camelot's log hut now ignites suburban tract housing. The medieval robbers who had emerged from the woods now spring, like ambushing bullies, from a new wilderness—a suburban alley, with a can labeled "ASHES" in the background to help us recognize the setting. A scene of Lancelot with fellow knights at the Round Table from the first part of the cartoon becomes in the second part several boys gathered at a circular coffee table near the alley that the boy's heroism has made safe. "Fair maid Guinevere" herself is replaced by the girl from the photograph and again she needs to be rescued from a thug.

A boy dreams of emulating a knight in "Sir Lancelot," *Mel-o-Toons* (New World Productions, 1959).

Despite its juvenile demographic target, this short distinguishes itself through a thoughtful consideration of the boy's dream perspective. Secondary characters (Lancelot's enemies and the king) from *Knights of Old* become mere silhouettes or are cropped entirely from the frame in the boy's dream as he effectively *becomes* Lancelot. The boy conquers all the obstacles that Lancelot faced and then wakes at cartoon's end to discover that the bedside photograph itself has changed as a consequence of his dream. He blinks in astonishment. The girl who before stood next to him facing forward now holds his hand and gazes lovingly at him—his reward for emulating Lancelot. We should also observe, however, that while the cartoon's Sir Lancelot rescues Guinevere for his king, the boy obviously has his own designs upon the girl in this tale dangerously (albeit unintentionally) reminiscent of the adulterous relationship in Malory's *Le Morte Darthur*.

4. "What's Up, Duke?"

Meanwhile, ten years after *Crusader Rabbit*, Jay Ward was again assembling talented people who wanted to make edgy television cartoons. His latest concept was a limited-animation cartoon variety show focused on a pair of mismatched protagonists—the same formula that had made *Crusader Rabbit* successful. Audiences would come to know these two new characters as Rocky and Bullwinkle on ABC's *Rocky and His Friends* (Jay Ward Productions, 1959–61). Three times in the first season on the air, Ward's crew touched Arthurian themes in *Rocky*'s subsidiary short-feature series, *Peabody's Improbable History* and *Fractured Fairy Tales*.

Ward and his deeply iconoclastic, erudite writing partner Bill Scott were rarely reverent when it came to dealing with commonly accepted American values. Time and again *Rocky and His Friends* treated satirically the givens of the day—much to the chagrin of virtually every sponsor that the show ever had.[15] Hollywood's Arthurian films of the decade made excellent targets for their sharp pens. Indeed, by 1959 Ward and Scott were not alone in thinking that there perhaps had been a few too many live-action treatments of the Middle Ages, as several contemporaneous cartoon portraits of unattractive Arthurian courts suggest. Ward and Scott offered broad burlesque to make the point.

Mr. Peabody and Sherman's fifth voyage through the time-traveling WABAC Machine in *Peabody's Improbable History* takes to them to Camelot in "King Arthur" (1959). It is "the sixth century"—a minor script detail that the show's Mexican animators overlooked when they placed a calendar for "853 AD" on the castle wall. Arthur tells his visitors that they have come on a bad day: Black Tuesday, 6 April, a day that brings disasters to the kingdom every year. Already the king's Singing Sword is punningly "flat." Merlin has developed amnesia that leaves him unable to complete spells: "Abra.... Abra.... I wish I could recall how the rest of that goes." And a dragon is attacking the castle.

Sherman suggests fighting the beast. Arthur: "With what?" Sherman: "What about your knights?" Arthur: "Restless, lad, restless. Can't sleep a wink." Peabody specifies "the armored kind: Galahad, Launcelot," whom the king then deploys. But they are unable to defend the realm because they have showered in their armor. "Rust," Arthur sighs, "It is the thing we feareth most." Fortunately, Arthur's "most valiant knight" Sir Round has just returned "from a quest" and takes up the challenge straightaway. Yet just as quickly, the dragon sears Round's armor to dust. Arthur decides he must fight, even if his sword is out of tune. Excitedly he raises his sword in preparation and in the process severs a rope. A bell that the rope once held drops from above to knock the king unconscious.

As is usual in these episodes, Peabody must save the day. He gives bubble gum—"Double Bubble Bubblegum," Sherman insists, as if pandering to a network sponsor—to the dragon. The dragon chews it, tries to breathe fire, and unintentionally creates a hot air balloon that carries it away. Conscious again, Arthur would like to dub the helpful visitors knights, but the scourge of Black Tuesday continues. Termites are eating away at a square table that is becoming—you guessed it—the Round Table.

Ward and Scott's *Fractured Fairy Tales* version of "Tom Thumb" (1959) employs the same traditional premise that Jones and Noble use in 1963's "I Was a Teenage Thumb": Merlin overhears a woman's desire for a son no bigger than her husband's thumb. He is "so amused" by her wish that he giggles uncontrollably as he grants it. Little Tom has a tough childhood. His plowman father complains of "just another mouth to feed." His loving yet overprotective mother keeps him in a birdcage for safety.

At age 16, Tom's only friend is a butterfly. He runs away from home, riding his butterfly to "the big city," the heart of Arthur's kingdom. Reveling in his freedom, Tom calls himself Big Thumb, the ringleader of a band of punks known as the Big Thumb Gang — as he will say later, he becomes "the biggest man in the kingdom." He resembles Marlon Brando out of *The Wild One* (1954) as he rides his butterfly/motorcycle/hot rod (with "dual carburetors" and "oversized valves") to his first caper, a raid on a local candy store. But Tom and his pals do not get far. The police catch them just outside their hideout.

These events introduce a series of topical jokes about how (as a newspaper title howls) "JUVENILE DELINQUENCY GAINS IN KING ARTHUR'S KINGDOM." The entire realm is abuzz from Parliament to the man in the street. Everyone demands that the king do something about the national crisis—in truth, little more than some kids' thwarted scheme, blown out of proportion by the media. Ward and Scott's satire alludes to Eisenhower-era coverage of America's own aimless youth in the press and in such popular films as *Rebel Without a Cause* (1955), *Teenage Crime Wave* (1955), *Juvenile Jungle* (1958), *Riot in Juvenile Prison* (1959), and countless similar fare. Enter Arthur, who gruffly assigns Merlin the task of investigating and ending delinquency.

In a psychiatrist's office setting, Merlin talks to Tom. The magician discovers that his own spell created the social turmoil: Tom became a hoodlum to compensate for the feelings of inadequacy created by his thumb-sized stature. But Merlin cannot reverse the charm. Wizards have their limits, too. Then Merlin recalls the *language* of the wish for a boy no bigger than his father's thumb. And he sees a way out of the quandary: make the father's thumb *larger*. As Merlin makes dad's thumb grow, Tom gets bigger as well. When Tom is the size of other boys, he becomes a well-adjusted, conforming member of society. Arthur appoints him Keeper of the Royal Butterflies. The father retires from farming and his huge thumb is declared a national monument. Mom buys a bird for her cage. With the highly exaggerated national delinquency crisis solved, all can live happily ever after.[16] A network censor objected anyway:

> I find the whole tenor of this episode objectionable. Juvenile delinquency is not something to be treated flippantly. Please have Tom become something other than a mixed-up JD with a souped up butterfly, leading a juvenile gang on "candy heists." THIS EPISODE IS REJECTED [Scott 155].

Cooler heads won out. The episode aired as written.

Ward and Scott's most entertaining — and paradoxically most somber — Arthurian cartoon is "Sir Galahad, or The Tomorrow Knight" (1959), another of the *Fractured Fairy Tales* shorts. It tells the tale of the son of Harry Galahad, the world's most famous clown. Harry inadvertently christens his boy "Sir" when the Town Clerk asks dad if he has chosen a name for his son and Harry replies, "Yes, sir."

4. "What's Up, Duke?"

Harry wants little Sir Galahad to follow his footsteps into "show biz." Yet like Tom Thumb, this son also rebels when he gets to his teens. Rather than become the clown that his parents desire, Sir wants to be a knight. Sir has read about them in a book titled *Knights of the Round Table*. He knows that "knights get to wear armor…. Ride white chargers. Save lovely damsels from dragons." In the manner of all hero-worshiping boys, he has decked his walls with emblems of his goal: a triangular Camelot pennant and inspiring posters that encourage him to "BE A KNIGHT/EARN BIG MEDALS," "BE A KNIGHT/ARTHUR NEEDS YOU," and join in the rivalry of "CAMELOT VS. OXFORD."

One night Sir dreams he has become a knight. Yet being a knight turns out to be rather different from his idealized vision of it. His lackey gives him a nag to ride. His visor opens and closes with every step that his horse takes. It is hard to find a damsel. Killing a dragon proves difficult. Nevertheless, he overcomes all obstacles and finally wins a lovely princess for a bride. Unfortunately, his wife becomes less attractive as she bears their many children and keeps Sir at home, both because she does not want him rescuing any more damsels and because she requires her husband to tend the babies and wash the dishes. Sir laments, "I should have married the dragon."

We have now reached the point in the episode where Ward and Scott mark their target: this time, the Cold War. One day, "much to Sir's delight, a war broke out." The conflict allows Sir to leave his castle "to defend the kingdom from threatening invaders. Alone he sallied forth against overwhelming odds. And because he had fought bravely [we see him chased by many troops], he received a hero's welcome [we see trumpeters] with full military honors [panning shot to his grave, with weeping wife and child at graveside, and a cannon exploding]." "That's a hero's welcome?!" Sir exclaims, as the cannon's roar wakes him from the dream. Meanwhile, Sir's parents have also had a change of heart and decided to let their boy follow his dream of becoming a knight. Sir, however, comes to breakfast wearing a clown suit and juggling. He tells his folks that he would rather be in "show biz" than (it is implied) follow the chivalric ideals that will lead to his death. Ward and Scott thus show us what they hope the *tomorrow* knight will be: a pacifist.

Ward and Scott's brilliant use of Arthurian themes to explore contemporary social

The funereal "hero's welcome" that awaits warriors in "Sir Galahad, or The Tomorrow Knight," *Fractured Fairy Tales* on *Rocky and His Friends* (Jay Ward Productions, 1959).

issues was not easy to reproduce. Such piercing satire would not be seen again until Monty Python had its way with the legend. More typically, the early 1960s offered uninspired televised fare. With a shoestring production budget, Tooter Turtle punned his limited-animation way through the Arthurian realm in "Knight of the Square Table, or The Joust and the Unjoust" (Total Television, 1960) on NBC's *King Leonardo and His Short Subjects*. Popeye did the same in "The Black Knight" (King Features/Jack Kinney Productions, 1960) on the syndicated *Popeye* show. Astro Boy also traveled into the past for Arthurian adventure in "The Terrible Time Gun," an episode of *Astro Boy* (Mushi Productions, 1963) adapted from its Japanese original for telecast on NBC.

Both Total Television and Jay Ward Productions often relied on the same Mexican animation facilities, thus it is no surprise that the low-budget visual style of Tooter Turtle's "Knight of the Square Table" short calls to mind many Peabody and Sherman episodes of the day. The similarity does not end there. Tooter Turtle episodes strive for the same acrobatic, offbeat wordplay of the more successful *Peabody's Improbable History* and *Fractured Fairy Tales*. In "Knight of the Square Table," reading a book leads Tooter to ask Mr. Wizard (the Lizard) to send him to the land of "King Arturo" and his "Knights of the Square Table." Tooter wants to become a "knight-errand boy," because he is "bare-bursting with romantics and deeds of derring-do." Mr. Wizard offers to make him any knight he chooses. Tooter consults his book again and selects Sir Laffalot de Puddle.

It is tournament day as Tooter arrives in the Middle Ages. A sign announces the "Fight Today" between Sir Laffalot and Sir Mordred (mangled to "Sir Murdered" in Tooter's habitually garbled misreadings and mispronunciations). "Uh-oh," it dawns on Tooter. "That's me." A boxing-style referee introduces the contestants: Sir Laffalot of the Square Table, weighing one ton and riding his "white horse" (drawn as a dark gray horse with a light caparison by the animators), and Sir Mordred, "that scourge of the countryside," at two tons and riding a "black horse" (drawn as another dark gray horse but with black caparison). The referee reminds the combatants that the Camelot Jousting Commission has set the rules of conduct: "I want a clean fight, and in the case of killing, the other knight must retire to a neutral end of the field."

Tooter's unreadiness shows immediately. Even before the match begins, he fumbles the lance that a crane lowers to him, tumbles from his horse, and receives a five-point penalty from the referee. Tooter fares no better in his jousting pass at Mordred. He fails to connect with the target, plunges his lance into the ground, and receives more penalties. When the referee threatens to "disqualify" Tooter, Tooter chuckles goofily, "Seems to me more likely I'll be disjointed." Tooter next tries to battle Mordred on foot. He inexpertly hacks at his opponent until Mordred begins to fight back and forces Tooter to the ground once more. Fearing for his life, Tooter resorts to his formulaic call for Mr. Wizard to rescue him from an ill-chosen adventure. As in every episode in the series, Tooter admits his failings and Mr. Wizard advises him to accept his lot in life.

In director Ken Hultgren and writer Ed Nofziger's "The Black Knight" short, Professor O. G. WottaSnozzle's time machine—an unvarnished copy of Peabody's

4. "What's Up, Duke?"

WABAC — transports Popeye to Camelot for *Connecticut Yankee*—style adventures. Just after Popeye arrives in the Middle Ages, Brutus the Black Knight (reprising Bluto's role from 1947's "Wotta Knight") captures him, believing him to be a spy. The knight takes his prisoner to the rulers of the realm, "King Wimpy the Arthur" and "Queen Olive Guinevere." When Popeye begins to smoke his pipe, Wimpy fears the visitor is a witch. Popeye also incites the ire of Ethel Merlin the Magician (the Sea Hag),[17] who sees him as a potential rival and locks him in a cell until a joust between the Black Knight and the interloper can be arranged. To make sure that Popeye perishes in the bout, Ethel offers him no weapons or armor — only a "phony pony," a log with four posts supporting it.

The power of spinach allows Popeye to survive the Black Knight's four jousting passes. On the final pass, the hero shatters the knight's armor to bits, then reassembles the scraps into a wind-up car that he sends over the horizon with Brutus inside. King Wimpy wields his "medieval hamburger" joint of beef to dub the victorious Popeye "the Knight of the Spinach" just as the professor recalls Camelot's newest knight to the present day. The cartoon is unremarkable save for such specimens of fractured English as Popeye's "Where's the door atteth?" and a hackneyed string of (k)night puns designed to make viewers groan. With Wimpy in the role of King Arthur and Olive Oyl as his queen, Arthurianimation seemed to be scraping bottom.

Manga character Tetsuwan Atomu ("Mighty Atom," or "Astro Boy" as he is known in anglophone markets) also appeared in a time-travel plot borrowed loosely from Twain in "The Terrible Time Gun" (1963). Fred Ladd's English translation/adaptation of the Japanese half-hour cartoon tells the story of evil Dr. Tempo's plan to dispose of his adversaries, Dr. Elefun of the Institute of Science and his robot Astro Boy, by sending them to the Middle Ages. Many similarities to *Connecticut Yankee* appear: Elefun and Astro Boy read a book about the twelfth century before Tempo's time gun takes them there; a Sagramore-like knight challenges the time-travelers as they arrive in the Middle Ages; Princess Philomena falls in love with Astro Boy, her visitor from the future; court wizard Marvin the Magician and Elefun engage in a battle that pits magic against science; the newcomers foil a plot, hatched by an evil courtier and Marvin, to overthrow the king; and Astro Boy and Elefun return to their own time to defeat Tempo and see him confined to a hospital for the insane. Although translator/adapter Ladd is undoubtedly responsible for some of the Arthurian strokes, the many echoes of Twain's novel must be attributed to the Japanese crew at Mushi Productions who wrote and directed the original cartoon.

Beyond the theater and television screen, the increasing availability of 16mm projection equipment in schools across America opened another market for Arthurianimation: the educational film. Thirty years after creating the first Arthurianimation in "Bosko's Knight-Mare" and roughly twenty after an unsuccessful bid to bring *King Arthur and His Knights* to the big screen, Hugh Harman returned one last time to Arthur's realm with a twenty-minute animated reel destined for classroom use: Harman and Gordon Sheehan's *Tom Thumb in King Arthur's Court* (Coronet Instructional Films, 1963).[18]

Arthurian Animation

Coronet, the leading provider of social guidance films in the late 1940s and early 1950s, was updating its catalog. Timeworn live-action films about delinquency, drunk driving, and moral rectitude — the ones that many baby boomers still recall from their health, gym, and homeroom classes— needed to be replaced by pictures more in tune with 1960s youth. *How Billy Keeps Clean* (1951), *Dating Do's and Don'ts* (1949), *Why We Respect the Law* (1950), and dozens of similar stale entries in the studio's inventory were becoming less effective — if they ever were effective at all — in producing model citizens for a postwar America.

Although Coronet had little direct experience with animated films, Harman must have come highly recommended. He had already made one very lucrative film for the studio, an animated version of Charles Tazewell's 1946 children's classic *The Littlest Angel*. Harman's *The Littlest Angel* (1950), which Coronet translated into several languages for worldwide distribution, remains a Christmas viewing favorite. But the uneven animation and curious storyline of *Tom Thumb in King Arthur's Court* can scarcely compare to the vastly superior work of *The Littlest Angel*.

The Harman/Sheehan *Tom Thumb* covers much of the same familiar territory as Warner's "I Was a Teenage Thumb," also from 1963, the *Fractured Fairy Tales* "Tom Thumb" from 1959, and many nineteenth- and twentieth-century renderings of the folk tale. However, Coronet's distinctly different sensibility and social agenda control the approach. Narrative elements elsewhere played for laughs take on educational purpose. Coronet's Tom stands as an example of one who succeeds in life by always doing the best that he can, potential limitations (imposed by diminutive stature, in Tom's case) notwithstanding. In the words of one Round Table knight in the film, "true valor is not of size, but rather of courage, spirit, and resolve."

As in most retellings, Tom's parents try to nurture and shield their son as he struggles with the world around him. In this *Tom Thumb*, little Tom feels he is becoming a nuisance to his family and dreams of growing up (literally), finally deciding that he can solve his problems by running away to become "a knight, big and brave, like Sir Launcelot." The journey to Camelot begins. Tom's perilous trip parallels his journey in other versions of the tale: help from some (a wise old rabbit), temptations from others (a thief named Limbo and his trained spider Satan), and transport by animals (a raven and a fish) that carry Tom through the wilderness and by happy chance deliver him to his goal. After several adventures, Tom emerges from the mouth of an apparent "talking fish" on a serving dish set before King Arthur. His steps toward knighthood commence.

The king and his entourage are portrayed as dignified, noble, and kind to Tom as they welcome him to the court of "the bravest in all Christendom." Arthur agrees to Tom's request to become a knight. The queen gives Tom her thimble, sewing needle, and an ivory knitting needle to function as helm, sword, and lance. Galahad donates his belt buckle as Tom's shield. Launcelot's helmet becomes Tom's dwelling. A mouse serves as his mount. Tom learns to fight by sparring with Launcelot, sewing needle against teaspoon, and tussling with a hostile cat. But *Tom Thumb in King Arthur's Court* does not descend to silly portrayals of Arthurian characters. There is not the hiccupping

4. "What's Up, Duke?"

Merlin of "I Was a Teenage Thumb" or giggling Merlin of the *Fractured Fairy Tales* "Tom Thumb" or jackass Merlin of Monroe of "Knighty Knight Bugs" to be found; in fact, Merlin does not appear in the Harman/Sheehan film, perhaps because to introduce the wizard whom other cartoons of the day often portrayed as foolish would diminish the serious tone the film seeks to create around Tom, his ideals, and Camelot.

Tom Thumb protects Arthur's emerald amulet from Satan the spider in *Tom Thumb in King Arthur's Court* (Coronet Instructional Films, 1963).

One day as Tom practices his chivalric skills, Limbo and Satan arrive in Camelot. Unnoticed by all but Tom and his mouse mount, Limbo begins to loot Arthur's treasury. Limbo directs the spider to withdraw one coin at a time from the king's hoard. Tom alerts the court to the intruders and, after a difficult struggle, narrowly defeats Satan. (The spider seems to drown in the castle's moat.) Meanwhile, Arthur's knights subdue Limbo. The kingdom's treasure is saved.

It is time for the film's message. "The smallest of us," says Arthur as he dubs Sir Tom Thumb of the Round Table, can act "with the courage of the greatest," for "valor is not of size but of spirit." For exemplary service to the realm, the king grants Tom a boon. "Now," Tom asks haltingly, "may I go home, and see my mother and...?" The understanding king cuts Tom short. "We shall take you," Arthur laughs, "take you so that they may see the bravest boy in my kingdom, Tom Thumb." Beyond the film's overt message, perceptive students also take away a few deeper lessons about growing up, filial devotion, avoiding temptation, and even defeating Satan — all elements just below the surface of many a Coronet classroom film.[19]

Before passing from this period of active albeit uneven Arthurian cartoon production from roughly 1953 to 1963, let us take note of two peripheral entries in the annals of Arthurianimation. In 1955 Famous Studios reused part of the jousting sequence from 1947's "Wotta Knight" as a cartoon-within-a-cartoon penny arcade attraction that Bluto shows Wimpy in "Penny Antics," a theatrical short written by I. Klein (who had also worked on "Wotta Knight") and directed by Seymour Kneitel. The recycling of old material suggests that the studio wanted to offer "something Arthurian" to capitalize on the feature film and televised Arthurian offerings of the time but had nothing new to offer. Vintage footage from the vault thus found its way into the non–Arthurian "Penny Antics." Of all the moments that Klein and Kneitel could have used from "Wotta Knight," they chose to start with the banner that places us in the kingdom of "Ye Knights of Ye Round Table," even though, as already mentioned, nothing distinctly *Arthurian* appears in the cartoon beyond that banner. But one must catch the bandwagon before it passes, and many studios certainly tried.

Famous Studios's transparent attempt to capitalize on the era's Arthurian surge with a segment salvaged from "Wotta Knight" pales by comparison with a decision by producer/screenwriter Lou Rusoff and director/screenwriter Lee Kresel at Alta Vista/American International Pictures to assign an Arthurian name to a character in one of the first Japanese animated feature films to receive wide distribution in American theaters. *Saiyu-ki* (Toei, 1960) — edited, dubbed with a new storyline, rescored, and rereleased in 1961 to most English-speaking countries as *The Enchanted Monkey* but as *Alakazam the Great!* and *The Magic Land of Alakazam* in the United States — introduces the film's wise and powerful "Merlin the Magician," a minor character who "performs all kinds of secret magic on Lonely Mountain." In the film's Merlin sequence, Alakazam steals the wizard's book of magic and then extorts a promise from Merlin to teach him all its secrets. The American production team apparently chose the name "Merlin" for this character because writers wanted a familiar touchstone that anglophone audiences would instantly grasp. But the Merlin of *Alakazam the Great!* exists completely outside the Arthurian sphere and indeed bears no kinship to any traditional portrayal of the magician.

It may prove a small comfort to Arthurian scholars to know that *Alakazam*'s "Merlin" is not alone in receiving Western appellation. He joins Sir Quigley Broken Bottom, Herman and Vermin McSnarl, Philo Fester, Hercules, Moonpie, and others in a breathtakingly unhinged adaptation that also introduces into the plot the Japanese original's Buddha as the Latinized King Amo, "the supreme wizard extraordinary"[20] of Majutosoland, and his grammatically conjugate wife and son, Queen Amas and Prince Amat. The net effect of the wholesale rewrite often seems not far removed from that produced by Woody Allen in 1966's *What's Up, Tiger Lily?* For these reasons and several others, *Alakazam the Great!* well merits its place as the only cartoon to be included in Medved and Dreyfuss's *The Fifty Worst Movies of All Time* (21–25).[21] Arthurianimation had seen better days.

CHAPTER 5

The Sword in the Stone, a "Full-length Flop," and Arthurianimation's Decline

Broadway's hot ticket of the 1960 Christmas holiday season was *Camelot*. Based loosely on T. H. White's *The Once and Future King* tetralogy, Alan Jay Lerner and Frederick Loewe's wistful musical opened on 3 December and continued to unprecedented demand through 873 performances until its close on 5 January 1963. By the end of the run, the play had captured five Tonys, its soundtrack had been to the top of the Billboard charts, negotiations for a feature film adaptation had begun, and it had caught the attention of America's president and the world's most powerful animation studio. All signs pointed to certain success for an animated version of White's Arthuriad. However, Disney's *The Sword in the Stone*, released on Christmas, 1963, fell far short of expectations.

Fundamental miscalculations played a large role in the film's failure. On the stage Lerner and Loewe and on the screen Disney writer Bill Peet, composers Richard and Robert Sherman, and director Wolfgang Reitherman were all mining the same rich literary vein to create musical productions, but the results could not have been more different. The Broadway show aimed for an adult audience with a tragic tale of complex, mature relationships. The stage *Camelot* thus relied predominantly on the later, darker portions of White's tetralogy. The Disney film, on the other hand, reached primarily for a juvenile demographic. Its lighthearted tale focused on a boy's whimsical adventures in the company of a rather befuddled wizard. The target audiences had little in common beyond a shared interest in matters Arthurian.

To avoid the increasing gloom that White cast gradually into *The Once and Future King* to foreshadow Camelot's impending catastrophe, the Disney team disengaged the boy from the man he will become. Peet's highly sanitized adaptation of only the first novel of White's Arthuriad provided a roadmap. Peet and Reitherman were so successful in separating "the Wart" from King Arthur, however, that it seems almost incidental that the ungainly adolescent will one day become the nation's ruler. Likewise, White's carefully structured, nuanced narrative did not survive its Disney adaptation. In the novel, each of the boy's metamorphic lesson-adventures contributes to a larger Bildungsroman that recapitulates those very lessons at the climactic sword-pulling in which Wart demonstrates that he is ready to be the king. In Disney's *The Sword in the Stone*, on the other hand, White's architectonic design collapses into a loose agglomeration of transformations that Merlin *asserts* are educational, even if the metamorphoses and whatever Wart learns from them appear to be on the whole unrelated to the act of drawing the sword from the stone and becoming king at film's end.

Many concur with Raymond H. Thompson's balanced assessment of Disney's narrative failings:

> This pattern in which the weak overcome the strong affords ample opportunity for irony, but it does grow tiresome through repetition. Moreover, it obscures other ideas that are present in the film. The transformations teach Wart a number of lessons, but they are forgotten amid the hectic action of chases and neglected in the aftermath. Wart learns the power of love when he is pursued through the trees by an amorous female squirrel, but his vigorous defense of Merlin against the criticism of Ector emphasizes the importance of openmindedness rather than love for his tutor. And Merlin's transformations in the wizards' duel focus upon the comic effect of his bumbling impracticality, rather than the message that knowledge and wisdom bring power. The result is a film that offers little beyond the one basic message, and through repetition it becomes tiresome, despite the charm of individual scenes [111–12].

Thompson's view reflects a critical commonplace. As much as we would like to praise the first feature-length animated Arthurian film, Disney's *The Sword in the Stone* does not hold up well to analytical scrutiny. The public too judged it only a moderate success at its premiere (Jackson 63), recognizing occasional virtues in an otherwise monotonous storyline and its forgettable tunes. Today, *The Sword in the Stone* continues to leave most viewers feeling lukewarm at best. As John Grant observes in the *Encyclopedia of Walt Disney's Animated Characters*, "For some reason, few people actively like *The Sword in the Stone* very much. That said, few people actively dislike it" (262).

The film begins as do many of Disney's days of yore tales: with the opening of an old book, here an illuminated manuscript. We learn through ballad and narration that the king has died — the first of many significant departures from White's novel,[1] in which Uther's death does not come until almost the *end* of the first installment of the tetralogy — and that no one has been able to pull the sword from an anvil mounted on a stone, a "miracle" that will determine the heir to the throne. The film lightly modernizes Malory's well-known formula as the camera zooms to an inscription below the hilt: "Whoso pulleth out this sword of this stone and anvil is rightwise king born of England."

As time passes, everyone forgets the sword. The land falls into interregnal decay. "A dark age, without law, without order" rises, where the strong prey on the weak. To illustrate the point, the film moves from static manuscript illuminations into the action of the forest. A sinister, hungry wolf lurks near skeletal remains in the underbrush; a squirrel in the trees above narrowly escapes a hawk.[2]

The camera peers deeper into the woods to disclose Merlin. Disney's wizard is considerably cleaner than White's unkempt original. He is just as fleetingly crotchety, however, as he struggles with the mundane task of drawing water from a well, lamenting all the while the lack of twentieth-century conveniences. Bucket in hand, Merlin returns to his hut. He explains to his querulous owl Archimedes that an unknown visitor will soon arrive. The wizard's supernatural inner sight scans a clearing just beyond the

5. The Sword in the Stone ... *and Arthurianimation's Decline*

woods, seeking a glimpse of an expected "scrawny little fella about twelve." But first to come into view is Kay, a "big lad, ... close on to twenty," followed a few moments later by the anticipated guest, young Arthur.

This day Kay has gone hunting. Arthur ("Wart") has tagged along. Their relationship becomes clear in a representative, *Cinderella*-patterned exchange between the foster[3] brothers:

KAY: Quiet, Wart.
WART: I'm ... I'm trying to be.
KAY: Nobody asked you to come along in the first place.
WART: I'm not even movin'.
KAY: Shut up.

Kay cold-bloodedly takes aim at a young deer — one that might well be Bambi's mother in another film. But when Wart clumsily falls from a limb that has been serving as his observation post, he lands on Kay. The hunter's arrow veers off into the woods. The deer scampers away. Kay explodes in anger. Wart apologizes and sets out to retrieve the arrow from the forest — a dangerous region that Kay himself fears to enter. Oblivious to threats posed by a hapless Wile E. Coyote–style wolf tracking him through the wild, Wart is poised to recover the arrow from a tree deep in the woods when — once again — he tumbles from another branch, this time landing in Merlin's hut.[4]

Wart takes tea with Merlin and chats about life at home. Upon learning that Wart's education to date has consisted solely of tasks designed to train him to be Kay's squire, Merlin objects. "Real education," he declares, is "mathematics, history, biology, natural science, English, Latin, French...." The wizard decides that he must accompany Wart back to Ector's castle to serve as the boy's tutor.

Yet Merlin's proposed curriculum in the Disney film runs oddly counter to White's firm insistence on experiential rather than book-learning. In the novel, the most significant instruction that Wart receives comes during several outdoor excursions— emphatically *not* from the library that Disney's Merlin makes a show of packing for the trip nor from the kind of overregimented teaching that White himself disparages from the novel's very first sentence: "On Mondays, Wednesdays, and Fridays it was Court Hand and Summulae Logicales, while the rest of the week it was the Organon, Repetition and Astrology" (3). In White's view, children learn their greatest lessons out of doors, beyond formal classroom walls, where they may observe nature to discover what they will need to know to do well in life. Disney's Merlin, however, *initially* suggests a pedagogy more in line with one employed in the novel by Wart's governess— who is later discovered to have spent three years confined to an asylum!

It is one of the film's major inconsistencies that Disney's Merlin never employs a book-based curriculum at all. It would not be possible for Merlin to do so—contrary to the novel's storyline, Wart has not yet learned to read and write in the film. So Merlin's lessons in the film offer Wart a series of *potentially* educational animal metamorphoses that very loosely mirror the transformations found in the novel. It seems the Disney team could not choose a single direction for *The Sword in the Stone*, proposing at certain points that Wart's educational development be modeled on American classroom techniques of the 1960s and at other junctures that Wart follow the kind of practical pedagogy that White celebrated. Regardless of what might have gone on behind the scenes at the studio to create the inconsistency — Barrier tantalizingly compares writer Peet's 51-page story treatment to director Reitherman's "broad and careless" (567) production — the film as released contains deep contradictions even in the development of its essential theme of what constitutes true education.

As lessons begin, the audience sees that life at the castle of the Forest Sauvage has long been difficult for Wart. In addition to Kay's callous if not openly cruel attacks on Wart, his hot-tempered foster father Ector is quick to allot demerits, withdraw privileges, and assign additional kitchen hours as punishment for the least infractions. Similar troubles now extend to his tutor, too. Merlin must brook the petty indignities that Ector heaps upon "Marvin" — as the witless lord of the manor calls his guest. But with a tournament to decide who will be the next king coming on New Year's Day, Wart dutifully continues his squire-training by helping Kay prepare for the big day, supplemented by Merlin's own lessons to provide Wart a "real education" — that is, experiences in the natural world that will teach him about power, love, and the value of knowledge and wisdom.

Unfortunately, the film undermines each of Merlin's lessons with mixed if not incoherent messages. For example, as a perch, Wart escapes the pike's brawn not by outsmarting him — the purported objective of the lesson — but primarily through the owl Archimedes's intervention and a lot of luck. As a squirrel, Wart and Merlin escape the unwanted attentions of female squirrels with spells that make them human again. Unintentionally, this lesson attenuates the wizard's oft-repeated maxim that magic cannot solve all problems. As a sparrow, Wart is saved first by Archimedes and later by Merlin in a lesson that proves to be less about *what* Wart knows than about *whom* he knows. In sum, the lessons lack clarity, and precisely what Wart has learned seems in any event superfluous as the film heads into its final sequences.

New Year's Day arrives. Ector, newly knighted Kay, squire Wart, and Archimedes attend the tournament. (Merlin does not accompany them. Just after Christmas, he accidentally transports himself from the realm with an ill-considered "Blow me to Bermuda" oath. Later we learn that the potent words take the wizard around the globe and to the twentieth century.) Wart forgets Kay's sword at their lodgings — in the novel it is Kay himself who leaves it behind — and then goes to the inn to fetch it in a scene that thematically recalls Wart dashing into the forest to retrieve Kay's arrow earlier in the film. Finding the inn's door locked, Wart casts about for a solution. Archimedes spies a sword — *the* sword from the beginning of the film — stuck in an anvil on a stone in a neglected patch of churchyard. Archimedes tells Wart that he will "have a time pulling it out." Wart approaches the sword anyway. A heavenly choir sings softly and light begins to flicker from above. Despite the owl's admonition to "leave it alone," Wart pulls the sword from the anvil. The choir and light surge for a moment, then fade again.

Wart returns to the tournament, sword in hand. Kay snubs the weapon — "This is not my sword!" — till Ector reads the inscription and realizes it is the long-forgotten

5. The Sword in the Stone ... *and Arthurianimation's Decline*

sword that reveals the heir to the kingdom. Black Bart, a distinguished knight in the crowd, overhears the conversation and announces (with his voice backed by regal trumpets) to all, "Someone has pulled the sword from the stone!" Still, Ector does not believe Wart's yarn. The crowd laughs at the unknown boy's preposterous claim to have drawn the sword from the stone. To shouts of "Prove it!" all proceed back to the churchyard.

Ector reseats the sword and scoffs, "All right, boy, let's have the miracle." Before Wart can try, Kay steps in, followed by a riot of others. None succeeds in the task. Black Bart, seconded by family-friend Pellinore, insists that they "give the boy a chance." Fuming and determined, Wart pulls on the sword. Again it comes free, again accompanied by celestial music and light. Pellinore speaks for the assembly: "It's a miracle, ordained by heaven. This boy is our king." Black Bart wants to know his name. An astonished Ector reveals that the boy is "Wart—oh, uh, I mean, Arthur." The crowd begins to chant, "Hail King Arthur! Long live the king!" Ector and then more slowly and stubbornly Kay kneel and ask forgiveness before their new, bewildered king of the realm.

A narrator solemnly announces that "at last the miracle had come to pass" and "the glorious reign of King Arthur was begun." A cross-fade to a castle interior, however, discloses the truth of the matter: alone with Archimedes, the boy king sits uncomfortably on the throne, wearing an oversized crown and robes. He ponders running away—and Archimedes encourages him to try—but there is no escape from the adoring subjects encircling the castle. Wart's wish for Merlin's return summons the wizard back to the Middle Ages. Merlin attempts to assure Wart that all will be well. His knowledge of the future allows him to promise: "You'll become a great legend. They'll be writing books about you for centuries to come. Why, they might even make a motion picture about you."

As Merlin continues to fuss over whether Wart's crown looks better leaning one way or another and jokes about motion pictures being "something like television—without commercials," the camera draws back to a long shot of the hall. Regal trumpets sound and a chorus rapidly sings "Hail King Arthur! Long live the king!" The picture is over. Unfortunately, for the audience being rushed from its seats after this startlingly abrupt close, questions linger. How did Merlin's words put the boy at ease with his new role? How did Wart's animal transformations lead to this moment? How has his education prepared Wart to be king? The last few minutes of the film feel rushed and nonsensical—a perfunctory stab at bringing the story to an end, even if that end is not a conclusion.

Walt Disney reputedly had taken little interest in the film and after its release "criticized it repeatedly" (Barrier 568). Theme parks and the live-action *Mary Poppins* (1964) occupied the sexagenarian's attention in the years that *The Sword in the Stone* was in production. The project had been assigned primarily to Reitherman, one of the "Nine Old Men" who had been with the Disney operation from near the beginning. Ward Kimball, another of the Nine, has suggested that Reitherman rose to prominence within the organization less through talent than simple loyalty and an ability to churn out Disney "product" while Walt was busy with more pressing matters. Commenting on

Arthurian Animation

Disney's decision to select Reitherman as director for *The Sword in the Stone*, Kimball sourly opined: "[T]hey picked out a guy who wouldn't give them much trouble. Woolie was always subservient to the place" (Barrier 567). In this instance, subservience led to a lackluster film that the studio did not see fit to rerelease in American theaters until 1972 and then again in 1983.

If Disney's mighty studio could not craft a blockbuster from the matter of the Round Table, what hope of commercial or critical success was there to be for the handful of live-action Arthurian films that opened through the next dozen years? *Sword of Lancelot* (Emblem, 1963), *Siege of the Saxons* (Columbia, 1963), and *Gawain and the Green Knight* (United Artists, 1973) spent little time on theater marquees in their time and are largely forgotten today.[5] Even among devoted Arthurians, *Camelot* (Warner Bros., 1967) may stand alone as the only notable Anglo-American Arthurian film to emerge between *The Sword and the Stone* and *Monty Python and the Holy Grail*.[6] But the Warner Bros. *Camelot* failed to inspire animated spin-offs. Just as it was with the Broadway musical that spawned the film, *Camelot*'s mature themes did not lend themselves easily to cartoons that were increasingly being created solely for children.

Arthurian short cartoons that appeared in the dozen years following *The Sword in the Stone* generally show no more than a glimmer of respect for or knowledge of the Arthurian legend. Many are Arthurianimation by virtue of the slimmest of criteria. For instance, although a character named "Merlin" often appears as a wizard, he is divorced from any authentic Arthurian associations, medieval or modern. A few examples may suffice. In "Merlin's Magic Marbles" (Filmation, 1966) from CBS's *The New Adventures of Superman*, Lex Luthor uses an electronic viewscreen to look back in time to contact Merlin. The archvillain dupes the wizard into providing magic marbles that allow Luthor to disguise himself as a boy or turn invisible. Luthor employs his newfound powers to commit crimes until Superman stops him. On a subsidiary *Super Chicken* segment of ABC's *George of the Jungle*, the scrappy fowl and sidekick Fred confront an evil wizard in "Merlin Brando" (Jay Ward Productions, 1967). Merlin has learned from his magic mirror that Super Chicken is "the greatest one of all" and therefore plans to destroy him. But Super Chicken defeats the wizard by turning Merlin's own mirror—and powers—against him. Joining the in-name-only Merlins of *Superman* and *Super Chicken* there was also a Marvin. A botched spell transports a bumbling, leprechaunish wizard to the year 3000 for non–Arthurian adventures with Rocket Robin Hood and the Sheriff of N. O. T. T. (National Outerspace Terrestrial Territories) in the three-part arc of "Marvin, the Magician," "Who Do Voo Doo?" and "This Trick Will Kill You" (Trillium/Krantz Films, 1967) on the syndicated *Rocket Robin Hood*. One is hard-pressed to find anything even tangentially related to traditional Arthurian materials in such episodes.

Merlin's reputation continued to slide. In 1967 Warner Bros. introduced a new character, Merlin the Magic Mouse. This blundering, W. C. Fields–impersonating, vaudeville magician uses a flying carpet to carry himself and sidekick Second Banana from one non–Arthurian adventure to another. He appeared in only five cartoons and then disappeared as Warner Bros. shuttered its animation unit in 1969. Television view-

5. The Sword in the Stone ... *and Arthurianimation's Decline*

ers learned that Merlin's son, too, moved to the vaudeville stage in "Merlin, the Magician, Jr." (Mushi Studios/Rankin-Bass, 1970), one of the *Reluctant Dragon* shorts from ABC's *The Reluctant Dragon & Mr. Toad Show*. Fearing that Tobias the Dragon's daisy allergy will accidentally be sparked during a visit from neighboring royalty and perhaps precipitate "a world war," the king of Willowmarsh summons Merlin's son from Ye Old Vaudeville Theater for aid. The

Merlin tells Marcia that he wants to go home in "The Birthday Party," *The Brady Kids* (Filmation, 1972).

king asks junior to suspend the daisy-curse that Merlin long ago placed on Tobias. Unfortunately, although junior can shift the trigger from daisies to other vegetation, he cannot remove it completely. "You gotta hand it to the old man," Merlin Jr. observes, "he sure had a way with a curse." While Tobias does (as expected) roast the visiting royalty, the magician says that the event was unavoidable: "He's gotta blow up at something."

A larger — yet not much more considered — Arthurian cast appeared in the half-hour "The Birthday Party" (Filmation, 1972) from *The Brady Kids*, an animated spin-off from ABC's *The Brady Bunch*. The kids' magical mynah bird Marlon plans to celebrate his birthday with near-namesake Merlin. Marlon's transport charm sends him to the past, yet it also inadvertently summons a W. C. Fields–inspired Merlin to the present. The two displaced magicians and their magic books create havoc with spells that disrupt both timelines. Horses vanish from Camelot as Merlin summons them to the twentieth century to pull cars and trolleys. Marlon's search through Merlin's library for a spell to take him home succeeds only in sending to the present Julius Caesar, Cleopatra, Alexander the Great, Wyatt Earp, Leonardo da Vinci, and Magellan. At the Round Table, a beleaguered Arthur, Launcelot, Gawain, Modred, and Galahad try to stay clear of Marlon's inept spell-weaving. The wizards finally cast the spells needed to put everybody back in his or her own time — except for Arthur and a pair of knights who materialize in the present as the episode ends. They would like to punish Marlon for all the trouble he has caused.

A handful of non–Merlin, likewise marginally Arthurian cartoons was also produced in the wake of *The Sword in the Stone*. Launched from an exhibit at the Bedrock World's Fair, the Flintstones and Rubbles traveled to several points in their future in

"Time Machine" (Hanna-Barbera, 1964) on ABC's *The Flintstones*.[7] At one stop, the Stone Age companions finds themselves in the Middle Ages, where a castle holds a round table—"the biggest dining room table I've ever seen," Wilma remarks—and empty seats labeled for Galahad and Lancelot. The locals mistake Fred for Lancelot and force him to a joust with the Black Knight to see who will gain the hand of Princess Lenore, the daughter of the unnamed king and queen of the realm. Fred bumbles to victory; wife Wilma objects as the king insists on Fred's marriage to Lenore; yet before this *Honeymooners*-style misunderstanding can go further, all are swiftly transported to another time.

A four-part "Pain Strikes Underdog" (Total Television/Leonardo Television Productions, 1965) appeared on NBC the following year on *The Underdog Show*. In part one, Underdog guards a train carrying England's collection of Excalibur Swords, which are en route to San Francisco for display. Meanwhile, Riff Raff attempts to steal the treasure. The train derails during an unsuccessful heist, leaving the otherwise invulnerable hero with inexplicable back pains. The collection arrives at the museum in part two. Riff Raff takes the swords. Although still in pain, Underdog pursues the villain through part three. At last, with Riff Raff in police custody and the swords recovered, part four reveals the source of the Underdog's obscure hurt: when the train went off the tracks in part one, a sword became lodged in Underdog's cape. It is this sword that has been causing him to suffer whenever he bends over. Excalibur is the one weapon (it is implied) that can harm the superhero.

In the same television season, dim-witted Peter Potamus and his level-headed, simian sidekick So-So employed their time-traveling hot-air balloon to float to the Middle Ages in "What a Knight" (Hanna-Barbera, 1965) on the syndicated *Peter Potamus and His Magic Flying Balloon*. In this short, Peter pulls a sword from a stone—"an oddball thing," he calls it—to fulfill a local legend and become the kingdom's reluctant champion. As the defender of the unnamed king of the realm, Sir Peter fights a two-headed ogre and later "the scounderly Black Knight." Peter confronts both opponents in his usual fashion: run away; try to talk his way out of the scrape; and finally defeat them with So-So's help and his once-per-episode signature secret weapon roar, the Hippo Hurricane Howler. Before Peter can be called upon yet again to serve the kingdom, So-So suggests that it is time to leave the Middle Ages. As they drift away, Peter exultantly brandishes his newly acquired "nice sword," accidentally slashing the balloon to send them flying wildly over the horizon.

An eleven-minute episode of ABC's *Spider-Man* dropped Arthurian elements into a crime-fighting storyline in "Knight Must Fall" (Grantray-Lawrence Animation/Krantz Films, 1970). The tale opens at a theater. Now in its "third smash month," a stage play called *King Arthur* has again filled the till. Crooks try to make off with the day's ticket sales—as one of the villains recalls reading how long ago the king and his knights "went around knocking off robbers." Inexplicably (and never explained fully in the cartoon), Sir Galahad arrives to thwart the robbery because, as he says in quaint language, "King Arthur commands me to battle evildoers with my sword and shining lance." The knight uses his electrified lance to stun the criminals. Meanwhile, Spider-Man arrives on the

5. The Sword in the Stone ... *and Arthurianimation's Decline*

scene and Galahad stuns him, too. The knight takes the money and departs on a "trusty steed" (a motorcycle that can be called by whistling).

Galahad again acts more like a criminal than a hero as he robs an armored car of "stolen treasure" in the next sequence. Spider-Man enters to stop the theft. Once more Galahad defeats him and rides away with the cash. The knight and superhero face off a third time as museum officials arrive in New York with a box containing "a sword believed to have once belonged to King Arthur of legend." This time, Spider-Man wins the battle and captures the rogue Galahad—yet viewers are left scratching their heads over this confused cartoon. Has Arthur truly sent Galahad to the present, or is the knight merely (as characters in "Knight Must Fall" think) a "screwball"? Viewers must decide for themselves.

Arthurian in name or by implication only are the "Nuts of the Round Table" and "Myron the Magician" shorts from the syndicated *Batfink* (Hal Seeger Productions, 1967). "Nuts of the Round Table" chronicles superhero/superparody Batfink's struggles against a number of armor-clad (that is, *nuts* and bolts) robots. Despite the suggestive title, no "Round Table" or chivalric themes appear. Burglar Myron the Magician's theft of a portrait called "Whistler's Mother-in-Law" similarly lacks any Arthurian connection beyond the resonance of the villain's name.

Amid all the dross a few noteworthy, sometimes quite *good*, even arguably *educational* specimens of Arthurianimation did emerge. Riding high on the success of a 1962 NBC Christmas special retelling Dickens's *A Christmas Carol* with Mr. Magoo in the role of Scrooge, UPA launched an ambitious venture to cast the myopic protagonist into a number of other literary classics in NBC's *The Famous Adventures of Mr. Magoo* (1964–65). Abe Levitow and Bob McKimson[8] were the chief animators for Sloan Nibley's adaptation of *Le Morte Darthur*, "Mr. Magoo's King Arthur" (UPA, 1964), in which Magoo plays not the king but Merlin. Although the cartoon is rife with those errors that make medievalists cringe—the story is set in "London of the third century," but the walled city, Tudor architecture, and Gothic cathedral give one pause—it is nonetheless a competent albeit expurgated reworking of scenes from the opening sections of Malory's Arthuriad. "Mr. Magoo's King Arthur" enters the Arthurian narrative at a moment soon after Arthur's birth and ends shortly after he is crowned—just two of Nibley's many adjustments that allow UPA to sidestep prickly areas of the legend.

The half-hour cartoon begins backstage in the star's dressing room. Magoo talks about the role he has in tonight's tale of "medieval times—back when magic played an important part in people's lives." He will play Merlin the Magician, "King Arthur's sleight-of-hand man." Magoo's summary overview stresses (of course) his own crucial role in Arthur's rise to the throne.

As the story unfolds, "Mr. Magoo's King Arthur" presents many familiar though somewhat skewed incidents. We learn that it is a time of "fear and hunger" in the land as many petty kings struggle for ascendancy. To a castle a "half-day's journey to the north" of London, "kind and gentle" King Uther summons Merlin—the only wizard in England "who will not trade with the devil," Uther remarks—to *request* that the magician take his infant son into hiding for protection. Merlin is to conceal the boy's true identity until it is appropriate to reveal it. Uther weeps as Merlin carries Arthur from the court.[9] Merlin and his apprentice Spindle quickly (and comically) realize, however, that they cannot properly care for an infant. Merlin asks Ector to raise the child alongside Ector's son Kay in a distant castle.

Years later, teenage Kay and Arthur visit Merlin in London. They discuss the troubled times. Arthur shows his compassion for the hard-pressed citizenry as he affirms that "someday, someone must put an end to this misery." Kay explains to their host that they have come to the city so that he can participate in a tournament. When Merlin learns that all the nobles—including the brutish, power-hungry King Pellinore—plan to attend the meet, he agrees to accompany the boys. Having discerned Arthur's readiness to lead, Merlin confides to Spindle that "the time has come to change things in England."

On tournament day, Merlin covertly manipulates events to position Arthur for the throne. He places a mysterious sword in an anvil atop a stone in a churchyard.[10] He makes Kay's sword vanish so that Arthur will need to seek a replacement. He goads Pellinore to struggle futilely to take the sword from the stone before Arthur draws it easily. The wizard's stratagems have the desired effect: all the people of England recognize Arthur as their true king as he pulls the sword. When Pellinore continues to object to Arthur becoming king, Merlin reveals the boy's hidden pedigree to the crowd. Plans for a coronation in three days commence.

Pellinore and his brother Galron grimace menacingly as the new king begins to organize his court. Arthur charges Launcelot to complete the Round Table by finding fifty good knights. He also announces his intention to "share my throne with a wise and gracious queen," Princess Guinevere, daughter of King Leodegrance. Pellinore advises that Launcelot be sent to escort the bride. Viewers familiar with Arthurian films of the day—1963's *Sword of Lancelot*, for instance—may suspect that Pellinore's ploy is designed to spark an affair between the king's intended and his chief knight, but the villain's scheme is more straightforward. Pellinore wants merely to delay Launcelot from bringing more knights to court for a few days. In the interim, with Arthur unprotected, Pellinore and Galron will slay him.

Arthur and Merlin discuss changes for the medieval realm, proleptically addressing more modern issues as they make their plans. "First," Arthur says, "we must take all taxes off foodstuffs," and he wants to assure "a fair hearing" for anyone in prison. Galron interrupts them with news that an unknown knight is challenging passersby on a road to Camelot. Several knights have already been wounded, including Kay. Despite Merlin's cautions to wait until Launcelot returns, Arthur pledges to stop the knight immediately. As Arthur rides to the encounter, Merlin contacts his "old friend" the Lady of the Lake for help. Following "every word" of Merlin's instructions, she intervenes in the battle that Arthur is losing in order to give the king her scarf and the sword Excalibur[11]—which an arm eerily lifts to the surface of a nearby lake. Arthur then handily defeats the mystery knight, exposes him as Pellinore, and banishes both evil brothers with a threat to hang them if they are seen again.

A final segment shows Arthur and Guinevere happily enthroned. The king tells

5. The Sword in the Stone ... *and Arthurianimation's Decline*

his queen that he could have succeeded without Merlin's help. Merlin winks at the audience to remind us of his many behind-the-scenes machinations. This relatively reverent treatment of Malory's work can be viewed with pleasure even today.

A teenage Superman entered the Arthurian sphere in "The Black Knight" on CBS's *The Adventures of Superboy* (Filmation, 1966). Oscar Bensol's well-written short begins as Clark Kent's adolescent pal Timmy finds an old cape that once belonged to the Great Merlini, "a direct descendant of Merlin, King Arthur's court magician." The cape grants Timmy's casual wish to be "on a jousting field in the days of King Arthur and the Round Table." Clark changes to Superboy to "crash through the time barrier" and retrieve his friend from an unintended journey to the past.

Timmy's wish indeed lands him on Camelot's jousting field. Arthur and Merlin watch from the stands as the Black Knight and Galahad charge together with the boy in their paths. Superboy arrives just in time to shield Timmy from the knights' lances. Arthur upsets Merlin as he remarks of Superboy that "this strange young man's magic is greater than thine." Merlin's ire continues to grow as Superboy's powers become clear. The Black Knight is also angry: "Knave, thou hast broken my lance. For that, I shall break thy skull!" In the duel that inevitably follows, Superboy turns down Arthur's offer to use the king's own sword—"Thanks, I won't need it"—and then humiliates the Black Knight in combat. The "envy-ridden" Merlin and disgraced Black Knight plot their revenge.

Meanwhile, Arthur grants his time-traveling guests a tour. He shows them the "magic sword" in its anvil, commenting that "even now, he who can draw the sword from the anvil shall be the king of England." "Wouldst care to try it, Superboy?" Arthur asks. Modestly, Superboy accepts: "Well, okay." And out comes the sword easily! But Merlin and the Black Knight arrive at this moment. Merlin employs his magic to snatch the sword and give it to his evil ally. The Black Knight claims the throne. Superboy's meek "Come on, give it to me, please" fails to stop the committed usurper, so the Boy of Steel tricks the Black Knight into plunging the sword back into the anvil. Arthur imprisons the knight. Merlin vanishes with an "I shall return." Superboy whisks Timmy back to the twentieth century.

With the 1966–67 South Cadbury excavations that aimed to prove Arthur's existence in the news,[12] the animated Beatles traveled to Arthur's kingdom in "I'm Only Sleeping" (King Features, 1967) on ABC's immensely popular *The Beatles*. In this short directed by Jack Stokes—best known for his work on *Yellow Submarine*'s Pepperland sequence—animators from the United Kingdom, Canada, and Australia offered a tale that takes the Beatles to Camelot. The episode begins with John falling asleep as he reads a book to children: "And so the good King Arthur rode off with Merlin on further adventures...." The tale carries John into a dream. With visual backgrounds drawn from random pages of text from an unidentified edition of Malory's *Le Morte Darthur*, John (a "troubadour" and "slightly knight"), Merlin, Arthur, and finally the three other Beatles join forces to defeat a dragon, a "fire-breathing, man-eating monster [that] is smashing drawbridges and laying waste the countryside." While Arthur fights fearlessly and Merlin rather reluctantly, only the Fab Four can stop the beast. Taking Merlin's advice to lull the dragon to sleep with song—*the* song naturally of the episode's title—the Beatles conquer the dragon and bring peace to the land. As a grateful villager kisses John for accomplishing a feat that the king and his wizard alone could not, the dream ends and the Beatles return to the field where John fell asleep.

Media attention on the South Cadbury dig perhaps also prompted an Australian series of syndicated television shorts entitled *Arthur! and the Square Knights of the Round Table* (Air Programs International, 1968). Director Zoran Janjic's cartoons can best be compared to the kind of surreal humor that *Monty Python's Flying Circus* would bring to the British BBC1 mainstream the following year. We laugh at the unexpected juxtaposition of old and new, ideal and actual. Familiar characters—Arthur, Guinevere, Lancelot, Merlin, Morgana le Fay, the Black Knight, and others—engage not in traditional chivalric or amorous pursuits but in mundane acts such as jostling to get into the bathroom in the morning, planning parties, and shopping for hats. The series aims to deflate any idealized notions we might cherish about the kind of medieval life that was being discussed worldwide as archaeologists in Somerset sought definitive proof of the legendary king's existence.

Episodes of *Arthur! and the Square Knights of the Round Table* gesture toward legendary or folkloric storylines only to subvert them. Lancelot (a lisping, whistling knight) undertakes seven labors to restore youth to an old woman in "Seventeen Going on Seventy"—and then we learn that the old woman is simply senile, her tale of a being bewitched merely a product of her imagination. The Black Knight tries to steal Excalibur for Morgana in "Will the Real King Arthur Please Stand Up"—and then, as he is marched to the dungeon, he engages in psychobabble to blame the "very mixed-up childhood" that compels him to do evil. In an untitled sixty-second entry, Merlin works feverishly over a cauldron—all to prepare himself a warm bath. Arthur is the shortest adult in the kingdom, so we suspect irony when the proprietor in "The Inn" says that he recognizes the king by virtue of his "regal bearing," "commanding presence," and "royal figure." It is manifestly obvious that the sole characteristic that truly sets Arthur apart from others is "that crown on your 'ead," as the innkeeper says in his working-class accent.[13] Even the series *title* fails to observe Arthur's rank with anything more than an exclamation point. For the most part, the three dozen shorts created for the *Arthur! and the Square Knights of the Round Table* series are clever. They come from the minds of writers likely amused by the press that South Cadbury and "the real King Arthur" were receiving.

Two years later Janjic again directed and Michael Robinson[14] wrote an Arthurian animated film of a considerably different nature: a reasonably faithful rendition of Twain's novel in *A Connecticut Yankee in King Arthur's Court* (Air Programs International, 1970). The 72-minute edutainment cartoon was first broadcast on CBS during a ninety-minute block on Thanksgiving, 1970. Janjic and Robinson include more than a dozen pivotal episodes from the novel, but they subtly shift Twain's focus. The film emphasizes Merlin's role—removing Arthur to a large extent and Twain's attacks on the Church entirely. Janjic and Robinson also suppress virtually all of the Boss's negative qualities. Like its animated predecessors, this *Connecticut Yankee* also occasionally

5. The Sword in the Stone ... *and Arthurianimation's Decline*

updates technologies to twentieth-century levels: the storyline begins in a modern factory, knights come to rescue Arthur and the Boss on choppers rather than bicycles, etc.

In keeping with trends of the day, Janjic and Robinson revise Twain's narrative to keep it as nonviolent as possible for the intended juvenile demographic.[15] Thus the Boss defeats Sagramore by scaring him with the sound of his gun rather than following Twain's example of shooting him dead. The Boss and his small band of boys deploy electromagnets, rising steel walls, and water — but no electrocution — in the cartoon's version of Twain's "Battle of the Sand-Belt" episode. However, when the fighting ends, all the Yankee's enemies are still *alive*. The defeated troops, weighed down by their armor, are simply stuck in a newly created stream. Continuing to keep events bloodless after the battle, Twain's knight who stabs the Boss becomes one who clubs him instead, then (as in the novel) a disguised Merlin administers a potion designed to make the Boss sleep until his own time in the twentieth century.

When the Boss wakes in a modern hospital bed wondering if it has all been a dream, he asks his nurse for an encyclopedia. The entry for "Arthur" shows an illumination of the king — on a chopper! The story stops here on an upbeat note, thereby avoiding Twain's scene of the Boss's delirious memories of the wife he left behind in the Middle Ages and then his death. One can praise Janjic and Robinson for retelling as much of the story as they do, even if the cartoon does lack the soul of Twain's novel.

As a reminder that not only Britain but also Wales laid claims to Arthurian heritage, over five days in November 1970, Welsh actor Ray Smith offered young BBC1 viewers fifteen-minute installments of the Welsh Arthurian tale of *Culhwch and Olwen* from *The Mabinogion*. Under the title of "The Quest for Olwen," Smith's readings aired on the much-beloved *Jackanory*, a decades-long public service series that aimed to promote juvenile literacy by bringing high-profile personalities into the studio to read to children. Although no recording of these five episodes survives, it likely followed the more or less uniform *Jackanory* production scheme: cameras alternated between the celebrity's performance and illustrations from an existing book or newly commissioned for the show. While not animation in the strictest sense, the camera's gentle pans and zooms over the drawings simulate a cartoon-like effect to complement the star's recitation.

Shortly after Smith's performance aired, the BBC published the text that he read: Jenny Nimmo's adaptation of *Culhwch and Olwen, The Quest for Olwen* (1971), along with a dozen illustrations by Graham McCallum. Imaginative children could relive the television experience with a book of their own. Nimmo's version of the tale skillfully abridges the tale from *The Mabinogion* to make it palatable for kids. Gone are the lengthy catalogs of names and nested quests that might tax a child's patience. Nimmo concentrates instead on a few key adventures that Culhwch (spelled roughly phonetically as "Kilhooch") and six Arthurian knights pursue on their way to securing the items necessary for Culhwch to wed the giant's daughter Olwen. McCallum's illustrations help focus attention on key incidents: Culhwch's birth, his mother's tomb, assembling a group of Arthur's knights for the quest, Olwen's beauty that draws the hero forward, the cruel giant who kills men who court her, and so on, through to the closing illustration of the hero greeting his bride as his foot rests on the dead giant's arm. It is unfortunate that a recording of the *Jackanory*'s "The Quest for Olwen" has not survived.

Even as unlikely an organization as the United Kingdom's General Dental Council also pressed the Arthurian court into service for instructional purposes at the time. "Merlin and the Toothless Knights" (I. D. T. V., 1970)[16] uses the same animation technique as *Jackanory* productions: still pictures filmed so as to *seem* animated by camera pans and zooms. However, "Merlin and the Toothless Knights" also adds a few brief, rudimentary segments of cel- and collage-animation into the mix—moments that appear all the more striking because they surprise us.

The six-minute film targets the elementary school classroom demographic with an astonishingly unexpected Arthurian parable. "It all started when the king, Arthur," the narrator begins, "discovered that all his knights were losing their teeth." We learn that fire-breathing dragons are overrunning the land because Arthur's knights have allowed their teeth to rot. In fact, the nation's dental calamity has become so dire that the dragons will not even fight the knights anymore. Instead, the beasts "gnashed their own magnificent fangs and laughed at the toothless knights." Dragons abscond with any maidens they find, because "the maidens seemed to prefer being carried off by handsome dragons to rescue by ugly, toothless knights."

Merlin comes to court to discuss the realm's misfortunes. Cakes, snacks, and assorted dainties fill the large Round Table before Arthur and his assembly of brown- and gap-toothed, overweight knights. As the knights snack (to the sound of snuffling pigs), Merlin explains how healthy teeth decay when people eat "all the wrong food—sweets and sticky buns and soft drinks." "But what does all this got to do with teeth?" lisps the "very fat," nearly toothless Gawain. Merlin explains that he has discovered the role that sugary foods and plaque ("a coating") play in tooth decay. "No!" Gawain cries, seconded by all the others. The wizard tells the knights and the king that they need to eliminate the plaque to preserve their teeth.

Arthur orders Merlin to his cave in "the mountains of Wales" to devise a solution to save both the knights' teeth and the entire kingdom. Meanwhile, dragons continue to take maidens and the knights fall ill as they are unable to eat properly with so few teeth. Merlin returns from Wales after several weeks. He carries a small box containing the answer to their

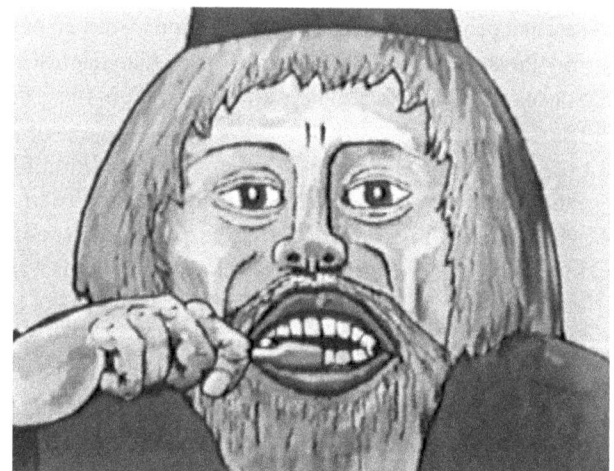

Merlin demonstrates proper brushing technique in "Merlin and the Toothless Knights" (I. D. T. V., 1970).

5. The Sword in the Stone ... and Arthurianimation's Decline

woes: a toothbrush (introduced with musical fanfare, a drum roll, and a few animated frames to suggest that the invention gleams). "What's this?" Arthur demands, "A magic wand?" But Merlin has not yet finished his presentation. He produces a second box, this one with toothpaste, "which when combined with the brush you hold in your hand will truly make magic." As if weaving a potent charm, Merlin demonstrates for the court how to use a toothbrush. "He who passes this magic brush over his teeth, with an up-and-down motion, after breakfast and last thing at night, shall by this magic ward off tooth decay." Merlin tells Gawain that if he must eat sweets, he should do so only "at mealtimes and not in-between."

Arthur decrees that henceforth knights use the toothbrush, and "so shall all in my kingdom who wish to become knights and sit at my Round Table." The narrator completes the tale: "And so it came to pass that in the days of King Arthur dragons were driven from Britain by knights with shining armor and strong, shining teeth." The newly fit knights adopt a fresh coat of arms: two crossed toothbrushes over a tube of toothpaste. Whether pediatric dental hygiene actually improved after students watched "Merlin and the Toothless Knights" cannot be known, though we must acknowledge the cartoon's ingenuity as it asserts that healthy teeth will be required for admission to the fellowship of the Round Table.

The years that followed *The Sword in the Stone* unquestionably brought some highly unusual instances of Arthurianimation to large and small screens. Perhaps strangest of all was Filmation's 1972 production of *Daffy Duck & Porky Pig Meet the Groovie Goolies* (*DDPPMGG*), in which the indefatigable duck produces, directs, and stars in his own film, a cartoon-within-a-cartoon entitled *King Arthur and His Knights of the Round Table*. In an online response to a reader's question, animation expert Jerry Beck ("FAQ-2") deemed *DDPPMGG* an obscure "'Lost Warner Bros. cartoon' that should remain lost, forever!" In a longer online critique ("The Bootleg Files"), cinema historian Phil Hall concurred: "[T]he film is not as bad as you might imagine — it is much, much worse!" Still others on Internet message boards have been reduced to one-word ejaculations: "infamous," "abysmal," and "abomination." For my part, I declared *DDPPMGG* "The Worst Arthurian Cartoon Ever" in a 2006 issue of *Arthuriana*. Fans of classic Warner Bros. cartoons continue to ask: How could Daffy sink so low? Fans of the Arthurian legend add: And how could he drag down the Arthurian legend along with him?

When Warner Bros. closed its theatrical animation unit in 1969, it began to license its characters to other studios. Filmation Associates, an operation specializing in low-budget television cartoons such as *The Brady Kids* and *The Adventures of Superboy*, obtained rights to use the Warner properties — all except for Bugs Bunny, Warner's crown jewel — in a one-off for ABC's hour-long cartoon anthology series, *The Saturday Superstar Movie*. Directed by Hal Sutherland and written by Chuck Menville and Len Janson, *DDPPMGG* features Filmation's own signature Groovie Goolies (Frankie, Drac, Wolfie, Hagatha, and Mummy) alongside about a dozen leased Warner Bros. characters in a chase cartoon that follows Daffy's attempts to make his Arthurian cinematic masterpiece while the Phantom of the Flickers (a disgruntled star from the silent era) puts roadblocks in his way. Yet even an all-star cast could not overcome *DDPPMGG*'s pedestrian draftsmanship, inconsistent voicing, humorless gags, stock music loops, and empty characterization—to name only a few of the many complaints that have been lodged against *DDPPMGG* over the years. The two segments—roughly thirteen minutes—devoted directly to Daffy's King Arthur film are no better than the rest of the cartoon that encompasses them.[17]

With an oblique nod to *Le Morte Darthur*, Daffy's film begins not with Arthur but King Uther "the chicken-hearted" (Foghorn Leghorn) pacing a castle floor. Uther learns he is a new father. He inspects a carton filled with diapered eggs and notes that the dark one is the "rotten egg" of the family. Uther gives this egg to the court jester (Sylvester) to abandon on "a long walk." The jester accepts the task, names the egg "Sonny—sunny side up, that is," and sets off into the forest.

The jester would eat the egg if not interrupted by Tweety[18] out of his concern that the jester's intended lunch might be an avian cousin. Tweety summons bulldogs to the rescue. The jester flees. The egg hatches. Arthur (Daffy, fully grown but wearing a baby bonnet) emerges from the shell. Despite newborn Arthur's objections that he could be named Lance, Rock, or even Daffy, Tweety nonsensically insists the hatchling be called Arthur "because my mommy's name was Arthur."

The first segment of Daffy's King Arthur film stops abruptly at this point. We learn that the Phantom of the Flickers has stolen the film from the television station broadcasting it. The Phantom announces to the world his intent to destroy every last frame of Daffy's work. The chase begins....

Later in *DDPPMGG*, a second, longer segment from *King Arthur and His Knights of the Round Table* reveals more of Arthur's youth and his rise to kingship. It begins as Tweety and Merlin (Porky Pig) escort Arthur to a carnival. There Arthur falls in love with Guinevere (Petunia Pig) as she peddles kisses for $49.95 (plus tax) at an arcade booth. Arthur buys a kiss and instantly asks Guinevere to marry him. She refuses, snobbishly insisting that she will wed only one of noble blood. Unaware of his royal lineage, Arthur offers to get a transfusion, yet he still cannot persuade Guinevere to accept the proposal. Tweety and Merlin try to comfort Arthur. Merlin casts a spell, aided by witch Hagatha (whom director Daffy has hired along with the other Goolies as stuntmen and extras for the film), but the spell goes awry and Guinevere falls in love with Tweety instead. Undeterred, Arthur says he will win Guinevere's heart yet.

A barker (Drac) at another carnival booth invites passersby to "remove the sword from the stone and win the crown of England." Arthur has no interest in the competition until Mordred (Yosemite Sam), tugging futilely at the sword for the 253rd time, tells the "kid" to go away because he is distracting Mordred from a difficult task. Arthur takes umbrage at being characterized as a "kid," pays the barker for a chance at the sword, and steps up to a sideshow test-of-strength device. The harder he pulls on a lever-like sword in a stone, the higher an indicator needle on the stone rises on an arc from pauper to king. Arthur strains at the sword and finally raises the gauge to the top of the scale. Then he wrenches the sword completely out of the stone and tumbles across a field. Arthur's head is still spinning as a Goolie extra (Frankie) proclaims him king

5. The Sword in the Stone ... *and Arthurianimation's Decline*

and crowns him. Others shout their approval. Meanwhile, Mordred still has eyes on the throne and his henchmen (the inexplicably cast Pepe le Pew and Wile E. Coyote) urge him on.

This second clip continues in a new setting. Arthur and Guinevere occupy a castle together. (We do not learn how or why Guinevere abandoned Tweety for Arthur. Perhaps Merlin's love potion wears off? Perhaps she decides that Arthur's sword and crown are sufficient proof of noble blood?) A herald announces that tomorrow "young King Arthur" and Guinevere will

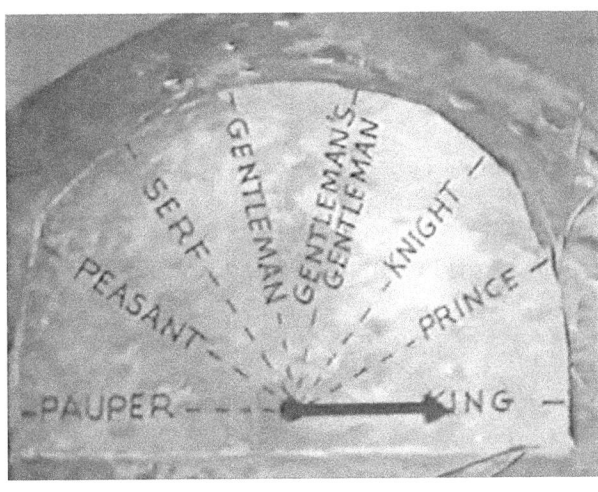

The stone's scale of regality in *Daffy Duck & Porky Pig Meet the Groovie Goolies* (Filmation, 1972).

marry. Mordred sends a message challenging Arthur to joust for both the crown and "that cute little filly." Arthur accepts. The joust begins and Arthur has won the initial pass as the second segment breaks off. Once again, the Phantom of the Flickers has stolen Daffy's film and the chase begins anew.

By almost any standard, Daffy's *King Arthur and His Knights of the Round Table* is painful to watch. If the rest of the cartoon were any better, one could argue that Daffy's producer/director/actor effort is *supposed* to be deeply flawed—as it is, for example, in 1938's "Daffy Duck in Hollywood" (Daffy posing as a director and then being mistaken for the real thing), 1946's "Hollywood Daffy" (Daffy posing as a director and "casting" a studio guard to try to gain entrance to the "Warmer Brothers" lot), or 1950's "The Scarlet Pumpernickel" (scriptwriter Daffy pitching his project to Jack Warner and envisioning himself as the lead). These three earlier cartoons were fine Warner Bros. releases that entertained even as—and because—they underscored Daffy's arrogance and many foibles. But Daffy's embedded Arthur film is as unrelentingly weak as *DDPPMGG* itself. There is no joke here—but there is Arthurianimation.

Extracting the Arthurian narrative threads from *King Arthur and His Knights of the Round Table* reveals several similarities to well-known versions of the tale. Uther gives up his child (still in embryo in Daffy's film). Tweety takes the role traditionally assigned to Ector, protecting and guiding the young Arthur until he comes of age. Merlin joins Tweety in this role in the second segment from Daffy's film. Merlin participates in Arthur's attempt to win Guinevere. Arthur is unaware of his ancestry (and remains so in Daffy's film). A sword in the stone exploit elevates Arthur to kingship. Mordred challenges Arthur for both the realm and his wife (his betrothed in Daffy's film). Mordred fights Arthur, though the outcome remains uncertain because the joust is ongoing as the second segment ends. There is little point, however, in trying to identify particular sources for these similarities. The Arthuriana in Daffy's film runs no deeper than common knowledge, a pastiche of highlights from the legend that any young person might recall from Malory, Tennyson, and/or T. H. White—or, perhaps more likely, from diluted film and television versions of the day.

It seems no coincidence that on 16 December 1972, less than a week before Disney rereleased *The Sword in the Stone* on 22 December 1972 for the first time since its 1963 premiere, ABC aired Filmation's *DDPPMGG*. ABC hoped to attract the same demographic that Disney had in its sights. The network brazenly sought to capitalize on an anticipated Arthurian resurgence for which Disney's advertising dollars were paving the way. But other factors were also at work in ABC's timing. By the fall/winter of 1972, CBS was in its third year of broadcasting Janjic's animated *A Connecticut Yankee in King Arthur's Court* every Thanksgiving. NBC, home to the weekly *Wonderful World of Disney*, was promoting the rerelease of *The Sword in the Stone* both during the Disney program and via advertising. At ABC, head of children's programming Michael Eisner — years before his stint as Disney's CEO — was not to be left out of what must have seemed 1972's competition to bring Arthurianimation to screens big and small.

But Filmation's *DDPPMGG* scarcely entered the contest. Despite the conclusion of *DDPPMGG* that shows Daffy proudly accepting an "Ozzie" for *King Arthur and His Knights of the Round Table* and making a speech in which he thanks himself repeatedly as producer, director, star, etc., the rest of the world took a dimmer view of Filmation's cartoon. After its premiere, the network broadcast it only once again, a year later on 29 December 1973 (Lenburg 284), before consigning it to the vaults.[19] Although the Phantom of the Flickers was speaking exclusively of Daffy's Arthurian film when he judged it a "full-length flop," his condemnation could easily be extended to *DDPPMGG* and much of Arthurianimation in the 1960s and early 1970s as a whole.

CHAPTER 6

The Profane and the Sacred: What Hath Monty Python Wrought?

More than any other single event in the 1970s, the release of *Monty Python and the Holy Grail* (Python Pictures, 1975) rejuvenated widespread popular interest in the Arthurian realm—and obliquely Arthurianimation as well. Most who have seen the comedy troupe's caustic satire of medieval life and modern films about the Middle Ages can readily recall—and many can recite if not reenact—the film's live-action scenes. But it takes a truly devoted fan to remember in any detail the movie's several brief *animated* sequences. These cartoon interludes mark the start of episodes ("The Tale of Sir Robin," "The Tale of Sir Galahad," and so on) or carry the film through stretches that would have been prohibitively expensive to produce using actors and/or costly special effects (God and his angels proclaiming the Grail quest, the telescoping of time and space on the way to meet Tim the Enchanter, and Arthur's confrontation with the Black Beast of Aaargh). By embedding inexpensive collage animation and even an animator[1] at work *within* the live-action film, *Monty Python and the Holy Grail* invited animators to think anew of the possibilities offered by the Round Table.

The film's box-office, rerelease, and college-circuit receipts demonstrated that King Arthur could be funny—*very* funny—and *very* profitable for animators willing to follow the troupe's lead. Animation studios began to create episodes with multifaceted, albeit sometimes muddled Arthurian dimensions. Scooby-Doo, always abreast of the day's trends, padded to Arthurian adventure in the half-hour "Scared a Lot in Camelot" (Hanna-Barbera, 1976) on ABC's *Scooby-Doo/Dynomutt Hour*. Shaggy's uncle Shagworthy, one of the world's richest jewel dealers, lives in "Camelot Castle," a structure that he has had transported from Old England to New. The castle's "ghosts"—Merlin and his Black Knight servant—have apparently come to America as well and have kidnapped Shagworthy just as the meddling kids' Mystery Machine arrives. As in all *Scooby-Doo* episodes, the ghosts turn out to be mere mortal crooks—here, intent on stealing Shagworthy's gems—who are eventually ferreted out by Velma's customary detective work. Arthurian touchstones are plentiful yet chaotic: the episode's rhyming title that evokes Arthurian associations not once but twice ("a lot" and Camelot); the castle name and a reputed "curse of Camelot" that accompanies the stones from England; a book (*Knights of the Round Table*) that Shagworthy reads on the night that he is taken; Shagworthy's treasure (distantly recalling Arthur's famed trove) stored in a refrigerator; a secret room that holds a Round Table surrounded by armor-clad mannequins of King Arthur and his knights; and a red-caped, spell-weaving, cauldron-

Arthurian Animation

Merlin and the Black Knight coerce Shaggy and Scooby-Doo in "Scared a Lot in Camelot," *Scooby-Doo/Dynomutt Hour* (Hanna-Barbera, 1976).

brewing Merlin. What "Scared a Lot in Camelot" lacks in coherence is easily countered by its fresh enthusiasm for Arthuriana.

Meanwhile, Chuck Jones went to work on a much more ambitious project — though in its opening credits Jones openly acknowledges that he has "plagiarized" and "stolen" from Twain. The veteran director and his studio team gained permission from Warner Bros. to take Bugs to Arthur's realm a fourth time in *A Connecticut Rabbit in King Arthur's Court* (Chuck Jones Enterprises/Warner Bros., 1977), first broadcast on CBS on 23 February 1978. While it was shown under the same title that Thanksgiving, in 1979 CBS began to run the half-hour cartoon under the title one generally finds it today, *Bugs Bunny in King Arthur's Court* (Woolery 95). The title change suggests that both Jones — whose studio presumably supplied the replacement frames for the opening credits — and ratings-conscious network executives expected the combined reputations of Bugs Bunny *and* King Arthur to be a bigger draw than a title that referenced only the Warner lagomorph and hinted confusingly at a possibly educational (and therefore probably dull) retelling of an American literary classic. No doubt about it, Bugs and Arthur were more popular than Twain.

Allusions to headline issues of the late 1970s abound: the energy crisis, endangered species, protecting the environment, the antiwar movement, and so on. Many of the

6. The Profane and the Sacred

topical gags, however, have not stood the test of time. For instance, Bugs is burrowing his way to the Georgia Peanut Festival—remember that Jimmy Carter, famously a peanut farmer from Georgia, was president in 1977—but upon arriving in Camelot Bugs exclaims, "This don't look like plain old Georgia to me," in a nod toward Carter's hometown of Plains, Georgia. Such jokes are no longer amusing to most viewers. Perhaps they never were.

A Connecticut Rabbit in King Arthur's Court is an all-star special, casting familiar Warner Bros. properties in prominent Arthurian roles: Daffy Duck as a disinterested, world-weary "Arthur, King of England, Etc." (from his nameplate); Yosemite Sam as the king's bloodthirsty magician, Merlin of Monroe, Baron of Yosemite; Sir Elmer of Fudde as the splenetic knight who captures the Yankee; Porkè [sic] of Pigge as the helpful varlet; and Bugges Bunnye of Carrot Patchville, U. S. A., once again playing the Yankee as he had in Freleng's 1947 "Knights Must Fall" and Jones's own 1955 "Knight-Mare Hare." Jones follows Twain's basic plot with departures suggested by many feature films and network television productions: capture of the Yankee; conflict with a troublesome knight and Merlin; the newcomer gaining the king's favor by "ending" the eclipse[2]; the Yankee's factory-building and his inventions to reform medieval society; battle and defeat of Merlin and his allies; and end of story through some means other than the violent, sad one that Twain had described.

Jones packs time-honored Arthurian references into his bright and cheerful cartoon. There is a Round Table at this Camelot. There are pavilions flying the pennons of Lancelot and Galahad. The Merlin of Monroe mailbox and his tower resurface unaltered from "Knight-Mare Hare." Jones introduces a charmed sword at the end to complete the story, as Bugs innocently pulls a "neat carrot slicer" from a stone. A disembodied, stately voice proclaims Bugs the "rightful king." Daffy quickly abdicates and relinquishes the crown to Bugs, the new ruler in "King Arth-Hare's Court" (nameplate). "The pun is mightier," Bugs quips, "than the sword."

With Daffy unseated, Bugs ruling the realm, and all Camelot's subjects pledging their allegiance to the new king, Jones slyly rebukes Filmation for its dreadful *Daffy Duck & Porky Pig Meet the Groovie Goolies*. Jones's long history with the Warner Bros. menagerie had taught him what fans also knew: only Bugs could ever be king. "It is sort of ridiculous for King Arthur to be a duck," Daffy concedes as *A Connecticut Rabbit in King Arthur's Court* comes to a close. After the relatively dry spell of the 1960s and early 1970s, creative Arthurianimation was on the rise again.

Animated superheroes, often originating in comic books, also frequently entered the Arthurian sphere in the late 1970s.[3] Sometimes with as little thought as in the 1960s, writers invoked Arthurian names, again especially Merlin's. Superman, Wonder Woman, Batman, and several of the other Super Friends resorted to the "rods of Merlin" to conquer the resurrected spirit of Gentleman Jim Craddock in the half-hour "The Ghost" on ABC's *The All New Super Friends Hour* (Hanna-Barbera, 1977). Yet beyond the use of Merlin's otherwise-unattested seven golden rods that the Super Friends obtain from researchers at Metropolis University, the episode contains no Arthurian dimensions.

Arthurian Animation

Little better came from the following year's half-hour "The Time Trap" (Hanna-Barbera, 1978) on ABC's *The Challenge of the Super Friends*. Sinestro sends the Super Friends through time as part of a scheme to loot famous treasuries. One target is Arthur's hoard. The Green Lantern and Samurai travel to "about 500 A. D." to Camelot, a medieval land devoid of familiar Arthurian characters. Sinestro and the Green Lantern joust. The villain escapes with the treasure, leaving Super Friends to take the blame. Knights imprison Green Lantern and Samurai for robbery, but Superman later rescues them and all three join the other Super Friends to return stolen gold to rightful owners. Despite the invocation of Camelot, neither King Arthur nor his knights appear in the episode.

Also negligibly in the realm of Arthurianimation is the Merlin, "master of magic," who accompanies Isis, Hercules, Sinbad, and Super Samurai as they fight evildoers in *The Freedom Force*, a subseries from *Tarzan and the Super 7* (Filmation, 1978–80). This Merlin brings to the Freedom Force's superpower arsenal a haphazard collection of magical and paranormal abilities—and a flying carpet. He promotes the Freedom Force's lessons of peace, tolerance, and understanding as he fights a range of villains, including one named Morgana. Again, deeper Arthurian facets remain undeveloped.

Merlin-inspired characters could also find themselves on the wrong side of the law, as Merlo does in "The Super Globetrotters vs. Merlo the Magician" (Hanna-Barbera, 1979), a half-hour episode of the Harlem Globetrotters' short-lived NBC animated series *The Super Globetrotters*. In this episode, Merlo and his Knights of the Crooked Table are stealing prominent world monuments because the wizard intends to rename them as a tribute to himself: the Great Pyramid to become "the Great Merlomid," the Statue of Liberty to become "the Statue of Merlo," etc. Just as Merlo seizes London Bridge—and as luck would have it—the Globetrotters have come to England to play an exhibition game for the Queen. The heroes transform to the diversely empowered Super Globetrotters to battle the villain. He imprisons them in his dungeon. Globetrotter Nate tricks Merlo to gain their freedom. "If your powers are so strong," Nate asks, as if throwing down a gauntlet, "How's about hitting the courts?" Merlo falls into the verbal trap: "No court can match my powers. King Arthur, Charlemagne, Richard the Lion-Hearted—I've conquered them all!" "Well, how's about the kind with two baskets on it?" Merlo has no choice but to allow the team onto a basketball court for an encounter that pits mounted, armed knights against the players. Merlo's knights lose, falling to the potent combination of the Globetrotters' athletic prowess and their superpowers. Beaten in fair combat, the magician admits defeat. Merlo concedes that "by the laws of chivalry" the monuments will be returned to their original locations.

More silly cartoons with Arthurian characters—along the lines of *Scooby-Doo* and *The Super Globetrotters*—also appeared on shows all but forgotten today. Cowardly Crazy Legs Crane ventured to the Middle Ages in "Fly by Knight" (DePatie-Freleng, 1978), a short for a subsidiary segment of ABC's *The All New Pink Panther Show*. Crazy Legs wants his son to be proud of him. Encouraged by his son's desires and a multitalented Merlin—whose tower advertises an eclectic skill set ranging from "MAGIC

6. The Profane and the Sacred

BLACK AND WHITE" and "KNIGHTHOOD TRAINING!" to "PARTY TRICKS" and "INCOME TAX"— Crazy Legs unenthusiastically agrees to slay the land's tiniest dragon, a dragonfly, in order to qualify for a Round Table seat. But the fire-breathing, Mexican-twanged dragonfly repeatedly defeats Crazy Legs, despite all the help that Merlin can provide. Merlin then recalls that *another* dragon is available, but it is much larger than the troublesome insect. As the cartoon comes to an end Crazy Legs is indeed "slaying" the big dragon the only way that he can — with vaudeville jokes.

Comedy was not the only approach. Entries such as the half-hour "Space Knights of Camelon" (Hanna-Barbera, 1979) on ABC's *The World's Greatest Super Friends* attest to a growing interest in action-adventure Arthurian cartoons. In a plot better developed than earlier *Super Friends* episodes, the resurgence of Arthurianimation and the pervasive influence of *Star Wars* combine as Superman develops amnesia after colliding with a radioactive meteor. He lands on the planet Camelon. Lightsaber-wielding "rebel forces" convince the disoriented superhero to become the Black Knight and help them overthrow King Arthur VII — astonishingly pronounced "Arthur Seven" throughout the episode, probably by subconscious analogy with titles from contemporaneous motion pictures such as *Rocky II* and *Emmanuelle III*. Arthur VII's intergalactic distress call brings other Super Friends to Camelon, but Superman and the rebels imprison the new arrivals along with the king. Superman becomes the new king and, on the advice of the rebel leader, begins to tax the citizenry into poverty. Still more Super Friends arrive to bring Superman back to his senses with the aid of a glowing "laser lance" and so restore Arthur VII to the throne. This blend of Arthurian past and *Star Wars* future offered pulsating, space-age updates of conventional medieval weapons and hovering mechanical equine mounts for Arthur's knights to ride into battle. Putting aside Wonder Woman's snarky puns about "demo(a)ting" knights as she plunges them into Camelon Castle's defensive ditch and another as she knocks the rebel leader unconscious with a "good night for your knighthood," "Space Knights of Camelon" earnestly attempts to engage several medieval and Arthurian motifs within the framework of a Saturday morning superhero cartoon. Monty Python's satiric approach was not the only possible road through the Arthurian realm toward the end of the 1970s.

Freshly popular Arthurian characters were also again used to edutain America's youth. In *Merlin's Magic Cave* (World TV, 1977), a ninety-minute animated feature designed for syndicated, classroom, and home use, Morgana reads from Merlin's book to tell children stories of "The Magic Pony," "Thumbelina," "The Three Wishes," and other non–Arthurian folk and fairy tales. No Arthurian dimensions appear beyond the name-dropping to capitalize on the Round Table's revitalized currency. Morgana and Merlin could have been called Bert and Ernie instead; *Merlin's Magic Cave* would have been much the same film regardless.

New live-action feature films further reinvigorated interest in Arthuriana. With *Monty Python and the Holy Grail* and Chuck Jones's *Connecticut Rabbit* fresh in people's minds, Disney turned to Twain's venerable standard with a live-action, comedic, space-age overhaul that debuted as *Unidentified Flying Oddball* (1979). Disney executives apparently had second thoughts about the wisdom of the "U. F. O." title. *Unidentified*

Arthurian Animation

Flying Oddball was rereleased under the patently more marketable *A Spaceman in King Arthur's Court* and *The Spaceman and King Arthur* in the 1980s.

Other live-action films moved in the opposite direction, away from comedy, in a worldwide cinematic Arthurian renascence. Reverent homages to the legend's graver elements could be found in Eric Rohmer's *Perceval le Gallois* (Gaumont, 1978), Tom Donovan's *Tristan and Isolt* (a.k.a. *Lovespell*; Clar Productions, 1979), Rodney Bennett's televised series of *The Legend of King Arthur* (BBC, 1979), Richard Blank's *Parzival* (West Deutsche Rundfunk, 1980), Veith von Fürstenberg's *Tristan und Isolde* (a.k.a. *Fire and Sword*; Genée and von Fürstenberg Filmproduktion, 1981) and — in almost simultaneous U. S. releases — George Romero's *Knightriders* (United Film, 1981) and John Boorman's *Excalibur* (Orion, 1981). While few saw Romero's limited-release reinterpretation of Arthurian values as they play out among a motorcycle-riding cast of characters traveling a festival circuit across rural Pennsylvania, Boorman's sword-and-sorcery hit drew the middlebrow crowd that had been eagerly awaiting a new Arthurian picture. For American audiences, *Excalibur* fueled widespread public appetite for movies about the Round Table, even as many critics panned the film.[4] As *Monty Python and the Holy Grail* had shown audiences that Arthurian themes could be funny and demonstrated to industry moguls that they could be profitable, *Excalibur* had a similar effect for serious dramatic treatments of the legend.

Less noticed at the time yet more important in the development of Arthurianimation's future course was another form of Arthurian film spreading across the globe. It began with a 1979 Japanese television series. Translations soon followed. By the end of the 1980s *Entaku no Kishi Monogatari: Moero Arthur* had been dubbed into English, French, Spanish, German, Italian, and Portuguese, and subtitled in many more languages for worldwide distribution. In 1981 the thirty-part serialized half-hour anime adventures of *King Arthur and the Knights of the Round Table* (Toei Animation) reached American television syndication. The first half dozen episodes were also sold directly to consumers on increasingly ubiquitous Betamax and VHS videocassettes. A new chapter in the story of Arthurianimation had begun.

The series strives to combine diverse, complex Arthurian traditions together into a coherent whole — just as Boorman in Ireland and Romero in America were attempting and Malory had

Tristram, Arthur, and Launcelot meet anime in *King Arthur and the Knights of the Round Table* (Toei Animation, 1979).

6. The Profane and the Sacred

done in England centuries before. Scriptwriters Kensyo Nakano and Mitsuru Majima begin their tale at King Uther's Camelot, where rulers from many surrounding kingdoms have gathered to celebrate Prince Arthur's third birthday.[5] King Ban graciously declares that the tot will become greater than either Uther or Ban himself. He predicts that Arthur will one day rule not only his birthright of Camelot but the whole of a united Britain. Ban points to the child's fleur de lis birthmark as proof of his future eminence. As the kings imagine a realm joined under Arthur, we meet the chief villain of the series: King Lavik of Ruggles, who fears the loss of his own authority should Arthur ever become the country's high king. Channeling *Macbeth* as he contemplates the deaths of those who stand in his way, Lavik's vicious thoughts inadvertently summon the ghostly witch Melissa. Lavik initially tries to reject her, yet her offer to help him become Britain's supreme ruler clearly appeals to his dark ambitions. Melissa explains what must be done: kill Uther with Ban's sword (conveniently provided to Lavik by Melissa) and Arthur as well, then, having implicated Ban, murder him too to divert blame. Lavik believes that the resulting power vacuum will allow him to become king over all Britain. Thunder and lightning fill the skies.

The scene shifts to Uther and wife Igrayne in another part of the castle. An old prophecy troubles Uther. While riding in the North Woods four year ago, Merlin appeared to Uther to warn him to beware on his son's third birthday — today. Cut to the castle exterior for an attack by masked and armored ninjas (called "black knights" in the English dub). Uther dies in the assault, though not before slashing and exposing the face of the black knights' leader, Lavik, and helping Igrayne and Arthur escape immediate peril. Merlin meets the fleeing mother and son in an isolated passageway. He explains to Igrayne that he will protect the boy by having Arthur raised by "some brave knight." Igrayne weeps and Arthur calls for his mother's arms as Merlin hurries the boy from the castle. As flames engulf Camelot, the black knights tell Lavik that Arthur has perished in the fire and Ban has been slaughtered in retribution for his alleged crimes.

Thirteen years have passed when next we meet Arthur. He has no memory of the events that brought him to live in the country with retired knight Ector and his son Kay. An incident with Gastar, Lavik's mean-spirited sheriff, reveals Arthur to be both fleetingly "short-tempered" and keenly sensitive to offenses against commoners — traits he will continue to evince as he comes to maturity through the series.

The years since Uther's death have also allowed Lavik to increase his power. He has decided the time has come to assert authority over the entire land, despite the quiet opposition of many, including Ector and King Leodegrance. The Archbishop of Canterbury calls a mass at which Lavik expects to be named the high king. All nobles and their families (including Arthur) attend. But the archbishop surprises everybody when he sonorously announces that "a divine revelation has been received." With Leodegrance's beautiful daughter Guinevere at his side (serving as an altar girl), he tells the surprised assembly that kingship will be determined by pulling the "holy sword" Excalibur from an anvil in the courtyard.

Reluctant to engage in the archbishop's public contest, Lavik nonetheless takes the first pull — and fails. The archbishop next asks Leodegrance to make an attempt. He also fails. Lavik's ally, King Longinus, fares no better. Lavik interrupts the proceedings. He insists that a "bogus game" should not be used for the "serious business" of selecting a king. The archbishop reminds Lavik that to challenge the contest is to doubt God's word. Lavik backs down, then ironically turns the contest into a game as he suggests that his strong-man sheriff try next. Gastar's clumsy, comic, failed attempt amuses the crowd, especially young Arthur, who cannot suppress laughter at the sheriff's public disgrace.

An enraged Lavik demands that Arthur try the sword next. He warns the teen that he will spend his life in a dungeon should he fail. Insouciantly, Arthur catches Guinevere's eye, casts a wink, and with some effort extracts Excalibur from the anvil (accompanied by electronic sound effects, blinding light, and trumpet fanfare), surprising himself as much as the onlookers. "I did it. Excalibur is mine. I guess that makes me king of Britain, huh? Ha, ha, ha!" Arthur's joy is reflected in the faces of Guinevere, Ector, Kay, and Leodegrance. Lavik accuses the boy of witchcraft and wants him jailed.

The archbishop intervenes. He draws from Ector the story of Arthur's true lineage and an account of how Merlin asked Ector to raise Uther's heir. But Lavik counters that Merlin's involvement only proves that witchcraft is involved and, further, that he remembers from long ago that the baby Arthur had an unusual birthmark—which Lavik now sees this annoying teenager bears on his shoulder! Lavik grumbles that he will not accept the outcome of the contest and in an aside vows to finish what he started when Arthur was a toddler. Both nobles and commoners surround the confused youth to celebrate their new king.

This first episode's complexity signals what the rest of the series will bring as Arthur expands his circle of followers, rebuilds Uther's Camelot, takes many missions and quests, rights wrongs, gets occasional advice from Merlin and the mysterious Green Knight, and stays one step ahead of Lavik and Melissa—all while growing up, making friends, gaining self-confidence, and learning self-control. The series is not kiddie fare but aims instead for a young adult male demographic. There are intricate subplots, political intrigues, and character development, all set within a framework that draws freely from Malory, *Sir Gawain and the Green Knight*, Shakespeare, and elsewhere. Familiar Arthurian characters—Arthur, Ban, Leodegrance, Guinevere, Launcelot, Tristram, Percival, and Merlin—stand alongside newcomers such as Lavik, Melissa, and Gastar in adventures that bring Arthur to the position forecast on his third birthday: Britain's high king.

Thirty episodes were not enough. Toei producers apparently thought that Arthur's story remained incomplete—and that additional storylines and profits were possible. Foreign invaders threaten Britain as the Japanese series continued in 1980 with a 22-part sequel, *Moero Arthur: Hakuba no Oji*. The English-language version was soon syndicated to American television as *King Arthur: Prince on a White Horse*. In the sequel series, Arthur rides incognito through the land making new friends, gathering new allies, fighting new enemies, and protecting his kingdom from threats internal and external. Both Toei series contributed significantly to the notion that, even in animation, the Arthurian world offered much more than a medieval backdrop for comedy.

CHAPTER 7

Many Returns of the King: The 1980s

Since the early 1980s, each year has witnessed the premiere of new live-action films set in medieval times. Harty's *The Reel Middle Ages* catalogs more than five dozen "medieval" films released in the 1980s alone. At least a dozen of these films are overtly Arthurian in nature. Cinematic approaches to the legend range from tragedy to comedy, fantasy to action-adventure, science fiction to musical to mystery to romance and beyond. An abbreviated roster of the decade's Arthurian "historical" live-action features—that is, films with all or most of the action set in the Middle Ages—includes *Excalibur* (Orion, 1981), *Arthur the King* (a.k.a. *Merlin and the Sword*; Martin Poll Productions, 1982), a telecast of a Broadway revival of *Camelot* (HBO, 1982), *Sword of the Valiant* (Cannon, 1983), *Le Morte Darthur* (BBC2, 1984), and *A Connecticut Yankee in King Arthur's Court* (NBC, 1989). This inventory includes only Anglo-American entries. It would be longer if we cast a wider net. Also omitted from this roster are films that deploy Arthurian themes in nonmedieval settings, such as *Knightriders* (United Film, 1981), *The Natural* (Tri-Star, 1984), *Indiana Jones and the Last Crusade* (Lucasfilm/Paramount, 1989), two entries in the *Star Wars* (Lucasfilm/Twentieth Century–Fox) saga in the 1980s, and isolated television episodes that aired on series spanning from *The New Twilight Zone* to *MacGyver* to *Highway to Heaven*. Arthur was suddenly everywhere.

Arthurianimation followed suit with a rich assortment of cartoons that drew their inspiration and marketing impetus from contemporaneous films, literature, comics, toys, and board games. Audiences welcomed more than two dozen Arthurian cartoons of varying length, quality, and degree of engagement with the legend. The potent, variegated brew of *Monty Python and the Holy Grail*, *Excalibur*, and kindred films both comic and serious prompted many animators to explore sundry paths though Arthur's realm.

Disney made two—some would argue three—passes at Arthurian legend in the 1980s. On NBC, ABC, the Disney Channel, and in syndication, *Disney's Adventures of the Gummi Bears* (1985–90) introduced the self-important old knight Sir Gawain, grandfather to the show's protagonist Cavin. Yet beyond the name, this Gawain, a pleasant duffer and long-time knight in the court of King Gregor of Dunwyn, has no discernible Arthurian literary roots.

Writer Mark Zaslove dug deeper into the legend for the amusing Arthurian-themed "Sir Gyro de Gearloose" (Disney, 1987) broadcast during the first season of the Disney

Channel's *DuckTales*. The half-hour episode follows Huey, Dewey, Louie, and inventor Gyro as they journey via time-traversing bathtub to the duck-inhabited, Arthurian-suffixed land of Quackalot. The realm is ruled by King Arty with the aid of his magician, Moreloon. King Arty warns his visitors not to confuse him with the "dull" King Arthur of an adjacent kingdom we never see. Moreloon feels threatened by Gyro's science and the two face off in a Twain- and White-inspired struggle of rival "magicians." Moreloon conspires with Arty's evil nephew, Lessdred, to destroy Gyro. Lessdred has his eyes, moreover, on the crown itself. Moreloon and Gyro eventually resolve their differences to join forces and save Quackalot from Lessdred.

Disney also produced a *possible* third contribution to Arthurianimation with its feature-length *The Black Cauldron* (1985), which Grant (262) contends marked the studio's first significant return to Arthurian themes since *The Sword in the Stone*. But whatever Arthurian elements exist within *The Black Cauldron* have been filtered twice, first through J. R. R. Tolkien's *The Lord of the Rings* and then through Disney's immediate source, Lloyd Alexander's *Chronicles of Prydain* series. The film's ever-changing parade of directors, assistant directors, writers, and animators[1] seems largely unaware of the deeper Arthurian underpinnings of the novels that it was adapting for the screen. *The Black Cauldron* was a missed opportunity for Arthurianimation.

Hanna-Barbera Studios, the industrious engine behind many of the decade's Saturday morning television cartoons, played the legend for light chuckles. Richie Rich stepped from the pages of Harvey Comics and newspaper funnies into a shared ABC animated series, *The Richie Rich/Scooby-Doo Show — and Scrappy Too!* As the twelve-minute "Richie of the Round Table" (1981) begins, Richie discovers that a book chronicling his ancestors in the kingdom of Richalot lacks its final page. Richie turns to Prof. Keenbeam's time machine to visit the Middle Ages to learn how the story ends. There he saves Princess Glorianna from the wizard Morecash's plot to seize the title deed to the realm. While the episode hints at Arthurianimation with yet another *-alot* kingdom and a villain whose name evokes *Mor*dred and *Mor*gan, "Richie of the Round Table" relies on the same hackneyed armor, moat, dragon, and castle gags that the audience had seen many times before. If not for a *Star Wars*–inspired "light sword" that Richie uses in battle against Morecash, "Richie of the Round Table" could have been made in the 1950s.

Hanna-Barbera writers and animators employed a time-traveling spaceship for another jaunt into the medieval past in the half-hour "Gone with the Wand" (1981) on ABC's *The Fonz and the Happy Days Gang*, an animated spin-off of the long-running ABC sitcom *Happy Days*. The Fonz saves Camelot from the Dark Knight and his fire-breathing dragon in a storyline that portrays Merlin as a wizard incapable of casting a proper spell, Arthur as a teenager who spends much of the episode trapped in his own dungeon, and Fonzie as the true hero as he takes the captive king's place in a joust to determine control of the kingdom.

Scooby-Doo also returned to the Arthurian world in "Excalibur Scooby" (Hanna-Barbera, 1984) on ABC's *The New Scooby-Doo Mysteries*. In this short, Shaggy, Scooby, and Scrappy thwart a rogue wizard who has been trying for "over 400 years" to "pull this sword out of this rock" in order to become the king of England. Scrappy draws the sword, then abdicates in favor of Scooby, who in turn nonsensically relinquishes the sword to the wizard's large toad—apparently the new amphibian king of the realm as the episode comes to an end.

Hanna-Barbera kept tapping the Arthurian spring. Yogi Bear and ten Hanna-Barbera properties assembled to save the planet from colliding with Bailey's Comet in "Merlin's Lost Book of Magic" (1985) on the syndicated *Yogi's Treasure Hunt*. The half-hour episode revolves around a search for a book needed to divert a comet bound for Earth—a topical allusion to Halley's Comet that would in fact be visible in the skies in 1986. Their *Charlie's Angels*–style mission takes the company to London, where Snagglepuss draws a sword from a stone ("a blade in a boulder, a rapier in a rock") on display at Madame Tussaud's Wax Museum. Everyone is magically transported to a castle. Newly elevated "King" Snagglepuss takes the opportunity to confer titles on his friends: "Sir Yogi of Bears, Sir Boo Boo of Boobs, Sir Snooper of Blabs, and Sir Blabber of Snoops, ... a round of knighthoods for everyone!" In the adventure that follows, King Snagglepuss releases Merlin from an enchantment that has changed him to a dragon, then Merlin leads the gang to Stonehenge to recover his book and cast the incantation needed to save Earth from destruction.

As the 1980s came to a close, Hanna-Barbera returned to Arthuriana once more. After hundreds of episodes, the final season of the NBC and globally syndicated *Smurfs* (1981–90) turned to time-travel plots for its half-hour escapades. "The Smurfs of the Round Table" (1989) deposits the small blue creatures in Arthur's kingdom, a location disclosed in a stilted exchange: "Fear not, Merlin, my trusted adviser," says Arthur, "for as long as I hold Excalibur, Camelot will be safe." These cues bring the Dark Knight and Morgan le Fey to the stage to steal the magical sword so that the witch can use it to destroy the realm. Empowered by the sword in her hand, Morgan changes Merlin to a talking stone, shrinks Launcelot to "Launcelittle," transmutes Arthur and all within Camelot to wax, and finally increases the sun's heat so that all knowledge of the king and his achievement "will melt from the memories of man." With Merlin and Arthur unable to defend the realm, it is the Smurfs who must defeat Morgan and her henchman, recover Excalibur, reverse the witch's spells, and save Camelot and Arthur from vanishing into a sticky puddle. Once restored to power, the king invests all the Smurfs with knighthood for their outstanding service to the realm and the implicit preservation of Arthur's heritage well into the future.

Smaller studios also offered their own brief Arthurian comedies. The newspaper comic strip *U. S. Acres* (better known as *Orson's Farm* beyond America's borders) was the rough inspiration for the animated "Hamelot" (Wang Film Productions/Lee Mendelson Films, 1989), a *U. S. Acres* subseries short on CBS's *Garfield and Friends*. It is a hot summer day on the farm. Orson Pig cools himself in a mud bath, passing the time with a book that recounts tales of King Arthur and his knights. His barnyard buddies are also seeking a way to escape the heat, but the farm's outdoor shower is broken. Orson thinks a leaky milk pail stored high on a shelf could relieve them all. Yet in trying to fetch the bucket, Orson takes a tumble that propels him into a pun-laden dream kindled from day residue. And thus King Orson and his "Knights of the Round Waller ... embark on a glorious quest for the glory of Hamelot." They will seek the Hol(e)y Pail. Accompanied by silly ditties that could have been sung by a minstrel from *Monty Python and the Holy Grail*, King Orson and his "knights" (series regulars Roy Rooster, Wade Duck, Booker, and Sheldon) confront a hungry griffin that guards the well-protected Pail — that rests on an obelisk amid a garbage heap behind barbed wire. Orson learns that he will need help from the Lady of the Lake (Lanolin Sheep) to win the prize. She rises from the waters to present him with a horseshoe magnet. Clever Orson employs the magnet to draw the Pail from behind the griffin's defenses and prevent his friends from being devoured. When Orson wakes from his dream, he knows to use a magnet to pull the old bucket safely from the shelf. Finally, with a shower head devised from the holey pail and a garden hose, (King) Orson brings relief to his subjects.

It was another unexpected tumble that transported Tom to the Middle Ages in "A Connecticut Mouse in King Arthur's Cork" (Filmation/MGM, 1982), a short for CBS's *Tom and Jerry Comedy Show*. In this one, Tom pursues Jerry to the top of a bookshelf. The mouse escapes the cat. Tom is left with nothing to grasp but a book titled *Camelot*. As Tom plummets to the floor, he uses the time profitably — to read the book — thus gathering the day residue that will next appear in his dream. By the time that Tom hits the ground (and, as we later discover, loses consciousness), he has moved from present to past; however, the chase continues in the new medieval setting. The Dread Knight (Jerry) terrorizes the populace. A crowned, mustached cat rushes to Tom with an offer. "Hey, you! Yeah, you! I'm King Arthur and need you to get rid of the Dread Knight for me, okay? Now, you won't go unrewarded. If you get rid of the knight, you'll have half of my kingdom and my daughter Gwen's hand in marriage." A silent Gwen is displayed as the prize. A chase cartoon set against a medieval background follows with expected drawbridge, catapult, and castle gags and a few more unusual ones: a locomotive-powered potbelly stove that serves as the Dread Knight's armored assault vehicle and Tom's mechanized catapult-cum-basketball-backboard contraption that allows him to capture the rodent menacing Arthur's realm. As Arthur prepares to dub Tom his newest knight, the Dread Knight escapes and the chase resumes. In pursuit of the escapee, Tom plunges through a castle window into the shark-infested moat below. This second fall returns Tom to the present. He wakes to find that he is dripping wet. Jerry has continued to antagonize the sleeping Tom by dumping a glass of water on him. As is true of many details in this fast-paced short, the title's "Cork" wordplay is never explained. And given that it is Tom's dream rather than Jerry's, would not "Connecticut *Cat*" make more sense than "Connecticut *Mouse*" in the title? Finally, we learn little more of Arthur or the king's daughter Gwen, despite the fact that the camera zooms back to the *Camelot* book again as this not altogether coherent cartoon comes to a close.

Sometimes mildly didactic agendas attached themselves to the comedy. In the half-hour "Sports of the Round Table" on the comic book–inspired *Sport Billy* series (Filmation, 1979–80; in American syndication in 1982), evil Vanda travels to the Middle Ages to prevent soccer — King Arthur's brainchild, the episode informs us — from ever being invented. Vanda's actions in the past ripple into the present, changing the world

7. Many Returns of the King

and turning colorful Madrid—one of several Spanish cities in fact hosting the 1982 World Cup tournament—to a bleak, abandoned cityscape. Series protagonist and soccer-aficionado Billy, companion Lilly, and their talking dog Willy journey through time to Camelot, A.D. 940, to rectify the disrupted timeline. They discover that Vanda has incarcerated Merlin, King Arthur, and every Round Table knight except for Gawain. Billy and pals join forces with Gawain to find and free the missing king. Ultimately, they release the captives and Vanda slips away to continue the fight another day. As the victors celebrate with food and games, the newly christened "Sir Sport Billy" suggests to Arthur that his favorite ball-kicking pastime be called "soccer." An epilogue reminds viewers of the value of teamwork—in struggles against Vanda, on the soccer field, and in life.

Sir Launcelot Penguin (Tuxedo Sam) watches as the Kitty of the Lake of Lost and Found (Hello Kitty) presents Excalibur to Arthur (Chip the Seal) in "Paws of the Round Table," *Hello Kitty's Furry Tale Theatre* (DIC, 1987).

The Japanese Sanrio corporation's Hello Kitty franchise phenomenon found its way to animated cartoons—and warmly didactic Arthurianimation—in the 1980s on CBS's *Hello Kitty's Furry Tale Theatre*. In writer Tony Marino's eleven-minute "Paws of the Round Table" (DIC, 1987), the Hello Kitty characters mount a stage production in which they take on Arthurian roles. Guided by the wizard Furlin the Wise (Grandpa Kitty), the diminutive and timid Arthur (Chip the Seal) pulls "the royal sword Excalibur from the enchanted stone" to demonstrate that sometimes small folk can succeed where larger ones fail. Yet the brawny Black Knight (Grinder the Bulldog) and his muscular friends refuse to acknowledge Arthur's rule, even after Arthur repeatedly draws the sword that no one else can. Furlin explains that the "boy king" needs to earn the people's respect by performing an impressive feat. He already has one in mind: Princess Bunnyvere (My Melody the Bunny) needs to be rescued from a dragon that has fallen in love with her. Arthur's quest to save Bunnyvere carries him into conflicts with Morgan le Fur (Catnip) as she attempts to steal Excalibur, an alliance with Sir Launcelot Penguin (Tuxedo Sam), and a visit to the Kitty of the Lake of Lost and Found (Hello Kitty) to recover his sword when it falls into a lake during combat with the Black Knight. As events play out, Arthur gains self-confidence, rescues Bunnyvere, defeats Morgan, wins the Black Knight's respect and allegiance, and appoints the lovelorn dragon as "royal cook and personal bodyguard" to Bunnyvere at his Round Table. Although "Paws of the Round Table" is far from *Le Morte Darthur*, perceptive viewers will recognize several parallels between the two in this refreshingly thoughtful adaptation of the legend.

Arthurian Animation

The Muppets also offered laughter mixed with gentle lessons about playing well together in writer Hank Saroyan's half-hour "The Pig Who Would Be Queen" (Marvel/Jim Henson Productions, 1988) on CBS's *Muppet Babies*. Although the toddler Muppets do not have a time machine in their nursery, they possess craft supplies and vibrant imaginations in abundance that allow them to journey anywhere — in much the same way that *Hello Kitty's Furry Tale Theatre* used the stage. In this episode, the babies' combined art projects take the cast to the Middle Ages. Imperious Miss Piggy naturally wants to rule, but she learns that a convoluted quest and her friends' support will be necessary to become queen. Merlin (Beaker) explains the labyrinthine, alliterating journey: the Muppets must pass through the Whispering Forest to the Laughing Lake in order to retrieve the Singing Sword from the Stone of Silence (a floating block of ice that stifles the Singing Sword's otherwise-uncontrolled folk-singing), then brandish that sword at the Slithering Serpent (Animal) in the Swamp of Silliness. With the assistance of their Muppet companions, Sir Kermalot of the Lily Pond and his "manservant" Sir Fuzzalot (Fozzie Bear) successfully complete the tasks to place Miss Piggy on the throne — just as caretaker Nanny enters the nursery with lunch and draws the Muppet Babies from their medieval reverie. Dotty ballads by a minstrel (Rowlf), Fozzie's coconuts that make the sound of hoofbeats, talking trees in the Whispering Forest, and Skeeter's questions from atop a castle wall recall moments from *Monty Python and the Holy Grail* in this pleasant, mildly instructional Arthurian outing.

Arthur returned to native soil for sophisticated humor in thirteen ten-minute episodes of Thames Television's *Alias the Jester* (Cosgrove Hall Productions, 1985), which won a 1986 BAFTA in the Best Animated Film category. Writer Brian Trueman's series introduces Alias of Zogma, an interplanetary traveler transported "from the middle of space to the Middle Ages" and stranded on Earth. To keep his true identity and extraterrestrial powers secret, Alias takes the role of jester in the humdrum court of King Arthur of Houghton Bottoms. Arthur's working-class diction and pedestrian concerns about paying the bills and sacking the help must have called to mind for its original British audience a sanitized, medieval *Till Death Do Us Part*, just as many Americans will think of *All in the Family* as they watch the series. Haughty and airheaded Queen Edith, timorous Princess Amaranth, scatterbrained magician Meredith, and lisping knight Sir Pinkley round out the court. When not trying to entertain the king, Alias spends his time discreetly rescuing the court from various mythical creatures and foreign intruders invading Houghton Bottoms in every show.

Trueman was back the following year with more rapid-fire, intelligent, irreverent fun in the half-hour "Where There's a Well, There's a Way" (Cosgrove Hall Productions, 1986) on *Danger Mouse*, Thames Television's long-running animated parody of the secret agent adventure genre. When archaeologists unearth Merlin's secret book, Danger Mouse and his hamster assistant Penfold are charged with finding the wizard's wish-granting inkwell before it can fall into the hands of some blackguard. A sequence of interlocking messages take them — via Stonehenge, Gawain's tomb, a witch, and Druids — ever nearer their goal. Metal-nosed Copper-Conk Cassidy, the episode's villain who plans to use the inkwell's power to rule the world, pursues them closely. But at

7. Many Returns of the King

the end of their quest, the inkwell's one wish falls to Penfold. He unintentionally uses it to ask that the inkwell had never existed.

While the Arthurian legend's characters, themes, and motifs provided ample opportunities for laughs in the 1980s, some studios tapped these same elements for action-adventure fantasies energized by Boorman's *Excalibur* and the anime *King Arthur and the Knights of the Round Table*. Superheroes whose roots can be traced to comic books, toys, role-playing games, and video games appeared in Arthurian episodes on many Saturday morning action cartoons. A medieval fair and exhibit at Peter Parker's Empire University in writer Donald P. Glut's half-hour "Knights and Demons" (Marvel Comics Animation, 1981) on NBC's *Spider-Man and His Amazing Friends* brought the web-slinging hero to a new Arthurian adventure. Spider-Man, Iceman, Firestar, and an unusual *good* Black Knight unite to battle a malevolent wizard named, also quite unusually, Modred. Even though Merlin himself does not appear, his *name* does. We learn that Merlin created both the Black Knight's Ebony Blade, long ago used to exile Modred to the Land of Shades, and Merlin's medallion. The latter, when used at Stonehenge, allows passage to and from the Land of Shades. The heroes use the medallion to return Modred to banishment. In "Knights and Demons," fidelity to the legend seems less important than demonstrating engagement with the Arthurian universe, even if that engagement runs little deeper than the names invoked.

Writer Bill Dubay's half-hour "Terror in Time" (King Features/Marvel Productions, 1986) on the syndicated *Defenders of the Earth* also dropped Merlin's name into a storyline in which the wizard again does not make an appearance. When Ming the Merciless forces the show's D. O. E. superheroes through a time vortex to "the days of King Arthur," the futuristic crime-fighters team up with Prince Valiant, Queen Aleta, and teenage son Arn to retrieve Merlin's crystal ball "Eternity Stone," the source of all magic, from the medieval realm's evil Warlock. Medieval mission accomplished, Aleta employs the Eternity Stone to help the superheroes back to the future. Just before they go, Defender Jedda gives Arn a kiss and a D. O. E. identification badge—"a greater honor than sitting at King Arthur's table," Valiant remarks.

Writer Douglas Booth's half-hour "A Decepticon Raider in King Arthur's Court" (Sunbow Productions/Hasbro/Marvel Productions, 1985) on the syndicated *Transformers* begins with—and almost as quickly abandons—Twain's novel for a half-hour adventure in which the honorable Autobots and treacherous Decepticons continue their ceaseless battle in a Camelot of 543 A. D. After being drawn through a hengework's time vortex, the two robotic armies find themselves in the middle of a local power struggle between Sir Wigend and Sir Aetheling (Old English for "warrior" and "noble"). With Autobots on Aetheling's side and Decepticons on Wigend's, the Transformers serve as mounts for jousting knights and later participate in full-scale assaults on the nobles' castles. But when the Decepticons kidnap Aetheling's spunky daughter Nimue, Wigend realizes that the villains are helping him only for their own nefarious ends and, more importantly, that he feels affection for Nimue. For her part, Nimue's love for her father and her father's rival allows a rapprochement. Wigend and Aetheling settle their differences and unite their armies against the Decepticon threat. The unaffiliated wizard

Arthurian Animation

Beorht joins with the combined armies to defeat the mechanical villains. Both Autobots and Decepticons—enjoying a temporary détente—battle a dragon and then pass again through the hengework that is revealed to be Beorht's time-travel portal. All Transformers return to the present, taking them far from the Middle Ages that an allusive episode title, some name-dropping, and a few familiar motifs fleetingly associate with Arthurianimation.

Two syndicated, half-hour adventure cartoons shared the title "Excalibur" in 1985. Identical titles notwithstanding, these cartoons took rather different approaches to the legend. On *G. I. Joe: A Real American Hero* (Sunbow Productions/Hasbro/Marvel Productions), the animated action figure and his multiracial commando buddies travel to England to install an anti–Cobra radar system in writer Dan di Stefano's Arthurian episode. An aerial battle between the Joes and Cobras sets the plot into motion. A Cobra soldier crashes his aircraft into a lake, at the bottom of which he finds the Lady of the Lake and Excalibur. He takes the sword, escapes the water, and begins to wield his new weapon. The weather turns wild as the Joes and Cobras continues fighting.

A burring Scotsman named Beamish arrives to tell the Joes "about the sword— Excalibur-r-r-r-r it is." "You mean, like in King Arthur?" asks Lady-Jaye. "Aye, this be the home of the Lady of the Lake, keeper of Excalibur.... Legend says that if Excalibur

Mumm-Ra (disguised as King Arthur) and Excalibur vs. Lion-O and the Sword of Omens in "Excalibur," ***ThunderCats*** (Pacific Animation/Rankin-Bass, 1985).

7. Many Returns of the King

is taken from the Lady, she will raise up her hand and drown the British Isles." While skeptical of the Scot's mad tale, the Joes take simultaneous actions on several fronts: protecting the radar equipment and nearby villagers from the rain and winds; fighting Cobra soldiers; rescuing their comrades; and, finally, recovering and returning Excalibur to the lake to quell the tempest. The storm destroys the radar system, but England itself is saved as the Lady of the Lake raises her hand from the waters to repossess the sword and calm the weather. In the original run of the series, the episode was followed with the Joes delivering a short public service announcement, very likely on storm safety, and then the show's PSA tagline, "Now you know, and knowing is half the battle."[2]

The syndicated *ThunderCats* (Pacific Animation/Rankin-Bass) offered 1985's second "Excalibur" in writer Peter Lawrence's half-hour episode for the fantasy-adventure series. As in *G. I. Joe*, the famed weapon falls into the wrong hands. This time, the "ancient spirits of evil" tell villain Mumm-Ra of Excalibur, the world's one matchless sword that can defeat ThunderCat leader Lion-O's potent Sword of Omens. A dense intercalated backstory narrative channels Boorman and Malory to explain how the supremely powerful Merlin created the weapon long ago in "a time of darkness, evil, and war." Merlin set the sword in a stone and prophesied that whoever could remove it would bring the land "peace, justice, and happiness." All failed to win the sword until "an unknown youth," Arthur, drew it from the stone and launched the legend. One day as Arthur traveled through the realm fostering justice and honor, he used Excalibur to rescue an unnamed maiden (Guinevere?) from an enchanted castle. At this point, Mumm-Ra interrupts the ancient spirits of evil's storytelling. He wants to know how to obtain this sword. The backstory narrative resumes at the moment "when King Arthur's reign was ended" and relates that Bedivere returned the sword to the Lady of the Lake to await the day that Arthur will reclaim his crown.

Mumm-Ra knows what he must do. He masquerades as Arthur to trick the Lady of the Lake into giving him Excalibur, then taunts Lion-O to a joust and the inevitable clash of the two mighty swords. A few minutes into Mumm-Ra and Lion-O's skirmish, both swords unexpectedly leap from the warriors' hands to engage in an airborne dogfight in which Excalibur drains the Sword of Omens of its power. All ThunderCats fall unconscious. Mumm-Ra's triumph passes quickly, however, because Merlin arrives to banish the villain back to his crypt and recharge Lion-O's sword. The wizard tells Lion-O that Excalibur is also now his, if he wishes it—thus hinting that Lion-O may be Arthur returned—yet Lion-O asks that Excalibur be restored to the Lady of the Lake; he already owns "a sword that fights for justice, truth, honor, and loyalty." Later, in the show's educational, social guidance moment,[3] when asked why he refused the only weapon better than the Sword of Omens, the hero considers his own failings: "I didn't earn it.... I should never have fought [Mumm-Ra].... I let him get to me, and until I can control that, I've got a long way to go." Meanwhile, Merlin returns Excalibur to a hand that rises from the lake, placing the sword where Arthur expects to find it on the day that he will return.

Writers Herb Englehardt and Kip Gordy offered yet a third Excalibur storyline the following year as crime-fighting mission-leader Crystal Kane and her companions encountered diverse, intricate Arthurian strands in the half-hour "Merlin" (Ruby-Spears, 1986) episode of the syndicated *The Centurions*. While passing the day at a medieval fair, Crystal's former university professor tells her of his recent discovery at London's Riverfront Library: a map that reveals the exact location of Merlin's tomb at Stonehenge. A struggle presently arises between Crystal and the exoframe-assisted Centurions on one side and on the other cyborg Doc Terror and his minions, who wants the map as part of a scheme to harness Merlin's powers for world domination. Ultimately at stake is Excalibur, "the most powerful weapon in the universe." Before the adventure ends, Englehardt and Gordy introduce several additional old and new Arthurian elements: Melinda, an embittered descendant of Morgana le Fey, who owned the sword before "that knave Arthur stole [it]"; Merlin's mirror,[4] the key item required to release and awaken the sleeping wizard; and Arthur's crown, which is used in an incantation to make the Lady of the Lake surrender the powerful sword that she protects. After several back-and-forth struggles, a final battle sets everything right again. The Centurions defeat Doc Terror and thwart Melinda's plan to double-cross Doc Terror and seize power for herself. Excalibur is returned to a hand that rises from the lake. The villains slink away. Merlin returns to sleep underground with Arthur's crown. The mirror is launched into space, where it causes a sword-shaped constellation to shimmer. In the episode's closing education segment, Centurion Jake Rockwell explains how Stonehenge functioned as a calendar and was used long ago to know when to plant crops.

The decade's burgeoning fantasy role-playing market and related video game industry were also naturally drawn to the adventure-filled medieval landscape offered by Arthurianimation. Writer Mark Evanier's half-hour "The Night of No Tomorrow" (Toei Animation, 1983) for CBS's *Dungeons & Dragons* brought the show's six young D&D–inspired characters to a floating castle. The friendly occupant claims to be Merlin, a wizard renowned for trapping the land's marauding dragons a millennium ago. In truth, this "Merlin" is Venger, the series antagonist, in disguise. Merlin/Venger tricks the show's young magician (Presto) into using his powers to reverse the true Merlin's original spell that has long kept the dragons in check. Upon discovering Venger's treachery, Presto and his friends employ their diverse D&D role-playing abilities to eliminate the fire-breathing menaces before they can destroy a local village. There was not a continuous narrative thread from one episode to the next through the series; however, the Arthurian "The Night of No Tomorrow" served as the series-opener to *Dungeons & Dragons*'s two-year network run.

An amusement park ride first carried the *Dungeons & Dragons* kids into their fantasy universe. Kevin and his dog Duke of *Captain N: The Game Master* found another way: continually playing Nintendo video games until they were pulled through the television screen into Videoland, an electronic domain inhabited by malefactors spawned from various Nintendo game cartridges. In writer Jeffrey Scott's half-hour "Nightmare on Mother Brain's Street" (DIC, 1989) for NBC, Kevin/Captain N travels to "Excalibur, the land of wizards and warriors" to fight the sorcerer Malkill and rescue Princess Lana from Mother Brain's latest plot to gain mastery of Videoland. Although the episode

7. Many Returns of the King

shares more in common with *Sleeping Beauty*, *Tron*, and Freddy Krueger films than it does Arthurianimation, "Nightmare on Mother Brain's Street" indicates how far some shows reached to drop a trendy Arthurian element or two into their storylines.

Perry Martin's script for the fifteen-minute "King Mario of Cramalot" on another Nintendo-franchised, syndicated television series, *The Super Mario Brothers Super Show!* (Sei Young Animation/DIC, 1989), contained more developed Arthurian facets than did "Nightmare on Mother Brain's Street." In this episode, the resourceful plumbers travel down the drain and warp to a world of "damsels in distress and knights in shining armor" where despotic King Koopa has usurped a kingdom. Mario, Luigi, and Princess Toadstool call upon Mervin the Magician for help. Their adventure leads Mario to draw the Golden Plunger from the Sacred Sink to become the rightful king of the realm. Later, after Mario is compelled to sacrifice the Plunger to Koopa in order to save the Princess, Mervin guides the heroes to a lake from which Mario obtains Excalibur, the Plumber's Snake, "the mightiest tool of good deeds in the realm." Mario battles Koopa, Snake against Plunger, until Koopa is vanquished. With the people's backing, Mario becomes the land's new ruler. But Mario soon abdicates when he learns that the king has to diet to maintain a trim figure! Mario passes the crown to Mervin. The Nintendo characters depart for other adventures.

A few toy store aisles from the board and video games that engendered these last three cartoons, stuffed animals were also making the plans to enter Arthurianimation. In the second half of the 1980s, the Care Bears branched from their American Greetings card and then plush toy origins to headline theatrical and television cartoons in *The Care Bears Movie* (Nelvana, 1985), two rapidly spun movie sequels, and ABC's *The Care Bears* series (Nelvana, 1985–88) aimed at the toddler-to-ten demographic. But beyond a smattering of unconnected names and motifs—the Care Bears' castle of Care-a-lot, the heart-shaped table around which they gather, the character Love-a-lot, and so on—the franchise did not make any consistent or sustained use of Arthurian veins it scratched.

The cuddly Pound Puppies also came to television and cineplex screens. In the theatrical feature release of *Pound Puppies and the Legend of Big Paw* (Wang Film Productions/Cuckoos Nest Studios/Tonka/Family Home Entertainment, 1988), direc-

Digalot and Arthur in *Pound Puppies and the Legend of Big Paw* (Wang Film Productions/Cuckoos Nest Studios/Tonka/Family Home Entertainment, 1988).

tor Pierre Decelles and writers Jim Carlson and Terrence McDonnell offered up seventy-six minutes of product-pushing plot with an Arthurian backstory in the mix. It is the present as the action begins. Canine Uncle Whopper tells his niece and nephew two tales, one from 1000 years ago (a five-minute segment) and another from the 1950s when he was growing up (the bulk of the movie). Whopper's first tale explains how humans and their dogs gained the capacity to talk to each other. "Puppy Power," as their ability is called, emerged "in the Dark Ages," when Digalot, young Arthur's dog, helped his master pull Excalibur from the stone by releasing its linchpin, the Bone of Scone. Arthur became king and the legend began — all thanks to his pup.

This learned allusion to comparatively arcane lore — the fact that the Coronation Chair ("King Edward's Chair" in Westminster Abbey) of the United Kingdom contains beneath its seat the Stone of Scone, a symbol of Scottish monarchy dating back to the Middle Ages[5] — undoubtedly passed far over the heads of the preteens in the audience. Children also likely overlooked certain Arthurian touches that the writers quietly slip into Whopper's opening tale. Not only is Excalibur lodged in *stone*, the stone itself rises from a *lake* in a clever conflation that fuses both of Arthur's swords from *Le Morte Darthur*.

The film continues with esoteric jokes that only Arthurian specialists might recognize. The sword is said to be guarded by Big Paw, a mysterious creature known solely by the giant footprints he leaves behind until late in the movie. Here Carlson and McDonnell gesture toward Nennius's ninth-century description in the *Historia Brittonum* (para. 73) of one of Britain's marvels, a supernatural stone that preserves the print of Arthur's dog Cafal. Like a faithful hound, this stone always finds its way home:

> There is a wonder in the country called Builth. There is a heap of stones there, and one of the stones placed on top of the pile has the footprint of a dog on it. When he hunted [the boar] Twrch Trwyth[,] Cafal, the warrior Arthur's hound, impressed his footprint on the stone, and Arthur later brought together the pile of stones, under the stone in which was his dog's footprint, and it [the stone] is called Carn Cafal. Men come and take the stone in their hands for the space of a day and a night, and on the morrow it is found upon the stone pile.

The picture is a mine of similar recondite allusions, Arthurian and not, that probably puzzled more often than pleased. During one musical number alone ("The King of Everything") sung by the film's villain, the animators insert visual sequences parroting Eisenstein's *Ivan the Terrible*, Chaplin's *The Great Dictator*, and Thorpe's *Jailhouse Rock* (starring, of course, the *King* of Rock and Roll). While kids watched the baffling montages and tapped their feet to canine-themed covers of 1950s and 1960s rock and roll ("At the Hop" recycled as "At the Pound," "Duke of Earl" as "I'm a Puppy, Too," etc.), their parents' minds may have drifted from the film to its allusions. The cinephilically inclined could relish iconic moments from well-known film classics. Arthurians could be amused by the inventive redeployment of history, pseudohistory, and legend. For many viewers, however, *Pound Puppies and the Legend of Big Paw* must have seemed simply a peculiar bit of heavy-handed merchandising masquerading as a kids' movie.

Whopper's second tale recollects his puppyhood in the 1950s. To celebrate the millennial anniversary of the Bone of Scone, a museum has brought the bone and a cast of Big Paw's famed print to town. The exhibit brings out Marvin McNasty, a descendant of Arthur's ancient rival. McNasty wants the bone in order to rule "the pound, then the country, then the world." Young Whopper and his pals, the descendants of Digalot, rise up to protect the Bone of Scone from McNasty's many attempts to use it for evil ends. Big Paw (or perhaps it is Big Paw's descendant?) also joins in to preserve Puppy Power and make sure that good triumphs over evil. *Pound Puppies and the Legend of Big Paw* demonstrated that Arthurianimation could arise in the most unexpected of places by the late 1980s.

Few might have predicted that Hungary's Pannónia Filmstúdió would also release an animated Arthurian feature film as the 1980s came to close, though the many cartoons arriving from across the Atlantic must have provided strong incentive to do so. Directed by Tibor Hernádi, 1989's 78-minute *Sárkány és papucs* (*Dragon and Slippers*) takes an unorthodox approach to the legend's central love triangle. We meet a middle-aged Arthur in the opening scene. He enjoys the many hours that he spends with his Round Table knights watching tournaments, telling stories of days gone by, and listening to his jester's banter. Yet the king's happiness comes at a price: the film's lead character, Queen Guinevra, feels that Arthur neglects her.

Guinevra's handmaiden Peggy advises her to consult the court's bumbling, Disneyesque Merlin for a love potion that will help the queen recapture her husband's attentions. Guinevra bakes the magician's philter into a plum pudding to disguise its taste. But her plan crumbles when Arthur—who does not like plums—gives the dish to a teenage Lancelot. The youth who once had feelings for handmaiden Peggy now falls hopelessly in love with the queen. A comedy of errors follows.

In slapstick fashion, young Lancelot awkwardly courts the adult queen with gifts, messages, song, and grand public and private displays of affection—usually injuring Guinevra in the process. By three-quarters of the way through the film, the queen has lost her front teeth, a tuft of hair, her chamber's furnishing to fire, and all of her dignity. Lancelot's amorous pursuit has also given the queen a black eye and forced her to hobble about with a crutch. At wits' end, Guinevra insists that Arthur do something to halt the lovesick lad's unwanted advances.

King and queen concoct a quest to make Lancelot leave court. Under the pretext that the dragon Góliát has stolen Guinevra's best slippers, the royals send Lancelot to retrieve her footwear. And with Lancelot gone, Arthur at last carries his bedraggled bride to the bedroom. Presumably engaged in long-delayed connubial passion, the king and queen exit from a film that still has twenty minutes remaining!

Meanwhile, on his quest, Lancelot learns in adventures with witch Matilda (a clone of Disney's Mim) and the dragon that Góliát knows nothing of the slippers and has little interest in fighting the knight over the alleged theft. Nevertheless, little Lancelot fruitlessly stabs and slashes at the huge dragon until Peggy arrives on the scene. She reveals that the knight has been on a fool's errand. Annoyed, Góliát kicks the pest away. The impact expels from Lancelot's stomach the undigested, potion-laced pudding—which plops into Matilda's open mouth. Matilda falls in love with Góliát. The dragon soon sets out for Loch Ness to escape her embrace. With Lancelot free of the potion's power, he and Peggy find love at last as *Sárkány és papucs* comes to a close.

Sárkány és papucs dabbles playfully in Arthuriana as it develops its overlapping love stories. The well-known motifs of Launcelot's feelings for the king's wife and the misapplied philter from the *Tristan* legend — revised almost beyond recognition in this unusual retelling — serve as the backdrop to a tale of how a frustrated wife regains her husband's affection and her handmaiden wins a young knight's heart. Merlin's potion is ultimately effective in renewing Arthur's passion for his wife, though it achieves its results in a way that even he did not foresee.

While some cartoons of the decade motioned briefly — and routinely only in the final minute of the show — toward educational agendas, at least one studio rehearsed the legend exclusively for didactic ends. Aimed at the homeschool and middle-school library markets, two direct-to-video entries in director Greg Beeson's *Fables and Legends: English Folk Heroes* series (Donald Thompson & Associates/Milliken Publishing, 1986) offered sober, bowdlerized, instructional abridgements of Arthurian tales. These tales are presented within frame narratives in which live-action adults and children recite campfire stories of tales of heroes of old. As each fable or legend unfolds, a narrator supplies historical and literary background — while a camera slowly pans and zooms across static illustrations to create a sense of movement without the expense of true animation (à la *Jackanory* and "Merlin and the Toothless Knights"). The camera continues to drift over the pictures as other voices enter to recount a hero's exploits.[6]

In Beeson's ten-minute "Arthur and the Sword," a voiceover introduces King Arthur as a "semimythical," "Christian," "minor Roman-Saxon chieftain" in the "south of Britain" who fought against the "invading Saxon pagans." A condensed narrative follows with a sanitized *Le Morte Darthur*, more or less, from Uther's final days to Arthur's coronation. Several omissions, elisions, and outright changes strike the attentive viewer. Uther's reign is described as *peaceful*, a time "when knights fought each other only in friendly jousts." Uther's adviser Merlin, characterized as "wise and crafty" and possessing an ability to control all powers of good and evil, is never openly called a "magician" or any synonymous darker term to which some parents might object. And although Merlin moves to protect Arthur after Uther dies, no mention is made of the boy's *mother* — which would involve sensitive threads that Beeson shrewdly chooses not to pursue. For many other details, the director traces Malory's text directly or through plausible inference: the interregnal turmoil after Uther's death; Merlin revealing the sword in the stone to the Archbishop of Canterbury; a New Year's tournament to determine the next king; the unknown boy's drawing the sword; Merlin's revelation of Arthur's true identity and his explanation of why Ector raised Arthur in secret for the boy's own protection; and the coronation of the young king. As far as it goes — and in only ten minutes — "Arthur and the Sword" provides a reasonable synopsis of many key moments from the opening of *Le Morte Darthur*, stressing the importance of Merlin's guiding hand and the importance of the Church, even as it glosses over or silently omits other crucial details.

Beeson's fifteen-minute "The Table Round" follows a similar pattern in its strate-

7. Many Returns of the King

gically packaged account, departing ever further from Malory as the narrative develops. Merlin has continued to serve the royal household. Arthur builds Camelot and rules with equanimity. He eventually marries Guinevere. The bride vows to be "his true and faithful wife forever"—and in "The Table Round," she will not abandon this pledge. The Round Table fellowship grows. In a nearby castle, Morgan le Fey plots to overthrow her "brother" Arthur. There are many reasons for Morgan's actions, all painted in darkest terms: she is "evil"; "filled with envy"; "had not accepted the true Church"; "followed the ancient and dark ways of the false Druids"; and "through terrible pagan ceremonies ... became a sorceress of great power."

Meanwhile, Arthur warmly welcomes young Launcelot to Camelot, though not without some jealous grousing among his knights, primarily from the duplicitous Modred, Morgan's son. The narrative then skips quickly through much of *Le Morte Darthur*, lighting and adjusting here and there: the empty Siege Perilous; Launcelot's journey to King Pelles's land and his deadly vengeance on Morgan's Black Knight; Launcelot's marriage to Pelles's daughter Elaine; a maiden (Morgan in disguise) whose potion causes Launcelot to forget his wife; Launcelot's return to Camelot; and the birth of Galahad and death of Elaine.

Fifteen years pass. Camelot has declined. Launcelot and Guinevere alone remain steadfastly loyal to the king. Modred foments dissent and eyes the throne. Merlin is nowhere to be found. Arthur longs for the one who will fill the Siege Perilous and heal the kingdom. One day a hermit (Merlin in disguise) brings Galahad to Camelot. Launcelot's memory of Elaine returns and he welcomes his son. The hermit chastises the "false" court and its "vain and petty" king, telling them all that their one hope of saving Camelot lies in a perfect knight's quest for the Holy Grail. Only young Galahad is "brave and pure enough" to accept the mission. Galahad does at last find the Grail—"but it was too late." As an image of an elderly Galahad weeping at the foot of a decaying castle appears on screen, the narrator explains: "Time and the nature of man had conquered Camelot. The dreams of King Arthur and the Table Round had become only ashes and faded memories."[7]

The program turns again to live-action and the campers seated around the fire. They model a few of the lessons that viewers are to have learned:

> ADULT 1: Can you believe how mean Morgan le Fey was? What a witch!
> TEEN: She sure was!
> CHILD 1: I like Sir Launcelot because he was bold and brave....
> CHILD 2: ... and forgetful.
> CHILD 1: That's because Morgan le Fey put a spell on him.
> CHILD 3: Can somebody really put a spell on someone else?
> ADULT 2: Well, that's what the legend said.
> ADULT 1: Ah, but remember, legends have a way of twisting things.

And so does Arthurianimation.

CHAPTER 8

Arthur, Arthur, Everywhere: Short Animation of 1990s

Live-action feature films for theaters, television, and direct-to-video release continued to deliver an abundance of Arthurian-themed material to an eager public in the 1990s. Anglo-American premieres through the decade included *Gawain and the Green Knight* (Thames Television, 1991), *The Fisher King* (Columbia, 1991), *Army of Darkness* (Universal, 1992), *Merlin* (a.k.a. *October 32nd*; United Filmmakers, 1992), *Guinevere* (Lifetime Productions, 1994), the Welsh *Ymadawiad Arthur* (Tiger Bay for S4C, 1994), *The Four Diamonds* (Disney, 1995), *First Knight* (Columbia, 1995), *A Young Connecticut Yankee in King Arthur's Court* (Filmline, 1995), *A Kid in King Arthur's Court* (Disney, 1995), *Dragonheart* (Universal, 1996), *Lancelot: Guardian of Time* (Alpine Pictures, 1997), *Kids of the Round Table* (Melenny Productions, 1997), *Merlin: The Quest Begins* (a.k.a. *Merlin: The Magic Begins*; Seagull Entertainment, 1998), *A Knight in Camelot* (Disney, 1998), a *Merlin* miniseries (Hallmark, 1998), *Arthur's Quest* (Crystal Sky Worldwide, 1999), and *The Excalibur Kid* (Canarom Productions, 1999). Animators contributed their share, too, to what was to become the richest years ever for Arthurianimation.

Several animated serial productions kept the legend continually on the airwaves. Two seasons each of *The Legend of Prince Valiant*, *King Arthur and the Knights of Justice*, *Princess Gwenevere and the Jewel Riders*, and *Blazing Dragons*, and a single season of *Tristan & Iseult: La légende oubliée* collectively proffered 169 first-run half-hour episodes of Arthurianimation and countless reruns. A child growing up in the 1990s might have concluded that Arthur was unfailingly only a click of the remote away.

The Legend of Prince Valiant (Sei Young Animation/Hearst Entertainment/King Features/Family Channel, 1991–94) in many ways recalls Toei's *King Arthur and the Knights of the Round Table*. In sixty-five ambitious, complexly structured episodes, this medieval soap opera presents a flawed yet often idealistic world — in other words, a place not unlike our own. Season one follows young Valiant (voiced by Robby Benson) and his family into exile, chased by Cynan from their land of Thule; Valiant's dream vision of faraway and perhaps merely imaginary Camelot, Arthur, the Round Table knights, and Merlin; the new friends Arn and Rowanne that Valiant makes as he seeks Camelot; their arrival at court and training to become knights; diverse adventures that help Valiant and his companions mature; Valiant's acquisition of the Singing Sword, the "sister" weapon from the same forge that produced Arthur's Excalibur; the hero's return to Thule to reclaim the land from Cynan; and finally Valiant's investiture as he joins the Round Table and sets off on his first quest as a Round Table knight.

8. Arthur, Arthur, Everywhere

Sir Bryant teaches Valiant to use a lance in *The Legend of Prince Valiant* (Sei Young Animation/Hearst Entertainment/King Features/Family Channel, 1991).

We hear many familiar names: Arthur, Guinevere, Gawain, Mordred, Morgana, Merlin, Kay, and so on, but the characters have often been redefined. Mordred is roughly Arthur's age (and thus cannot be his son) and long-time ally, yet he often disagrees with Arthur's desire to be a peacemaker and at last leads a full-scale uprising against the king in season two. Morgana is Arthur's half-sister and Mordred's erstwhile lover. Her knowledge of alchemy and herbals rivals Merlin's similar powers. Merlin's own abilities can border at times on the supernatural, yet in most episodes he acts purely as a wise old adviser and military/political strategist. As in Foster's original newspaper strip, the series eschews magic in favor of realism. Guinevere is faithful to Arthur — an easy matter perhaps without a Launcelot anywhere in the series to complicate her storyline. Arthur is an intelligent, pragmatic ruler who safeguards his people by forging treaties and alliances when he can and fighting when he must. Some new and some revised characters, loosely based on Foster's work, also enter the Arthurian sphere. Rowanne, a blacksmith's athletic daughter who aspires to be "the first female knight of the Round Table," and Arn, a peasant whose family was slain by Vikings, are coming of age along with Valiant. Both are welcomed into knighthood in season two.

Episodes express hope for a better world and offer implicit roadmaps and social agendas to create Arthur's "New Order." Women stand as men's equals, if not sometimes their betters. Bryant, a Moorish knight sure to be understood as African American by most young viewers in the United States, is the most thoughtful, respected member of the king's inner circle after Merlin and Guinevere. Bryant's actions often contrast starkly with those of another of Arthur's advisers, the hot-tempered, impetuous—and white-skinned—Gawain. Although all Arthur's adherents swear to support right over might, each episode shows knights-in-training Valiant and his two close companions, experienced knights, and even Arthur himself struggling to control passions that would make them no better than their enemies, both domestic (Mordred, Morgana, alliterating newcomer Maldon, and several single-episode bad guys) and foreign (primarily Cynan and sundry Vikings).

Season two traces Mordred's rebellion. His "New Dawn" coalition of outright evildoers and merely misled folk strain Arthur's New Order to the breaking point. As the series approaches its close, Camelot's end seems certain. In "The Death of Arthur" (episode 63 of 65) the king devises a last-ditch plan to fake his own death in order to draw out his foes, then "return" from the dead to deal with them—a new spin on the old legend. But Arthur's plan collapses when an explosion nearly kills him and causes everybody to think that the king has truly perished.

For the good of her people and because Arthur would have wanted it, Guinevere announces that she is abdicating and appoints to the throne the man Arthur loved as a son and considered his spiritual heir, Valiant. The penultimate episode explores Valiant's many difficulties in his new role, compounded again by threats from Morgana and now Kay as well—yet he does not need to think about them for long. The final episode brings outside help from Princess Aleta of the Misty Isles (Valiant's betrothed since episode 42) and then Arthur, whose surprising return from "death" stuns everybody. Following a long-anticipated battle between Valiant and Mordred, Arthur rallies his people to decisive victory over the New Dawn. Mordred is marched away in tears. The series closes on the note that ideals embodied by Camelot's New Order will continue, presumably with Valiant one day assuming Arthur's role once more.

Story editor-in-chief Dianne Dixon's reinterpretation of Foster's comic garnered a Humanitas Prize and a Silver Angel Award for promoting positive, family-friendly values in a television landscape that many viewers at the time perceived as increasingly unsuitable for children. But *The Legend of Prince Valiant* is by no means pablum. In many episodes someone dies by sword or poison, though the forces of good and justice do always prevail in the end in a kind of animated *Bonanza* for the 1990s. No doubt many parents joined their children to watch the engaging, popular series every week, first on the Family Channel's Tuesday night primetime line-up and later on weekend mornings.[1] Nintendo and Game Boy video games and music from the soundtrack on CD were released while the show was still in its first run.

The Legend of Prince Valiant's success invited weaker imitations. Bohbot Entertainment rolled out two syndicated Arthurian series in the 1990s, *King Arthur and the Knights of Justice* (C&D Asia/Golden Films/Bohbot Entertainment, 1992–93) and *Princess Gwenevere and the Jewel Riders* (Hong Ying Animation/New Frontier/Enchanted Camelot Productions/Bohbot Entertainment, 1995–96; *Starla and the Jewel Riders* in many foreign markets), the former for boys and the latter for girls. Both Bohbot entries were integrated with larger marketing campaigns designed to put VHS cassettes, trading cards, actions figures, and related merchandise into the hands of children watching the shows—which at times seem to be little more than half-hour advertisements for items that were available at toy stores. These Bohbot series enjoy the rare distinction of holding *two* spots—first and fifth, respectively—on Todd Ciolek's 2009 online list of "The 10 Most Ridiculous Adaptations of Arthurian Legend."

As writer/producer Jean Chalopin's story opens for the twenty-six episodes of *King Arthur and the Knights of Justice*, Morgana has already imprisoned King Arthur and his Round Table knights in the Cave of Glass. Then her accomplice, Warlord Viper, kidnaps Guinevere. All seems lost until the female spirit of the Round Table directs Merlin to travel into the future to find those who can save the past. Merlin's magic brings New England Knights football star Arthur King and his high school teammates to Camelot. These young men must become the Knights of Justice to rescue the king and queen — or else their own future may never exist. Along the way, they learn lessons of loyalty, honesty, and comparable Boy Scout virtues as they seek the Keys of Truth that will allow them to return to the present. Action figures and trading cards sold to young boys encouraged them to continue the adventures in their imaginations. Nintendo followed with a video game in 1995, just as it had in 1992 for *The Legend of Prince Valiant*.

Girls too buy toys, of course. Bohbot next wooed young female viewers with twenty-six episodes of creator/director Robert Mandell's *Princess Gwenevere and the Jewel Riders*. Bohbot's *Amazin! Adventures* website announced at the time:

> Gwenevere is the sixteen-year-old bold and beautiful Princess of Avalon, ... ready to face the challenges that await her as she rides the wings of her destiny to become the next Queen of the kingdom. She has certain traits that she has inherited from her famous namesake—courage, a strong will, and impulsiveness. She also has a fiery temper and can sometimes be snobby and pretentious. Happily, she has bonded with a rare and stunning winged unicorn named Sunstar who works with the young princess to help her realize her potential and develop her inner beauty. Sunstar will teach Gwenevere to make the right decisions, and keep a positive outlook, always. Gwenevere's (human) best friends, Fallon and Tamara, are a great source of happiness for the princess and contribute enormously to her growth as a young woman and future leader of the kingdom.[2]

It was "amazin'!" indeed to see the Princess of Avalon display these purported qualities "inherited from her famous namesake" each week as she battled the wicked women of the land, Morgana and Lady Kale (an anagram for "Lake"). When Gwenevere needed more help than her female companions could provide, she turned to Merlin and Drake, "the dashingly handsome leader of The Pack, knight protectors of the Crystal Palace" ("Princess Gwenevere Homepage"). Accessories were sold separately. Batteries were not included. A *Princess Gwenevere* video game did not materialize; however, for young girls who missed the show once its run ceased, Rachel Roberts penned the *Avalon: Web of Magic* series of books (2001–10) based loosely on the Bohbot production.

Although the Python troupe toyed with brief Arthurian cartoon elements in *Monty Python and the Holy Grail*, it was Monty Python's Terry Jones, along with Gavin Scott,[3] who fully engaged Arthurianimation in *Blazing Dragons* (Nelvana/Ellipse Animation,

1996–98). The amusing, occasionally droll series premiered in Britain and Canada before being syndicated to (and mildly censored by) the Disney Channel for American distribution. *Blazing Dragons* takes us to Camelhot, a realm where fire-breathing dragons sport draco–Arthurian names. Portly, middle-aged King Allfire has seen better times. He still wields Excaliburn, drawn from a stone years ago, but his glory days of leading the Knights of the Square Table into battle are behind him. Queen Griddle is Allfire's *second* wife — the series does not reveal what happened to the first — who shares little in common with the traditional Arthurian queen whom she replaces. Shrewish and prone to outbursts, Griddle makes Allfire's home life difficult. Camelhot's court befits its rulers. Indolent knight Loungealot routinely avoids battle, leaving the kingdom's defense to his inventive squire Flicker and Princess Flame, Allfire's daughter from his first marriage. Sir Burnevere "the Overly Educated," Sir Galahot "the Proper," Sir Hotbreath "the Not So Proper," Griddle's flamboyant (and often Disney-bowdlerized) son Sir Blaze "the Smartly Dressed" from an earlier marriage to Herman the Nearsighted, and others populate the silly, fun, allusive realm of Camelhot. *Blazing Dragons*'s tone recalls both *Alias the Jester* and *Arthur! and the Square Knights of the Round Table*, Pythonesque animated Arthurian fare that a British audience likely would have recognized as precursors of the series. More importantly, *Blazing Dragons* channels much the same kind of creative wit that produced *Monty Python and the Holy Grail*.

Camelhot is the usual medieval turf of quests, tournaments, and protecting the kingdom from invaders— here, the dragons' natural enemy, man. One man in particular repeatedly threatens Allfire's rule, "the Dread Count Geoffrey de Bouillon, Oppressor par Excellence of the Poor and Weak," from nearby castle Threadbare. Geoffrey's court makes Allfire's look admirable by comparison. A spy in ill-fitting dragon disguise, klutzy evil knights ("One," "Two," and "Three" by name), and the sharp-tongued sorceress Merle the Wizard bumblingly attempt to execute Geoffrey's many schemes. But the count's master plan to abandon ramshackle Threadbare and move into comparatively palatial Camelhot always comes to naught, thwarted most often by Flicker and Flame. A *Blazing Dragons* video game allowed hostilities to continue on Sony PlayStations and Sega Saturns after the series ended its initial run.

Director Prakash Topsy and writer Pierre Métais's Camelot-adjacent adventures of *Tristan & Iseult: La légende oubliée* (Arès Films/France 3/Cartoon Express/CNC, 1999; *Tristan & Isolde: The Lost Legend* in anglophone markets) came to French television and then worldwide syndication as the decade came to an end. Arès's online promotional video trumpeted: "On the eve of the third millennium, *Tristan and Isolde*, the greatest love story ever, is brought to the small screen for the first time" (*Arès Films*). But the twenty-six episodes of the series avoid entering the Arthurian sphere directly, offering a plot that focuses instead on the lovers' exploits in King Mark's Cornwall:

> Set in the lush rolling hills of western England, our story begins with the brutal kidnapping of Tristan, the young and handsome heir to the throne. When the pirate ship on which he is held prisoner shipwrecks, Tristan escapes to the kingdom of good King Mark, where he meets and falls in love with the ravishing Isolde. Though bound to one another by a secret love potion, the young couple's union will be destroyed unless they can recover this strange

8. Arthur, Arthur, Everywhere

world's most precious object — the Magic Blue Stone, hidden in the Crystal Palace [*Arès Films*].

Viewers may feel that Arthur's kingdom lies just over the next hill, yet the series does not journey there. Métais draws many traditional incidents from the *Tristan* legend — the Morholt, a love potion, rival Iseults, a venomous dragon, and so on — but ultimately he concedes to his youth audience and avoids the medieval tale's core conflict: that the potion that binds Tristan to Isolde also dooms them. Some areas of the old story remained unsuitable for children.

Each of these series explored the Arthurian world by traveling avenues producers believed to be underexplored. Each had its marketable "hook" and target demographic. *The Legend of Prince Valiant* showed us Camelot through the eyes of young adults discovering the Arthurian world, its principles, and their own values as well. *King Arthur and the Knights of Justice* and *Princess Gwenevere and the Jewel Riders* gave us a pair of Arthurian fantasy worlds designed for middle-schoolers willing to plunk down their allowances on many toys. *Blazing Dragons* suggested that even mythical beasts could live according to Arthurian ideals — and offered jokes that adults could appreciate while their kids were entertained by the slapstick on screen. *Tristan & Iseult* added to the growing Arthurianimation corpus of the 1990s a young adult tale of medieval love, magic, and adventure to parallel the more familiar legend of Launcelot and Guinevere.[4]

At the same time that these five series were offering regular televised installments of Arthurianimation, one-off Arthurian episodes also premiered in many cartoons where viewers would not necessarily expect to find the legend making an appearance. Predictably, most of these cartoons took a primarily comic approach. They drew their inspiration from the same sources as before: live-action films, literature, comic books, toys and games, and even other cartoons.

Some of the best-written comic Arthurianimation in the 1990s appeared on two series executive-produced by a prominent director: *Steven Spielberg Presents Tiny Toon Adventures* (Warner Bros./Amblin, 1990–95) and *Steven Spielberg Presents Animaniacs* (Warner Bros./Amblin, 1993–98), more often known simply as *Tiny Toons* and *Animaniacs*. Both shows were syndicated to Fox and later shown on The WB network. Children and college-age adults enjoyed the madcap, allusive nature of the series. Writers ventured into Arthurian territory three times in the early 1990s: "Day for Knight" (1991) on *Tiny Toons*, "Spell-Bound" (1993) on the *Pinky and the Brain* subseries of *Animaniacs*, and "Sir Yaksalot" (1993) on *Animaniacs*. Peals of laughter rose in living rooms and dormitory lounges across the nation.

Co-written by Earl Kress, Tom Minton, and Jim Reardon, "Day for Knight"[5] takes us to the Middle Ages for a richly referential short. When the overworked, vaudeville-era quips of the king's jester (Babs Bunny) fail to amuse an unnamed, rotund monarch, he consigns her to death in a dragon's lair[6] — roughly refashioning the start of Warner's own Arthurian "Knighty Knight Bugs" from 1958. But the sweaty, bespectacled, red-haired, neurotic dragon — a transparent Woody Allen caricature — turns out to be in no hurry to toast Babs. Instead, he befriends her, in spite of his worries about violating the Geneva Convention by "fraternizing with the enemy" and incurring the wrath of "the union." Babs coyly notes that he is being "a *reluctant* dragon"—and on several levels calls to mind the effeminate beast of Disney's "The Reluctant Dragon" segment from 1941's *The Reluctant Dragon*.

Meanwhile, the realm's least capable knight (Buster Bunny) embarks on a rescue mission that carries him through scenes lifted from *Monty Python and the Holy Grail*. A frog claims a witch turned him to a prince, but he "got better" and is again a frog. A troll issues challenges that recall those posed by the Knights Who Say "Ni" and the Keeper of the Bridge of Death. Sir Buster of Acme presses on, despite being maligned as a "Camelot coward" and taking a "wrong turn at Bath—or was that Bidet?" When challenged by the "Beige Knight," Buster reaches for a sword lodged in a nearby stone. An angelic choir sings. When Buster discovers that he cannot extract the weapon, he heaves both sword and the attached boulder to crush his opponent.

Several other adventures further delay Buster from reaching Babs. By the time he arrives at the dragon's cave, she no longer requires his aid. Babs has psychoanalyzed and "rehabilitated" the nebbishy dragon. "I've channeled all my latent hostility into music," the dragon says, as he announces that henceforth he will be a clarinet-playing pacifist. As the cartoon comes to a close, Buster integrates the dragon into the social order as a short-order cook at Ye Old Tacos. Babs performs her comedy routine for patrons. They enjoy her tired jokes no more than the king did at the beginning.

While "Day for Knight" repeatedly referenced Arthuriana, traditional Arthurian characters did not appear in the cartoon. But when many of the same studio team from "Day for Knight" reassembled a couple of years later for *Animaniacs*, perennial favorite Merlin returned to Warner Bros. cartoons. In writer John P. McCann's half-hour "Spell-Bound," *Pinky and the Brain*'s two genetically altered mice ("one is a genius, the other's insane") find themselves in England in the year 1194. "WELCOME TO CAMELOT," a sign beckons with the castle's name in black letter, "ASK ABOUT OUR ROUND TABLE."

The mice have come to Merlin's workshop. A self-important wizard speaks to himself: "Only I, the all-powerful Merlin, have the wizardly skills to create matter from nothing. I am fat with magic! Ha, ha, ha, ha, ha!" He recites a charm from the book before him:

> Sonny Tufts, Sonny Bono,
> Lorna Luft, Yoko Ono.
> Paula Abdul, Chip and Dale,
> Hillary Clinton, Quentin McHale.
> I win, you win, Edwin Newman,
> Lee of Kathy, Regis Philbin.

Yet Brain's hopes of learning "the secrets of the universe" from Merlin vanish quickly. The spell produces blueberry pie! Brain condemns the "pathetic waste of magic" used to create "mere pastry." Merlin completes his task and leaves the workshop to eat dessert in seclusion. He knows that Arthur and his knights—the "bunch of pigs," as Merlin calls them—will expect him to share the pie that is "yummy and good and all mine."

8. Arthur, Arthur, Everywhere

Pinky and the Brain are left alone with Merlin's book. Brain seizes the chance to find the incantation that will allow him to accomplish the goal he seeks in every episode: world domination. But a potion-mixing mishap soon sends the mice on adventures into a fairy tale wilderness to obtain a missing ingredient, a red dragon's toenail. With Merlin's wand at their side, the mice venture forth and eventually find the needed item. Yet just as Brain is about to complete the spell, Pinky distracts him and botches the charm. Brain's scheme to rule the planet fails, as it always must. Meanwhile, we hear nothing more of Merlin and Arthur's porcine court in "Spell-Bound."

In another office on the Warner Bros. lot, however, Paul Rugg was developing a script for a deeper treatment of the Arthurian court. His 1993 *Animaniacs* short, "Sir Yaksalot," brings Yakko, Wakko, and Dot to Camelot, "the most celebrated kingdom in the history of Britain." In this idyllic realm, a sign near the castle apprises visitors that there is "NO RAIN 'TIL SUNDOWN"—one in a string of witty homages to Warner's 1967 *Camelot*. Although the land is normally one of "peace, prosperity, and singing," a dragon currently menaces the populace, blithely stomping and incinerating anybody who gets in its way.

With the realm's knights in cinders, Arthur (admirably voiced as an over-the-top Charlton Heston or Kirk Douglas) instructs Merlin (a caricature of illusionist Doug "It's maaaa-gic!" Henning)[7] to summon "a brave and powerful knight to slay the dragon." Merlin's conjuring fetches the Animaniacs instead. Arthur grovels before Yakko, kisses his feet, and begs the Animaniacs to save the kingdom from destruction. The new arrivals agree to help, but Yakko insists that peasants stop yelling "Dragon!" Breaking the fourth wall, an animator complies by dropping an anvil on a noisy offender—a violent turn on Groucho Marx's *You Bet Your Life* "secret word" game. One crushed peasant later, there is quiet.

The heroes discuss a plan of action. They make a brief visit to a war room—a brilliant forty-five seconds of rapid-fire nods to *WarGames*, *Dr. Strangelove*, *Godzilla*, and *Perry Mason*[8]—before deciding to defeat the dragon through the power of comedy. While Yakko pretends to be "Henny Dragon," a vaudevillian whose jokes cause the dragon to laugh until he begins to snort flames, Dot places dynamite where it will surely be ignited. "Hey, how about that Lady in the Lake? I mean, how long can she hold her breath?" Rim shot from Wakko. "Hey, how about that King Arthur, huh? You know, I'll never forget the first time we met—but I'm trying!" Another rim shot. "Hey, what's green and stands in a corner? A naughty frog." Boom!

As pieces of dragon drizzle from the sky, one surprise remains: the invading beast was not a dragon at all but a robot piloted by none other than series-crossover the Brain. He admits to Arthur that he was "trying to destroy Camelot in yet another attempt to take over the world." The Brain and Pinky depart. The grateful king dubs the Animaniacs Sir Yaksalot, Sir Waksalot, and Lady Dotsalot. The newest members of the realm conclude the episode as Sir Yaksalot asks that someone stop the shouts of happy citizens celebrating the end of "The dragon! The dragon! The dragon!" A crowd-sized anvil drops from the sky.

Warner Bros. also distributed Arthurian-themed episodes from other studios in the 1990s. Fueled by Tim Burton's success with the live-action *Beetlejuice* (Warner Bros., 1988), ABC and later the Fox network offered four seasons of *Beetlejuice: The Animated Series* (Nelvana/Geffen/Warner Bros., 1989–92), a show loosely derived from the feature film's core elements. Two half-hour episodes brought the crude yet likable ghost Beetlejuice and his offbeat goth tween pal Lydia into the Neitherworld for pun-filled adventures with Arthurian ingredients. In writer Michael Edens's "Family Scarelooms" (1991), the protagonists go searching for Beetlejuice's missing coat of arms in the Land of Lost Stuff, a realm ruled by the famed Sir Lostalot from his camel-shaped, two-humped castle of Camelost. Yet Lostalot fails to live up to his inflated reputation as "the noblest knight of all"; he is, in fact, a greedy bully who steals even from children. Beetlejuice, mounted on a burro, jousts to victory over his better-equipped opponent. Although Beetlejuice's heritage may not be as storied as Lostalot's, everyone in the Neitherworld comes to recognize who has the finer spirit.

In writers Jim Carlson and Terrence McDonnell's allusive "King BJ" (1991), Lydia reads a book about Merlin that makes her long for a meeting with "the most perfect magician ever." Beetlejuice obliges and transports her to Camelot. (It is the same camel-shaped structure as in "Family Scarelooms.") He cautions her that the castle's name ought never be spoken, because mentioning it invariably causes a *lot* of *camels* to stampede across the screen—a verbal/visual gag used well several times through the episode.

Lydia and Beetlejuice pass the skeletal trilithons of Bonehenge and enter the court. They discover a world far different from the one that Lydia hoped to see. With a vulture on his shoulder, Merlin is scheming to usurp the throne. The rulers of the land—an aloof King Arthur and a queen whom he calls "Whenever," despite the lady's insistence that her name is actually Guinevere[9]—are unaware of the threat from within the court. Arthur's knights are also blind to Merlin's nefarious machinations. They are an unimpressive band save for the sparkling wordplays that illuminate their characters: the overeating Sir Lunchalot, beach bum Sir Fing, caducean Sir Gery, bovine Sir Loin, ophidian Sir Pent, and insane Sir Tifiable. Beetlejuice fittingly takes on the role of court jester in this crazed Camelot.

With magical powers of his own, Beetlejuice now stands in the way of Merlin's ambitions. The wizard launches increasingly violent attacks on the newcomer and imprisons Arthur and Guinevere in a tower in order to prepare an avenue to the throne. In the middle of a joust that Merlin has arranged to kill the jester,[10] Beetlejuice quite unexpectedly becomes the ruler of the land when he blindly draws the Board from the Bone (a plain piece of lumber lodged in a rock) and the people proclaim him king. Lydia laments that Camelot "isn't nearly as fun as in the books" as she realizes that her idealized Arthurian world does not exist. Even worse, she knows that her friend Beetlejuice is ill-suited to serving as an example for the people and leading the land.

Merlin does not relent. He sends a huge beast—the pungent, punning, and medieval-sounding B. O. Wulf—to destroy Beetlejuice. Meanwhile, with the future of Camelot itself in jeopardy, levelheaded Lydia frees the true king and queen from their prison. Arthur explains that B. O. Wulf can be stopped only with aid from the Lady in the Cake. Near a table where Lunchalot continues his incessant feasting, a hand rises from within a cake to proffer the Golden Scrub Brush to Lydia. She then gives the weapon to Beetlejuice to use against the beast. In Beetlejuice's hands, the Golden Scrub Brush becomes a toothbrush to remedy B. O. Wulf's personal hygiene troubles. The newly cleaned and reformed B. O. Wulf chases Merlin from the land. Arthur offers to reward Beetlejuice for all that he has done. Lydia stops Beetlejuice from accepting anything. He has already done enough for — and to — Arthur's reputation.

Other cartoon comedies offered their own takes on the legend. In the twelve-minute "Quest for the Holy Pail" (Anivision/Klasky-Csupo/Nickelodeon, 1996) on Nickelodeon's *Aaahh!!! Real Monsters*, frightening portents cause schoolmaster Gromble to send monster-in-training Ickis on a mission to find "the ancient garbage cans, the Holy Pail." Armed only with an assortment of human refuse and his own quick thinking, Ickis's journey leads him through perils echoing Indiana Jones and Monty Python adventures to a reclusive monster at "the top of the [garbage] heap." "Why have you come?" the hermit asks sonorously. "I've come for the Holy Pail," replies Ickis. The hermit's peremptory, colloquial response startles the young quester: "Sorry, fresh out. That's it. We're done. I'll see ya." The hermit gives Ickis a used toothpick for his efforts and sends him on his way.

Ickis returns home without the Holy Pail. Standing before the schoolmaster and his classmates, he admits defeat and dejectedly reports the many dangers that he survived on a fruitless journey. Gromble reveals that he expected Ickis to fail, just as he himself once failed — and he has his own toothpick to show for it. Gromble explains the true significance of the quest: "If you travel through life with your eyes open, you'll never come home empty-handed. Now you have memories, experiences, and, if you ever have anything stuck between your teeth, you have a very attractive toothpick." Viewers learn that meaning lies in the life one leads on the journey, not its goal or the destination — an interpretation of questing at least as old as Lowell's *The Vision of Sir Launfal*.

Storyboarder Paul Rudish and director Genndy Tartakovsky's eleven-minute "D & DD" (Hanna-Barbera, 1997) for *Dexter's Laboratory* on Cartoon Network imagined a *Dungeons & Dragons*–like game called *Monsters & Mazes* for Dexter and his buddies to play. Their goal: "the magic Grail," a cup whose powers are determined by game master Dexter. But when Dexter's sister Dee Dee becomes the game master, she redefines their quest along lines more appealing to girls. Dee Dee adds an enchanted pixie prince, a decapitated dragon that spills candy rather than blood, and a fairy queen (Dee Dee herself) who grants Dexter's game character the "magic Grail." Its power? "You can drink from it," she explains flatly, "and it will never spill." Dexter is not amused: "That's it?! Lame!"

The Grail was not the only prized Arthurian object sought by comic cartoon characters. The eleven-minute "Neptune's Spatula" (United Plankton Pictures/Nickelodeon, 1999), co-written by Chuck Klein, Jay Lender, and David B. Fain for Nickelodeon's *SpongeBob SquarePants*, moved the venerable sword-in-the-stone motif to the show's Fry Cook Museum.[11] While posing for a snapshot, SpongeBob unintentionally pulls a golden spatula from a bucket of aptly named "ancient grease." The act proves him wor-

Arthurian Animation

SpongeBob draws Neptune's spatula from a bucket of grease in "Neptune's Spatula," *SpongeBob SquarePants* (United Plankton Pictures/Nickelodeon, 1999).

thy of becoming King Neptune's royal cook. Everyone applauds SpongeBob's feat — except for Neptune. The King of the Sea cannot believe that a "lowly yellow sponge, puny, insignificant, a commoner" could ever be a mighty god's fry cook. Other museum patrons step forward to testify that SpongeBob truly did extract the spatula, but Neptune continues to raise objections to taking him to Atlantis.

At last Neptune decides that SpongeBob must prove his skills in a cook-off against the king. Neptune's divine powers allow him to prepare 1000 burgers in the time that it takes SpongeBob to make just one, yet SpongeBob's single patty is the only tasty one of the bunch. Neptune admits his opponent's worth and prepares to take him to Atlantis. But when SpongeBob learns that he cannot bring his friends with him, he declines the position. As the episode ends, SpongeBob is back at his burger-flipping job at the Krusty Krab. The Krusty Krab's new fry cook trainee Neptune is learning that "perfect patties are made with love, not magic," and that a commoner's abilities can sometimes surpass those of nobles — a theme with roots reaching far into the past.

Writer Holly Huckins's eleven-minute "The Lost Ball" (Beantown/Disney, 1998) for the Disney Channel's *Recess* offered another example of a character with unexpected Arthurian dimensions. Fourth-grade milquetoast Gus Griswald daydreams in class as he reads a book titled *King Arthur*. In the reverie, an armored king interrogates a small young knight (Gus): "Did ye do it, Sir Knight? Did ye take the sword Excalibur and mislay it in yonder Cave of Doom? Did ye make a blunder so terrible it could bring down our beloved England? Did ye? Did ye?!" Gus the knight trembles behind his poultry-emblazoned shield as the king presses the question, asking whether Gus will bravely proceed to the cave to recover the missing weapon and regain his honor "or shall ye just chicken out and be a loser geek like always?" Gus screams as he wakes from his dream. "This King Arthur guy just keeps getting scarier and scarier," Gus remarks.

This Arthurian prelude provides the subtext for the day's playground events. At recess, Gus accidentally kicks a new ball over the fence into the Yard of No Return, from which no one has ever retrieved an errant ball. His schoolmates humiliate him for the loss. Gus's overactive imagination haunts him with visions of a life ruined. At last, Gus summons the courage needed for a recovery mission. Urged on by playground companions and armed in football shoulder pads, an army helmet, and earmuffs, he scales the fence. He forges on, past eerie topiary and lawn ornaments, until he locates the missing ball. As he turns to leave with the prize, Gus encounters the property owner—sheathed in terrifying exterminator's garb! But the conflict with terrible forces that Gus feared does not materialize. The owner turns out to be simply a pleasant old lady spraying her exotic plants to protect them from bugs. She happily returns Gus's lost ball and then gives him and his schoolmates hundreds of balls that have sailed over the fence through the years. Everyone proclaims Gus a "real hero." He alone accepted the quest that they would not and returned with a treasure to share with the people for his courageous efforts.

Animation writers of the decade tended to focus more on Arthurian themes and motifs than on particular Arthurian characters, yet Merlin remained a convenient touchstone. Beyond his appearances as a less-than-effective wizard in *Animaniacs* episodes and a power-hungry sorcerer in the animated *Beetlejuice*, Merlin also tussled with Felix the Cat in the eleven-minute "Middle Aged Felix" (Rough Draft Studios/Film Roman, 1995) on CBS's *The Twisted Tales of Felix the Cat*. In a storyline by Jeremy Kramer and Timothy Bjorklund, Felix and gal-pal Sheba discover *Merlin's Book of Spells* while cleaning Felix's grandmother's garage. As Sheba reads aloud from the book, she and Felix are swept suddenly to a medieval setting. Merlin wakes, emerges from his home in a tree trunk,[12] and demands the return of his property. Felix refuses. The two struggle over the book, using their considerable powers against each other in several battles that Felix always wins by dint of superior ingenuity. Meanwhile, Sheba invokes the book's "How to Return Home" spell to carry all three to the present. Merlin becomes the object of grandma's passions. Even though Sheba returns Merlin's book to him, it cannot help the old warlock escape geriatric lust. The Animaniacs, Beetlejuice, Felix the Cat, and even Felix's grandmother all proved themselves more powerful than Merlin through the decade.

Two eleven-minute episodes of *Angry Beavers* offered another character with origins in Arthurian lore. Writer John Derevlany's "Alley Oops" (Gunther-Wahl/Nickelodeon, 1998) brings us to the medieval-themed Camelot Lanes bowling alley, an apt setting to debut the pear-figured (or perhaps pin-shaped?) and tubercular repairwoman

Laverta Lutz, the Lady of the Lanes. Beaver Daggett's wayward bowling ball knocks Laverta from her hydraulic boom lift. Dazed, she rises in a snarl of wires and fluorescent tubes (Daggett: "celestial light") to present the gift that she claims he alone can touch: Excaliball, the bowling ball that guarantees a strike with every toss. With the confidence that Laverta's deranged endorsement inspires and a wad of gum she uses to stick Excaliball to his hand, Daggett instantly becomes an expert bowler.

Everyone is impressed — except for the Otto brothers, local bullies who challenge Daggett to a doubles tournament to determine control of Camelot Lanes. Daggett convinces his reluctant brother Norbert to join him in a match against the Ottos. The habitually quarreling rodents temporarily put aside their differences to unite as a team and defeat the thugs. Laverta proclaims a victory not only for the beavers but for all: "You freed the lanes from the tyranny of them there Otto guys."

Derevlany reprised the Lady of the Lanes in "Sang 'Em High" (1999). This time, Laverta is fishing on the beavers' lake when Daggett — angry with Norbert and wishing he could one day beat him in an argument — throws a rock into the waters behind their dam and inadvertently topples Laverta from her boat. Daggett recognizes the confused, submerged victim as "that strangely shaped magical-mystical woman from the bowling lanes, the Lady of the L ..., L ..., La.... Pond." Laverta has lost her memory again but speaks to Daggett as if she understands his outrage. Standing in the lake, she explains cryptically that no argument is ever over "till the fat beaver sings."

Returning to the lodge, the brothers continue to argue. Yet now, as Daggett's anger swells, so does he, until a morbidly obese Daggett bursts into melodious song. Norbert does not know what to say and Daggett wins several arguments in a row. But when Norbert begins to *enjoy* his brother's singing, Daggett's ability to win arguments vanishes. Without Norbert's anger to fuel his girth, Daggett can no longer become fat on command. His singing turns to screeching. Norbert makes his own wish now: that Daggett never sing again. Laverta crawls out of the lake to grant it. The brothers decide that they have had enough of Laverta's dubious assistance. They put aside their differences to agree on one thing: the Lady of the Lanes (Pond) must go. Just as she begins to regain her memory, the beavers toss Laverta far into the lake and out of their lives. Life at the lodge returns to "normal" as the brothers nonsensically decide to express themselves through modern dance rather than argument — at least until the next episode.

The Simpsons (Gracie Films, 1989–present) on Fox offered many cursory comic gestures toward Arthuriana in otherwise non–Arthurian episodes through the 1990s. Let us review. The Sir Putts-a-Lot Merrie Olde Fun Centre miniature golf course appears in "Dead Putting Society" (1990), "I Married Marge" (1991), "Natural Born Kissers" (1998), and various aerial views of Springfield through the decade. "Rosebud" (1993) reveals that Mr. Burns's *Citizen Kane*–inspired vault contains Excalibur; it is lodged in an anvil as in *Le Morte Darthur* and *The Sword in the Stone* and kept alongside other treasures such as "the only existing nude photo of Mark Twain" and "that rare first draft of the Constitution with the word 'suckers' in it." In "Homer Goes to College" (1993), Bart and Homer kidnap Springfield A&M's mascot, a pig named Sir Oinkcelot. Marge and Homer attempt to rekindle their ardor at the Aphrodite Inn Fantasy Rooms

8. Arthur, Arthur, Everywhere

and Conference Center, passing by the medieval-themed Camelot Room on their way to a utility closet in "Grampa vs. Sexual Inadequacy" (1994). In "A Fish Called Selma" (1996), the family watches a television movie called *The Muppets Go Medieval* in which Miss Piggy addresses a knight (Troy McClure) as "Sir Lies-a-lot" and Kermit asks Piggy to follow him home to Hamelot. In a slap at the Care Bears franchise, Homer receives a helmeted, sword-bearing "Sir Loves-a-lot" plush toy in "Trash of the Titans" (1998). Homer attempts to consume a sixteen-pound beef tenderloin to win the "Sirloinalot challenge" in "Maximum Homerdrive" (1999).[13]

Sometimes *The Simpsons* lingered longer in the realm, riding the wave of Arthur's popularity as the 1990s came to a close. In a perceptive episode, director Bob Anderson and writer Ian Maxtone-Graham's "E-I-E-I-D'Oh" (a.k.a. "E-I-E-I-[Annoyed Grunt]"; 1999) questioned the verisimilitude of the day's historical films. On a family outing to the thirty-six screens of the Springfield Googolplex Theatres, the Simpsons settle in for an evening's entertainment. The coming attractions preview a war film — which we recognize as a thinly veiled version of the World War II beachhead scene from 1998's *Saving Private Ryan*. An American kills a German, then takes a can of Buzz Cola from the dead soldier's kit. He drinks the soda with relish and gives a thumbs-up to the camera — and to the audience. The trailer's voiceover narrator drives the point home: "Buzz Cola. The taste you'll kill for." The dead German soldier revives. He too has a message to deliver: "Available in zee lobby." Although Lisa registers her stern disapproval of "cheapening the memory of our veterans" to sell merchandise through conspicuous product placement, Homer is already making his way to the snack bar.

By the time that he returns to his seat, the main feature has begun. *The Poke of Zorro*, a historical patchwork parodying at least two more of 1998's big-budget period films, *The Mask of Zorro* and *The Man in the Iron Mask*, fills the screen. Zorro enters, kills the Three Musketeers with a single thrust, then turns to the Man in the Iron Mask to slash an initial into his shirt:

> (on screen)
> MAN IN THE IRON MASK: What? N? What does N stand for?
> ZORRO: No, no. It's a Z. I am Zorro. Z for Zorro! I have come to return King Arthur to the throne.
>
> (in audience)
> BART (excitedly): It's a history lesson come to life!
> LISA (with disgust): No, it isn't. It's totally inaccurate.
> BART: Quiet! Here come the ninjas.

As *The Poke of Zorro* continues its geographically and time-muddled romp, all pasts collapse into one. Zorro chases the Scarlet Pimpernel from his loge at the opera. One box over, a regal, bearded character celebrates Zorro's triumphs: "I, King Arthur, declare Zorro the new king of England!" Arthur tosses his crown to Zorro. *The Poke of Zorro*'s credits roll, revealing Cheech Marin as the actor incongruously cast as Arthur.[14] Lisa's "totally inaccurate" condemnation scarcely begins to correct Bart's "history lesson come to life." Arthur could appear seemingly anywhere, at any time. Decades of Arthurian film and animation had proved it — and *The Simpsons* took note.

Arthurian Animation

Animators in the 1990s also produced Arthurian-themed adventure cartoons to complement the decade's many comedies. Two half-hour episodes of *Fox's Peter Pan & the Pirates* transported characters freely derived from J. M. Barrie's classic tales into the Arthurian matrix. In writer Bruce Schaefer's "Tootles and the Dragon" (Southern Star Productions/Fox, 1990), Peter and the boys are playing a game of make-believe that they call "King Arthur and Camelot," inspired by a tale that Wendy has read to them. Yet they lack a crucial prop: the sword in the stone. Luckily, Peter says that he knows where to find one. He leads the boys to Dragon's Rock—a stone jutting above the sea—from which a large, mast-like object protrudes. Peter assigns his followers random Arthurian names—Launcelot, Gawain, Galahad, Perceval, Kay, Pelleas, and Tristram—but none can draw the object that Peter calls "Excalibur" from the stone to become king of Neverland for the day. Even Peter cannot extract it—a failure he nonchalantly dismisses as he loses interest in the game.

Tootles arrives. Peter tells him that there is no point in trying the sword that has already foiled everybody's attempts, but Tootles remains at Dragon's Rock after the others have flown away. He gingerly pokes at "Excalibur." The entire stone trembles and frightens Tootles away. The camera passes below the water's surface to reveal that Dragon's Rock is an actual dragon that has turned to stone.

Tootles returns to the scene later, his confidence bolstered by Wendy's kindness toward him. This time, gently twisting rather than vigorously tugging the object allows Tootles to remove it—and we see that it is not a ship's mast or a sword but rather a key to a locking harness that the petrified dragon wears. We learn shortly that the harness has long kept the dragon frozen in place. Yet free now, the dragon ravages Neverland. All efforts to stop it fail. Wendy helps Tootles again. As Tootles laments, "I just wanted to be a king," she explains that being a leader goes beyond "giving orders" to "taking responsibility"—a lesson that Tinker Bell later underscores. Tootles puts his fears behind him, approaches the dragon, and inserts the key in the harness again. The beast turns to stone once more and sinks into the bay. All celebrate Tootles, a more capable knight this day than any of the Arthurian ones that Peter lightheartedly christened. Peter tries to take all the credit for subduing the dragon, but we know better.

In writer William Overgard's "Knights of Neverland" (Southern Star Productions/Fox, 1991), Wendy's storytelling leads the boys to a marginally Arthurian adventure. This time, Wendy fashions herself Guinevere and Peter adopts the role of Arthur in the day's make-believe. Peter adds a rule intended to make the game more realistic: no flying allowed. Elsewhere on the island, Hook's men are preparing to eat an endangered wolf. When ecology-minded Wendy learns of the captain's plans and wants to stop the game to save the animal, Peter and the boys weave Hook's activities into their role-playing. As fast as Peter can dispatch the boys on "quests" to rescue the wolf, they find themselves snarled in the ship's rigging. And rather than fight Hook, Wendy tries reasoning with him, but he binds her to a mast. Finally, Peter battles Hook. Hook makes the mistake of cutting away Peter's armor. Without his armor, Peter claims that he is released from his "Arthurian obligation" and the game is over—and the Arthurian

8. Arthur, Arthur, Everywhere

dimension of the cartoon as well. Able to fly again, Peter quickly rescues everybody, including the wolf.

Series creator Greg Weisman's syndicated *Gargoyles* (Disney, 1994–96) combined several mythologies and literary traditions in its sprawling saga of a small clan of medieval Scottish stone-by-day/flesh-by-night gargoyles who wake after 1000 years of sleep to discover that their castle now sits atop a New York City skyscraper. Five half-hour episodes directed by Dennis J. Woodyard and written by Brynne Chandler Reaves and Lydia C. Marano for the 1995–96 season present a complex, multitimeline Arthurian story arc that moves from archaeologists' discovery of Merlin's scrolls in "A Lighthouse in the Sea of Time," to a journey to the Middle Ages and Arthur's premature awakening in the three-part "Avalon," and then follows Arthur's voyage to present-day New York to retrieve Excalibur and begin a quest to locate Merlin in "Pendragon." The arc remained incomplete, however, because the original *Gargoyles* series ended and new personnel were hired for the sequel series, *The Goliath Chronicles* (Disney, 1996–97). The new writers did not continue the Arthurian storyline. Thus, in the way of many a medieval narrative, Arthur's quest remains an unfinished thread in *Gargoyles*.

Reaves and Marano introduce the intricate narrative of "the sleeping king" who rests in the "hollow hill" in Avalon in episode 17 (of 52). In "A Lighthouse in the Sea of Time," viewers learn from power-hungry Macbeth[15] the story of how Merlin

> took a ragged boy, and with magic and wisdom turned him into the greatest king this world will ever see. The king ruled with justice and compassion, and took the torn remnants of warring tribes and knit them into a country of beauty and civilization, with Merlin always by his side, until it fell.

The Scottish king imagines himself as Arthur's successor.

Macbeth steals Merlin's scrolls from the archaeologists who found them. He expects to learn powerful spells that will help him to the throne but instead finds only the wizard's diary describing his time with Arthur: "He was a scabby, bony boy when first I saw this once and future king. Had I not known what his destiny held I would have laughed aloud.... Though young and not yet formed, his mind was open and eager...." Macbeth stops reading and casts aside the scrolls as worthless. Even Goliath, the gargoyle leader, is ready to destroy the scrolls because of the trouble that Macbeth has already stirred by seeking them. It takes the simple wisdom of a subordinate gargoyle to recognize that "they *are* magic.... It's Merlin's life in his own words. When you read them, they take you there. It is magic, Goliath, precious magic." Merlin's scrolls are preserved.

Seventeen episodes later *Gargoyles* returned to the Arthurian thread in "Avalon" (episodes 34–36). In a time-traversing plot, a threat to a clutch of gargoyle eggs[16] hidden on Avalon brings Tom, a young man from medieval Scotland, to the present to seek Goliath's aid. Goliath and the clan magically sail from the present to tenth-century Avalon. They soon wake and enlist the legendary Arthur to fight Goliath's longtime enemy, the Archmage, and others seeking to destroy the "eggs" that have in fact already hatched into a brood of young gargoyles.

Arthurian Animation

In these episodes we learn more of the mysterious sleeping king, reputed to be "the best warrior who ever lived." Because he has been resting "till his country needs him," he is understandably puzzled when roused: "You have awakened me early. I have neither Excalibur nor my knights nor my old friend Merlin." Still, he offers his help, and together the gargoyles and their human allies conquer the evildoers to save the last of Goliath's kin from destruction. As episode 36 ends, Arthur announces his plan to explore this world into which he has awakened. He sets sail from the isle, knowing that the waters surrounding Avalon will take him across time and space to wherever he needs to go to fulfill his destiny.

Twelve episodes farther along in the series, *Gargoyles* picked up the Arthurian thread again once more in "Pendragon" (episode 48). From out of the mists, Arthur's boat appears on the Thames as Big Ben chimes—and we understand that Arthur has come to present-day London. Arthur enters a church and approaches a throne with a block of stone beneath its seat. The writers do not explain—though Anglophiles and Arthurians must note—that Arthur has come to Westminster Abbey and that the throne before him is the Coronation Chair of the United Kingdom. Arthur does not know the church or throne by these names, of course, though he does recognize the one item in the church that is older even than himself: the Stone of Destiny (that is, the Stone of Scone). Drawn by its power, Arthur focuses on a gap in the Stone's surface: "I'd hoped Excalibur had returned to you," he says, as the *Gargoyles* refashions the legend to link the Stone of Destiny to the stone from which Arthur traditionally draws a sword to become king.

The Stone speaks to Arthur. It reveals that, because he has "returned to the waking world unbidden," he must again prove his worth to wield Excalibur by passing several mental and physical challenges. With the help of Griff, a gargoyle who oversees the abbey, Arthur solves a riddle. Both gargoyles are magically transported across the Atlantic to New York. They join Goliath's clan and proceed through several adventures. Arthur summons the Lady of the Lake from a pool in Central Park. She says that she had not expected to see him "for some time," but because "the world does need a leader and that leader needs the sword," she offers him another test and then another riddle to move him closer to his goal. Arthur and the gargoyles enter a garden maze, fight Macbeth for possession of an "Excalibur" shortly revealed to be counterfeit, battle a dragon statue sparked to life by lightning, and then solve the final riddle to discover that the true Excalibur lies hidden within a gemstone on the dragon's breast. Arthur smashes the jewel. Flames shoot from the gemstone. The real Excalibur appears. The beast disintegrates in the fire.

Macbeth at last acknowledges that Arthur is "the one." He declines an offer to become one of Arthur's knights, but he pledges his support should the need ever arise—thus planting seeds for further episodes if *Gargoyles* had continued with Reaves and Marano writing it. Arthur announces that he will next find his "friend and teacher" Merlin. To join him on the quest, Arthur dubs the abbey gargoyle his first twentieth-century knight, Sir Griff. And here *Gargoyles* abruptly ended its Arthurian thread.

Series creator Rick Ungar's syndicated adventure/comedy franchise of *Biker Mice*

8. Arthur, Arthur, Everywhere

from Mars offered a two-part "Biker Knights of the Round Table" (New World Animation, 1995). In these half-hour episodes, evil Limburger extends his pillaging of the planet's natural resources to the past as he and his henchmen excavate the land around Camelot and then send the plunder through a time vortex to the present. The Biker Mice also pass through the vortex from present to past and quickly ally themselves with Arthur,[17] Guinevere, Launcelot, and Merlin to stop the devastation. Along the way, Limburger draws the king into a tournament that promises the deed to Arthur's kingdom to the victor. Later, Mordred joins in Limburger's plot, too. Much signature rocking, rolling, and riding later, the mice defeat the villains to preserve Camelot for the king and his people.

Before the battles begin, however, a glimpse into Arthur's castle reveals the fun-loving, rough-and-tumble, daily life of the court. A banquet scene that includes wrestling, staff-fighting on the tables, throwing food, eating without utensils, uninhibited farting, and Guinevere's hearty burp presents a Camelot likely to appeal to the young audience drawn to the series. But viewers learned little about the traditional legend from *Biker Mice from Mars*.

Mid-1960s cartoon star Jonny Quest returned to television in *The Real Adventures of Jonny Quest* (1996–97) on TNT, TBS, and Cartoon Network. In the half-hour "The Alchemist" (Hanna-Barbera, 1996), writer Peter Lawrence presents the story of greedy scientist/archaeologist Montegue, who uses the recently unearthed Philosopher's Stone to transmute scrap into gold. Spirits rise from the Stone to dissuade the scientist: the eagle that laid the egg that became the Stone, an Eastern monk who took it from the eagle's nest, Faustus (who cautions Montegue about selling one's soul for worldly goods), and finally Merlin all try to convince Montegue to leave the Stone alone. Merlin recalls his own attempt at alchemy's supreme feat: "Not even I, Merlin, succeeded in turning base metal to gold — and everyone knows I was the best there is!" Yet the words of the famed (and pompous) wizard go unheeded and Merlin soon vanishes from the storyline. Montegue's thirst for gold continues — entangling Jonny and his pals in the narrative — until at last the Stone causes Montegue's lab to burst into flames and kills the man who reaches too far.

As in the 1970s and 1980s, product franchises targeting the young extended their reach with occasional Arthurian cartoons. Characters originating in video games, comic books, and manga found their way to Arthurianimation in the 1990s. In writer Jeffrey Scott's half-hour "Hedgehog of the 'Hound' Table" (DIC/Bohbot Entertainment, 1993) on the *Adventures of Sonic the Hedgehog*, the plucky hero follows evil Robotnik and his minions through time to medieval Mobius, where a feline Merlynx the Magician and canine King Arfur dwell. Merlynx is a bumbling wizard, trying (and failing) to master a spell to make him young again as the villains enter his cave. Robotnik forces the magician to help him become invincible against all enemies. Merlynx explains that there are two steps to invincibility: obtaining a powerful emerald (that Merlynx possesses) and becoming king of Mobius. The small, beagle-like king and his Hound Table knights prove no match for Robotnik. Sonic, as the Holy Hedgehog foretold by prophecy, rescues the kingdom by defeating Robotnik in a joust, then sends the villains

Arthurian Animation

though time to face hungry lions in the Colosseum. King of the realm once again, Arfur dubs his newest knight Sir Sonic the Speedy.[18]

Comic book superheroes also crossed again into Arthurianimation. As the *Teenage Mutant Ninja Turtles* branched from comics into half-hour cartoons on CBS, the lure of an Arthurian episode proved too strong to resist. In writers Francis Moss and Ted Pedersen's "Shredder's New Sword" (Fred Wolf Films, 1993), while touring the British Museum, the Turtles initially scoff at the story of the Round Table as "a fantasy." Yet their opinion soon changes when series nemesis Shredder steals Excalibur from Arthur's tomb and uses its magic to create transtemporal chaos—and become king himself. Merlin awakes from a portrait at the British Museum. (The Turtles describe him as a "strange old dude" wearing "really wigged-out threads.") The wizard explains that though his powers have grown "rusty" in the "nearly 2000 years" since he fell asleep, he has come to the present to stop Shredder's misuse of Excalibur.

Meanwhile—in what amounts to an almost educational travelogue of London that includes a tour of the British Museum, Big Ben, the Tube, Royal Albert Hall, and so on—Shredder steals the Crown Jewels, takes the Turtles' human friend April O'Neil as his queen (after Merlin mistakes her for the Fair Maid of Astolat in an unglossed non sequitur), takes up residence in the Tower of London, and conjures two "evil black knights" to serve him. Merlin and the Turtles mount opposition to Shredder but to little effect. At last, Merlin proposes a trip to Camelot to retrieve his book of spells. But Shredder arrives in Camelot before the heroes, finds the book, and thus controls Merlin's powers in addition to Excalibur's.

With Merlin and the Turtles facing certain defeat, Excalibur itself summons Arthur and Guinevere from the past. Shredder has no fear of "an ex-king." Arthur insists on a tournament between his reptilian champions and Shredder's henchmen to settle possession of the sword. The Turtles conquer Shredder's men, then wrest Excalibur from his hands. The Heroes in a Half Shell present the sword to Arthur, the true king. The villains slink away until the next episode. For their services—and offering viewers one more unglossed allusion—the king dubs the Turtles the "Green Knights of the Round Table."

The comics also fueled writer Hilary J. Bader's "Target" (Warner Bros., 1997) on a half-hour Superman segment of The WB's *The New Batman/Superman Adventures*. Edward Lytener, a scientist fired from Lexcorp for helping

Clark Kent removes a crystal Excalibur from Lois's trophy in "Target," ***The New Batman/Superman Adventures*** (Warner Bros., 1997).

8. Arthur, Arthur, Everywhere

Lois gather information for an award-winning exposé, decides to kill the reporter for ruining his life. As the adventure unfolds, the episode repeatedly toys with — but ultimately fails to make meaningful use of — several Excalibur references. Lois accepts an Excalibur Award for Outstanding Investigative Journalism — an award presumably so named because Lois's insight is as penetrating as Excalibur's blade, though "Target" does not explicitly draw the connection. The award itself comes with a trophy, a small crystal sword that pierces a stone base. At the presentation ceremony, Lytener makes his first attempt on Lois's life by causing a large crystal sword suspended above the dais to crash to the stage. Superman arrives to bear the force of the impact and the sword shatters. But if the audience is supposed to draw from the incident some conclusion about the outcome of a Superman vs. Excalibur contest, the episode does not clearly delineate it.

Additional references to the famed sword serve only to muddy what Excalibur represents in the episode. As Lois and Clark drive home from the ceremony, Lytener uses his computer skills to remote-control their car in order to force a highway accident. Clark pulls the trophy's sword from its stone base and cuts through the convertible's fabric roof to open an escape route from the car. While the episode appears to tap traditional Excalibur lore as Clark/Superman draws the small sword from its small stone, the significance of the allusion remains unclear. We scratch our heads. How is Clark/Superman like Arthur? Finally, the Excalibur trophy appears once more when, in a dream, Lois try to stop an attacker with it. The trophy drops from her hands. Its crystal sword shatters. While the audience may wonder about a weapon that fails its owner — as Arthur's sword does in *Le Morte Darthur* and elsewhere — what Excalibur signifies in "Target" remains a confused puzzle.

A more coherent yet less authentic Arthurianimation entry appeared the same season in writer Stan Berkowitz's "The Demon Within" (Warner Bros., 1998), a half-hour Batman segment of *The New Batman/Superman Adventures*. The episode tells the story of a struggle over Morgan's branding iron — a device with no precedent in traditional Arthurian legend but with a DC Comics backstory conveniently supplied by the sardonic auctioneer selling the piece: "It is rumored to have been the personal branding iron of the Arthurian-era witch Morgan le Fey. Legend has it this piece has some sort of magical power — Gotham Auctioneers Limited makes no such guarantee!"

Its power is real. Teenage "witch-boy" Klarion steals the branding iron to control Etrigan, a demon whom Merlin[19] long ago summoned to defend Camelot. We learn that after Camelot's fall, Merlin fused the demon Etrigan with Jason Blood, a nobleman of Arthur's court. Merlin hoped that Etrigan/Blood would continue to serve humanity's best interests through the ages. But with Morgan's stolen branding iron in hand, Klarion splits Etrigan from Blood, then orders the demon on a rampage through Gotham. Batman fights Etrigan and Klarion. Then, with aid from Blood and Robin, Batman again binds the demon to the man, just as Merlin intended.

Sabrina the Teenage Witch, a character raised from the pages of the *Archie Comics* of the 1960s, enjoyed a resurgence of popularity in the late 1990s with a live-action television movie, live-action series, and a cartoon series, all broadcast on ABC. In writer

Arthurian Animation

Glenn Leopold's half-hour "Hexcalibur" (Hong Ying Animation/DIC, 1999) on ABC's *Sabrina, The Animated Series*, tween witch-in-training Sabrina is struggling with a term paper on the theme of "Merlin's Mystical Contributions to Wizardry." Even Sabrina realizes that the *Encyclopedia Enchantica* offers her only desiccated factoids:

> Merlin the magician, the founder of medieval magic. Merlin was the official wizard to England's King Arthur and his knights of the Round Table. With the help of the magical sword Excalibur, Merlin and Arthur made Castle Camelot the ultimate symbol of chivalry and gallantry for all time.

Sabrina predicts that her essay will be a "yawn" unless she can consult her aunt Zelda's autographed "first edition" of Merlin's writings for juicier material. But when Sabrina and her feline familiar Salem accidentally destroy Zelda's prized volume, they decide they must take "the 4:15 back to the Middle Ages" to get a replacement directly from the author himself.

Arriving in the sixth century, the two discover that they have traveled a few years too far: Merlin (surnamed Schmerlin) is only twelve years old! Moreover, Sabrina learns that the young sorcerer has yet to master the skills that will later make him worthy of an encyclopedia entry. She gently encourages him to keep practicing his craft in order to become the powerful wizard whom she knows he will become and, at the same time, urges him not to follow his father Hurlin into the local catapult industry. Sabrina also recognizes that Merlin's clumsy young friend, "Dude Arthur" (series regular Harvey, Sabrina's boyfriend), seems unlikely to grow to legendary stature without a course correction:

> ARTHUR: I dream of being a great knight and riding on a bold, white charger.
> SABRINA: Ever consider raising your sights a bit higher — say, king?

As if in an episode of *Peabody's Improbable History*, Sabrina nudges both lads toward their destinies, quietly using her powers to help them along the way.

While Merlin and Arthur ponder the bright futures at which Sabrina hints, a sword in a stone mysteriously appears in a nearby clearing—caused, perhaps, by Sabrina's presence in the medieval timeline and the sequence of events that she is initiating. However, no one notices the sword immediately, except for young Morgan le Fey (series regular Gem, Sabrina's rival for Harvey's affections) who watches the scene through a demonic crystal ball. The crystal reveals that whoever holds the sword will one day rule the kingdom and that prophecies say Morgan's own half-brother Arthur will become king. "Not if I get that sword first," she exclaims, as Morgan and servant Launceloaf raise several ultimately thwarted attempts to stop the boys from taking their places in history.

"Hexcalibur" teases the audience with allusions to a larger legend beyond the periphery of the immediate story on the screen. Although Arthur is repeatedly described as Morgan's half-brother and she taunts him with childhood memories of wasting his allowance on "chocolate Holy Grails," such details have potential meaning only in the minds of those who know more Arthurian lore than the episode actually provides. Similarly, near the end, with Morgan defeated, Excalibur[20] firmly in the future king's hands, and both Merlin and Arthur having demonstrated the promise of what they will become, a stranger arrives unexpectedly from another part of the legend: "Excuse me. I'm lost. Can you tell me how I can get to the once and future Camelot? My name is Guinevere." Arthur tells her that though he has not been to Camelot,[21] "I'll bet I can find it." He invites her to travel with him. As the couple rides away, Sabrina muses: "There'll come a time when Arthur will be sorry he...."

Salem interrupts Sabrina to remind her that they must get home before Zelda does. That term paper remains to be written. Sabrina can now complete it thanks to her direct knowledge of the subject. And her aunt's precious volume needs to be replaced. Sabrina has that replacement in hand, because Merlin gives her a book of magic that he has just penned — his first. Merlin requests an honest review. "Be brutal," he declares to the teenage witch who shows herself in this episode to be the first teacher of the greatest wizard of all time. Sabrina and Salem return to their own time, believing that Zelda will never learn that they destroyed her book. Yet, as Sabrina sets the new book on the old shelves, the bookcase collapses and all the volumes disintegrate. "Oh, man!" Sabrina cries, as dust rises, the credits roll, and the audience feels that the story of "Hexcalibur" is about to begin all over again.

An animated series based on the Japanese *Flint the Time Detective* manga introduced America's Fox network viewers to a young King Arthur in search of confidence and courage in the half-hour "Leafy" (Sanrio/Saban Entertainment, 1999), written and adapted for anglophone markets by Mark Ryan and Steve Apostolina. Resurrected caveman Flint, his futuristic human companions Sarah and Tony, and their menagerie of helpers from the Bureau of Time and Space travel to "sixth-century England," where time-shifter Leafy's presence threatens to disrupt the tapestry of time. They find a clearing with a sword in a stone. Sarah recognizes it as "the famous Excalibur." An old man, wearing a cross and carrying a dragon-headed staff, tells her that the sword has long awaited the one who can extract it to save the land in a time of woe. Many have tried; all have failed. As Sarah begins recounting what she learned in school about Arthur and Excalibur, Time Protector Pterry interrupts her. Pterry reminds Sarah that she cannot reveal future information to those in the past without disturbing the very timeline that the Bureau of Time and Space is pledged to safeguard. Meanwhile, Flint uses his Cro-Magnon strength to draw the sword from the stone. He replaces it when Pterry reminds him of the reason for their mission.

The old man describes his people's longing for the destined one who can wield the sword. "Legend says the king will come in our time of need to claim Excalibur, and our need has never been greater than it is now." The Witch beyond the Waterfall (series nemesis Petra Fina's role in this episode) has used Leafy's powers over nature to make crops fail and filled the fields with strange vegetation. The old man presses Sarah to finish the story that Pterry cut short. As she temporizes, a young boy arrives in the clearing nearby. He draws the sword easily. The old man believes that their savior has come at last. But this boy — Arthur, we soon learn — says that he is interested only in replacing his brother's weapon, a weapon that Arthur himself lost while bearing it to Nottingham. (Arthur's brother is not named. Nor does "Leafy" reveal why the sword is needed in Nottingham.) Arthur timidly explains his modest plan to borrow the sword and then return it later. The old man tells him that higher ambitions must now guide him. Arthur's actions have made him "the future king of England" and his people are in trouble.

Arthur hesitantly joins Flint's group. After a back-and-forth battle, they defeat Petra Fina and Leafy to return the land to health — though not without destroying some stone structures and leaving ruins that the audience recognizes as present-day Stonehenge. (Sarah notes precociously, "If the Druids come back, they're going to be mad.") The battle also teaches Arthur lessons about the courage, friendship, and self-confidence that he will need in his new role: "I'd have been lost without your help.... I have a lot to learn to be a king, but I do feel as though I've found a source of power and strength within me that will help me to heal this land." With England in good hands and the timeline stabilized, Flint and his fellow Time Protectors return to headquarters for their next mission.

At least seven Arthurianimation titles with pointedly didactic agendas aired in the 1990s as well. In 1991, PBS's award-winning *Long Ago and Far Away* series featured an episode centered on *Merlin and the Dragons* (Shanghai Animation Film Studio/ Lightyear Entertainment, 1990), written by Jane Yolen and directed by Dennis J. Woodyard and Hu Yihong.[22] In a rich, 24-minute adaptation that builds directly on the writings of Geoffrey of Monmouth and Nennius, *Merlin and the Dragons* introduces its elementary- and middle-school audiences to several names from the Arthurian legend usually reserved for the college classroom: Vortigern, Ambrosius, and a young wizard identified through much of the story only by his Welsh name Emrys. In prefatory and concluding segments for the PBS series, show host James Earl Jones invited young viewers to ponder what the legend might mean and to explore similar stories at local libraries.

Merlin (voiced by Kevin Kline) narrates events of a night long ago. A violent storm rages over a darkened castle. Lightning strikes an anvil (without a sword) mounted on a stone in the courtyard. The camera enters Arthur's chambers, where the tempest and the boy's nightmares combine to trouble his sleep. The new king is haunted by worries about his ability to lead. In a dream, Arthur draws a sword from an anvil atop a stone, but, as he tries to heave it aloft, it tumbles from his hands and to the ground. Adults suddenly materialize around him. They mock his failure.

Unnerved, Arthur wakes. He looks at the sword hanging on the wall, gathers the crown from the floor where it had been "tossed carelessly aside," and seeks comfort from the only other occupant of the castle: old, bespectacled Merlin, dozing in a chair near the fire in a cozy study, an owl resting on his shoulder. Arthur explains that he has previously had unsettling dreams similar to this night's and that all his dreams share a common theme: "a fatherless boy becomes king just because he pulls a sword from a stone." Merlin believes that the way to help Arthur better understand his dreams — and the anxieties that plague him — is through a tale of a similar teen.

"There once lived in the wild, rugged mountains of North Wales a lonely, fatherless boy called Emrys," Merlin begins. Like Arthur, Emrys is a thoughtful, inquisitive, sen-

8. Arthur, Arthur, Everywhere

sitive outsider — and also prone to obscure dreams and visions that perplex him. An old man from the mountains near Emrys's village helps the young wizard learn to understand his abilities. Emrys's talents make him popular, then frightening, and finally an outcast. The villagers cannot make sense of the boy's apparent power over birds, nature, and the sun.

Meanwhile "proud" and "stubborn" Vortigern, having "unjustly declared himself high king over all Britain," comes to Emrys's village to erect a tower to serve as his castle. Using the villagers as slave labor, Vortigern completes the structure. It promptly collapses overnight. Every attempt to rebuild it results in a new collapse. Vortigern turns to his magicians for a solution. The stymied charlatans offer what they believe to be an impossibility: to find "a fatherless child, spawned by a demon," and sprinkle his blood on the foundation stones. Yet to their surprise, a local boy says that strange Emrys is just such a child — or at least that is what the superstitious villagers *believe* him to be.

Vortigern summons Emrys from his mountain solitude with the intent of slaughtering him. Emrys's many dimly understood dreams and visions now become clear to him. With ever-increasing confidence in his powers, he explains why the tower has repeatedly crumbled. In a pool deep beneath the tower's foundation, two unhatched dragons slumber. Each night the dragons' dreams cause tremors that shake the tower above until it falls. Vortigern orders workmen to excavate. They unearth two stone eggs and split them open, unleashing a white dragon and a red one. The dragons immediately begin to fight. Vortigern fires an arrow at the red dragon, distracting it for a moment. The white dragon takes this opportunity to kill the red, then breathes fire to incinerate it. Emrys boldly tells Vortigern that he will suffer the same fiery fate as the red dragon.

The boy returns to the mountains. Emrys and a hawk enjoy a "communion" that allows him to control the bird and see through its eyes. Through the hawk, Emrys spies "a vast army, led by two noble knights" nearby. "These were Vortigern's enemies, the true heirs to the throne, coming to rid the country of the murderous king." The army's leaders interpret the hawk as a good omen and follow it toward

Vortigern orders Emrys to reveal his dreams in *Merlin and the Dragons* (Shanghai Animation Film Studio/Lightyear Entertainment, 1990).

the village. Meanwhile, Emrys confronts Vortigern again. He describes the approaching army and makes another prediction: "I dreamed that you were attacked by righteous knights and that you were defeated." At this moment, the army arrives and challenges Vortigern on account of his abuses. Abandoned even by his own men, Vortigern retreats into his half-built tower. A cross-fade from the flames that destroy Vortigern in his tower to the flames in Merlin's fireplace moves the narrative back to Merlin's study. In the midst of his own tale, the wizard has fallen asleep.

Arthur wakes him and begs to hear more. Merlin footnotes the final events: the knights leading the army were both kings, two brothers called Ambrosius and Uther Pendragon. Arthur recognizes Uther's name as that of the last high king of the realm. He wonders whether one of Uther's sons might come to claim the throne that he now holds by virtue of the sword. Merlin sees that it is time to disclose a secret that he has long kept: Uther had only one son, Arthur. In a single moment, Arthur realizes that he is not fatherless, that he is the rightful heir, and that he is king "not just because I pulled a stupid sword from a stone" but because drawing the sword proved that he was a king's son and "qualified to rule all of Britain." Arthur's dreams, Merlin riddles, awakened the boy to a truth about himself: Arthur was "always king," even if he doubted it. Merlin reveals one last secret this night: the boy Emrys went on dreaming and following his visions, making "a career of it." Emrys is (of course) Merlin himself.

With his anxieties behind him and a clearer appreciation of his role, Arthur dons his crown, returns to his chambers, and confidently raises the sword above his head — as the blade pulses with light and a trumpet fanfare sounds. Although the sun has already risen, Arthur can now sleep soundly. The emblems of his authority, the crown and sword, rest carefully next to the young king's bed. Merlin (in voiceover) recalls that that stormy night marked a turning point in Arthur's path to becoming the "truly great king" who would assemble the knights of the Round Table — a tale for another time, Merlin yawns, because "magicians need their sleep, too."

Merlin and Arthur also appeared on television in *Tom Thumb* (Gary Delfiner Productions, 1991), a 25-minute, direct-to-video release aimed at the elementary school and home markets. Producer/director Delfiner closely follows Richard Jesse Watson's 1989 children's book — which in turn draws its inspiration from earlier *Tom Thumb* variants, with Watson making appropriate narrative adjustments and abridgements for his juvenile audience. Delfiner's film offers an engaging, well-paced, video tour of the book. Narrator Dom DeLuise reads Watson's text as pan-and-zoom camera work traverses Watson's finely detailed illustrations. The result is a pseudoanimated storybook that can be used as a read-along exercise for children with the book in their hands. Indeed, a note at the end of the credits advises viewers to "Watch the video and read the book."

"Long ago, in the days of knights and giants, wizards and fairies," the tale opens, "there lived a poor farmer and his wife." One day, they welcome into their home a man (Merlin) disguised as a beggar.[23] Merlin is grateful for the food and hospitality that he receives from the humble folk, but their sadness puzzles him. They explain that they have no children. To repay their kindness and because it "tickled his fancy," the wizard

8. Arthur, Arthur, Everywhere

decides to grant the wife's wish for a child—even one no bigger than her husband's thumb. With help from the Queen of Faeries, "the tiniest of tiny boys" is soon born. Faeries assemble to name the child Tom Thumb and clothe him in delicate natural materials such as spider webs and thistledown.

The curious, high-spirited tyke grows older but no bigger. As he does so, he falls into diverse perils, despite his parents' best efforts to protect him from harm. "Tom was sorry to add to their hardships, and often wished he could be useful to his parents and help to ease their lives." One day, a raven snatches Tom from the farm. A chain of further adventures—involving the giant Grumbong and a seashell's sound that soothes him (until Tom startles the giant and the shell is destroyed), a fish that swallows Tom, royal fisherman who catch the fish, and scullions who discover the boy within the fish—delivers Tom to King Arthur's court.

Tiny, entertaining Tom becomes a royal favorite—and then falls from favor when he is unfairly blamed for ruining the king's dessert one day. Arthur imprisons Tom in a cage designed for mice. Tom languishes in the mousetrap, worrying about his parents back on the farm and his own safety if the king decides to punish him further. A kindly mouse befriends the boy. He tells Tom not to worry about Arthur, because the king and his knights are busy fighting a giant who has attacked the kingdom. It is Grumbong. Tom knows how to stop him.

Castle mice help Tom escape from his cage. Forest animals join them as they seek a shell and then carry it to the battlefield. The fighting rages so fiercely, however, that little Tom fears to enter the fray. Tom and his animal companions all join together to blow into the shell as if a horn. The piercing blast brings everybody to a halt. Tom delivers the shell to the giant. Comforted again by the shell's soothing ocean sound, the giant returns to his castle.

Arthur rewards the hero. He dubs him "Sir Thomas Thumb" and offers him as much of the royal treasury as he desires "to take back to his parents." But Tom cannot carry any gold. Lifting even a single coin is beyond his strength. So the king orders that small animal-drawn carriages be made for the gold. Everyone at court cheers the miniature wagon train and Tom, atop his mouse mount, as they set out for the farm. "And so it was that Tom Thumb, in the end, helped his parents and earned his place as the smallest knight of the Round Table." Gentle lessons to be gleaned from Delfiner's film mirror those offered by Watson's book: generosity is rewarded; ingenuity overcomes superior strength; cooperation is the key to victory; and children should honor and support their parents.

Arthur's legendary Welsh connections were celebrated on native soil, too. Relying on Welsh professor, translator, and poet Gwyn Thomas's script, Valeri Ugarov's Soviet cel- and collage-animation team created *The Quest for Olwen* (Metta and Soyuzmultfilm/S4C and HTV, 1990). This 22-minute adaptation of *Culhwch and Olwen* from *The Mabinogion* intelligently condenses the Welsh original's many interlocking tasks that Arthur's kinsman Culhwch undertakes to win Olwen from her father, the giant Ysbaddaden.[24]

Following a thirty-second, live-action segment that presents landscape scenes of "the misty, mythical land of Wales, ... a land of kings and heroes with magical powers," the story begins. Thomas abridges strategically to streamline and fuse Culhwch's adventures, trimming the original's thirty-nine nested tasks to four pivotal ones: gathering and planting the flax seed necessary for Olwen's bridal veil; finding the hunter Mabon needed to track a huge boar (Twrch Trwyth); recovering scissors, comb, and a razor from the boar to groom Ysbaddaden; and obtaining the blood of the Black Witch, needed to soften Ysbaddaden's beard and prepare him for the wedding day on which the giant is fated to die. Although Thomas's script echoes his source well — given that even the original relates the details of only a few of Culhwch's adventures — *The Quest for Olwen* focuses primarily on the tale's *love* story and what Culhwch must accomplish to remove all obstacles that stand between him and his bride. And as in the original, Arthur and his knights contribute to Culhwch's quest, but the emphasis remains on Culhwch's exploits.

The animators take more liberties than the scriptwriter. For instance, Olwen, the object of Culhwch's quest, appears on screen more than a reading of *The Mabinogion* might suggest. Her increased presence further recasts the tale as a story of young love — and the visuals often highlight the heroine's new narrative importance.[25] Ugarov's unit fleshes out a depiction of Arthur's court as well. The king resides in a Romanesque castle high on a hill. Beyond the portcullis entrance and long stone halls, Excalibur hangs on a wall above the king's throne. The sword throbs electrically as voices whisper "Excalibur." The king's Round Table looks to be a cross-section cut from an ancient, immense tree, perhaps to suggest the king's (and legend's) connections to primeval times. Court proceedings, as Culhwch requests aid and Arthur grants it, appear formal and ritualistic — which is perhaps as much a matter of the animators' intent as it is a product of the limited movement available in collage animation.

The animators take a few unexpected liberties, too. The Black Witch seems derived most probably (and most inappropriately) from *Monty Python and the Holy Grail*. Anyone familiar with Tim the Enchanter's pyrotechnics and the carnage left by the Killer Rabbit of Caerbannog has a hard time suppressing a giggle as the Black Witch cackles before his cave and hops about the skeleton-littered landscape by means of whirlwinds and lightning strikes. And when a knight defeats the witch with his laser-shooting sword, *Star Wars* likely springs to mind. But these minor excesses aside, educators can profitably employ *The Quest for Olwen* to help their students better understand the medieval tale that inspired the animated adaptation.

After *The Quest for Olwen*, S4C returned to Arthurianimation once more later in the decade. In association with BBC Education, BBC Wales, and HBO, S4C commissioned six studios in Moscow, London, and Cardiff to animate Jonathan Myerson's screenplay of *Geoffrey Chaucer's* The Canterbury Tales (Christmas Productions and Right Angle/S4C, 1998–2000), a dramatization of ten tales and their narrative links. The charge for an animated adaptation of Chaucer's *Wife of Bath's Tale*, the story of an Arthurian knight who rapes a maiden and then comes to understand the wrong he has done, went to Joanna Quinn's Beryl Productions.[26] Quinn's six-minute "Wife of Bath's Tale" (1998) offers several insights into the court: the ferociously angry, axe-wielding

8. Arthur, Arthur, Everywhere

Queen Guinevere who sentences the knight-offender to death unless within a year he can discover "what women most desire"; her ladies of the court, who alternately gasp and laugh as the queen physically and mentally tortures the knight to punish him for his heinous deed; and the knight himself, who grasps the error of his ways only when compelled to marry the hag who revealed to him the secret of what women want, to learn from her the true nature of *gentilesse*, and to grant her the sovereignty that women desire above all else. Arthur pointedly does not appear. As in the original poem, the king gives the knight's fate over to Guinevere and then vanishes from the narrative. In Quinn's animation, an empty throne next to Guinevere's provides the only visual trace of the king.

Many BAFTA and Emmy awards that came to Quinn for bringing to the screen an excellent adaptation of Chaucer's sole Arthurian tale notwithstanding, some educators may find the "Wife of Bath's Tale" too raw for all but high school and college audiences. Like its source in the *Canterbury Tales*, this animated version pushes beyond the boundaries of what many school districts deem acceptable. The film's depiction of the hag's pendulous breasts and the intercourse enjoyed by the knight and hag — as her form fluctuates between aged crone and young beauty — may well disturb some viewers. Likewise the rape scene that sets the plot in motion — even though it is handled discreetly, more via implication (the knight's rearing horse, the flower dropped from the maiden's hand) than direct portrayal — makes this adaptation suitable perhaps only for older students.

The creators of the direct-to-video *The Legend of Percival* (Gateway Films/Vision Video, 1993) aimed their half-hour evangelical production at much the same middle-school audience that the *Fables and Legends: English Folk Heroes* series targeted in the late 1980s. Blending and lightly bowdlerizing narratives drawn primarily from Chrétien de Troyes's *Perceval* and Wolfram von Eschenbach's *Parzival*, writers Joan Thiry and James Robertson used "the legend as a teaching device for moral development" (2) as they asked young viewers to ponder "basic questions we all must face on our pilgrimage through life" (1).[27]

A narrator recites the story as a camera pans and zooms over a sequence of still images to tell the familiar tale of Percival's upbringing in the Welsh woods, initial encounter with Round Table knights, departure from mother and home to seek Arthur's court, the kiss and ring stolen from an unwilling maiden, combat with the Red Knight, the teachings of Gournamonde, first visit to the Grail Castle, and so on, through dozens of scenes derived from medieval Perceval romances. And *The Legend of Percival* is reasonably faithful to its sources — to the degree that direct comparison with any one of them is possible — but the Thiry/Robertson storyline breaks off before the hero finds the Grail Castle a second time. The study guide that accompanies the video argues that conclusions offered by medieval authors who attempted to *finish* threads of Chrétien's incomplete romance missed its deeper meaning: "Percival's search is symbolic of the quest we all have as human beings" (6). Percival is Everyman, engaged in a lifelong quest to seek salvation through Christ: "Jesus is our goal, our Grail, and living the Christian life is our quest" (10). Thus *The Legend of Percival* continues a tradition begun long ago, offering yet one more *possible* conclusion to Chrétien's enigmatic, unfinished tale.

Education leavened with laughs may be one of the most effective pedagogies for young minds. Led by executive producer/series creator Tom Ruegger, the subversive talents at Warner Bros. Television Animation mixed instructional Arthurianimation with burlesque for a seven-minute segment of the half-hour "*Histeria!* Satellite TV" (Wang Film/Warner Bros., 1998), an episode of The WB network's overtly educational *Histeria!* ABC's contemporaneous late-night news program *Nightline* provides the touchstone for a parody in which Lancashire-born newsman Ted Koppel is replaced by a thinly disguised "Sir Fred Moppel" and the show becomes *Medieval Knight-Line*. The evening's guest is King Arthur ("Knight, Founder of the Roundtable, Nice-Guy" in the chyron). Moppel skeptically introduces Arthur as a character widely believed to be "merely a popular legend." Speaking with an accent that betrays an upbringing nearer New Jersey than Cornwall, the potbellied king disputes the host's assertion. Arthur contends that "everything you heard about me and my guys is absolutely true." A rapid-fire potpourri of Arthurian lore follows. Arthur dismisses as "pure fairy-tale fantasy stuff" the yarn that he became king by pulling the sword from the stone. Instead, he insists that he obtained Excalibur "the regular, old-fashioned way"—when "the Lady of the Lake reached up out of the water and gave it to me." A flashback transports the audience to the moment that an elderly, overweight woman (series regular World's Oldest Woman), wearing a bikini as she floats on an inflatable pool lounger, threw Excalibur at Arthur as he dozed near a lake. Arthur: "And next thing I know, boom! I'm Arthur, king of Camelot, with the knights of the Round Table and the works. Hey! Talk about being in the right place at the right time!"

Moppel's disbelief continues to grow as he questions other guests who appear on the studio's television monitors to vouch for Arthur's historicity. The host welcomes to the show Merlin, "the mystical sorcerer and prophet who allegedly raised" the king. But Merlin undermines his own credibility as he describes himself as an "enchanted lifestyle facilitator" and then rants until the host turns off his screen. The next guests are Monty Pythonesque Lancelot and Galahad ("Good Knight" and "Good Morning" in the chyron). They appear to be inventing their story as they tell it. Lancelot: "Being a knight of the Round Table.... Yes. Well, first off, we'd, uh, we'd sit around the, uh, Round Table for a bit, I suppose," and so on. Meanwhile, Galahad acts out the characters that Lancelot describes: a shrill damsel in distress, crafty gnomes, undead zombie knights,[28] fire-breathing dragons, and unicorns. Moppel cannot conceal exasperation: "Oh, come on.... That's the stuff of fairy tales.... I find this totally unbelievable."

An unexpected guest, speaking with a refined (albeit contrived) British accent, suddenly appears on another monitor: "Hear, hear. Please don't let these fictitious frauds further degrade the noble profession of knighthood with their romanticized rubbish." The newcomer identifies himself as Sir Thomas Malory ("Famous Author"), "thirteenth-century [*sic*] English author and drinker of raspberry smoothies"—one of which he holds in his hand. Rejecting as "pure poppycock" the fables that the other guests have offered, Malory sketches a literary genealogy of the legend back to "the earliest of these stories [that] appeared about A.D. 1136 in *Historia regum Britanniae* by the Welsh poet [*sic*] Geoffrey of Monmouth."²⁹ Arthur disputes Malory's account and his sobriety: "If you axed me, I'd say he's had one too many sips from the Grail, *capisce*?" "Pish, posh," counters Malory, "Sir Lancelot was invented by the twelfth-century French poet Chrétien de Troyes." This last remark rankles Lancelot, who is still listening to the discussion from another monitor. Lancelot will not accept that "history's greatest English knight [was] made up by a French man." Lancelot and Galahad begin to trade insults ("mythical moron," "fictional French fop," "metaphorical meathead," etc.) and blows as the interview spins out of control à la *The Jerry Springer Show*.

Moppel turns to Arthur to accuse him of breaking "the most sacred knightly oath of all: honesty." He challenges the king to single combat. Arthur shies away from the sword-wielding host. In a panic, Arthur begins to contradict himself — insisting now that his power derives from pulling the sword from the stone — while his knights refuse to help the king because they are (as they insist) "mythical." Arthur runs from the set. Malory looks on and records the events with quill on parchment. With one final bow to ABC's *Nightline*, "*Histeria!* Satellite TV" offers a fractured version of Koppel's signature "Good night" sign-off: "Until next time, I'm Sir Fred Moppel, a real good (k)night."

PBS's Peabody and Emmy-winning educational series *Arthur*, based on the young adult book series by Mark Brown, brought its eponymous protagonist to Arthurianimation with "The Return of the King" (CINAR/Cookie Jar, 1999). Writer Peter K. Hirsch's thirteen-minute episode follows young Arthur Read and his Lakewood Elementary schoolmates on a field trip to a medieval fair to compete for the Golden Griffin, a trophy given annually to the class that demonstrates the greatest knowledge of medieval history. But when the privileged students of Glenbrook Academy and their supercilious teacher arrive, Arthur's little cohort can guess who will likely win the day. As Arthur's group loses one competition after the next, the episode casually presents a pastiche of information about the Middle Ages. We learn of the invention of tennis, the geocentric universe, the rude contours of a Norman fortification, and a "Wheel of Fortuna" that jocularly offers "Permanent Exile," "Black Death," and a trip to the "Stocks" as possible outcomes. "Haggis," "capon," "crenellations," and "arrow slits" introduce medieval vocabulary and terminology. A modicum of linguistics also comes into play: "In Old English," a judge pedantically explains to Arthur's team as he comments on their pennant for a losing entry in a castle-building contest, "Lakewood would have an -*e* on the end." The arrogant Glenbrook kids taunt their opponents in both Latin and (almost) Middle English: "Veni, vidi, vici!/We will defeat ye!"

Only an Arthurian-themed competition can keep Lakewood from being trounced. Arthur has been thinking about it all day and already tried it twice without success: pulling a sword from a stone at one of the fair's many stations designed to help youngsters learn about the Middle Ages. To save his people from defeat, Arthur must do what his famous namesake did long ago. The sword-station attendant's riddle offers

Arthurian Animation

one clue: "All your might won't set things right./'Tis a gentle hand 'twill rule the land." Two brute-force attempts having failed Arthur, he ponders the riddle anew, then realizes that he must first *twist* the pommel *lightly*, then tug, to release the sword from the stone. Sword in hand, Arthur is proclaimed king of the fair. The Glenbrook teacher cannot but acknowledge that Arthur has been taught "to think for himself," perhaps the most valuable lesson of all.

CHAPTER 9

Four Roads to Camelot: The Feature Film Bumper Crop of 1997–98

Spurred by the phenomenal popularity of televised Arthurianimation in the 1990s, four animated Arthurian feature-length films appeared almost simultaneously toward the end of the decade: *Quest for Camelot* (Warner Bros. Feature Animation, 1998) and three direct-to-video releases that pinned their profit expectations on how well *Quest for Camelot* would perform at the box office. The "financial coattails" strategy was simple. If Warner Bros. succeeded with its Arthurian cartoon, the copycat productions would likely benefit as well. If, on the other hand, *Quest for Camelot* failed, the three far less expensively produced knock-offs could be quickly remaindered on superstore tumble tables. In any event, with considerably lower production and advertising costs than those incurred by Warner Bros., the direct-to-video films would likely recoup their investments regardless of *Quest for Camelot*'s profit/loss margin.[1]

Any studio attempting to capitalize on *Quest for Camelot* had ample opportunity to learn of plans on the Warner Bros. lot. Even as production was underway on the hybrid live-action/animated *Space Jam* (1996), the first film to tap the resources of Warner's newly formed Feature Animation unit, gossip swirled in trade magazines and Internet newsgroups about difficulties the fledgling unit was already experiencing with the *next* film in its queue, the fully animated *Quest for Camelot*. Producers, writers, directors, staff, and voice talent appeared to change weekly. Would Christopher Reeve, paralyzed in a 1995 horse-riding accident, accept the rumored offer of Arthur's voice? He did, but Pierce Brosnan replaced Reeve before the vocal tracks were recorded. How closely could the writers preparing the screenplay adhere to Vera Chapman's novel of rape, revenge, and redemption in a film that had to stay squarely within the MPAA's guidelines for a G-rating? At first blush, Chapman's *The King's Damosel* seemed intractable material on which to base a kids' film. The trite smokescreen explanation of "creative differences" was advanced as one person after another exited through a revolving door at Warner Bros. An effects supervisor on the set at the time later confessed to Beck for *The Animated Movie Guide*:

> People were giving up. The head of layout was kicked out, the head of background, the executive producer, the producer, the director, the associate producer—all the heads rolled. It's kind of a hard environment to work in [217–18].

And all the while the Feature Animation unit's delays with *Space Jam* were moving *Quest for Camelot*'s production timeline into an ever more distant future and the costs kept climbing to well over $100 million.[2]

The tumult became the subject of parody even inside the studio perimeter. Writers at Warner's *other* animation unit, the one responsible for television hits such as *Tiny Toon Adventures*, *Pinky and the Brain*, and *Animaniacs*, could not resist mocking their colleagues across the lot. In part 1 of the *Animaniacs*'s "Hooray for North Hollywood" (first broadcast on 3 January 1998 on The WB), writers took jabs at a fictional Warner executive's disastrous hodgepodge of a film that "crashed on take-off." This film was called *Jamelot*, an obvious lampoon fusing the recently released *Space Jam* and the developing *Quest for Camelot*.

Smaller studios might have observed the harbingers warning that *Quest for Camelot* would not be a blockbuster with ample skirts to ride. Yet the enduring lure of Arthuriana, the prospect of drawing the same audience that television had been grooming through the decade, and the ability to benefit obliquely from Warner's hefty advertising budget for its own Arthurian film were too potent to resist. Three production companies rushed to release direct-to-video films in 1997 and 1998, all with "Camelot" figuring prominently in the title. All three were available in stores before *Quest for Camelot*'s May 1998 premiere.

One. *The Sword in the Stone* meets the 1967 *Camelot* meets *First Knight* provides a thumbnail index to several major threads of director William R. Kowalchuk and writers Lisa Moricoli-Latham and Elizabeth Logun's seventy-minute *Camelot: The Legend* (Tundra Productions/GT Merchandising & Licensing Corp., 1998). Scrolling text and stately brass music set the scene as the film opens:

> Once upon a time, in England, there was a sword that magic had firmly wedged in a stone. Legend told that only the future king of England would be able to remove the sword. Though many tried, none succeeded until...
>
> A young lad called Arthur came along. He pulled on the sword — just a little — and...
>
> Out it came!
>
> So, Arthur became King and should have lived happily ever after. But the wicked witch, Morgan le Fay, tricked Arthur into fathering a son, Mordred. She then schemed against Arthur to put Mordred on the throne.
>
> Oblivious to this plot, Arthur took the beautiful Guinevere as his queen and together they dreamed of uniting England. Arthur was guided by Merlin, the magician, who did his best to protect the naive Arthur. And they all lived in...
>
> Camelot...

Voiceovers provided by Merlin,[3] several musical numbers, and details dropped haphazardly into the storyline advance the film's traditional and invented Arthurian lore. The audience learns that the wizard raised Arthur — already in his forties in this film — but the king's prehistory and biological origins are never revealed. Mordred's parents, on the other hand, are known to all: he is Arthur and Morgan's son, the product of an unexplained "trick." Now in his early twenties, Mordred skulks about Camelot, biding

Cover art of Merlin, Arthur, Guinevere, and Lancelot, *Camelot: The Legend* VHS tape (Tundra Productions, 1998).

his time until he and his mother can make a play for the throne. While Arthur optimistically hopes that Mordred will develop into a "valiant knight," Guinevere distrusts him from the outset — and, besides, she wants a son of her own.

One day, Arthur, Guinevere, Merlin, Mordred, and a small group of knights set out for a conference in Cornwall that Arthur hopes will bring peace with rival kings. Merlin is skeptical: "Sit down together and talk their problems out, like grown-ups are supposed to? ... It's not very realistic. People fight. It's human nature." In fact they never even arrive at the summit. Mordred has hired mercenaries to slay the king and queen in transit.

The attempted assassination turns the plot in another direction. As Arthur insists on clinging to his ideals while a thug holds a sword to his wife's throat — "Even if you kill us both," Arthur avers, "Camelot will live on forever!" — newcomer knight-adventurer Lancelot arrives from France to save them both. Arthur decides to return to Camelot, concerned that it too may be attacked next. We do not hear again about the peace conference in Cornwall. It is one of the film's many abandoned threads.

Although Merlin imprisoned Morgan in a cave twenty years ago, she has continued to try to steer events in Camelot from the grubby subterranean lair that holds her. In a metrically irregular, broken-rhyme, half-spoken song ("Mine"), she touches allusively on traditional Arthurian narratives, asserting that she was once an heir to the throne, "the princess supreme" of the land, until Arthur stole her birthright by pulling a sword from a stone. Is this "princess" perhaps half-sister to the king? *Camelot: The Legend* will not tell us. Morgan also reminds the audience of the sword in a stone that marked Arthur as king — but no further details are forthcoming. Morgan's next stanza reveals that Merlin has already prophesied Arthur's fated end (his death?) at Mordred's hands. Again, the film *introduces* Arthurian information but then does not *integrate* it meaningfully into the storyline.

These Arthurian particulars and many others recede far into the background as the visual silliness of Morgan's performance draws our attention. Spiders pluck their webs like harp strings and rats drum discarded bottles that litter the cave as the witch sings and go-go dances about the room in a short pink dress stretched over a pudgy frame. Only a viewer intently seeking the Arthurian dimensions of *Camelot: The Legend* finds them in these moments — and then only with repeated viewings. The children for whom this film was presumably created, however, likely fail to notice most of its casually inserted Arthuriana. Instead, the final words of "Mine" probably linger longest in young memories as Morgan promises to make Merlin "lick my feet" when she one day triumphs over the wizard who put her in the cave.

As Mordred's first plan to seize the throne fails and he begins others, the rest of the story unfolds, tapping into various facets of the legend as it proceeds. Lancelot and Guinevere become close, but no more than friends, as he teaches her to use a sword and offers easygoing companionship to a lonely spouse. Meanwhile, Arthur is preoccupied, fearing for Camelot's safety in the unstable land and seeing no way to enlarge his stock of men-at-arms without a court of nobles from which to draw. Practical Guinevere proposes that Arthur consider knighting the townsmen who are busy fortifying the city walls. The king agrees to her plan and assigns Lancelot the task of selecting commoners worthy of elevation. To make all people feel equal as laborers join together with royals as Arthur's new knights, the resourceful queen suggests using "that wedding present, the big round table" for their meetings.[4]

Morgan and Mordred continue working covertly to destroy Arthur's realm. They contrive to make the king doubt the queen's fidelity by insinuating that Lancelot and Guinevere are in love. After a battle of Disneyesque shapeshifting magicians and a mock trial of Guinevere for treason — a trial designed to draw Mordred into the open — the villains' plans are at last fully exposed and thwarted. Along the way, Arthur realizes that he must treat his wife better than he has been, that he cannot spend every moment thinking about the kingdom.

A warped *First Knight*–inspired ending closes the movie, though not with Arthur's death but instead with the king, queen, and Lancelot happily singing together on a platform that only a moment before had served for the sham trial. Merlin delivers his final voiceover as doves take wing over Camelot: "Arthur and Guinevere reigned together for many years to come, Lancelot by their side as first knight. And so the legend of Camelot lives on in the hearts of all those true believers who want equality, justice, and opportunity for all people."

Confused? Rather than a steady plot with a clear intent we find a movie that at base cannot decide whether it is drama or comedy and whether its audience is old or young. On the sober side, we have Morgan and Mordred conspiring to kill people and relishing detailed thoughts of their enemies' deaths, suspected adultery, Arthur's plan to banish Guinevere to the forest despite her plaint that she will perish if thrust into the wild, Lancelot's and Merlin's roles as teachers to both king and queen, and Morgan spouting uncharacteristically philosophical notions such as "Mordred is a spell I formed in flesh." It is difficult to reconcile these serious elements with the relentless, awkward gambits at humor on the film's comic side. Item, Morgan's repeated use of a Clapper to activate a makeshift sword in the stone/projection television that she employs to keep an eye on events in Camelot. Item, Lancelot's song (and barroom chorus number) about what it means to be a "parfit, gentil knight," which manages to bring together in a single stanza a knight's chivalric duties to fight battles and convert pagans with the more mundane obligations to rescue children from wells and kittens from trees — as everyone dances like Rockettes. Item, a damsel-tossing competition that reveals how the rustic townsmen entertain themselves. Item, an overworked gag that rises from Morgan's accidental substitution of sneezing powder for a love potion. Item, slapstick pratfalls accompanied by overamplified cartoon sound effects. Item, cross-dressing to stir laughs. And so on.

After as little as half an hour of oscillating randomly between straight drama and low comedy, the picture becomes largely incoherent. When Merlin reminds us at film's end of the message the production team apparently once had in mind — to show Camelot as a symbol of democratic values — one has to wonder why this theme was scarcely explored. Although Arthur does raise some reformed locals to knighthood and although he does eventually recognize that his queen can handle a sword and can offer useful advice on how to rule the kingdom, the conclusion seems unrelated to most of the film that we have just seen.

A few other notes are in order for *Camelot: The Legend*. Arthurian scholars may snicker as Lancelot is senselessly assigned the Siege Perilous—according to most traditional versions of the legend, a vacant Round Table seat that only the Grail knight Galahad can occupy without suffering the eponymous "peril" it offers—despite the work of the "historical consultant" listed in the credits. Literary critics may ponder the Freudian significance of gifts that Morgan sends to entwine and implicate Guinevere and Lancelot in adultery: a phallic sword to the queen and vaginal gloves to her knight. On the technical side, the animation from Colorland Animation Productions (Shenzhen, China) is occasionally crudely drawn and lacking in continuity; the audio, especially in the musical sections, is muddy; and, in an unintentional nod to Franco Nero's performance in 1967's *Camelot*, Lancelot's faux-French accent is absurd.

Two. Imagine the musical *Camelot* framed by Marion Zimmer Bradley's *Mists of Avalon*, with a few touches added from *The Sword in the Stone*, and you have the intriguing mix brought together in director Greg Garcia and writer Peter S. Beagle's *Camelot* (Golden Films/Sony Wonder, 1997). The dense, fifty-minute film covers Arthur's entire life from the moment that Merlin saves an abandoned baby[5] from a modest hut in war-torn Britain to the wounded king's journey to distant, eternal Avalon at film's end. Between the rescue and his final passage to the otherworld, Arthur grows up in Avalon, returns to Britain, and founds, rules, and finally witnesses the collapse of Camelot.

In Avalon, Arthur is raised by "Aunt" Viviane, her sister Morgause, and the other wiccans who inhabit the isle. The women teach him to fight, ride, and dance, while Merlin transforms the boy into various animals à la T. H. White to show him the connectedness of all things in nature. Morgause also teaches Arthur about love and then marries him in accord with the gynarchy's hope that Arthur will carry the rational, peaceful, female spirit of Avalon back to his testosterone-ravaged homeland.

Shortly after the marriage, a white stag appears and Morgause vanishes—events, like many others in this fast-paced film, without explanation — as Merlin emerges from a tree to take Arthur to a cavern in which the island's inhabitants have gathered. Merlin orders Arthur to pull a golden sword from a stone in order to fulfill his destiny of building Camelot as a haven for "the weak and the humble." "For centuries," Merlin explains, "thousands have tried [to draw the sword], but only the new rightful king of England can pull it from its place." Viviane tells "Arthur of Avalon" to wield Excalibur honorably. Foster parents Merlin and Viviane then push their young adult ward from the nest. The time has come for Arthur to leave both Avalon and wife Morgause, for "she cannot exist in the real world" of mortals to which Arthur must now travel. As Arthur sails for England, Viviane pledges that one day he will rejoin his wife.

Arthur has aged enough to sprout a light beard by the next time that we see him. He meets Guenevere when he rescues her from a fire-breathing dragon. She is a runaway with "nowhere to go"—escaping from parents who would have married her to a wealthy landlord twice her age — and so she becomes Arthur's riding companion. As they journey, Arthur explains his Avalonian plans for the new realm of Camelot. He intends to

Cover art of Guenevere, Arthur, and Merlin, *Camelot* VHS tape (Golden Films/Sony Wonder, 1997).

stop the strong from oppressing the weak. Guenevere (as does Merlin in *Camelot: The Legend*) believes it will be a difficult task on British soil, because she knows that "that's what strong people do."

Arthur rides the countryside gathering knights one by one and eventually settles in Cornwall, a spot chosen because "sometimes you can see Avalon from there." The Cornish inhabitants band together to help Arthur build a castle and then democratically "choose" him to be their king. Merlin's spirit appears behind Arthur at the Round Table to turn all the knights' swords golden (like Arthur's), thus underscoring their equality, as dark-skinned (Moorish?) Palomides, Arthur's tactical adviser, leads them in shouting "Might for right!"

Merlin urges Arthur to wed Guenevere. (Bigamy is apparently not an obstacle if your other wife lives in the mists.) Then Arthur sets off to solidify his control over the kingdom by fighting battles and arranging treaties. Left at home, Guenevere feels slighted by her inattentive husband and turns to Lancelot for companionship. Autumn leaves blow across the screen to signal the beginning of the end.

Arthur's hair has silvered in the next scene. The king knows that his queen and Lancelot are attracted to each other, but his only response is sadness—and yearning for Morgause whom he left behind in Avalon long ago. Meanwhile Lancelot and Guenevere become more reckless. One day Meliagrance discovers the two as they are holding hands. Only Viviane's magical intervention prevents Lancelot from killing the witness to the suggested infidelity. Viviane tells the lovers that she has stopped Lancelot to protect Arthur—not his disloyal wife or the knight—and exits icily, "If you can't be faithful, try to be kind."

The stage is set for the surprise arrival of Mordred of Avalon, hitherto unrevealed son of Arthur and Morgause. He will also be unable to balance the demands of faithfulness and kindness as he righteously and without hidden agenda reveals to Arthur the affair that the king has ignored for over twenty years. Echoing the 1967 *Camelot*, Arthur is powerless to stop the growing gossip, the plan that follows to take Lancelot and Guenevere in her chambers, and the deaths of several knights as the lovers escape to Joyeuse Garde.

Arthur and Lancelot meet privately to arrange a treaty, yet both know that Mordred will not let the two men find peace. At a public ceremony the next morning, Mordred goads Lancelot until the latter pulls his sword and the final catastrophe ensues. In the fighting, an unidentified knight wounds Arthur. Before the king loses consciousness, he reconciles with Lancelot, Guenevere, and Mordred. Arthur tells Mordred that it is now his responsibility to "carry the peace of Camelot forward." Mists rise, Viviane and Merlin come for Arthur, and they sail to Avalon where the king is reunited with Morgause at long last. Merlin's voiceover recalls Arthur's accomplishment—"hope of a world at peace, beyond all fear"—and reminds us that Arthur waits in Avalon until his time comes again.

Arthur has no overt enemies in this film. Instead, conflicts arise as Arthur strives to make Camelot mirror Avalon. Near the film's close, as Arthur realizes that the end of his dream must come soon, he tells Merlin: "I blame only myself. I don't blame

9. Four Roads to Camelot

Guenevere and Lancelot for anything. I don't even blame Mordred. I am the one who lost Camelot." It takes Merlin's reply to reveal a broader perspective:

> Nonsense. You are the one who built it. No one else could have done that. The Lancelots can't build. They can only defend. And the Mordreds have good intentions but cannot see the bigger picture.... Because of you now there is a Camelot to remember, a Camelot to dream about, a Camelot to rebuild and rebuild, over and over, and every time to come. It will fall again, each time, and return again. Only Avalon is forever. And you are part of Avalon.... You are one with Avalon — always, Arthur, always.

Sony Wonder's *Camelot* is a much better film than Tundra's *Camelot: The Legend*. The storyline and use of traditional Arthurian material are far more coherent, despite a number of telegraphic gestures toward Bradley's feminist reinterpretation that only viewers familiar with her novel are likely to understand. The film's robust, memorable ballads help to further the narrative, even if one ("Camelot") calls to mind the signature theme of the 1967 *Camelot* and another ("Dreams of Avalon") echoes "Colors of the Wind" from Disney's 1995 *Pocahontas*.[6] The animation from Hong Ying Animation (Suzhou, China) pleases the eye. Sony Wonder's *Camelot* must certainly pique the interest of Arthurian scholars; however, whether this complex, allusive, quickly moving film could hold a child's attention is another matter.

Three. At the same time that Sony Wonder's *Camelot* was arriving in stores, another animated film with the same title and the almost identical runtime of forty-nine minutes appeared next to it on the shelves: director Richard Slapczynski's *Camelot* (Burbank Animation Studios [Australia]/Anchor Bay Entertainment, 1997), from a storyline developed by Roddy Lee and Roz Phillips and screenplay by Paul Leadon. The bulk of the animation was rendered at Colorland Animation Productions, the same company that animated *Camelot: The Legend*, though the general artistic competence is much higher than in the Tundra film.

Unlike the Tundra and Sony Wonder films, Slapczynski's *Camelot* borrows little from previous Arthurian features, with the exception of some shallow correspondences to *The Sword in the Stone* that may be inevitable because both films focus primarily on the life of young Arthur leading up to the moment that he becomes king. *The Sword in the Stone*'s opening movement of the dangers and rapaciousness of the forest — symbolic of the land's political unrest — is recalled in Slapczynski's opening scene of a storm ripping through the forest outside a darkened castle. Within the castle, King Gerdlach imparts final commands from his deathbed. Knowing that chaos will follow his death, Gerdlach orders court magician and adviser Merlin to watch over his infant son Arthur for twelve years, at which time the lad will be old enough to claim the king's hereditary sword Excalibur, castle, and the land as his own.

Merlin carries the child to Stonehenge, sets the sword in a granite block within the circle for safekeeping, then passes through a column with his young charge to a spacious cave beneath the hengework. Quick vignettes show the turmoil that follows Gerdlach's death, the slow disintegration of Camelot castle, and Merlin raising Arthur into adolescence. Along the way Arthur befriends gal-pal Cynthia, an adolescent "foundling" who turns up one day inside Stonehenge and is taken in by Merlin,[7] and four animal sidekicks.

Cover art of Arthur and his animal companions, *Camelot* DVD (Burbank Animation Studios, 1997).

9. Four Roads to Camelot

Arthur longs to be a magician, but when it becomes clear that Cynthia is the one with the gift, he leaves his underground home in search of a destiny that Merlin cannot yet reveal. To protect the future king as he leaves the safety of the cave, Merlin transforms Cynthia into a falcon and sends her after him. Then Merlin broadcasts a message heard throughout the country: all warring clans should gather at Stonehenge in order to determine who can pull Gerdlach's Excalibur from the stone and thus become the next king.

Enter the complication: short-tempered, thick-headed Sir Baldrick, who learns from his page Runcibel that Arthur seems to be able to move the sword. (Even Arthur does not yet know of his power over Excalibur. Runcibel noticed the sword quivering when Arthur accidentally brushed against it on his exit from the Stonehenge cave.) Aspiring to be king himself, Baldrick captures Arthur to learn his secret. When Arthur cannot answer Baldrick's questions, the villain casts both Arthur and Runcibel into a dungeon to be eaten by a dragon. Falcon Cynthia and the other animals rescue them.

Merlin's Stonehenge convocation is underway and each clan's champion has already tried to pull the sword when Arthur, Runcibel, and their animal companions arrive. Despite Baldrick's taunting of the "puny infant" whom he believes could not possibly budge Excalibur, Arthur draws the sword and thereby demonstrates to all that he is their king. Clouds part and the sun appears in the sky. The darkness that has long held the land disperses. Merlin leads the assembly in hailing "Arthur, king of Camelot." Merlin's voiceover relates that in the years that followed, Arthur rebuilt Gerdlach's Camelot, banished Baldrick, established the Round Table "to insure no knight would ever abuse his powers again" as Baldrick did, appointed Runcibel as his adviser, rewarded the animals, and accepted Cynthia as his new court magician when Merlin retired to write his memoir, "The Secret of Camelot"—a title introduced so clumsily that one can only assume that at some stage it may have served as this production's working title.

Burbank's *Camelot* has a fine sense of its target audience, which the DVD case for the film advertises as "ages 4 to 9." The storyline proceeds cleanly from start to finish with a single, simple complication. Potentially frightening moments, even while in Baldrick's dungeon, are innocuous, and these threats are further undercut by wisecracking Runcibel and comical talking animals at Arthur's side. This *Camelot* stands apart from contemporaneous rivals in offering no songs—a prudent decision for a film apparently made on a relatively meager budget.[8] Burbank's *Camelot* sets a modest goal and achieves it—an accomplishment that distinguishes it from the other two direct-to-video Arthurian releases of the day.

Four. Director Frederik Du Chau's *Quest for Camelot* disappointed many viewers. The screenplay by Kirk De Micco, William Schifrin, Jacqueline Feather, and David Seidler claimed to be based on Chapman's *The King's Damosel*. Yet anyone familiar with Chapman's romance novel of betrayal, rape, torture, revenge, forgiveness, personal redemption through love, and spiritual regeneration through a Grail quest, had to wonder why Warner Bros. ever acquired the rights in the first place if it intended to make a children's film. Indeed, only a few surface similarities to the novel remain in the 86-

minute feature. Both offer a strong heroine — Lynett in the novel, Kayley in the film — essentially Malory's sharp-tongued Lynet of *Le Morte Darthur*'s Gareth tale (Caxton's book VII), whose narrative Chapman reenvisions, continues, and enlarges in her novel. There is in both the heroine's love-interest, a young and blind hermit — Lucius in the novel, Garrett in the film — certainly an important character for the development of Chapman's heroine, but far more crucial to the storyline in *Quest for Camelot* than to the plot of *The King's Damosel*. The protagonists must naturally face villains — Chapman offers several distilled from Malory and Tennyson, who are all compressed into the film's Ruber. Falcons again figure prominently in these tales of Camelot, too — Chapman's falcon accompanies the heroine; in the film Merlin sends it to protect Garrett in the wilderness. Finally there is in both a quest — in *The King's Damosel* for the Grail that could heal the heroine's psychic scars and potentially restore Garrett's sight, reduced and secularized in *Quest for Camelot* to an adventurous search for the stolen Excalibur.[9] Nothing anywhere in Chapman's sober tale gives rise to the comic relief that screenwriters invent for a kids' movie: Devon and Cornwall, a two-headed, bickering dragon that can neither fly nor breathe fire until its two personalities learn to cooperate.

If *Quest for Camelot* is far from a straightforward adaptation of *The King's Damosel*, then what is it? Reviewers who saw the premiere were not sure. Joe Leydon's *Variety* review (10 May 1998) tepidly spun the film as "a lightweight but likable fantasy that offers a playfully feminist twist to Arthurian legends." Most critics were more severe. The online *ScreenIt: Movie Reviews for Parents* (9 May 1998) deemed *Quest for Camelot* an undistinguished Disneyesque formula piece that rated only 5.5 on a 10-point scale. *ScreenIt*'s anonymous reviewer remarked that the quality of animation was "well below what we've come to expect from Disney and now Fox" and that the musical numbers, "while all competent and decent, are nothing to write home about." Roger Ebert in the *Chicago Sun-Times* (15 May 1998) and dozens of his peers across the nation struck similar chords and awarded middling ratings:

> "Quest for Camelot" is still another big studio attempt to wrest the crown of family animation away from Disney. It's from Warner Bros., which scored with the bright and amusing "Space Jam," but now seems to fall back into the pack of Disney wannabes. The animation isn't vivid, the characters aren't very interesting, and the songs are routine.

Two out of four stars. A few years later, with all the receipts tallied and the perspective that hindsight affords, Beck's entry for *Quest for Camelot* in *The Animated Movie Guide* chronicled the studio disorganization, resignations, and firings that culminated in "a colossal artistic and box-office failure, nearly ending the legacy of Warner Bros. Animation" (218).

Yet perhaps the most penetrating critique appeared even before *Quest for Camelot* opened. It came again from the Warner lot itself. In the *Animaniacs*'s "Jokahontas" (first broadcast on 14 September 1996 on The WB), a parody of Disney's *Pocahontas* that takes swipes at *The Little Mermaid* and *Beauty and the Beast* as well, the score caustically summarizes (and predicts) the formula of most of the decade's "strong heroine" cartoons as mere "rerun," "retread" copies of well-worn heroines from the past. And *Quest for Camelot*'s Kayley indeed did turn out to be the predictably spunky animated

Lobby poster of Garrett and Kayley, *Quest for Camelot* (Warner Bros., 1998).

mainstream heroine of the 1990s: a goo-goo-eyed brunette; strong, but always less so than the males in her life; beautiful and tomboyish at once, though ready to trade her trousers for a dress by movie's end; a girl who wants to be a boy — at least until she meets one. (Sound familiar?) Her signature tune, "On My Father's Wings," overtly reveals Kayley's reliance on the patriarchy at the beginning. A "Just Knighted" sign tied to a horse's hindquarters as she and Garrett ride off at the end suggests the connubial "just hitched," even if we witness no actual marriage ceremony in the film.

Kayley must learn to play the role that society intends for her. In a revealing moment early in the film, the heroine fidgets as her mother Lady Juliana[10] tries to fit her for a new dress. Kayley explains that she would much rather join the menfolk in their search for the recently stolen Excalibur.

> KAYLEY: But, Mother, Excalibur is missing. I must go after it.
> JULIANA: That's a job for the knights, not for a young girl.
> KAYLEY: But I want to be a knight. I'll go on grand adventures, fighting evil, rescuing damsels in distress.... What is a damsel, anyway?

Kayley will eventually learn of course that *she* is a damsel. And the damsel must inevitably don the dress— which Kayley in fact does as *Quest for Camelot* comes to a close with a knighting ceremony that also ambiguously doubles as a marriage service. In Disney fashion, the light gray homespun shift from the fitting scene reappears as the snowy gown Kayley wears at the end. In the cathedral-like setting of Camelot's main hall, with Kayley dressed in luminous bridal-white apparel and sporting a floral circlet in her hair, she *appears* to marry Garrett — as the audience has long anticipated she would.

On the studio's *Quest for Camelot* website promoting the film during its release, producer Dalisa Cooper Cohen remarked that Kayley "wants to be a knight, something unheard of in her era, but she's not so single-minded that she's immune to the charms of a handsome young man who comes to her assistance, either." Or, as sensitive Devon explains to his gruff companion Cornwall, Kayley needs "someone who'll hold her in his arms, who'll run his fingers through her hair, look deeply in her eyes, and make her feel like a real woman." And so, rather than offer a truly independent, strong heroine, Warner Bros. ultimately relied on a conventional, conservative formula. *Quest for Camelot* reaffirmed dominant paradigms of proper behavior for girls. To pioneer a different path risked too much for a release that cost an estimated $120 million. Again, "Jokahontas" offered telling commentary as it baldly acknowledged the fact that in Hollywood profits often take precedence over innovation: getting "your seven bucks" for admission outweighed any desire to "try something new."

Quest for Camelot's storyline opens with Kayley's father Sir Lionel preparing to leave his rural home for King Arthur's plenary court at Camelot. Before he goes, he rehearses a well-worn tale for ten-year-old Kayley. He recalls that on the day that she was born, Arthur pulled Excalibur from the stone.[11] Around that stone and the ancient Ring of Stones hengework that encompassed it, Arthur and his knights proceeded to build Camelot and "the greatest kingdom on Earth." As Lionel departs, Kayley shouts after him, "I'm coming with you, Daddy." "Yes, one day when you're old enough," he replies, "I will take you to Camelot." Lionel has already passed beyond earshot as Kayley

9. Four Roads to Camelot

confides to her mother, "One day, I will be a knight, like Father." The opening credits roll and the film's "United We Stand" theme song (reminiscent of 1994's drum-thumping, call-to-gathering prelude from *The Lion King*) begins, as Lionel and a growing company of knights travel a road that comes to a fork. A sign points right to Camelot and left to the Forbidden Forest. They pass to the right.

Our initial view of Camelot's interior reveals a bustling castle and its leadership. A boy practices skills necessary to become a knight. Lovers and old friends greet as riders arrive from across the kingdom. All join in singing the theme. A long shot that tellingly forecasts his unimportance in *Quest for Camelot* introduces the king. Arthur stands with Merlin at his side at the top of stairs leading into the main hall. Indeed, Arthur will remain spatially, narratively, and emotionally distant throughout the movie. The close-up treatments reserved for principal characters never fall on the king — who is, in fact, not listed until the *seventh* position in the closing credits, following even Devon and Cornwall. Brosnan's laconic, detached voicework for Arthur further diminishes the king's significance for the audience. Merlin, voiced by John Gielgud, likewise scarcely draws our attention. On the sole occasion that Arthur asks his putative wizard whether they could use *magic* to recover Excalibur — a fair question that even children might pose — Merlin blandly replies that they will need to rely on the courage of the citizenry to find it. Eleventh in the credits, Merlin is as inconsequential as the king he serves.

As the "United We Stand" chorus continues, fifteen knights and the king enter the hall. They take their places at a sixteen-seat Round Table decorated with interlocking rings said to represent Camelot, Arthur, and Excalibur, the trinity unifying the spirit of the realm. Arthur contrapuntally reminds the court of the convocation's dual purpose: to celebrate the collective goals that have built Camelot over the past decade and divide the realm "in equal shares." Each knight uses his shield to reflect light to the rafters and then cries aloud one of the mixed bag of democratic ideals that the fellowship pledges to uphold: liberty, justice, trust, freedom, peace, honor, goodness, strength, and valor. They hang their swords behind their chairs, place their shields on the table, and sit. Most of these knights do not appear in the film again after this scene.

One knight (Sir Ruber) brings the "charming sing-along" to an end as he loudly adds "Me!" to their catalog of values. Ruber argues that he has been impatiently waiting for ten long years, helping the others secure the realm, and he wants his share of lands *now*. But the ostensibly proto–Marxist Arthur calmly (and contradictorily) explains that the division into "equal shares" means that "the lands will be divided according to each person's needs." Ruber counters that he needs more territory than any of the others and, moreover, deserves to rule Camelot. Although the mind reels at the extremely odd jumble of politics and virtues at work in Arthur's court, the film moves forward quickly so that the audience does not have time to ponder the profound philosophical contradictions at the Round Table's political, economic, and ethical cores.

Lionel objects to Ruber: he will not follow a false king. All knights leap from their seats while Arthur remains seated. In the frenzy that follows, Ruber kills Lionel and then lunges at the king. Arthur rises slowly from his chair and raises Excalibur to deflect

Ruber's mace. As if the sword and mace carry opposite electrical charges, a shock propels Ruber across the room. Ruber swears that "one day that sword will be in my hand" and then escapes from the hall. Arthur and his knights bear Lionel's body home for burial.

Ten years pass. Kayley becomes a young woman. She still dreams of following her father's footsteps to knighthood. She practices her fighting skills with a pitchfork as she springs athletically about the farm.

Meanwhile, Ruber has continued to plot to gain Excalibur. He orders a servile griffin (Griffin) to invade Camelot and steal the sword. Griffin injures the king's arm while snatching the prize. Arthur then all but disappears from the movie until the end, with the one significant exception of the scene mentioned above in which he tries to stir himself to action only to be stopped by Merlin, who tells the king that he is too weak to seek Excalibur and therefore must rely on his people to recover it.

Griffin flees with Excalibur in his talons. Merlin orders his falcon Ayden to stop the thief. Ayden and Griffin tangle in aerial combat. Griffin drops Excalibur into the Forbidden Forest. Alarms go out across the land, eventually reaching Kayley's home. She wants to join those seeking Excalibur, but Juliana reminds Kayley of her domestic duties—"boring" chores, Kayley grumbles—and besides, Juliana adds, "The knights will find the sword, and they'll do it by working together."

Ruber still lacks Excalibur, but Arthur does not have it either, so the villain proceeds with plans to seize power from the wounded, vulnerable king. Ruber and several cretinous minions invade Kayley and Juliana's home. He takes the women hostage and commands that Juliana serve as cover to help him sneak into Camelot. If Juliana refuses, Kayley will die. Ruber next resorts to a Warner Bros. "Acme" magic brew that fuses organic tissue and metal objects to transform one of the barnyard fowl into a chicken/hatchet amalgamation (Bladebeak) and then all his followers into an assortment of weaponized cyborgs. As Ruber admires his horrific abominations, Kayley escapes.[12]

Kayley's unwitting entrance into the Forbidden Forest by way of the road's left fork brings her into contact with the handsome blind hermit Garrett. As he later reveals in his backstory, Garrett once lived in Camelot and aspired to be a knight. But one night, while bravely rescuing animals caught in a stable fire, a horse kicked him in the head. As Garrett's vision ebbed, his dream of knighthood would have faded as well if not for Lionel's intervention. As "the only one" in Camelot who "still believed in" the sightless lad's ability to become a knight, Lionel mentored and trained him.[13] Yet when Ruber killed Lionel, not only did Kayley lose her father but Garrett lost his teacher and friend. Garrett abandoned Camelot for the wilderness. Merlin discreetly sent the seeing-eye falcon Ayden to protect the boy from dangers.

Garrett has lived alone for the past decade. He has become an expert woodsman during his time alone. He moves through the forest with the aid of a staff, avoiding or confronting perils as Ayden's screeches direct him. Chapman's corresponding blind character, Lucius, emits his own bat-like whistles to navigate. The screenwriters for the children's film wisely modified the potentially disconcerting portrait.

Garrett and Kayley initially dislike each other. Formulaically, however, their feelings soon warm to love as he transitions from antagonist to mentor to boyfriend. Their adventures in pursuit of Excalibur—which Kayley wants to return to Arthur so that the king can save her mother and the kingdom from Ruber—occupy the bulk of the film's non–Arthurian midsection. Ruber chases the young heroes through forest, dragon country (where Garrett and Kayley take Devon and Cornwall into their company), an ogre's cave (where the animators introduce a visually disjunct CGI monster that uses Excalibur as a toothpick), and at last out of the forest, sword in hand. Ruber and his cyborg army follow always one step behind.

Through these midsection exploits viewers observe that the fighting skills that Kayley believes she has acquired with her pitchfork cannot compare with the true expertise that Garrett reveals in his actions and signature "I Stand Alone" melody. The audience also learns Garrett's key battle tactic: take position, face your fears, hold your ground until the last possible moment, and then wait for a signal (from Ayden, in Garrett's case) to strike or evade the danger. Kayley must learn to follow Garrett's ways to achieve her goals. In many respects, Garrett serves as a replacement for Kayley's dead father, a new man's wings on which she can fly.

Although Garrett and Kayley have fallen in love along their journey, the mission nears its end. Kayley need only follow a short road to enter Camelot and return Arthur's sword. Unexpectedly, Garrett says he will not continue on to the castle. Camelot holds no place for a blind man, he says. Garrett turns back to the comfort of the woods. "In Camelot, she'd only see me though their eyes. Not a knight, not a man, not anything." Immediately after he leaves, Ruber and his hostage Juliana arrive. Ruber captures Kayley and Excalibur. Devon and Cornwall find Garrett to tell him what has happened. All three simultaneously realize that, despite any differences that divide them, they all love Kayley and must again unite to help her.

Ruber prepares for the assault on Camelot by Acme-fusing Excalibur to his arm and using Juliana to conceal his entry into the castle. Kayley escapes Ruber's clutches once more. She raises an alarm and the final struggle begins. Kayley tries to alert Arthur to Ruber's presence by climbing into the keep. A mere twelve seconds into her attempt, Griffin and the cyborgs cause her to fall. Garrett suddenly arrives astride a newly flight-capable Devon and Cornwall to save Kayley from death. To the metaphoric wings of both her father and Garrett, *Quest for Camelot* now adds Devon and Cornwall's literal wings to support the heroine. The reunited company moves forward to stop the assault on Camelot.

Kayley and Garrett now use their skills in concert to defeat Ruber, "working together" in the way that Juliana once told Kayley that Excalibur would be recovered. For her part, Kayley's sight allows her to help Garrett avoid several dangers as they cross the courtyard. For his, Garrett draws on boyhood memories of unlit passages beneath the stables and his ability to move easily through the darkness to help Kayley access the main hall from below. As she enters Arthur's hall, Ruber fights the invalid king. Arthur is losing.

Kayley cannot match her opponent physically, yet she does see a way to win by outwitting him. Kayley lures Ruber toward the stone from which Arthur first pulled Excalibur. With Garrett at her side, she puts into practice the tactic that he has taught her. Garrett stands before the stone. Ruber moves in for the kill. At the last possible moment, Kayley signals Garrett to jump out of the way. Ruber plunges the sword into the stone. As the rogue knight's evil nature comes in contact with the stone's innate goodness, a shockwave spreads over the land to reverse the Acme potion's effects, restore the king's health, and disintegrate the bad guy. Arthur pulls the sword from the stone again to demonstrate his complete recovery.

The final scenes reveal Kayley in her sparkling white investiture-cum-wedding gown. Acknowledging her daughter's wish to follow Lionel's path, Juliana gives her the knight's old shield as she moves across the hall toward the king and Garrett. Garrett and Kayley kneel before Arthur. He dubs them "knight" and "lady"—and not at all surprisingly honors Garrett before Kayley, despite her leading role in the rescue. Arthur then rather confusingly claims that they will both sit at the Round Table as "knights." Kayley's dream of knighthood comes true.

Arthur reflects on what this adventure has taught him: "that a kingdom's strength is not based on the strength of the king, but the strength of the people." For their parts, Kayley has learned much from Garrett and Garrett's time with her has allowed him to discover a few things about himself, most importantly that he cannot "stand alone" forever. Kayley blissfully turns to Garrett, "Is this everything you've ever wanted?" "Not quite everything," he replies, as the two kiss at last.

Cut to the heroes riding from Camelot on one horse, the "Just Knighted" sign on its rear. Kayley leads and Garrett sits behind her, both because the blind man cannot guide the horse and because Kayley has become as much of a strong heroine as she will ever be. We realize that she finds this strength, however, by learning to follow Garrett's teachings and apparently by marrying him. The audience gets the usual happy ending it expects.

In fact, the audience could have predicted the conclusion before the first reel rolled. The five lobby posters for *Quest for Camelot* told prospective viewers much of the story even before they took their seats: one composite shot of the principal virtuous characters, one of villainous Ruber, one of the transformed chicken/hatchet Bladebeak, one of Devon and Cornwall, and—as inseparably linked as the two-headed dragon—*one* of Garrett and Kayley. This last poster carried the caption: "A noble warrior and a brave girl find the magical sword." Try as she might, the best Kayley can manage in *Quest for Camelot* is to be "a brave girl," and only then when flying on the wings of and relegated to second billing after the film's "noble warrior."

Box office response was far less than Warner Bros. had hoped for the Feature Animation unit's first fully animated film. Although it cost an estimated $120 million to produce, ticket sales totaled only approximately $23 million domestically and another $15 million abroad according to figures reported on the *Internet Movie Database*. But merchandise sales helped boost the bottom line as Warner Bros. licensed the *Quest for Camelot* trademark widely. Garage-sale remnants of the marketing push can still be found today on eBay. From these eBay items, we see that older fans bought the soundtrack, porcelain collectible figurines, and cookie jars depicting Devon and Cornwall tussling over a snack. For the younger set, there were several books based on the film:

9. Four Roads to Camelot

An assortment of *Quest for Camelot* prizes distributed with Wendy's Kids' Meals in 1998 (photograph by Joel Salda).

a Scholastic novelization, a DC comic, a simplified-vocabulary reader, and a pop-up book. Children also enjoyed a video sing-along and played Gameboy and personal computer games nominally based on the film. They were enticed to dress in Kayley and Garrett costumes at Halloween, exchange *Quest for Camelot* cards on Valentine's Day, and celebrate birthday parties with an assortment of movie-themed plates, napkins, conical hats, and horns. They could wear *Quest for Camelot* tee shirts as they carried their matching lunchboxes to school, then play with Ruber action figures and Kayley dolls until they trundled off to bed clutching a Bladebeak plush toy. Wendy's won the contract to include *Quest for Camelot* trinkets in Kids' Meals. The summer's goodies included plastic miniatures of the stars (Kayley, Garrett, Devon and Cornwall, Bladebeak, and Griffin), a Go Fish card game, interlocking Viewmaster-style castle components that coaxed children to return to Wendy's for the additional parts needed to build an ever larger citadel and gain additional "views" within, and a leatherette "passport" portfolio filled with a map, "coins of the realm" bearing Arthur's likeness, an identification card with a space for "ye photo here," and a pocket guide to the film's "heroes" and "evil doers" that tellingly includes neither the inconsequential king nor his aged adviser.

A few weeks after *Quest for Camelot*'s premiere, Disney released its own strong heroine film, *Mulan*. In Hollywood's contest to deliver the next animated "brave girl"

Arthurian Animation

to the screen, Disney clearly won. *Mulan* sold as many tickets in its opening weekend as *Quest for Camelot* did in its entire three-month run.[14] *Quest for Camelot* was forgotten as it moved to bargain theaters and soon vanished. Max Howard, president of Warner Bros. Feature Animation, resigned. Warner's animation unit was reorganized. *Quest for Camelot* merchandise and the three also-ran direct-to-video releases that hitched their hopes to an unlucky star were shortly repriced for clearance. A steep wager on an animated Arthurian feature film turned out to be a losing bet.

CHAPTER 10

Where Lies Arthur? Arthurianimation Since 2000

Arthur, his court, and themes of the realm remain a cinematic staple. Since 2000, Anglo-American live-action feature films for theatrical, television, and increasingly direct-to-video release have included *Merlin: The Return* (Peakviewing Productions, 2000), *The Mists of Avalon* (Constantin Film/TNT, 2001), *Wheelmen* (Timberwolf Productions/Crossroads Productions, 2002), *King Arthur* (Touchstone Pictures, 2004), *Cup of My Blood* (X Ray Productions, 2005), *Tristan + Isolde* (Twentieth Century–Fox, 2006), a *Merlin's Apprentice* miniseries (Hallmark, 2006), *The Da Vinci Code* (Columbia, 2006), *The Last Legion* (Quinta Communications/Ingenious Film Partners, 2007), *Merlin and the War of the Dragons* (The Asylum, 2008), *Merlin and the Book of Beasts* (Front Street Pictures/Starz Media, 2010), *Avalon High* (Disney, 2010), *Adventures of a Teenage Dragonslayer* (Razor Sharp Productions, 2010), and *The Sorcerer's Apprentice* (Disney, 2010). An Australian-Canadian co-production offered two seasons of *Guinevere Jones* (Crawford Productions, 2002), the tale of a present-day adolescent girl who not only struggles with the typical angst of growing up but also must come to terms with the knowledge that she is the reincarnation of her famous namesake. Two other series have explored the early days of Arthur's realm in five seasons of the BBC1's fantasy drama of *Merlin* (Shine Limited, 2008–12) and a single season of premium cable's gritty *Camelot* (Starz Media, 2011). Farce has also continued as a popular avenue into the kingdom in two seasons of *Sir Gadabout: The Worst Knight in the Land* (Alibi Pictures, 2002–03) on Britain's youth-oriented CITV and six seasons ("livres") of rapid-fire satiric glimpses into *Kaamelott* (Alexandre Astier/M6, 2005–10) on France's M6.[1] Meanwhile, on the stage rather than the screen, *Spamalot* (in various runs starting in 2004) has kept the torch of *Monty Python and the Holy Grail* burning brightly.

Animated versions of the legend, however, have debuted at a slower pace than in the 1990s. *Quest for Camelot*'s disappointing box office warned studios that audiences had perhaps grown a bit weary again of Arthurianimation. Parallels can be drawn to a similar decline in Arthurian cartoons in the 1960s following the anemic reception granted *The Sword in the Stone*.

Since 2000, only two full-length animated Arthurian features have seen theatrical release—and it was necessary to look abroad for the first. Director Thierry Schiel's eighty-minute *Tristan et Iseut* (Oniria/Neuroplanet, 2001; released to European theaters in 2002 and later dubbed into English for a 2010 DVD-only rerelease under the title *Tristan & Isolde*), from studios based in France and Luxembourg, falls under the

Arthurian Animation

Arthurianimation rubric, even though King Arthur himself does not make an appearance. As in the 1999 French television series of *Tristan & Iseult: La légende oubliée* that helped develop a market for Schiel's film, this *Tristan et Iseut* also sets the famous love story in the Camelot-adjacent lands of Cornwall, Lyonesse, and Ireland. Again, several key incidents from the Tristan legend inform the storyline. Once more, these events appear in simplified, sanitized fashion: Tristan's departure from Lyonesse and arrival in Cornwall, the home of his uncle, the good King Mark; Anguish of Ireland's demand for an annual tribute of Cornish children to serve as slaves; the defeat of Anguish's champion, the Morholt, in single combat with the hero[2]; the poisoned wound that Tristan receives in the fight; Tristan's journey to Ireland for a cure; the syllable-reversing "Tantris" disguise that the hero adopts to conceal his identity from his healer, Iseut, daughter of Anguish and niece of the Morholt; the growing attraction between Tantris and Iseut, followed closely by his banishment when Tantris is revealed to be Anguish's enemy Tristan; and so on, through many events drawn from the medieval *Tristan* tales. These incidents are presented to the audience through a mix of animated action and the narration of a garrulous, know-it-all wood-sprite named Puck.

As in the legend, a love potion designed to bond Iseut to the king of Cornwall before their wedding comes into play and, also as in the legend, Tristan rather than Mark drinks the brew. *Tristan et Iseut* avoids the customary tragic denouement, however, in a clever revision in which Mark abdicates so that his nephew can become the Cornish king and therefore marry Iseut. With the marriage, the Irish tribute comes to an end. Cornwall and Ireland forge a lasting peace.

In the film's final moments, Puck tells us that the story is only *beginning* and that Tristan and Iseut still have "a few trips to make ahead of them." Yet whether their journeys might continue through branches of medieval *Tristan* narratives that follow the knight to Camelot and a seat at the Round Table cannot be said, because a voracious forest plant gobbles up the talkative wood-sprite before he can finish his tale.

Arthur played a significant role in the decade's second Arthurianimation feature film, director Chris Miller and co-director Raman Hui's 92-minute *Shrek the Third* (DreamWorks Animation, 2007). The young king, however, is not the film's star. In fact, he is billed *ninth* in the closing credits. This second major sequel in DreamWorks's lucrative *Shrek* franchise focuses primarily on the further Bildungsroman adventures of the eponymous ogre as he nervously prepares to become a father and — in a thematically related plotline — steers a diffident Arthur to the throne. Shrek's time with the teenage "Artie" allows both to grow and learn to accept their new responsibilities — Shrek as a dad and Artie as a king.[3]

Shrek the Third continues threads from the earlier films in the series. Fiona's father Harold, the Frog King of Far Far Away, has grown old and ill. Shrek and Fiona fill in for the ailing amphibian, an assignment Shrek dutifully yet reluctantly accepts. The heavy-handed ogre proves particularly ill-suited to the duties of court life. He (apparently) kills a knight during a dubbing ceremony. He sinks a ship while christening it. He lights a hall aflame. Yet as Harold's life slips away, he names maladroit Shrek his heir. (Although Shrek and Fiona are both described as "next in line" for the throne,

10. Where Lies Arthur?

Harold never considers putting Fiona in charge. Nor does the film explain why Harold's wife, the capable Queen Lillian, could not take the reins. Everyone in Far Far Away silently assents to the premise that Harold's successor must be male.) When Shrek protests that an ogre would not make a good king, Harold reveals that there lives one other possible heir: Arthur Pendragon, Fiona's cousin.

After Harold's death, Shrek sails to find Arthur. Meanwhile, in a second narrative thread, the opportunistic Prince Charming — still smarting from losing Fiona and the kingdom to the ogre in earlier *Shrek* installments — marshals an army of fairy tale "losers" (a *Cinderella* stepsister, the Wicked Witch, Captain Hook, Rumpelstiltskin, etc.) to help him seize the realm. A third thread, following Fiona and the film's other female principals (Queen Lillian, Rapunzel, Snow White, Sleeping Beauty, Cinderella, and the other *Cinderella* stepsister), keeps the action moving briskly albeit rather anarchically. Here, we concern ourselves primarily with the Arthurian storyline.

Shrek, Donkey, and Puss discover the future peers of the Arthurian kingdom at Worcestershire Academy, a Potteresque boarding school. Teenage Arthurian characters engage in diverse activities. Young "Mr. Percival" is learning to drive a coach across the courtyard. "Gwen" and a coterie of self-absorbed medieval Valley Girls are seeking their next dates:

> GWEN (to Shrek): This is, like, totally embarrassing, but my friend Tiffany thinkest thou vex her so soothly. And she thought perchance thou would wanna ask her to the Homecoming Dance, or something?
> SHREK (surprised): Uh, excuse me?
> GWEN: It's, like, whatever. She's just totally into college guys and mythical creatures and stuff. [GWEN pops her bubblegum to punctuate the sentence.]

Nearby, a large, aristocratic youth hones his jousting skills. With a blow of his lance, he effortlessly tosses a smaller boy far across the field. Shrek believes that he has surely found the next sovereign of Far Far Away. "Strong, handsome, face of a king," Shrek remarks, "Does Arthur look like a king, or what?" But the jousting patrician is revealed to be Lancelot, a class bully. His sparring muggins, we learn shortly, is "Artie," an unassuming teen who has long served as the butt of Worcestershire abuse.

Shrek soon locates Artie again at a school assembly. Before all Artie's classmates, Shrek delivers the message that brings him to Worcestershire:

> SHREK: You're the new king of Far Far Away.
> ARTIE (incredulously): What?
> LANCELOT (sneering): Ha, ha! Artie a king? More like the Mayor of Loserville!

The crowd laughs. Shrek assures Artie that it is not another joke at his expense, that the teen is truly heir to the throne — "the one and only," fibs the ogre. Artie takes advantage of the moment to chastise those who have made his school years miserable and, further, declare that he has always loved Gwen — a non sequitur for the film but an open secret known to everybody seated in the cineplex. In response to Artie's mortifying public disclosure, Gwen groans an "Ew!" Artie revels pompously in thoughts of his new power to reshape the world — until Shrek has heard enough and carries him bodily from the assembly.

Arthurian Animation

They set sail for Far Far Away. Shrek inexpertly moves into the role of surrogate father as he strives to convince Artie that the boy will be able to handle the duties that await him. Puss and Donkey counter with the many troubles that monarchs face each day. As Puss and Donkey's litany of famine, plague, and assassination grows, Artie's courage falters. To prevent their ship from continuing toward its destination, Artie grabs the wheel and wrecks the vessel. They are stranded in unknown territory. Shrek lectures Artie:

>SHREK: If you think this is getting you out of anything, well it isn't. We're heading back to Far Far Away one way or another, and you're going to be a father!
>ARTIE: What?
>DONKEY: You just said "father."
>SHREK: I said "king"! You're going to be king!

Shrek's verbal slip reveals that he too has unresolved issues about responsibilities that await him at home. Both Shrek and Artie will confront their problems with the help of the land's sole occupant, Merlin.

Shrek the Third's Merlin is a disheveled, comic character. An addled former Worcestershire magic teacher relieved of classroom duties after a "nervous breakdown" and currently a resident of a Neolithic tumulus, he leads his guests on a New Age journey of self-exploration to unveil their deepest fears. In the wizard's Fire of Truth ceremony, Shrek sees a baby carriage. The vision leads him to confide to Artie that he understands "what it's like to not feel ready for something. Even ogres get scared, you know, once in a while." For his part, Artie's vision of a father bird that abandons its son and leaves the forsaken hatchling terrified that it will fall from the nest reopens an old emotional

Merlin prepares to send Donkey, Puss, Shrek and Artie to Far Far Away in *Shrek the Third* (DreamWorks Animation, 2007).

wound: Artie's father "left" him, and he has lacked confidence in himself ever since. "Even my own dad knew I wasn't worth the trouble," Artie reflects. "He dumped me at that school the first chance he got and I never heard from him again." The ogre and the future king discover that they have much in common.

The next day, Shrek learns that during his absence from court, Charming has seized the throne. Fiona is in danger. Merlin transports the heroes to Far Far Away for a showdown. After a series of adventures, Shrek allows Charming to capture him in order to protect Artie's life, though not without hurting Artie's feelings in the process.

The final confrontation brings all three narrative threads and everybody to the stage — literally. We have learned that Charming turned to writing plays and acting after his failure to win the kingdom in *Shrek 2*. Thus it is in character that he plans to mount an operatic extravaganza for the citizens of Far Far Away — and no surprise that he intends to use the opportunity to kill Shrek during the performance. As Charming directs and stars as himself in the self-produced *It's a Happily Ever After, After All*, his many enemies swarm the stage. The battle teeters toward victory for Charming and his army of losers. Artie arrives unexpectedly and convinces the army to throw down its weapons — thanks, naturally, to a lesson about self-affirmation that Artie learned under Shrek's tutelage. But Charming refuses to surrender. He continues fighting until a prop tower crushes him. Artie's final moments on screen — still standing in front of the audience assembled for Charming's musical as *Shrek the Third* builds to a metatheatric mise en abîme — show the newly confident youth accepting the crown, the people's adulation, and the kingdom.

As the film ends, Shrek and Fiona return to their beloved swamp to begin to care for new baby triplets. Arthur is quickly forgotten by all but the fans of Arthuriana in the theater. The Lancelot and Gwen characters do not resurface after Worcestershire. Merlin returns briefly to reverse side effects of an imperfect spell, but he is inconsequential. The Arthurian narrative itself is subordinated throughout to Shrek's and Fiona's adventures. Questions linger. Why did Artie's father (brother to the Frog King? to Queen Lillian?) abandon him? Who is Artie's mother and what happened to her? Will the young Gwen, Lancelot, and Artie grow into their traditional roles? Will Percival ever earn his driver's license? Who is the "Bohort" (a variant spelling of the Arthurian "Bors") listed in the credits? No doubt such questions are not really meant to be asked. Despite the ostensibly direct engagement with Arthurianimation in *Shrek the Third*, Arthur and his future court remain shadowy figures on the edge of the *Shrek* corpus.[4]

Although Arthuriana rode into American theaters in 2007 only on Shrek's ogresized coattails, *Shrek the Third* may have been a sign of a new Arthurian resurgence percolating in recent years. Another indication that American animation studios were again testing the popularity of Arthurian themes appeared in directors Chris Renaud and Michael Thurmeier's 72-second Arthurian segment of the seven-minute "No Time for Nuts" (Blue Sky Studios/Twentieth Century–Fox Animation, 2006), a theatrical-style short released as a DVD bonus feature with *Ice Age: The Meltdown* (2006). Prehistoric squirrel-rat Scrat's unending, hyperkinetic, and always ultimately frustrated efforts to gather and safeguard acorns lead him to unearth a nut-shaped electronic device buried beneath the ice. As he examines the find, it energizes, sending Scrat's precious acorn to another time. He shakes the device angrily, causing it to activate again and again. Scrat finds himself beamed along a transtemporal journey to recover his dinner.

As Scrat and the acorn materialize at various points in time, every landing is filled with new perils. Chariots and lions at the Colosseum nearly kill Scrat. A French Revolution guillotine is poised to chop off his head. The *Titanic* bears down on an iceberg where he stands. Rockets ignite over his head. And so on, as the device keeps moving Scrat's meal just beyond his grasp.

In the cartoon's longest (and first) teleportation segment, the acorn lands under a teetering boulder. As Scrat struggles to extract it, he becomes aware of a glowing object (accompanied by the sound of a synthesized choir) in the forest clearing behind him: a sword in a stone. Scrat momentarily stands transfixed in awe, then realizes that the sword could be used as a tool to free the nut. He draws the sword with ease and holds it aloft triumphantly. A hail of arrows immediately descends upon him. As he flails the sword to defend himself—miraculously deflecting every dart—a lucky stroke dislodges the acorn trapped under the boulder. Scrat seizes his quarry. Meanwhile, the sword is forgotten on the ground as Scrat scurries up a tower and into a hole for safety—only to be fired from a cannon and back into another volley of arrows before jumping to another time, where the quest for the acorn begins anew.

"No Time for Nuts" does not explain its Arthurian allusions, yet it is clear that Scrat has landed in a conflict with the sword at its center. He who pulls the sword that heralds the next king—as Arthur does in legend and Scrat (apparently) does here—also becomes everybody's target. Perhaps we are to imagine Scrat falling unawares into the tumultuous interregnum between Uther and Arthur? The cartoon leaps manically forward before we can answer. In any event, Scrat has no interest in becoming a ruler. He thinks only as far as the next nut.

There have been no recent American animated television series prominently featuring the king and his court, but the legend has remained a source of inspiration at Canadian, British, French, and Japanese studios creating for the small screen. An Arthurian storyline wound through forty half-hour episodes of lead director Didier Pourcel's medieval fantasy adventure of *Xcalibur*. Produced at the Canadian and French units of Ellipse Animation (a.k.a. Ellipsanime) from 2000 to 2002 for Canada's YTV and later syndicated internationally, the motion-capture, CGI-animated series explored the complex, turbulent world surrounding the preteen[5] heir to the throne, Arthus. The king's French/English composite name—a conflation of the French "Artu"/"Artus" and English "Arthur"—and unorthodox orthography for his sword exemplify *Xcalibur*'s approach to the legend, where elements of the Arthurian story appear in a universe at once both familiar and strange.[6]

The son of murdered King Edwyn and "missing" Queen Lorna, Arthus is a relatively minor figure in a power struggle for control of Edwyn's Xcalibur, "the Sword of Justice." *Xcalibur*'s plot traces the shifting alliances and battles among many adversaries: the demon Kwodahn, usurping regent Bragan, warring sylphs of the enchanted forest of Broceliande, obscurely Eastern "Shogi" monks, seafaring Viking (?) "barbarians" who harry the land, and the sixteen-year-old Princess Djana who bears and protects the sword through much of the series. While everyone fights for or against the interests of the future king who will one day wield Xcalibur, Arthus himself makes only brief appearances and does so in fewer than half of the episodes.[7] His actions stir few ripples in the storyline.

Instead, the plot focuses on the exploits of three "outlaw" teenagers defending the naive heir from threats that he rarely recognizes. Djana, who gains possession of Xcalibur after Edwyn's death, leads the trio. She is accompanied by Herik, one of the last Shogi monks, whom the Grand Magus has entrusted with the multipurpose Book of Life that contains knowledge needed to heal wounds, generate holograms, perform DNA analysis, and watch over the kingdom via a surveillance system that recalls the Marauder's Map introduced in 1999's *Harry Potter and the Prisoner of Azkaban*. Tara, a "barbarian" (she prefers to be called a "woman of the sea"), completes the group as a brusque combatant whose demeanor and garb call to mind the contemporaneous *Xena: Warrior Princess*.

On the rare occasions that Arthus comes to the screen, the audience sees an innocent, duped, and sometimes petulant child. He would like to follow Edwyn's just ways, but with no parents to guide him, his wicked uncle Bragan easily steers him along darker paths to further Bragan's own agenda to the throne. Only very late in the series, as the heroes expose Bragan as Edwyn's killer, defeat Kwodahn, reunite the missing Queen Lorna with her son, and present Xcalibur to the future king, does the audience *begin* to see in the boy glimmers of the man he will one day become. Yet Arthus remains merely a child as we leave him, speaking to Lorna, with his parting words in *Xcalibur*: "Am I doing all right, Mother?"

Series originating on opposite sides of the English Channel have recently offered audiences a pair of zany impressions of the Arthurian world. Creator Jan Van Rijsselberge and director Jean-Christophe Roger's *Patates et dragons* (Alphanim/CINAR, 2003; *Potatoes and Dragons*) takes us to the Middle Ages for seventy-eight shorts originally broadcast on French television and then syndicated internationally. The affably unhinged King Hugo III presides over a small court of leguminous subjects in Potatoland, a "medieval" realm in which characters employ modern conveniences such as computers, cars, and telephones. With his daughter, jester, and wizard Merlin at his side, Hugo's days would be happy save for the kingdom's one menace: a dragon that wants to burn everything in sight. The series traces Hugo's unremittingly failed efforts to banish the beast. Although Hugo draws on Merlin's somewhat shaky talents and the services of "knights" passing through the kingdom, the dragon cannot be chased from Potatoland. Hugo does not realize that his daughter and jester have befriended the dragon and alert it to all impending threats.

In addition to Merlin's presence throughout the series, writer Jacques E. Bouchard's "Lancelot, chevalier de la chaise longue" ("Sir Lance a Lot, Knight of the Round Coffee Table" in the English dub) brings a knight from Arthurian legend to Potatoland. Lancelot's reputation as a valiant warrior gives Hugo hope for an end to his troubles.

But the vain, pink-armored, ascot-bedecked fop is far from what the king expects and needs. Further, Lancelot says that he will not even fight unless challenged first. (The jester then warns his dragon pal not to antagonize the visitor.) As Lancelot spends his days lazily lounging about the castle and regaling the court with grandiose tales and songs of his exploits, his welcome wears thin. The dragon at last unintentionally provokes a fight. Lancelot proves to be the coward that his demeanor has already telegraphed. The knight leaves the realm in shame. The dragon continues to harass Hugo as life returns to normal in Potatoland.

Across the channel, co-creators Paul Parkes and Will Ashurst's *King Arthur's Disasters* (Zenith Entertainment/Coolabi Production/Neptuno Films, 2005–06) aired on the United Kingdom's CITV in 26 half-hour episodes directed by Ed Bignell (season 1) and David Freedman (season 2). In the tradition of *Arthur! and the Square Knights of the Round Table* and *Alias the Jester*, a diminutive king strives to serve his considerably taller lady, for whom he will do whatever is asked. However, in *King Arthur's Disasters*, Arthur and Guinevere have not yet married—in fact, the imperious, materialistic princess will not even allow the ardent suitor through her doors.

Episodes follow an uncomplicated formula. The overblown voiceover of a narrator ("the shouty bloke," as Arthur calls him, speaking openly to the narrator throughout the series) cheekily sets each tale in Cornwall. From her balcony, Guinevere demands that the king bring her a present before they can wed. Arthur rides to Camelot to ask Merlin's help in procuring the desired item. After a quest that brings Arthur into contact with various "Dark Forces," Merlin's hit-or-miss efforts to aid the king, and encounters with rivals such as (another) vain Sir Launcelot, ballad-singing Robin Hood, and samurai-inspired Sir Martyn "of the East," Arthur obtains and delivers the gift—or, most often, an ersatz version of what Guinevere requested. She always rejects it. Defeated, Arthur can but wonder if his beloved will ever agree to marriage. At the conclusion of the last episode of the series, he wonders still, though her resolve appears to be weakening.

Comic, thumbnail allusions to Arthurian legend arise throughout the series. In "The Yodelling Dolphin of Kirkwall," Merlin prompts Arthur to recall that when Arthur and Launcelot were boys, it was "Launcelot who felt that he was the rightful king." A thought bubble opens over the king, flashing back to a memory of the wizard requiring claimants to try their hands at the sword in the stone to determine "the true king of England." Accompanied by a tune reminiscent of Survivor's "Eye of the Tiger," svelte Launcelot flexes his muscles as he walks to the stone. But unable to withdraw the sword, Launcelot is dismissed from competition. Short, stocky Arthur mocks Launcelot's failure, then moves forward to try his luck. Out of spite, Launcelot trips him, sending Arthur hurtling toward the stone. Arthur blindly grabs at the sword on his way to the ground. The sword comes free in his hand. Launcelot's legitimate protests about the "accident" notwithstanding, Merlin proclaims Arthur the king of the land. Arthur has been quietly chuckling about how he came to the crown ever since.

Many additional Arthurian characters and motifs are introduced, although always with a twist. Arthur has banished his sister "the Lady M" to France for tormenting him as a child. She appears in several episodes disguised as Sir Margaret, a swashbuckling outlaw knight. Arthur encounters the "old crone" Morgan le Fey, Sorceress of the Forest—but not his *kin*—in "The Bear Necessities." The king antagonizes the peace-loving, hippy Druids of Stonehenge in "Baa Baa Green Goat." He causes their temple to collapse into the ruins that we see today.[8] The restorative powers of "the misty Isle of Avalon" are revealed in "The Fountain of Youth." When Guinevere discovers her first gray hair, the king braves many dangers to fetch a vial of the fountain's waters. Yet by the time that he returns, Guinevere has already discovered the age-reversing effects of an ordinary bottle of dye. In "King of the Moon," cave paintings in the mountains of North Wales tell the story of the giant Reitho—a name and scenario loosely borrowed from Geoffrey of Monmouth's *Historia regum Britanniae* (X.3)—who conquers his opponents and makes "a cloak from their beards and a loincloth from their mustaches." Arthur inadvertently revives Reitho, but this time (contrary to Geoffrey's account) the king is no match for the giant. Arthur, Launcelot, Bors, Kay, Merlin, and Martyn bring the Round Table from Norway in "The Viking Venture." When Guinevere rejects the gift,[9] the king decides to keep it for himself rather than risk a perilous return to Viking lands. "And so it was," the narrator says, "that King Arthur's knights became the legendary knights of the Round Table." Playful, occasionally learned, and always irreverent, *King Arthur's Disasters* time and again dips into legend for wry jokes likely to put smiles on the faces of adults watching the show along with their children.

Arthurian themes have surfaced prominently in at least four recent Japanese series as well. Type-Moon's interactive, software-driven "visual novel" paved the way for 24 half-hour anime episodes of *Fate/stay night* (Studio Deen, 2006) broadcast on Japanese television and later syndicated internationally. Director Yuji Yamaguchi and writer Takuya Sato's series sought to present in animated form a subset of the many possible roads through the visual novel's adventures of the fifth Holy Grail War. This fifth war is only the latest clash in a recurring tournament that periodically pits seven teams against each other. Each team consists of a human Master (or "Magician") chosen by the Grail and a Servant (or "Knight") whom the Master summons from the spirits of all legendary heroes to fight at his or her side. The last Master or Servant to remain standing in the ensuing battle royale wins possession of the Grail.

Yet this particular Grail comes with attributes that distinguish it from the holy vessel that Arthurian knights often seek in medieval legend. Although *Fate/stay night*'s Grail offers limitless power, it also grants the possessor whatever he or she desires, be it good or evil. Its energy can annihilate entire cities and even the Grail itself can be destroyed, as occurred at the end of the fourth Holy Grail War. It is an object of power stripped almost entirely of its conventional Christian and medieval Arthurian spiritual significance, a vessel more fitting for an Indiana Jones adventure than for Chrétien's Perceval.

It is through Shirou, an orphaned teenage schoolboy who becomes a Master as the series commences, that *Fate/stay night* advances its Arthurian storyline. Without understanding how he does it, Shirou summons as his Servant a teenage female knight-warrior called Saber, a generic name for the sword-wielding class of heroes in the tale's mythos. Her true identity remains a mystery, however, until halfway through the series. Episodes 12 and 13 reveal that her invisible sword is called Excalibur (also "Caliburn") and Saber, when she first lived, was Arturia Pendragon (also "King Arthur"), the female ruler of medieval Britain.

Master Shirou and Servant Saber experience several shared dreams that open windows into an Arthurian world drawn principally from the opening and closing sections of Malory's *Le Morte Darthur*. Familiar scenes include pulling the sword from the stone, as an old man (presumably Merlin) counsels Arturia (episode 13); the revelation that Excalibur's missing scabbard is more important than the sword, because the scabbard grants the bearer invincibility (episode 16)[10]; a decisive battle between Arturia and her son on a hilltop, surrounded by a field of dead warriors (episode 21)[11]; and Arturia's orders to Bedivere (also a woman)—who does not hesitate to follow the king's command as the parallel character does in *Le Morte Darthur*—to return Excalibur to the waters of the Lady of the Lake, followed by the start of the king's long sleep in Avalon (episode 24). Although a viewer may not need to know *Le Morte Darthur* well to follow *Fate/stay night*'s Arthurian storyline, the allusions can be misunderstood by those who come to the series without having read Malory's romance. Comments posted to Internet message boards often construe Arturia's sleep as her *death*—an unlikely interpretation for viewers who come to the series with Malory as their guide to the legend.[12]

As the injured Arturia drifts in and out of consciousness in the final episode, she raises the mindbending notion that Saber's struggle in the fifth Holy Grail War and the love that she feels for her Master Shirou have perhaps been nothing more than the elaborate, delirious *dream* of a wounded medieval king. If true, Saber, Shirou, the Holy Grail Wars, and all modern events recounted in the series evanesce to hallucinatory figments, Arturia's vision of a *future* time in an inverted *Connecticut Yankee* scenario. Yet, as with Twain's similarly fevered Boss in *Connecticut Yankee*'s final chapter, Arturia is eager to return to the dream. "My slumber this time might be a bit long," she tells Bedivere, as she lapses off again to pursue the vision and *Fate/stay night* comes to a close.[13]

By contrast with *Fate/stay night*'s thoughtful and intriguing attention to Arthurian legend, director Goro Taniguchi and writer Ichiro Okouchi's *Code Geass: Lelouch of the Rebellion* (Sunrise, 2006–08) only narrowly offered the minimum criteria necessary for Arthurianimation. Despite a plentiful and promising assortment of familiar *names* introduced into fifty half-hour episodes spread over two seasons, the series

Arturia Pendragon (Saber) in *Fate/stay night* (Studio Deen, 2006).

10. Where Lies Arthur?

failed to developed coherent *themes* that might produce an Arthurian storyline. The series flirts with Arthuriana throughout: robotic mechwarrior "knightmare frame" exoskeletons named "Lancelot," "Gawain," "Gareth," "Galahad" (with its huge "Excalibur" sword), "Percival," "Tristan," and "Mordred"; an elite battle squadron of "Glaston Knights" and another called the "Knights of the Round"; a weapons research team designated "Camelot"; the flying battle cruiser "Avalon"; and a recurring stray cat named "Arthur." Yet these names are divorced from their legendary associations. If, for instance, the mechwarrior Gawain were instead to be called Mordred, the story that *Code Geass* tells would remain unchanged. It seems that the Arthurian nomenclature has been introduced only because of the contemporaneous popularity of *Fate/stay night*.

A slender yet amusing Arthurian thread casually meandered through director Takuya Igarashi and co-writers Akatumi Yamatoya and Megumi Shimizu's 51 half-hour episodes of *Soul Eater* (Bones, 2008–09), based on Atsushi Okubo's manga of the same title. At the simplest level, it is also a story of several teenage masters-in-training ("Meisters" or "Technicians") and their evolving servant-weapons ("Partners") in a battle to protect the world. But where *Fate/stay night* struck melancholy chords, *Soul Eater* finds laughter. Among the many weapons that the Meisters encounter in their training at the Death Weapon Meister Academy, they encounter the insufferably supercilious Excalibur. This potential servant-weapon can become a peerless golden sword capable of splitting the cosmos, yet it prefers to manifest itself in animal form: a penguin-like figure outfitted with top hat, ruffed collar, waistcoat, and cane.[14] The preposterous appearance accords well with Excalibur's personality. Throughout the series, the sword (in its animal form) endlessly spins overblown, improbable yarns in celebration of alleged past glories. No one believes the tales that Excalibur tells.

Three episodes (9, 17, and 32) showcase the Arthurian character/weapon.[15] In the first, a library book entitled *Excalibur* leads Meisters Black Star and Death the Kid to a fairy cave behind a waterfall. They hope to find "the Holy Sword" that makes a hero of the Meister who pulls it "from the ground." According to legend, "someone who obtained Excalibur in the past went on to become a mighty king." But upon arriving at the cave, the young Meisters are surprised to discover that *anyone* can draw the sword—easily. The possessor of the sword, however, must agree to its outlandish terms: listening to nonsensical rants about Excalibur's importance throughout history, adhering to one thousand quirky stipulations that the Partner sets for its Meister, and being ceaselessly tongue-lashed as a "Fool!" Appalled at the prospect of binding themselves to such a life, the Meisters push the sword back into the earth and leave the cave. One observes sarcastically, "Anyone who would put up with him *is* a hero!"

In episode 17, when studious Meister Ox Ford comes to the fairy cave, *Soul Eater* continues the story of "the mighty king" who once partnered with Excalibur. Excalibur treats Ox Ford to absurd tales of its stage performances and crime-solving for Sherlock Holmes, then turns to an adventure from the time "just after my legend began in the twelfth century, when I accompanied the Meister King Arthur on an expedition to Rome." The scene moves to Arthur standing at the edge of a bluff. He is alone with Excalibur (in animal form). A sizable Roman force approaches on the plain below.

ARTHUR: Facing an army of this magnitude will be arduous, Excalibur.
EXCALIBUR: Saying such a thing isn't like you, Arthur. You mustn't lose heart.
ARTHUR (hesitantly): Excalibur....
EXCALIBUR: The knights of the Round Table never give up, no matter what. You must remember that. You swore an oath.
ARTHUR: Of course, you're right. I forgot myself. My comrades are depending on me.
EXCALIBUR: We fight on for their sake.
ARTHUR: Yes, we fight for them, Excalibur. Will you lend me your strength now?
EXCALIBUR (changing to a sword): Of course!

Galvanized and emboldened by his Partner, Meister Arthur charges down the hill. The outcome of the seemingly hopeless battle between the king and thousands of Roman soldiers is not revealed. Instead, Excalibur's narrative trails off: "And thus my journey with King Arthur continued on...."

When Ox Ford notes inconsistencies in the Holy Sword's description of itself (as singer, sleuth, king's confidant, and so on) from one tale to the next, Excalibur silences him with a barrage of non sequiturs, more untenable fables, a vacuous song and dance, a recitation of the many conditions that Excalibur sets for its possessor, and a reminder that the young Meister is a "fool!" Yet because Ox Ford has at least *listened* to the thousand stipulations, Excalibur changes from penguin form to sword: "You are chosen! It shall all be yours! Victory and glory! ... You shall rule the world, reigning above all others as a mighty warrior-king! So let us go forth together, for victory and for glory!" Ox Ford unexpectedly plunges the sword into the earth. He explains that he already has a Partner. He journeyed to the cave solely to gather information for a school report. Besides, Excalibur's tales have convinced Ox Ford to find another topic for the assignment. "You're lame," the Meister declares, "So forget it."

In episode 32, Meister Hero, a meek, "miserable loser" who hopes to change his life by allying himself to an invincible Partner, agrees to all Excalibur's terms. Hero swiftly becomes as overbearing as his Partner, using his newfound powers to invade a girls' locker room, lift girls' skirts, bully other students, and defeat the Academy's three strongest Meisters. Meanwhile, Excalibur continues recounting unbelievable exploits, singing the brainless tune from episode 17, and imposing each of the one thousand conditions on Hero. The grateful Meister cheerfully endures everything. But one day Excalibur suffers a sneezing fit that triggers Hero's fierce germophobia: "Sneezing's gross. Spit, snot go flying. It goes everywhere. I can't stand it! Seriously, the damn thing would be better off dead!" With the bond between Meister and Partner shattered, Hero returns Excalibur to the cave. The fairies are not happy to have it back.

Excalibur returns to the storyline at the end of *Soul Eater*'s run. In episodes 46–51, Excalibur (in animal form) resurfaces for several cameo appearances to remind various Meisters, Partners, and Academy teachers that they continue to be "Fools!" Just when the Holy Sword's self-professed powers would be most useful — as the forces of good face off against the forces of evil for a fight to the finish — Excalibur stops seeking a Meister. Perhaps the Holy Sword has learned at last that no one wants it as a Partner? Perhaps it has no true power to offer and all its alleged accomplishments are merely lies? Regardless of the answers, a viewer could well conclude that Arthur's legendary sword has no part to play in the final battle. Despite Excalibur's renown in the Western tradition, *Soul Eater* intriguingly asserts that the weapon is finally no more than an inconsequential windbag endlessly embroidering fabricated stories about itself.

As was the case with *Fate/stay night*, software-driven storylines earlier in the decade played a large role in developing an audience for 26 half-hour anime episodes of *Tears to Tiara* (White Fox/Aquaplus, 2009). Directors Tomoki Kobayashi and Masahiko Nakada and writer Toko Machida's series took an unconventional approach to the legend with an Arthurian narrative that draws from both Celtic myth and Roman pseudo-history. The series traces the emotional and martial growth of teenage Arthur, First Warrior of the Gael clan and son of the dead Elf King Pwyll, as he rises to power in Albion, a land ravaged by internal tribal warfare and Roman colonization. His adventures introduce a diverse cast of allies: his priestess sister Riannon, the apostate "Demon King" Arawn from the Celtic otherworld of Annwn, busty Gaelic guerrilla fighter Morgan,[16] expert swordswoman and Roman defector Octavia, minstrel and later king of the Brigantes clan Taliesin, sledgehammer-wielding "mine elf" Rathy, Avalonian "house elves" Limwris and Ermin, sea sprite Llŷr, and a mystical sage named Ogam. From Arthur's base in elf-magically protected Avalon Castle, he and his companions combat rival clans, the colonizing efforts of the Roman Empire, and the supernatural Council of White Spirits of Annwn that seeks to obliterate not merely Arthur but all Earth's creatures.[17]

An intricate plot moves freely from slapstick interludes to battlefield engagements to philosophical debates concerning free will, fate, and the connections that exist between the unknowable high god Watos, the ambiguously angelic or demonic Council of White Spirits, and the human and elfin beings of the Earth. The Arthurian legend is thus not as much the *subject* of this series as it is a *springboard* to explore many contemporary issues. Although traditional motifs such as Arthur's round meeting table and a sword in a stone[18] figure into the plot, these elements often seem little more than background details in *Tears to Tiara*'s inquiry into far-reaching political and metaphysical uncertainties.

In the lingering shadow cast by *Quest for Camelot*, American producers have remained understandably reluctant to offer series-length excursions to Camelot. *Glancing* references to Arthur's realm, however, have cropped up in episodes of many series. Fleeting allusions—often introduced for comic or ironic effect—have surfaced unexpectedly in the midst of otherwise non–Arthurian half- and quarter-hour installments of two seasons of *Mike, Lu & Og* (Kinofilm/Cartoon Network, 1999–2001); *Sheep in the Big City*'s "Baaa-ck in Time!" (Curious Pictures, 2000); *South Park*'s "It Hits the Fan" (Braniff Productions, 2001); *The Brak Show*'s "Brakstreet: Men in the Band" (Wild Hare Studios, 2002); *Home Movies*'s "The Wizard's Baker" (Burns & Burns Productions/Soup2Nuts, 2004); *The Fairly OddParents*'s "Beach Bummed!" (Frederator, 2005); *Family Guy*'s "The King Is Dead," "Jungle Love," and "Bango Was His Name, Oh!" (Fuzzy Door Productions, 2000, 2005, 2006); *Ugly Americans*'s "An American Werewolf in America" (Tookie Wilson Productions/Augenblick Studios/Cuppa Coffee Studios, 2010); *MAD*'s "Twigh School Musical" (Warner Bros., 2011); *American Dad*'s "Season's

Beatings" (Fuzzy Door Productions, 2011); *Regular Show*'s "Eggscellent" (Cartoon Network Studios, 2012); and no doubt others as well.

In these episodes, allusions to legendary touchstones often pass with lightning speed as writers and animators gesture toward what they trust is the common knowledge of a shared cultural heritage acquired in the classroom, from movies, television, and the Internet, and from reading material of all kinds. Item, *Mike, Lu & Og* introduces the recurring female character Launcelot, a silent pet turtle utterly devoted to—and sometimes savior of—her imperious mistress Princess Lu. Item, *Sheep in the Big City*'s General Specific, believing that a time machine has teleported him to the past, draws a sword from a stone and proclaims himself king of England. He is in fact at a modern Renaissance fair. Security guards haul the supposed lunatic away. Item, Chef and the boys of *South Park* travel to "the land of castles, knights, and kings"—the Excalibur Casino and Hotel in Las Vegas—to help the Knights of Standards and Practices stop a plague and a dragon spawned by widespread overuse of a "curse word"/"word of curse": "shit." Item, *The Brak Show*'s high school rap contest presents Marlon, who materializes onstage to perform "for the wizards in the cazzazle." Judges open a trapdoor to drop Marlon from the stage after only one verse. Item, *Home Movies*'s Coach McGuirk tries in vain to barter his "exact replica" of Excalibur for beer and chips. No one wants the "cutlery" that he purchased from a shopping channel, despite McGuirk's tepid and unproven assurances that "it has magical powers." Item, *The Fairly OddParents*'s Cosmo and Wanda are searching the beach for their missing fairy wands when Cosmo unearths "*another* Holy Grail." A halo floats above the clearly labeled chalice, but he casually tosses it aside. Item, *Family Guy*'s Brian auditions for a community theater production of *The King and I* with his rendition of "If Ever I Would Leave You" from the 1967 *Camelot* ("The King Is Dead"). Item, *Family Guy*'s cutaway scene introducing Peter's ancestor, King Arthur Griffin ("Jungle Love"):

> MAIDEN: Oh, Arthur, if you are able to draw the sword from the stone and prove to me you truly are the sole king of Camelot, I will make love to you right here in the clearing.
> KING: What if I could just move it an inch? Will you touch me?

Item, *Family Guy*'s Peter recalls the time that he went on a "last crusade to find the Holy Grail" à la Indiana Jones. He correctly identified a coffee mug with "Jesus" on it as the sacred vessel ("Bango Was His Name, Oh!"). Item, when *Ugly Americans*'s boozing warlock Leonard Powers resigns from his job at New York City's Department of Integration, he learns that he must relinquish his Excalibur-in-the-stone "magic pen set" desk accessory and Merlin mousepad, too. Item, in a fifteen-second *MAD* sketch inserted in an unrelated episode, a knight tugs repeatedly on a sword in a stone. His frustration grows until the stone begins to putt as if powered by a small engine. The triumphant knight rides his newly mechanized stone—as if it were a lawnmower—out of the frame. Item, on *American Dad*, Roger's plastic "pimp cup" is revealed to be the Holy Grail in a plot that motions toward *The Omen*, *The Da Vinci Code*, and Indiana Jones movies. Item, in another nod to *Indiana Jones and the Last Crusade*, *Regular Show* characters Rigby and Mordecai attempt to consume a restaurant's twelve-egg, chili-

10. Where Lies Arthur?

cheese omelet in under an hour to win a trucker's hat emblazoned "I'm Eggscellent." As Mordecai finishes the meal, he is transported to a room filled with various helmets, crowns, and caps guarded by a medieval knight who tells him to choose correctly or die. Mordecai selects the prized trucker's hat and then leaves—at which point we learn that the guard has an entire closet filled with identical hats. The episodes in which these Arthurian references emerge make no attempt to explain the allusions or integrate them meaningfully into larger storylines. Context-free Arthuriana is the punch line to a joke never fully told. Whether a particular free-floating allusion stirs a knowing smile or merely a puzzled head-scratch differs for every viewer.[19]

While many shows have taken their Arthurian potshots, a few comedy series have occasionally thrust deeper into Arthuriana, though perhaps rarely along expected routes. Marlon returned with (brother?) Merlin at his side in "The Time Machine" (a.k.a. "Diff'rent Braks"; Wild Hare Studios, 2002), an eleven-minute episode co-written by Jim Fortier, Andy Merrill, and Pete Smith for Cartoon Network's *The Brak Show*. When Dad tells Brak that he cannot go to his favorite restaurant because he skipped the previous night's homework to play video games instead, Brak and Zorak time-travel a day into the past to remind themselves to study. Many trips through a time machine, however, inevitably lead in each iteration to the same result: every Brak and every Zorak play video games and no schoolwork is ever done. As their home fills with more and more time-looped Braks and Zoraks, the original Brak wishes that homework had never been invented at all. Zorak proposes one last journey through time to solve the problem at its source.

Cut to a castle. Merlin and less-talented Marlon are competing to produce new inventions. Their creations materialize as the wizards announce them:

MERLIN: The microscope.
MARLON: The flying lawnmower.
MERLIN: Penicillin.
MARLON: The golden shower head.
MERLIN: The combustion engine.
MARLON: Behold, the double-beer hat! Check it out!

Brak and Zorak arrive to tell Merlin and Marlon that one of their inventions has "destroyed the future." Posing as one of "the Presidents of the Future," Zorak describes the devastating effects of homework: starvation, suffering, and streets "filled with wickedness and filth." Merlin says that although he was "just about to invent" homework, Zorak's prophecies have convinced him not to unleash such a scourge upon civilization. Moreover, Merlin and Marlon decide to destroy *all* their inventions to prevent unintended harm to the future.

Brak and Zorak return to their own time. They are delighted to learn that homework no longer exists, yet their tinkering with history has changed many other things as well. No one has heard of Brak's favorite restaurant. In fact, they now live in an altered world where one can be "snatched up by a gigantic terrible bird and torn limb from the limb on a lonely mountaintop," as Dad explains in his not-quite-fluent English.

Arthurian Animation

Rather than use a time machine to voyage to Arthur's realm, Timmy called on his fairy godparents for transport in "Knighty Knight" (Frederator, 2002), a twelve-minute episode directed by Sarah Frost and Butch Hartman and co-written by Hartman, Steve Marmel, and Jack Thomas for Nickelodeon's *The Fairly OddParents*. Young Timmy's excitement runs high as the fairies provide horse and armor for a day of role-playing fun at a local reenactment fair, the 595th Camelot Festival. He approaches a tall teenager dressed in armor:

TIMMY: Greetings, fellow knight! Shall'st we quest for the Grail?
TEEN: Um, I don't think so. I'm just here to point to where the Porta-Potties are.

To make matters worse, the teenager is soon exposed as just a small boy standing on a ladder, behind a piece of wood painted to look like armor.

Timmy's initial burst of enthusiasm rapidly sours to disappointment. The Festival lacks authenticity at every turn. Temporary scaffolding supports flat façades of castle towers. A vendor hawks Cleaning Wizard spray that pledges to tackle even manure "and make almost all of it go all away." The promise of a dragon offers only a flimsy sideshow attraction: a dog with a papier mâché shell on its head. Timmy wants something better: "I wish we were all in the real Middle Ages." "Here it's just called The Ages," fairy Cosmo says, as he whisks Timmy to the fifteenth century.

But Timmy has made a mistake in formulating the wish: his parents also travel with him to the past. Mom and Dad are shortly snatched away by a real dragon as

Merlin urges Artie Leibowitz to pull Excalibur from the stone in "Knighty Knight," *The Fairly OddParents* (Frederator, 2002).

10. Where Lies Arthur?

Timmy's wish for "authenticity" takes shape. Timmy's quest to save his parents now begins to transect a hodgepodge of Arthurian storylines. Timmy pulls Excalibur ("the big, glowing, magical sword over there") from a stone. He finds the Holy Grail ("a cup"). He helps wimpy, near-sighted Artie Leibowitz gain the confidence and corrective lenses needed to defeat the dragon and thus save Timmy's parents. Finally, Timmy exposes Artie's "uncle" Merlin as a gold-digging charlatan who backs Artie's rise to power solely for the wealth it will bring him. Before returning to the present, Timmy insures that the legend will develop along established lines. He urges that "the Shining Blade of Leibowitz" instead be called "Excalibur" and Artie's "pentagonal ottoman" be replaced with a round table.

The 595th Camelot Festival's hokum paled by comparison with a similar reenactment celebration depicted in "Renaissance" (Burns & Burns Productions/Soup2Nuts, 2002), a half-hour episode of Cartoon Network's *Home Movies* from director André Lyman and co-writers Bill Braudis and Brendon Small. Viewers familiar with these fairs easily recognize the targets being skewered.[20] There is an overzealous teacher and "county chairman of all medieval activities" who speaks—and insists on badgering others to use—an "Elizabethan dialect" that he has not himself mastered. Vendors' booths offer "Meat for Thee," "Medieval Wands," and like products purportedly of yore. An ahistorical mishmash of makeshift-costumed participants, representing diverse eras and regions, wander the fairgrounds. A stereotypical nerd (role-playing as "a chaotic, neutral, eighth-level, half-elf, ranger illusionist") passes through scenes calling attention to historical inaccuracies. At one point he vehemently argues that scrimshaw could not have been used in a "wand of summoning" because there was no whale-hunting in King Arthur's day. Calmer voices note that the Porta-Potti ("Pee-Pod"), cell phones, and curly fries also did not exist in the Middle Ages. One final assault on the fair's verisimilitude comes from just across an open field where sci-fi aficionados and their robots are enjoying their own celebration—"a huge conflict of interest for geeks," one boy observes.

The teacher/county chairman, dressed in a robe and conical hat as Merlin,[21] has hired several of his students to portray medieval characters for the fair's afternoon entertainment, a rock opera entitled *The Tragedy of King Arthur and Robin Hood*. The intentionally absurd musical combines elements from both legends, placing together on stage characters from different periods who should never in fact meet—thus ironically mirroring the motley fairgoers themselves. In act 1, Robin (à la Little John) defeats Arthur on a footbridge and then befriends him. Act 2 reveals that Robin remains a thief as he steals Arthur's treasure and (à la Launcelot) his "girlfriend" Guinevere. When a dragon kidnaps Guinevere, the two heroes put aside their differences long enough to rescue her. In act 3, Robin and Arthur duel for possession of Guinevere. Yet before a victor can be decided, the sci-fi fans invade the "Renaissance" fair. The play and both festivals collapse into mayhem.

German children's book author Knister was the storyteller behind Louise Geraghty's script for the half-hour "Lilli und König Artus" (Trixter Film/Magma Films/Vivatoon, 2007; "Lilly and King Arthur") on *Hexe Lilli* (*Lilly the Witch* in anglophone markets), a series first broadcast on Germany's public television network WDR and later syndicated internationally. In this episode, Lilli's little dragon sidekick Hector has a dream in which the two help an adult King Arthur defeat five sinister knights and then are invited to join his court. Upon waking, Hector convinces Lilli that they must make an actual journey to the past to meet the king.

Their transport spell appears to have gone awry, however, when they arrive at a crumbling castle in the Middle Ages. Lilli investigates a sculpture garden near the castle, passing "do not touch" warning signs as she explores the grounds. An addled and distracted Merlin enters and inexplicably tosses a bucket of water on her as she nears a throne made of stone. Merlin cannot tell her anything about Arthur and says that the king has been away for a long time.[22] He returns to carving stones for the garden.

Lilli and Hector's quest for the king brings them to a nearby training camp for knights. An arrogant young Launcelot runs the operation with an iron hand. They soon find Arthur, too — not the mighty king of Hector's dream but a poor, modest page responsible for the camp's laundry. Arthur also serves as the object of Launcelot's surly abuse. Lilli encourages Arthur to strive for higher goals and to believe in himself. She and Hector pledge to help.

Lilli's magic provides Arthur with a horse and armor so that he can begin to train in the woods outside the camp. Relying on knowledge gained from watching action films such as *The Karate Kid* and *Star Wars*, Hector instructs Arthur in swordplay, horsemanship, jousting, and archery. Launcelot belittles Arthur's training. He continues to believe Arthur useful only for menial tasks, but the other boys begin to envy Arthur's training drills because they are much more fun than Launcelot's stern regimen. "Knights never have fun," Launcelot insists. While Launcelot keeps ridiculing Arthur, it is becoming clear to all that Arthur has untapped talents. Lilli boosts his spirits again when she tells him that he can become the greatest knight ever.

On a return visit to Merlin's garden and a second bucket-dousing for again nearing the prohibited sculptures, Lilli learns that the king of the land will be revealed only after he passes several trials. It is suggested that one such trial somehow involves a garden sculpture of a stone with a sword planted in it. Meanwhile, just beyond the camp, Arthur is becoming a proficient knight. Yet when he petitions Launcelot to be allowed to demonstrate that he has mastered the skills requisite for knighthood, Launcelot turns to underhanded tactics to sabotage the aspirant's attempts to prove himself. Arthur ultimately triumphs over Launcelot's trickery — and dazzles the other boys, who slowly shift their allegiance from Launcelot to Arthur. Arthur impresses Lilli and Hector as well when he saves them from being crushed by a runaway cart. The unassuming lad they met at the start of their visit has become a confident young man.

Despite Arthur's evident fitness for knighthood, Launcelot still insists that he has failed the tryout. When other boys rise in support of Arthur, Launcelot decides to give him one impossible test: enter Merlin's garden without being soaked by the old man. As Arthur explores the garden, toying with the odd sculptures, he innocently draws the sword from the stone. Merlin arrives at this moment, sees what Arthur has done, and drops his bucket. Although Arthur tries to return the sword to the stone — as if having

10. Where Lies Arthur?

done something wrong—Merlin kneels and addresses him as "Your Majesty," since Merlin has long known that only the true king could pull the sword. The sword shimmers in Arthur's hands. Merlin brings some of the other sculptures to life to celebrate the event.

Merlin sounds a trumpet to summon all adult knights to the castle. With Arthur seated on the stone throne over which Merlin has been keeping watch, each knight steps forward to pledge allegiance to the new sovereign. As Lilli sees that the king will no longer need her assistance and prepares to leave, she spies a stone round table in the sculpture garden. She suggests that when Arthur's knights gather together, they meet at such a table. Launcelot and his few remaining followers try one last time to assert their authority, but King Arthur will not allow it. Lilli and Hector return to the present. They open a book about King Arthur and his knights of the Round Table, discovering proof of what they set in motion.

After nearly a decade of silence on Arthurian matters—another mark of *Quest for Camelot*'s chilling effect—*The Simpsons* have again begun to tease Fox audiences with comic allusions to the realm. In "Love, Springfieldian Style" (Gracie Films, 2008), Marge lists famous lovers of the past and present. These couples include "Romeo and Juliet, Arthur and Guinevere, [and] Brangelina." In an episode sparked by strains from Peter Jackson's 1994 *Heavenly Creatures*, the imaginations of Lisa and new friend Juliet transform the abandoned Clam-elot Seafood restaurant[23] into the mythical realm of Equalia in "Lisa the Drama Queen" (2009). Mrs. Krabappel works through a midlife funk in "Bart Gets a Z" (2009) by reading *The Answer*, a self-help system "discovered by the philosophers of ancient Greece, who hid it under a rock, where it was discovered by the knights of King Arthur, who placed it in a bottle and set it in the ocean, where it was found by Pat Sajak." The opening couch gag in "The Ten-Percent Solution" (2011) has Homer failing to pull a sword from the sofa, only to be bested by Ned, who draws it easily as the camera zooms to the inscription—"Property of Ned Flanders"—and Homer grumbles with resignation. Again, whether such references are funny or non sequiturs depends upon knowledge that the viewer brings to the episode, because the allusions have meaning only in an unspoken context that the writers do not supply.

As they have since the 1970s, animated series based on comic book superheroes have also contributed to contemporary revisionist Arthurianimation. Four action-adventure episodes featuring DC Comics properties along-

Clam-elot Seafood, the home of Equalia, in "Lisa the Drama Queen," *The Simpsons* (Gracie Films, 2009).

side Arthurian characters have premiered since 2000. All explore Morgan's schemes to gain a crown for her son or herself.

Director Butch Lukic and writer Keith Damron's "A Knight of Shadows" (Warner Bros., 2002), two half-hour episodes of Cartoon Network's *Justice League*, resumed and reworked the Jason Blood/Etrigan storyline that also appeared in 1998's "The Demon Within." This time, the tale begins as Blood, portrayed as Morgan le Fey's lover in this episode, betrays his fellow Arthurian knights by allowing the witch's troops into Camelot. Once inside, Morgan promptly double-crosses and poisons him. She reveals that she needed his assistance only to clear a path to Arthur's throne for her teenage son Mordred. As Camelot falls, Merlin imposes a curse on Blood for aiding Morgan. The wizard extends the traitor's life yet binds him to the hellspawn Etrigan, the manifestation of Blood's uncontrolled passion, his "inner demon."

The narrative jumps forward in time to Gotham City. Batman is investigating a robbery at an antiquarian bookstore as Blood arrives. Blood explains that the injured owner is "an expert in Arthurian lore" and Morgan has interrogated the man to the brink of death. She seeks the location of the Philosopher's Stone, "a gem from the hilt of Excalibur and the true source of the sword's fabled power." Blood continues: "When Camelot fell, Merlin was able to hide the Philosopher's Stone from her. Now she's returned to track it down again.... With it she can resurrect Camelot and place her son Mordred on the throne."

The search for the Stone ultimately carries Morgan, Mordred, and members of the Justice League to the mansion of Harv Hickman, an erstwhile archaeologist who has mounted the Stone on his bed in order to enjoy a lifestyle to rival (it is alliteratively implied) Hugh Hefner's. Wonder Woman cannot contain her disbelief: "Let me understand this. You possess the most powerful object in the world and yet all you wished for is money and women?!" The superheroes takes possession of the Stone, but Morgan then uses sorcery to seduce Leaguer J'onn into stealing it for her.

On Halloween, as Morgan waits for J'onn to deliver the Stone, she casts spells that change modern London into a medieval realm suitable for her son's reign. J'onn comes to realize, however, that Morgan can never truly fulfill her pledge to restore his annihilated homeworld and family; the past cannot be recaptured, no matter how much he desires it. J'onn crushes the Stone that would have sustained Morgan's transformation spell. London is restored. Mordred turns to Morgan, "Have we lost, Mother?" "Only this battle, my son," she replies, "but not the war." They vanish. In the final frames we see Blood walking out of Gotham and up a hazy hill of memories toward Camelot.

Morgan's war continued in director Joaquim Dos Santos and writer Henry Gilroy's half-hour "Kid Stuff" (Warner Bros., 2004) on Cartoon Network's *Justice League Unlimited*. Mordred seethes with tweenage petulance from the opening moments:

> MORDRED: This better be worth it, Mother. I mean it!
> MORGAN: If the legends are true, it will be.
> MORDRED: You've been saying stuff like that for, like, centuries. Nothing ever changes!
> MORGAN: Everything's changed — except you, Mordred — and that's because I want you to still be young when I give you your kingdom.
> MORDRED: I wanna be king *now*!

10. Where Lies Arthur?

In this episode, Morgan is scheming to grant Mordred a crown with power derived from the font of all sorcery, the Amulet of First Magic. Mordred, however, has plans of his own — plans that do not include his mother. Seizing the Amulet, he declares himself king of a world in which Morgan and other adults cannot tell him what to do: "I never want to see you or anyone older than me ever again!"

An energy wave spreads around the globe. Everyone older than Mordred's roughly twelve years is exiled to a phantom zone dimension. In this alternate plane, Morgan approaches the similarly stranded Justice League with a proposition: because Mordred's Amulet-fueled incantation affects only *adults*, she will change the superheroes temporarily to *children* so that they can return to Mordred's dimension and neutralize the spell. Superman, Batman, Wonder Woman, and Green Lantern reluctantly agree to their long-time enemy's plan.

The young-again Leaguers find a changed world. Mordred has transmuted the Disney-inspired (and nearly anagrammatic) theme park of Funseyland to his infernal home. A central fountain sculpture has become a guillotine. A gate into pastoral Sherwood is now a gnarled passage to a hellscape. Sleeping Beauty's Castle is replaced by a gloomy citadel. A sword in the stone display in the background, however, remains untouched by Mordred's magic. Mordred tells the orphaned children — left behind in the park when their parents were swept to the other dimension — that he is their king. Having no one else to guide them, the children hesitantly follow him to court. King Mordred soon discovers, however, that his new title also carries the responsibility to provide for his subjects. He wearily grants their petitions for toys and food.

The Leaguers confront Mordred. He uses the Amulet's magic to cast them into his dungeon, where an infant demon Etrigan belches fireballs at them. The three male superheroes battle Etrigan until Wonder Woman intervenes. She recognizes that Etrigan merely suffers from colic. Once burped, Etrigan sides with the Leaguers. All prepare to engage Mordred again as they escape the dungeon.

Meanwhile, chaos reigns in the streets of Funseyland. Unsupervised children run and fight wildly; some test the guillotine's blade on an empty suit of armor; others weep for their missing parents. Under Wonder Woman's maternal direction, the Justice League takes control:

WONDER WOMAN (echoing loudly): That's enough!
CHILD: You can't tell us what to do. You're not our mom.
WONDER WOMAN: No, but I promise you, we will find all your moms.... And I'm gonna tell!
CHILD: Well, what should we do?
WONDER WOMAN: Go outside [the park] and wait for your parents. Now!

The Leaguers and Etrigan engage Mordred in battle. The superheroes succeed in destroying the Amulet, but Mordred has already absorbed the last of its energy. Mordred draws Funseyland's sword from its stone base and prepares to exercise his "kingly duty" to slay his enemies. A tearful child interrupts him: "I want my mommy." Betraying his own repressed thoughts, Mordred futilely tries to convince her that a mother would only hold her back. The Leaguers recognize an opportunity to defeat Mordred with a ruse. They taunt him for being "a momma's boy" and "a boy doing a man's job." Mordred becomes enraged. He summons all his remaining magical force to make himself no longer a boy but an adult — and inadvertently banishes himself to the same phantom zone holding all the grown-ups.

With no power left in the Amulet to sustain Mordred's transformed world, everything returns to normal. True to her word, Morgan reverses the charm that made the Leaguers children. Her plan to give her young son a kingdom to rule, however, has come to an end. "My spell gave him eternal youth," she laments, "but now that he's broken it, all he has is eternal life." A final scene reveals the fate of the boy who would be king. Morgan cares for her "baby," now reduced to a drooling old man.

Director Ben Jones and writer J. M. DeMatteis's half-hour "The Day of the Dark Knight!" (Warner Bros., 2009) for Cartoon Network's *Batman: The Brave and the Bold* found yet more ways to fold Arthurian myth into the DC Comics multiverse. When Merlin Ambrosius's former pupil Morgan conquers her half-brother Arthur's kingdom and magically petrifies the king and his knights, the wizard seeks aid from the future.[24] The wizard summons Batman and Green Arrow to fifth-century Camelot. Merlin explains that the land's only hope rests in finding "the one who is worthy" to pull Excalibur from a stone in the Tower of Excalibur, then use the sword's magic to defeat the usurping witch. Merlin does not know, however, which of the two men before him is "the one." Adventures en route to the Tower will reveal whether Batman or Green Arrow — two fiercely competitive superheroes — will be able to draw the sword.

Morgan sends her knight-demon champion (Blood/Etrigan) to thwart Merlin's new allies. Etrigan introduces obstacles but finally fails to block the heroes' progress to the Tower. As they arrive, Merlin declares Batman to be "the one." "Sorry," Green Arrow objects sarcastically, "but the last time I checked, the mystic runes left this one up for debate." Batman and Green Arrow continue a jocular contest of superhero one-upmanship as they fight past ogres, Etrigan again, and Morgan's enchantments to make their way into the Tower and to Excalibur. Their competition takes a serious turn, however, when Morgan casts a possession spell over Batman and commands him to bring her the sword. "Can someone please tell me," Green Arrow asks plaintively, "why everyone just assumes Batman is the worthy one? You know, people, it could be me!"

Batman fights Green Arrow until the latter falls from the tower. Merlin then manages to free both Batman and Blood from the witch's influence. Morgan's anger rises. She becomes a fire-breathing dragon and begins demolishing the Tower. Merlin says that only Excalibur can save them now. Batman, however, cannot budge the sword from the stone. "Then you're not the one who is worthy?" Merlin asks. "Apparently not," Batman replies matter-of-factly. Dragon-Morgan proclaims the dawning of the "Age of le Fey" as she petrifies Etrigan and Merlin with her flames and prepares to do the same to Batman. Green Arrow suddenly arrives to distract her. Batman is saved from being turned to stone. Yet as Green Arrow cockily turns to challenge Morgan with Excalibur, he finds that he too cannot draw the sword.

Batman proposes a possible solution: "Maybe the *one* who is worthy is really *two*?" The friendly rivals pull together on the sword's hilt as the dragon's petrifying fire engulfs

10. Where Lies Arthur?

them. The flames lift to reveal Batman holding Excalibur. He tosses it quickly to Green Arrow, who uses his bow to launch the sword into the dragon's breast. Dragon-Morgan vanishes in an explosion, defeated by the combined actions of Batman and Green Arrow.

With Morgan's enchantments broken, Merlin says that Arthur will surely confer knighthood on the two for their service to the realm. Batman and Green Arrow, however, have resumed their ongoing argument over which of them is the more accomplished superhero. Exasperated at last by their bickering "conduct most unbecoming in candidates for knighthood," the wizard sends them home. Neither becomes an Arthurian knight this day — and it appears unlikely that either ever will.

Arthurian characters have made fewer "educational" animated appearances in recent years than they did in the 1980s and 1990s. One notable exception to this trend was first broadcast in 2002 on S4C, the Welsh-oriented programming wing of the United Kingdom's Channel 4. The gentle didacticism of *Sir Gawain and the Green Knight* provided writers Penelope Middleboe and Martin Lamb with the materials needed for director Tim Fernee's 24-minute *Sir Gawain and the Green Knight* (Vinegar Hill/Moving Still/S4C, 2002). The visually stunning film — made of computer-animated sequences that approximate a three-dimensional journey through moving stained glass panels that dissolve one into the next — won a 2002 BAFTA for Elaine Kinsella in the Best Animation category.

Fernee's film follows the fourteenth-century original closely yet with extreme economy, often employing visuals rather than words to convey many key narrative elements. The approach allows the film to condense the poem's first fytte of 490 lines to a spartan dialogue that runs just over three and one-half minutes. We begin in Camelot. Through the castle's windows, we see a knight in the distance galloping closer. Inside, the "thirty-something"[25] king welcomes his guests to Camelot.

> ARTHUR: Let Camelot commence its New Year's feast! I will join you once you have told me a tale of a fantastic feat.
> GREEN KNIGHT [entering on horseback]: Who is the commander of this court?
> ARTHUR: I am Arthur, head of this house. Dismount and dine with us.
> GREEN KNIGHT: I have not come to eat. [Arthur grips his sword as the Green Knight raises a holly bow in one hand.] I come in peace to test your reputation in a Christmas game. [The Green Knight lifts a huge axe in his other hand.] I offer this axe to any of you to deal me one blow, on condition that I can counter that blow in a year and a day. [Silence.] Am I in Arthur's house? Is this the noble band of the bravest knights?
> ARTHUR: Your request is foolish, sir, and there are no fools here to grant it. Give me your axe and I will administer your blow. [The king wields the great axe.]
> GAWAIN: My lord! This is not right! Let me be the one to take the risk. As your nephew, I owe my position here to my blood, not my virtue. I would be the least loss to your court.
> ARTHUR: God be with you, Gawain. Wield your one stroke well and you need not fear his.
> GREEN KNIGHT: Who now consents to my contest?
> GAWAIN: My name is Gawain.
> GREEN KNIGHT: Ah, Sir Gawain! I am grateful. Promise you will approach me alone, in a year and a day, for me to present my blow.
> GAWAIN: Who are you?! And where will I find you?!
> GREEN KNIGHT: I will tell you — oh, after you have struck me. And — if I am speechless — then you can stay safe at home. Now, take up the axe.
> GAWAIN (resolutely): Gladly, sir. [Gawain decapitates the Green Knight. Red blood spatters

the room as the head rolls toward Guinevere, but the blood is mysteriously green as it splashes on the queen's horrified face. The torso stands and retrieves its head.]
GREEN KNIGHT: Remember your promise, Gawain! I am the Knight of the Green Chapel. Greet me there, next New Year's morning, and I will repay you. Come, or be called a coward! Hyah! [He urges his horse forward and rides from the court, carrying his head by the hair.]
ARTHUR (somewhat uncomfortably): That was a marvel to suit the moment! More than enough to make me hungry. Hang up the axe, Sir Gawain. It's hewn enough for one day. [Later, to Gawain alone:] When will you go?
GAWAIN: After Halloween.

The adaptation of the next three fyttes follows a similar method, focusing viewers on a certain aspects of the poem while inevitably neglecting others. Students enjoy noting differences between the text and the film — then using those differences to come to a fuller appreciation of the Middle English poem itself. As a classroom tool, Fernee's film is quite effective, though the Green Knight's wife's bared breasts on the third day of temptations may make this Arthurianimation suitable only for more mature students, at least in American classrooms.

Since the 2002 premiere of Fernee's film, Channel 4's Learning website[26] has offered teachers and students access to an ever-expanding collection of classroom activities, study questions, short essays on dozens of topics related to the poem and the film, Middleboe and Lamb's script, and links to relevant resources aimed at helping students better understand *Sir Gawain and the Green Knight*. One must imagine that the original author would be proud of the way that his poem continues to find educational relevance more than 600 years after its composition.

Coda

Two closely juxtaposed images from 1993's "Sir Yaksalot" bring Arthurianimation's perpetually dual nature to crystal focus. As the camera zooms into a castle chamber in an establishing shot, viewers glimpse the perfection of the Arthurian dream: a tapestry (though we do not initially realize it is one) of a stately king and his knights solemnly seated at the Round Table. Two seconds later the camera tilts down to the unvarnished reality of the court at the table below: Arthur and his men do in fact eat like pigs (as Merlin observes in "Spell-Bound") as they indecorously slobber over large hunks of food. The two opposed images coexist, and they do so necessarily. The grander the ideal, the funnier its parody can be.

We can expect that these two poles—the reverent respect for an imagined past and the mischievous examination of it—will continue to exert their complementary forces on Arthurianimation. Some writers and animators will be drawn to an idealized vision of the legendary kingdom. Others will want to laugh at it. Both will be aware that the alternative outlook also exists not far away. Whether serious or comic, realistic or fantastic, aimed to entertain or to edify, the king and his court seem certain to continue to play roles in cartoons short and long for years to come.

More undiscovered Arthurianimation will come to light, too. As celluloid prints become increasingly accessible in digital form, new sightings of King Arthur and the Round Table must be expected. Meanwhile, as we await those discoveries, some may wish to pursue Arthurian avenues that here I have not. Clay and puppet stopmotion animation offers an adjacent area yet to be systematically investigated. From the Animagic puppetry of *Willie McBean and His Magic Machine* (1965) to the Claymation of *Gumby: The Movie* (1995) and plasticine stylings of Bob the Builder's *The Knights of Fix-a-Lot* (2003), from the handpuppets of "The Brush in the Stone" of

The ideal of King Arthur and his court at Camelot, "Sir Yaksalot," *Animaniacs* on **Steven Spielberg Presents Animaniacs** (Warner Bros./Amblin, 1993).

Coda

The Adventures of Timmy the Tooth (1994) and "Elvis the King and His Knights of the Round Table" on *Muppets Tonight!* (1996) to the posed dolls and action figures of *Robot Chicken*'s "Half-Assed Christmas Special" (2007) and "Chirlaxx" (2008), more work yet remains. *Arthurian Animation* aims to provide some road signs for pilgrims as they explore the many different animated paths to Camelot.

The reality of King Arthur and his court at Camelot, "Sir Yaksalot," *Animaniacs* on **Steven Spielberg Presents Animaniacs** (Warner Bros./Amblin, 1993).

Chapter Notes

Introduction

1. "Short" is used here for cartoons with a running time of ten minutes or less. Most theatrical shorts run approximately seven minutes, some a little more, others somewhat less. Animation made for television includes commercials in the running time. Thus a "half-hour" television cartoon is one designed to be shown, along with commercials, within a thirty-minute block on American television. The actual duration of such a "half-hour" cartoon is generally closer to twenty-two minutes than to thirty.

2. Sir Galahad Vodka, an inexpensive spirit distilled in Chicago in the late 1970s, is no longer made. It remains an open question whether the brewers were alluding sincerely to the knight's *purity* or ironically to his famed *temperance*.

3. In three essays grouped under an "Economics" rubric, Sklar (9–23), Isola (24–35), and Noble (36–43) examine the Arthurian marketing phenomenon in *King Arthur in Popular Culture*. Ortenberg's chapter on "Selling the Middle Ages" (225–36) in *In Search of the Holy Grail* provides a broader perspective on ways advertisers tap medieval themes to increase product appeal.

4. B. Lupack's introduction (xiii–xxi) to *Adapting the Arthurian Legend for Children* provides an illuminating survey of twentieth-century authors' recollections of their childhood initiations into the Arthurian realm. Thirty years from now, will today's authors acknowledge that Disney's *The Sword in the Stone*, *Quest for Camelot*, and Scooby-Doo joined Malory, Tennyson, Howard Pyle, and T. H. White as seminal influences during their formative years?

5. In this study, traditional (Malorian) forms of character names are normally employed: Morgan le Fey, Launcelot, Guinevere, Mordred, etc. In cases where it is clear from pronunciation, credits, or other internal evidence that a particular cartoon departs from this norm with "Morganna," "Lancelot," "Gwenevere," "Modred," etc., those forms are used.

6. The story of how cartoons came to be considered entertainment primarily for children has been told many times. Erickson's *Television Cartoon Shows* (5–46) offers a useful overview.

7. In order to set some boundaries to what constitutes "animation," I draw the line at the line drawn with pencil, pen, brush, and digital stylus. *Arthurian Animation* thus explores hand- and computer-drawn/painted animation as its central subject. Stopmotion-animated works, in which puppets and similar figures are manipulated and photographed to simulate movement, are not discussed.

8. Animation specialists may regret that I do not include complete information on the many directors, writers, artists, animators, musicians, and so on it takes to make a single animated short, much less the legions involved in a feature-length cartoon. In general, only the names of principal directors, writers, and/or animators that appear in the screen credits are provided here. Others may be irked even by the term "cartoon," though it does provide a convenient shorthand for the majority of animated works discussed in this book. Readers seeking more in-depth information should turn to the titles listed in the Works Cited, especially both Maltin and Lenburg (for theatrical cartoons), both Lenburg and Erickson (for television cartoons), Woolery (for animated television specials), Beck (for feature-length animation), Goldmark (for music), Shull and Wilt (for cartoons from the era of World War II), Beck and Friedwald (for Warner Bros.), Grant (for Disney), Barrier (for a comprehensive account of American animation), and Solomon (for the history of animation). Their fine reference works and studies have been at arm's reach as I have prepared *Arthurian Animation*.

Chapter 1

1. Warner Bros. has released only a few Bosko cartoons on videotape, laserdisc, and DVD over the years. (Not surprisingly, potentially inflam-

Notes — Chapter 1

matory MGM Boskos remain in the vaults, though unauthorized, often edited copies can be found on the Internet.) To date, "Bosko's Knight-Mare" has not been offered in any official Warner Bros. release. However, unauthorized copies of "Bosko's Knight-Mare," apparently recorded from Nickelodeon's late-night Bosko screenings, can be purchased on eBay and found on the Internet. These bootlegs show the efforts of editors who have trimmed as much as fifty seconds from a cartoon that originally ran seven minutes and twenty-five seconds. The description provided here follows the original, uncut version of "Bosko's Knight-Mare."

2. Gandhi frequently appeared in newsreels of the time and was often caricatured along with many other prominent people in the era's cartoons. In 1932 and 1933 alone, Gandhi shared animated stages with Bosko and the armored Round Table "knights" of "Bosko's Knight-Mare"; with several circus sideshow attractions in "I Love a Parade" (Warner Bros., 1932)— as snake charmer who makes a goat dance; with dozens of luminaries from Einstein to Al Capone invited to "Scrappy's Party" (Columbia, 1933)— as a sunbather who roller-skates to the event; with many of the same celebrities at the 1933 Chicago World's Fair in "The World's Affair" (Columbia, 1933)— as a dancer alongside Durante and others; with Al Jolson and Mae West in Cubby Bear's "Croon Crazy" (Van Beuren, 1933)— when a radio broadcast reaches India and reveals a belly-dancing Gandhi; and with Popeye in "I Yam What I Yam" (King Features/Fleischer Studios/Paramount, 1933)— when Popeye strikes a belligerent Native American chief so hard that the chief morphs to a meditating Gandhi. Today, these insensitive portrayals of the eminent Indian leader are usually excised on the rare occasions that the cartoons are broadcast.

3. "Bosko's Knight-Mare" reveals an uncertain moment of transition as America prepared for Prohibition's end. Production and sale of "intoxicating liquor" had been outlawed in America since the 18th Amendment took effect in January 1920 and would continue to be illegal until the 21st Amendment was ratified in December 1933. "Bosko's Knight-Mare" premiered in June 1933— as states were already ratifying the 21st Amendment, but still in the time of Prohibition— and thus the Black Knight's illicit liquor bottles provide another indication of his criminal behavior. On the other hand, by June, low-alcohol beer and wines were again permitted in America, thanks to the passage in April 1933 of the Cullen-Harrison Act that palliated the effects of the 18th Amendment even before Prohibition officially came to a close. The glee with which the Round Table knights drain their legal mugs of frothy brew must have been shared by many all across the nation.

4. Bosko leaves his armor/submarine at the lake.

5. Animators who once worked for Walt Disney— as had the creators of "Bosko's Knight-Mare" and the majority of others in the industry in the 1930s— seemed to delight at times in violating Disney's rule against the use of "bedroom crockery" in cartoons. Disney formalized the ban in a 1937 in-house style guide on "Tips to Remember When Submitting Gags" (see Klein 48–49). Another chamber pot appears in "Bosko's Holiday" (1931), a cartoon set entirely in modern times.

6. "Bosko's Knight-Mare" borrows many of its medieval elements and mise en scène from Disney and Ub Iwerks's silent "Oh What a Knight" (Winkler Productions/Universal, 1928) in the *Oswald the Lucky Rabbit* series. However, "Oh What a Knight" takes place *entirely* in the Middle Ages, has no dream frame, and offers no Arthurian dimensions.

7. Publisher Thomas Nelson and Sons (London, Edinburgh, Paris...) issued at least one-half dozen undated and sometimes abridged versions of Gilbert's work between roughly 1925 and 1935. Nelson's editions range from upscale publications containing a handful of Crane's original watercolors mixed with monochromatic pen and ink drawings by T. H. Robinson, to mid-priced editions with a color frontispiece and several pen and ink drawings (all by Robinson), and finally to small, inexpensive, pocket-sized editions that include only Robinson's monochromatic illustrations. During these same years across the Atlantic, Saalfield Publishing Co. (Chicago, Akron, and New York) also published many inexpensive, often undated, severely pruned editions of Gilbert's text, along with watercolors and pen and ink drawings by Frances Brundage. Saalfield's eccentric abridged abridgements appeared under the titles *King Arthur* and *King Arthur for Boys*.

8. Crane differs from illustrators such as Robinson and Brundage in the way that he depicts, for example, where a horse's saddle harnesses attach and in the kinds of hangings that drop from harnesses and reins. Bosko's horse's saddle, the decorative bridle, and the forest setting in which Bosko finds himself as the dream begins suggest that the animators had before them a copy of

Gilbert's *King Arthur's Knights* containing at least some of Crane's illustrations. Crane's portrayal of Beaumains on horseback ("Beaumains wins the fight at the ford," opposite p. 88 in the 1911 edition of *King Arthur's Knights*) in Gilbert's "Knight of the Kitchen" chapter seems to me a certain stylistic influence on "Bosko's Knight-Mare."

9. America's quest for a reliable mechanical lighter came to a close in the early 1930s as Zippo founder George Blaisdell first licensed an Austrian design for U. S. distribution in 1932 and then began to market his own model the following year (Baer and Neumark 13–16). While Merlin in the 1931 *A Connecticut Yankee* struggles with a pre–Zippo contraption, Rogers's Yankee can quip, "You gotta be a pretty good magician to work one of those." But by 1933, even Bosko's Black Knight can strike a flame with the flick of a thumb.

10. Only a few reels of the 1920 silent film survive. Harty has viewed the fragments and compiled additional evidence from reviews, industry notices, and contemporary summaries to provide the best description we may ever have of the film. See also his "Cinematic American Camelots Lost and Found" (97–98) for additional information.

11. See Schneider (34–39), Sartin (67–85), Jones (62), and Goldmark (16–21) for accounts.

12. *42nd Street* opened on 2 February 1933 and was in nationwide distribution by March. "Bosko's Knight-Mare" was released on 8 June 1933—too late to boost first-run ticket sales for *42nd Street* but a timely reminder to see the show at a second-run venue or to buy a record or the sheet music. Warner's animation music supervisors were pushing *42nd Street* at every turn throughout 1933, thrumming audiences relentlessly with the three show tunes that Busby Berkeley had choreographed for the musical. In addition to the Looney Tunes cartoons of "Bosko's Knight-Mare" and "Bosko's Picture Show" (18 September 1933), four of the studio's Merrie Melodies cartoons—"Young and Healthy" (4 March 1933), "The Organ Grinder" (8 April 1933), "Shuffle Off to Buffalo" (8 July 1933), and "The Dish Ran away with the Spoon" (24 September 1933)—also plied audiences with medleys from the score of *42nd Street*. Sartin contends that the Warner Bros. cartoons of the early 1930s were "particularly emphatic" in "showcasing music and letting songs dictate the development of the cartoon" (67). Sometimes, however, only the slimmest of connections between song and action can be found in cartoons whose musical selections were driven primarily by marketing decisions made by Warner Bros. executives.

13. As the dream ends, Bosko has been knocked cold and Honey remains trapped in the Black Knight's seedy bedchamber: a loss, it seems. But Bosko later achieves a measure of victory by smashing the empty suit of armor when he awakes, thus conquering while conscious what he could not in the dream.

14. Yet another emendation turns the lyrics of "A Warrior Bold" into the Round Table knights' drinking song. Their stanza concludes: "We drink a toast, to our good host—/ He knows we never pay."

15. See Bertino (105–09), Adamson (128–41), Solomon (100), and Schneider (34–43) for fuller accounts of Schlesinger's studio practices and actual (as opposed to credit-reported) division of labor at Warner Bros. in the 1930s.

Chapter 2

1. Harman and Ising's first two MGM cartoons continued to use the original inkblot Bosko character originally designed for Warner Bros. Beginning with the third MGM Bosko cartoon and continuing through the ninth and last of the MGM Boskos, the character was portrayed as an African American boy.

2. Barrier (188–92, 296–301) charts Harman's and Ising's complex, linked careers in their stormy relationship with MGM. Harman and Ising at first shared a contract—as co-owners of the Harman-Ising operation supplying MGM with cartoons—from 1934 until they lost the contract in 1937. The Harman-Ising studio went bankrupt in 1938. Harman and Ising next became MGM employees rather than independent subcontractors. Harman left MGM in 1941 to open Harman Productions. Ising remained with MGM until 1942, when he was commissioned as a major and put in charge of the military's animation studio, the First Motion Picture Unit. Ising rejoined his creative partner at Harman Productions after the war.

3. Maltin (341) lists the animators who defected to MGM with Harman and Ising: Carmen (Max) Maxwell, Rollin (Ham) Hamilton, Norm Blackburn, Larry Martin, Robert McKimson, Tom McKimson, and Robert Stokes.

4. I contacted Solomon in 1998 to try to learn more about the planned film. He reported that he had based his account on interviews with Shaw and Ising. (Harman had died by the time of Solomon's interviews.) According to Solomon, Shaw and Ising mentioned Harman's project only "in passing" (Solomon, e-mail to the author, 15 Sept. 1998) and thus he could not add more to the account published in *Enchanted Drawings*.

Notes — Chapter 2

5. According to Grant, "audiences voted with their feet by staying away. By and large, critics encouraged this attitude: they felt that the whole venture [compiling several unrelated short items to make a seventy-two-minute feature film] was something of a rip-off" (180).

6. Barrier acknowledged Kausler in *Hollywood Cartoons* for access to "items from Hugh Harman's papers" (xvi). This crucial lead steered me to the missing pieces of the puzzle.

7. Unless otherwise specified, all script quotations are drawn from the Second Revised Story Line and its addenda. Sequence letters and paragraph numbers come from the typescript.

8. Malory's Gareth arrives at court with two dwarves. However, these dwarves play no meaningful part in the action of *Le Morte Darthur* and have no comic function.

9. An event that requires capital letters in the script: "the Drawing of the Sword from the Stone" (A2).

10. Although spelled "Launcelot" (following British practice) on the unnumbered page containing the cast of characters, the story treatment itself uses the "Lancelot" spelling.

11. Merlin's voice in sequence A addresses Arthur as "my son" (A10), which is as ambiguous as it is suggestive in describing the foster father's relationship to the child "stolen"—by whom is never revealed—"from his parents" (A20) and raised by the magician.

12. The B15 addendum does not specify how Lynette responds. Her character, derived from Malory and most frequently described as "haughty" in the script's early scenes, perhaps refuses the anonymous stranger's untoward request. The alternative—that Lynette *does* grant Gareth some token—seems to me to run counter to the cultured/rustic contrast being established in the opening sequences. Lynette grows to love Gareth, but only after overcoming initial antipathy toward a lad whose arrogance sometimes rivals her own.

13. I have incorporated into the Second Revised Story Line's narrative all emendations indicated in the addenda's eighteen "re-revisions." The result is a composite text that best represents the authors' intentions as of 23 April 1941.

14. The writers fail to mention what happens to Gareth's *third* favor (first mentioned in B21) in either the Revised Rough Story Line or the Second Revised Story Line. The B4 addendum speaks of Gareth's *second* wish as if there might be only two rather than three gifts planned for *King Arthur's Knights* at the moment in late April 1941 when the B4 addendum was introduced. Two possibilities arise. (1) Harman and Edmunds's *next* (lost) revision of the screenplay settled on a two-gift storyline. Given that Gareth and Arthur find themselves on the same stage again only in the final intense battle against Modred and the invaders, no appropriate place for granting a third favor exists later in the plot. Or (2) the next script revision made Gareth's taking the rescue mission from Lancelot the second gift and then his request that Lancelot dub him knight in this scene (K9) the third (rather than second) wish. In *Le Morte Darthur*, the king grants the second and third gifts simultaneously, allowing Gareth to take the adventure of rescuing Lyonesse (gift two) and to be made a knight by Launcelot (gift three).

15. The language is somewhat ambiguous in the Second Revised Story Line. Having shot the arrow and returned Lynette to normal, "Gareth rushes in and, dispatching the dogs, rescues her" (R8). An American reader, though perhaps not a British one, could take "dispatch" in the sense of either "kill" or, more mildly, "send off" (alive). The earlier Revised Rough Story Line makes the deadly intent clear: "He dispatches the dogs with his arrows" (14).

16. While the overall trajectory of the final struggle is clear, sequence S has been more heavily revised than any other section—and needs still more attention before it will be complete. Some S addendum modifications—in particular, a battle that the magicians fight in the air above the human conflict on the ground—perhaps belong more properly to the action of sequence T.

17. Conspicuous by its unique appearance in sequence T (and the equivalent section in the earlier Revised Rough Story Line), the word "Saxon" occurs only once in the entire script. The oft-mentioned "invaders" from across the Channel are, in all other instances, simply "invaders" without qualification. Arguably, "Saxon" here suggests associations with events of World War II. However, it must also be noted that the invasion leader is Ban, whom readers of Malory will recall as Launcelot's father and one of Arthur's staunchest *French* allies. While "Ban" seems little more than a name regrettably chosen at random from the Arthurian canon, "Saxon" hints at the film's transhistorical message.

18. Presumably Gareth and Lynette do appear in sequence V as part of the assembly that Merlin addresses, but the Second Revised Story Line does not explicitly tell us what has become of them. The script's final mention of Gareth comes in T6: "Gareth kills Modred, after a tremendous encounter." Lynette exits the script in the preceding

Notes—Chapter 3

sequence as she tosses the rose to Gareth in S3. Although it is impossible to be certain what the next revision contained, I imagine that Harman and Edmunds must have brought their principal players back to the stage for the final scene.

19. Indeed, even Malory confuses the two swords at times, calling the sword from the stone "Excalibur" (Caxton I.9) long before the king receives Excalibur from the Lady of the Lake (Caxton I.25).

20. Rudolf (Rudy) Ising's brother.

21. I am deeply grateful to other successful eBay bidders through whose generosity the images in this chapter appear. I thank Bert Olton for alerting me to the sale, joining me in the auction, and donating a share of the spoils to me at the end. And I also thank Alan Lupack for providing images of the auction photographs now in his collection.

22. The sketches of Lynette, Morganna, Modred, and the jerkin-clad king were photographed while the original drawings were framed within or mounted upon dark mattes. (Some dark traces at the margins of Gobbo and Knight in Armor suggest that they too were likely in or on mattes at the time that they were photographed.) In one case, a character's name can also be found on the *front* of the photograph as well. Along the lower edge of one, "Lynette" has been written on the matte. In another photograph, where we would hope to find the name of the crowned, jerkin-clad figure whom I believe to be Arthur, the photograph has been composed in such a way so as to omit the bottom of the matte. As for the photographs as they are reproduced in this chapter: (a) the image of Lynette includes the matte that can be observed in the photograph; (b) the photograph of Gobbo is likewise reproduced in full; (c) Morganna has been trimmed to remove the matte; (d) Modred and the king have been cropped from full-length to three-quarter-length portraits and the mattes cropped as well.

23. Barrier's remarks spread through *Hollywood Cartoons* come closest to providing an outline of Stokes's career.

24. After Harman Productions had perhaps all but given up on ever securing the funds needed to make *King Arthur's Knights*, R. G. S.'s Lynette character did find love at last in the firm's *Easy Does It* (1946), a 22-minute industrial cartoon funded by Stokely Van Camp and probably intended to be shown at grocers' trade shows. While this cartoon's primary purpose is to convince store owners to carry the complete line of Stokely Van Camp canned fruits and vegetables, that message lies embedded within a narrative of young love between a stockboy and crimson-haired Anne, the grocer's daughter and—as a check of the R. G. S. sketches confirms—a curvaceous incarnation of Lynette. Screen credits for *Easy Does It* do not mention the contribution of Robert Stokes or anyone else with similar initials, though they do reveal that Robert Edmunds wrote the screenplay for the piece.

25. Lynette shares no scenes with Gobbo/Oscar. Thus it is unlikely, albeit possible, that a later version of the script develops a relationship between the two that in some fashion mirrors the functions Launcelot Gobbo performs for Shakespeare's Jessica.

26. Kausler, e-mail to the author, 1 July 2008.

Chapter 3

1. Little of this government-sponsored work has survived. Solomon (113–24) describes the kinds of projects produced by the First Motion Picture Unit (FMPU), which, under the wartime direction of Rudy Ising, made a wide variety of animated training segments and films for the military. Beyond the FMPU, civilian animators at Disney, MGM, Harman Productions, and many other studios contributed to the war effort on a contract basis. For additional information, see Shull and Wilt (80–89) and Barrier (501–04).

2. See especially Shull and Wilt (40–54) for examples of American wartime cartoons with caricatures of Hitler, Mussolini, Stalin, the Japanese, etc.

3. So, too, could live-action, cartoonish parodies be rapidly produced. Columbia anticipated its own 1949 release of *The Adventures of Sir Galahad* with a 1948 Three Stooges short subject, *Square Heads of the Round Table*. Columbia would do the same in 1954, releasing the trio's *Knutzy Knights* months before its Arthurian feature starring Alan Ladd, *The Black Knight*. In times of fervent production, with many projects on similar themes being created at about the same time, the line between what came "first" and what "followed" blurs.

4. In this Disney tour de force, Goofy plays all the principal roles, male and female.

5. Crosby finished recording the film's musical numbers in December 1947 (Zwisohn 74, 96, 115). Advance notices for the film were appearing in the press by May 1948 (Harty, "Comprehensive Filmography" 260).

6. On this consistent evasion, see Harty, "Cinematic American Camelots" (105 and note 16) and "Camelot Twice Removed" (113).

Notes — Chapter 4

7. One easy way to evoke Arthurian connotations is through the oft-used suffix *-alot*. Based of course on the final syllables of Cam*elot*, *-alot* has come to mean "of or relating to Arthur's kingdom," generally with a secondary pun on "excessively" or "in abundance." Although the etymology is a false one, *-alot* (along with the infix *-alot-*, phrase "a lot," and homophonic variants of both) stirs Arthurian associations for many people. For decades, Arthurianimation has employed *-alot* — a lot.

8. An inside joke. While Freleng and Pierce were working on "Knights Must Fall," Chuck Jones and Michael Maltese, their colleagues in a different animation unit at Warner Bros., were featuring Bugs Bunny in "Rabbit Hood" (1949) in which a live-action Errol Flynn from Warner's 1938 *The Adventures of Robin Hood* makes a cameo appearance.

9. Sklar reports similarly abridged print versions of *Connecticut Yankee* from the 1940s and 1950s. These adaptations were designed for juvenile audiences. See her "The Case of the Disappearing Text" (80–85).

10. Warner Bros. has since 2003 released a total of twenty-four DVDs in six boxed sets, each disc containing approximately fifteen classic cartoons, in *The Looney Tunes Golden Collection*. "Knights Must Fall" has yet to appear in the series.

Chapter 4

1. Studios in the 1950s produced a number of medieval films in the less expensive Academy aspect as well, among them *The Black Rose* (1950), *The Flame and the Arrow* (1950), *Rogues of Sherwood Forest* (1950), *The Golden Horde* (1951), *Ivanhoe* (1952), *The Sword and the Rose* (1953), *Lady Godiva* (1955), and *Saint Joan* (1957).

2. Harty's *The Reel Middle Ages* provides a related, worldwide perspective on the dramatic rise of the medieval film. There are twenty entries for films of the 1940s and sixty-two for the 1950s.

3. An inside joke, according to Brian's entry for "Knight-Mare Hare" on the *Hidden Gags in Looney Tunes and Merrie Melodies Cartoons* website. John Burton was a production manager at Warner Bros. whose name and likeness animators would occasionally introduce into their cartoons.

4. "My, he's a big one!" exclaims Bugs when he hears Sir O's full list of titles. Yet Sir O is also a huge man, mounted on an even larger horse.

5. The one exception to the pattern is 1931's *A Connecticut Yankee*, in which the always self-effacing Will Rogers questions his *own* sanity.

6. Say the name quickly three times and you have the joke.

7. Their table is in fact rectangular with rounded corners.

8. Merle Travis in 1955, the McGuire Sisters in 1956, Julie London in 1957, and Dean Martin in 1958 also released renditions of the unfailingly popular song that dates back to 1908.

9. Tom Thumb's tenuous toehold in the Arthurian court goes back at least as far as the Renaissance. For background, see Opie (*Classic Fairy Tales* 36–57), Lacy (*Arthurian Handbook* 154–55), Lupack (*Oxford Guide* 339–43), and Green.

10. Consider the glut of teen-themed films of the day represented by such features as *Teenage Crime Wave* (1955), *I Was a Teen-age Werewolf* (1957), *I Was a Teenage Frankenstein* (1957), *Teenage Monster* (1957), *Teenage Caveman* (1958), *Teenage Bad Girl* (1959), *Teenagers from Outer Space* (1959), *I Was a Teenage Mummy* (1962), *Teenage Tramp* (1963), and *The Teenage Psycho Meets Bloody Mary* (1963). Teens were hot; Arthur not.

11. An ironic allusion perhaps to the RMS *Queen Elizabeth*, the era's largest ocean liner.

12. A play on Lord Mountbatten, one of the most prominent British military men of the day. "Ralph K." perhaps hints at "Ralph Kramden," Jackie Gleason's character from television's *The Honeymooners*.

13. Formerly head of the Art Department at Harman Productions.

14. Abridgements range from utilitarian cuts designed to streamline the story to Eisenhower-era bowdlerizations. In the latter category, when Gawaine forgets his magic word and can recall only that it begins with an *R*, a dragon suggests in Broun's original that the hero may be seeking "reactionary Republican" (33). But there were many still employed at UPA in 1956 who certainly had not forgotten the fate of UPA's founder, John Hubley, at the hands of reactionary Republican congressmen. In the early 1950s, Hubley first refused to testify before the House Un-American Activities Committee and later appeared but without naming names. Hubley was ousted in 1952 from the studio that he had helped build (Barrier 533–35, Solomon 207–28). While "reactionary Republican" would have been a witty joke that took a swipe at the forces that had rent the UPA studio, the times were perilous. UPA's writers circumspectly replaced Broun's words with "repulsive reptile."

15. See Erickson (412–20) and Scott (143–59)

Notes—Chapter 5

for many amusing stories of Ward and Scott's devil-may-care attitude toward their sponsors.

16. Ward and Scott are not the first to invoke the Arthurian kingdom to solve "the boy problem" of juvenile delinquency; see Harty's discussion of the 1917 Edison/Boy Scouts of America film, *The Knights of the Square Table*, in "Lights! Camelot! Action!" (9) and A. Lupack's account of the Arthurian youth groups that preceded the Boy Scouts in "Visions of Courageous Achievement."

17. Wordplay implicitly links Ethel Merlin the Magician to American singer/actress Ethel Merman. A secondary pun leads from "Merman" to "mermaid" and then back to the Sea Hag's realm.

18. According to animation historian/animator Steve Stanchfield in an online posting ("Gordon Sheehan's Tom Thumb") in the *Golden Age Cartoons Forums*, Harman "started" the film that Sheehan later finished. But the Coronet film itself lacks any screen credits that might allow us to determine Harman's and Sheehan's precise roles in the production. Correspondence with Stanchfield (e-mail, 21 June 2009) and Kausler (e-mail, 18 August 2009) suggests that Harman's work (a story treatment? a storyboard?) on *Tom Thumb in King Arthur's Court* dates back to the 1950s, perhaps when Harman was working on another Coronet film.

19. For discussion of social guidance films from Coronet and competing studios, see Smith's *Mental Hygiene*.

20. *Sic*. Perhaps it is narrator Jonathan Winters's misreading of "extraordinaire" in the script?

21. Fred Patten, on the other hand, awards the strange movie three and one-half out of four stars in Beck's *The Animated Movie Guide* (10–11). The high ranking appears to be based less on *Alakazam*'s intrinsic merits than its effects as an early popularizer of Japanese animation in America.

Chapter 5

1. Grellner (118–20) inventories many of the changes from book to film.

2. Although perhaps all wolves, squirrels and hawks look more or less alike, these particular animals visually prefigure the wolf that pursues a tousle-headed squirrel (Wart) during Wart's second transformation and the hawk that chases a sparrow (Wart again) in his third.

3. Arthur identifies himself as an "orphan." Ector says he "took him in, adopted the lad, you might say." Arthur's biological parents are never revealed, which allows Disney's film to skirt difficult issues that even White touches only on the final page of *The Sword and the Stone*: namely, that it was Merlin who, years ago, carried the baby Arthur from Uther's court to Ector's. Such complications find no place in Disney's treatment.

4. Wart's cusp-of-pubescence ungainliness becomes a repeated, overused gag.

5. The direct-to-video *King Arthur, the Young Warlord* (Heritage Enterprises, 1975), a compilation based on a 1972–73 British television series, is likewise unmemorable.

6. Serious art house foreign films of the time treating Arthurian themes, such as Luis Buñuel's *Tristana* (1970), Yvan Lagrange's *Tristan et Iseult* (1972), and Robert Bresson's *Lancelot du lac* (1974), do not bear on the discussion here. They have no influence on cartoons.

7. One of these points is, as one might expect, the World's Fair that was happening in New York City in 1964.

8. The same McKimson who shared animation credit with Robert Stokes on "Bosko's Knight-Mare" three decades earlier.

9. Uther's "beloved wife" is mentioned, but she does not appear in the cartoon.

10. As in Disney's *The Sword in the Stone*, the usual Malorian "Whoso pulleth out this sword..." formula appears on screen as the sword is introduced into the narrative. In the Disney film, the words are engraved on the blade (as in Malory's *Le Morte Darthur*). UPA places the inscription on a plaque mounted on the stone.

11. In the prefatory backstage segment, we see the sword mounted on a wall. The label above the sword reads "THE EXCALIBER" [*sic*].

12. Although research and scholarship have moved forward, Ashe's *The Quest for Arthur's Britain* provides a valuable time capsule from an era in which many hoped (or perhaps believed) that definitive proof of a real, historical King Arthur was imminent.

13. The irony is compounded by Arthur's favorite endearment for Guinevere. He routinely calls her his "little queen" even though Arthur is but two-thirds her height.

14. Robinson was also one of five writers who worked with Janjic on *Arthur! and the Square Knights of the Round Table*.

15. Erickson (28–33) discusses the late–1960s movement to remove violence from children's television programming.

16. With some doubts, I adopt the date provided by the *British Film Institute Film and TV Database*. At least one earlier version of the database (accessed in 1996) gave the date as 1974. The

copy of "Merlin and the Toothless Knights" that I have viewed offers no date at all.

17. Both Beck and Hall provide for extended summaries of *DDPPMGG*. Beck concludes his entry with one hope: "If this plot synopsis spares even one of you from ever seeing this cartoon, then I have done my job" ("FAQ-2"). Here, we focus primarily on the portions of *King Arthur and His Knights of the Round Table* that are screened within *DDPPMGG*.

18. Although Daffy's film does not assign Tweety an Arthurian name (or any name), Malory's Ector would be the closest analogue.

19. Although Filmation produced the cartoon in color, ABC first broadcast it in black-and-white — but with color commercials and the opening color bumper used for all *The Saturday Superstar Movie* episodes. A somewhat abbreviated version of Filmation's original color production aired — in color — in the United Kingdom circa 1973. This abridged version lacks a four-minute segment in "Mad Mirror Land," a surreal through-the-looking-glass sequence in which three Groovie Goolies characters are replaced by costumed live actors— Filmation's writers and animators, filmed in pseudostopmotion "pixilation" style — who chase the Phantom into the real world before returning through the mirror to the cartoon world again. *DDPPMGG* has not been released on VHS or DVD; however, bootleg copies of both broadcast variants may be obtained through private collectors, on eBay, and sometimes online. Filmation later recycled the "Mad Mirror Land" segment as part of another Groovie Goolies cartoon, "The Haunted Heist" (c. 1978), on the syndicated *The Groovie Goolies and Friends* show.

Chapter 6

1. Portrayed by Terry Gilliam, who expires while drawing the Black Beast. The animator's death serves as a deus ex machina to save Arthur from the creature's attack.

2. Daffy fears and puns at the same time: "The sun! It's vanishing ... it's vanishing all right! What ... what will I do? It's the only sun I have. Everybody knows the king has to have a sun."

3. For explorations of the nexus of Arthuriana and the comic book, see Stewart's online "Camelot in Four Colors" and Tondro's *Superheroes of the Round Table*.

4. Harty's "Comprehensive Filmography" (263–65) itemizes the wildly mixed reviews. While *Excalibur*'s critical appreciation has improved somewhat since its opening, Harty's 1999 assessment remains undeniable: "The film has not ... aged well. It now seems too much a product of its times, dominated by a heavy musical score that is designed to cue audience reactions to scenes, sometimes before they are seen" (*Reel* 86). Despite well-deserved critical castigation, *Excalibur* remains a crowd-pleaser even today when screened on college campuses.

5. *King Arthur and the Knights of the Round Table* is another cartoon that can be difficult to obtain. A detailed summary of the first half-hour episode follows.

Chapter 7

1. Beck's *The Animated Movie Guide* (36–38) provides an account of Disney's turmoil at the time.

2. These safety PSAs are loosely linked to each episode's plot. Unfortunately, the PSAs are no longer screened with their original episodes and even DVD releases of the animated *G. I. Joe* include only random selections of the PSAs.

3. Presumably guided by advice from the "psychological consultant" listed in the end credits.

4. The notion of Merlin's mirror as an object of great power can be found in English literature at least as early as book 3 of Spenser's *Faerie Queene*. More recently, Andre Norton's science-fiction *Merlin's Mirror* (1975) has introduced many young adult readers to the mirror's powers. The wizard's mirror continues to evolve and exhibits whatever abilities a writer chooses to give it.

5. After 700 years in the possession of the kings and queens of the United Kingdom, the Stone was returned to Scotland in November 1996. It is now kept with the other Honours of Scotland in the Crown Room of Edinburgh Castle. The Queen has stipulated, however, that the Stone be returned to Britain and reinserted in King Edward's Chair for future coronations.

6. Other tales in the series cover Beowulf, Ivanhoe, Robin Hood, and Sir George and the Dragon.

7. This conclusion recalls the end of James Russell Lowell's *The Vision of Sir Launfal* much more than is does Malory's *Le Morte Darthur*. For a discussion of Lowell, see the Lupacks' *King Arthur in America* (10–13).

Chapter 8

1. Erickson (303) provides broadcast information.

2. From the long-since defunct *Amazin! Adventures* "Princess Gwenevere Homepage."

Notes—Chapter 8

3. Jones and Scott are credited with "concept" creation. A host of others was assembled to direct, write, and animate the episodes.

4. Meanwhile, seizing an opportunity to market the old as something new again, in 1990 New Pacific Pictures rereleased a scattering of episodes from 1968's *Arthur! and the Square Knights of the Round Table*. The 78-minute VHS compilation, retitled as *Camelot* on the video and *Camelot: An Animated Adventure for Children* on the box, certainly stretches the truth with its cover art promises: "Camelot comes alive with Daffy Dragons, Knutty Knights, Dippy Damsels, and his Wacky Highness Himself, King Arthur! Super animation brings to life the craziest version of The Legend of King Arthur ever seen! There are laughs galore in this delightful animated rendering of the Good King and his loyal but wacky subjects! The top cartoon program in England is now a fast-paced, hilarious feature film full of jousting jesters and just plain fun!" One wonders whether the cover designers actually watched any of the show. The compilation continues to be sold by East West Entertainment as *Camelot* (2005) on department store tumble tables across America. With more muted guarantees than New Pacific Pictures's enticements pledged, the East West DVD case informs viewers that they will be able to "[f]ollow King Arthur and all of his crazy brave knights of the round table as they battle dragons, evil wizards and The Black Knight in this hilarious collection of animated medieval shorts!"

5. The second of two *Tiny Toons* segments in the half-hour "Masterhare Theatre" episode entitled "Brave Tales of Real Rabbits."

6. As Babs sees it, an indignity beneath even those suffered by "Sir Shecky of Green."

7. Beyond the general similarities between magicians and illusionists that might have made animators employ Henning's likeness, Henning had co-produced and starred in *Merlin*, a 1983 Broadway musical/magic show.

8. This last reference requires the audience to recall that Raymond Burr played the newscaster spliced into the English-language release of *Godzilla, King of the Monsters* (1954) and that he was also a lawyer on television's *Perry Mason*. Convoluted allusions of this kind continue to make *Animaniacs* a cult favorite.

9. Arthur shrugs off his wife's annoyance: "Whatever."

10. Beetlejuice: "A joust? A joust?! Surely you jest? 'Twould be an unjust gesture for a jester to joust. A jester just jests. Get the gist?" Merlin: "Only just."

11. Online sites such as *SpongeBuddy Mania* report a more "Arthurian" (albeit more cryptic) working title of "The Spatula and the Stove" for the episode. ("Title changes" in the Works Cited.)

12. The roots of Merlin's tree reach back to medieval French prose romances, but it is likely that Kramer and Bjorklund had some more recent retelling in mind.

13. Still other episodes contributed decontextualized *-alot*s without any medieval weight attached: Mr. Burns criticizes Grampa Abe as a "Johnny Live-a-lot" in "Raging Abe Simpson and His Grumbling Grandson in 'The Curse of the Flying Hellfish'" (1996); a swollen-lipped Baron von Kiss-a-lot has a cameo in "Half-Decent Proposal" (2002); and *Stab-a-Lot: The Itchy and Scratchy Musical* premieres in "Girls Just Want to Have Sums" (2006). Beyond the suffix, none of these *-alot*s carries any discernible thematic links to the Arthurian sphere.

14. The credits add another layer to the joke by referencing actors and characters who play no part in *The Poke of Zorro*. Marin did not actually voice any of the roles in "E-I-E-I-D'Oh."

15. Sorcerer-king Macbeth has also crossed from medieval Scotland to the present and often finds himself at odds with the gargoyles.

16. These eggs were long thought to have been destroyed by the same Vikings who nearly obliterated Goliath's clan in the gargoyle genocide depicted in opening episodes of the series.

17. Voiced by Efrem Zimbalist, Jr., who had also provided the king's voice in *The Legend of Prince Valiant*.

18. An unrelated "Sonic Sez" educational message on using the buddy system while swimming followed the episode.

19. Young Robin can scarcely believe what Bruce is telling him: "Merlin? The knight-in-armor magician guy?"

20. Arthur names the sword after his goldfish — perhaps because both shine? (The sword itself is silver.)

21. Up to this moment in "Hexcalibur," Arthur has called his *horse* Camelot. Perhaps he will name his future kingdom after his horse?

22. Yolen later developed the script into a children's picture book, also titled *Merlin and the Dragons* (1995). Woodyard also revisited Arthuri-animation when he directed the five episodes of *Gargoyles* (1995) discussed above.

23. As Merlin's name is introduced into the narrative, the film crew adds a lightning-flash effect to the video and thunder rumbles in the soundtrack.

24. An earlier version of my remarks on *The Quest for Olwen* appeared as a review in *Arthuriana* 8 (1998): 159–60.

25. By contrast, Nimmo's adaptation and McCallum's illustrations for *Jackanory*'s "The Quest for Olwen" (1970) focus on adventure more than love.

26. Quinn came to prominence with her first short film, *Girls Night Out* (1987). Its themes of female agency and empowerment rise again in Quinn's treatment of Chaucer's romance.

27. From *The Legend of Percival Study Guide* that accompanies the video.

28. A glancing allusion, perhaps, to the undead of 1992's Arthurian *Army of Darkness*.

29. Geoffrey's *Historia regum Britanniae* is a prose work, not verse, although perhaps the "historical researcher" or the "educational consultant" (both are listed in the credits) employed by *Histeria!* was thinking of Geoffrey's verse *Vita Merlini*. To place fifteenth-century Malory in the thirteenth century, however, is simply a mistake.

Chapter 9

1. Parts of this chapter, under the title "Arthurian Animation at Century's End," appeared in *King Arthur in Popular Culture*, ed. Sklar and Hoffman (111–21), and as a review of *Quest for Camelot* in *Arthuriana* 8 (1998): 176–78.

2. Beck's *The Animated Movie Guide* (218) pegs the estimated cost at $120 million. It was an extraordinary budget for an animated film in 1998.

3. As Merlin or his master Blaise traditionally acts as the chronicler of the legend in Malory and his sources, so Merlin in *Camelot: The Legend* acts as an omniscient narrator. Merlin's voiceovers are often accompanied by images that depict him writing or reading from his journal of events, recalling a time that has already passed.

4. Malory tells the story to which Guinevere alludes: her father Leodegrance gave the couple the Round Table as a wedding gift (Caxton III.1).

5. The film does not further explore the boy's origins beyond a remark that his family was "destroyed" in the war. Arthur is, in effect, a foundling.

6. Sony Wonder bundled a complimentary audio "cassette sampler" with the videotape. The cassette features selected songs from the movie.

7. The film does not further explore Cynthia's origins.

8. A single credit for the "generic opening music"—an orchestral brass loop used throughout the film at moments requiring a stately backdrop—attests to the producers' lack of interest in (or budget for) music for the Burbank *Camelot*.

9. The fastidious viewer will remark that, despite the film's title, the quest is for *Excalibur*, not *Camelot*. Road signs literally point the way to Camelot; everyone knows where it is. Warner Bros. released the film in many countries under more accurate alternate titles that gave priority to the missing weapon rather than to the king's castle: *The Magic Sword: Quest for Camelot*; *Excalibur, l'épée magique*; *Das magische Schwert: Die Legende von Camelot*; etc.

10. In the novel, Lynett's mother died long ago. Lynett's *nurse* is Dame Juliana, a pragmatic governess who shares little with the film's warm-hearted Lady Juliana.

11. The prehistory and biological origins of the "true king" who pulls the "magical sword" from the stone to "unite the people" are never revealed. Lionel's story introduces him simply as "an unexpected hero," a beardless teenager able to draw the sword that others could not.

12. Ruber's threat to kill Kayley becomes moot with her escape. And though Juliana has said that she "would sooner die" than help Ruber take Camelot, she accompanies him—as his hostage—nonetheless. Such gaps in the narrative logic appear only in retrospect.

13. Given this particular Camelot's adherence to many other modern American values, it is surprising that the kingdom makes few provisions for the disabled.

14. *Internet Movie Database* figures.

Chapter 10

1. This inventory and the comparable ones in earlier chapters could be amplified with many isolated Arthurian episodes from decades of live-action television series. These series run the generic gamut: science fiction (*The Time Tunnel*, *Lost in Space*, *Land of the Lost*, *Blake's 7*, *Tekwar*, *Babylon 5*, *Millennium*, *Sliders*, *Andromeda*, *Doctor Who*), action-adventure (*MacGyver*, *The New Adventures of Robin Hood*, *The Secret Adventures of Jules Verne*, *V.I.P.*, *Adventure Inc.*, *Sir Arthur Conan Doyle's* The Lost World), western (*Bonanza*), fantasy (*ElectraWoman and DynaGirl*, *The New Twilight Zone*, *Fantasy Island*, *Highway to Heaven*, *Twin Peaks*, *Hercules: The Legendary Journeys*, *Xena: Warrior Princess*, *Charmed*, *Buffy the Vampire Slayer*), and comedy (*Northern Exposure*, *Sabrina the Teenage Witch*, *Red Dwarf*, *GvsE*, *Upright Citizens Brigade*). Olton's *Arthurian Legends on*

Notes—Chapter 10

Film and Television and his "Was that in the Vulgate? Arthurian Legend in TV Film and Series Episodes," Nastali and Boardman's *The Arthurian Annals*, Lacy's *The New Arthurian Encyclopedia* and its supplements, and Howey and Reimer's *Bibliography of Modern Arthuriana* contain additional information on many of these episodes.

2. Contrary to the medieval versions of the story, Tristan does not kill the Morholt. Instead, Anguish banishes the Morholt for losing the fight.

3. An earlier version of my remarks on *Shrek the Third* appeared as a review in *Arthuriana* 17 (2007): 176–78.

4. DreamWorks flirted with Arthuriana in the original *Shrek* (2001). A carriage parking lot surrounding Farquaad's castle contains banners to remind potentially forgetful visitors that "you are parked in LANCELOT," as Donkey tells Shrek that they have arrived in "Duloc" (a near-homophone of "du Lac"). From the start, an Arthurian kingdom existed somewhere only slightly beyond the periphery of *Shrek*'s revisionist once-upon-a-time cosmos.

5. One episode refers to the boy as eight years old; another has him celebrating his tenth birthday.

6. Unusual orthography also makes it easier to trademark the names for merchandising purposes, though apparently no toys or games based on *Xcalibur* were produced.

7. He also has few spoken lines. The French-language release puts Arthus seventh (of nine) in the voice credits. Producers for the English-language release must have realized that Arthus spoke so rarely that a single voice could perform both a major role and Arthus's minor one as well. The English version employed one actor for both the female lead and the boy king: Djana/Arthus is in first position in the English voice credits.

8. Winchester, home of Wanda the Wise, is likewise more modern than medieval. "Double Double Wizard Trouble" does not mention the city's traditional connection to the Round Table that still brings tourists to the Great Hall. Instead, the episode focuses on another well-known feature of Winchester—as a posh resort getaway—and proprietor Wanda knows Merlin well from his (apparently) frequent visits.

9. "That's not the table I ordered. It's too big. It's round. No one in their right mind would want a round table."

10. Episode 21 reveals that Shirou's foster father, a Master in the fourth Holy Grail War, concealed the scabbard in Shirou's body for safekeeping and to protect the boy. During the fifth War, Shirou removes it so that Saber can use it in a pivotal battle against the Servant Gilgamesh. See *Le Morte Darthur* (Caxton II.11 and the events of book IV) for Malory's account of the scabbard's power.

11. Animators seem to have turned to the final minutes of Boorman's *Excalibur*— with its glowing red sun that backlights and silhouettes events of the duel between king and son—for many elements of the mise en scène.

12. See, for example, the discussion titled "not the best ending ... SPOILERS" attached to the *Internet Movie Database*'s entry for *Fate/stay night* or the 490-post conversation that followed a summary of the final episode at the *RPG.net* forum. ("Fate/stay night: 'not the best ending ... SPOILERS,'" and "Where I Watch — Fate/Stay Night" in the Works Cited.)

13. Further animated entries in the *Fate/stay night* franchise have explored alternate paths through the software visual novel. An animated theatrical feature film, *Fate/stay night: Unlimited Blade Works* (Studio Deen, 2010), tells a tale with many of the same characters who appear in the 2006 series, but it traces a different storyline in which Saber/Arturia and Arthurian themes play a far more limited role in the adventures. And a televised anime prequel, *Fate/zero* (Ufotable, 2011–12)—based on a Type-Moon series of books (2006–07) intended for younger adolescents—returned to events of the fourth Holy Grail War for 26 half-hour episodes that provide a prehistory to the *Fate/stay night* narrative of the fifth War. While Saber figures prominently in the *Fate/zero* series, she is but one of several legendary and historical Servants who populate a dizzying narrative that brings Alexander the Great, Diarmuid from Irish myth, notorious fifteenth-century child-killer Gilles de Rais (Bluebeard), a mad Lancelot (as the Black Knight, summoned as a member of the Berserker class), and Gilgamesh (again) into the battle for possession of the Grail. With its ensemble cast, *Fate/zero* finds fewer opportunities than the original *Fate/stay night* series to introduce Arthurian lore.

14. The peculiar garb prompts one Meister to exclaim, "Why the hell isn't he wearing any pants?!"

15. Unlike Excalibur, the locomotive-driving, hook-weaponed Fisher King of *Soul Eater*'s episode 30 has no recognizable Arthurian reverberations beyond the name.

16. No blood ties exist between Morgan and Arthur in *Tears to Tiara*.

17. Myrddin (or "Merlinus") also appears in

Notes — Chapter 10

Tears to Tiara's backstory as a White Spirit and Arawn's spiritual father. As punishment for the Promethean crime of granting fire to humanity, the White Spirits destroyed Myrddin. Arawn then took Myrddin's place on the Council until he too rebelled against the White Spirits' plans, joining forces with Pwyll and later Arthur to defend elf- and humankind.

18. Late in the series (episode 22 of 26), Arthur pulls his father's sword Drynwyn from a block of stone. Drynwyn is said to be the "brother sword" to the one that Arawn wields. Arthur and Arawn carry these weapons as they move into decisive battles against the worst of the White Spirits and an army of golems brought to life by the Cauldron of Revival, a vessel from Celtic myth which can reanimate dead warriors.

19. Similar glancing allusions— but from beyond America's borders— have appeared in *Digimon: Digital Monsters*'s "Piedmon's Last Jest," "Apocalymon Now," and "The Fate of Two Worlds" (Toei Animation/Saban, 2000). As the first season came to a close, *Digimon* introduced Excalibur (along with many other potent weapons) into the storyline of a decisive battle between the Digidestined children and the Dark Masters. A thorough study of recent Japanese animation would likely reveal many more undeveloped references to the Arthurian realm.

20. Readers unfamiliar with such events may consult Price's "In the Lists" for descriptions and analysis of the Arthurian dimensions of such fairs.

21. In a fabricated dialect, he says his name is "Moylin."

22. Merlin's confusion appears to stem from his inability to determine whether time is flowing forward or backward.

23. As the episode reminds us, Clam-elot Seafood is just across town from Sir Putts-a-Lot's Merrie Olde Fun Centre, another of Springfield's Arthurian-themed venues.

24. Mordred does not appear in this episode. Morgan seeks the throne solely for herself. Writers freely vary the Arthurian matrix from one DC Comics–inspired episode to the next.

25. Middleboe and Lamb's screenplay for *Sir Gawain and the Green Knight* provides the detail of Arthur's age. Most critical interpretations of the poem, however, argue for a much younger monarch. Rather than the original's portrait of a boyish, beardless youth who refuses to eat until he hears a story or sees a marvel, Middleboe and Lamb explain in the stage directions that the mature king does not want to join the feast because he is "the epitome of the engaging host, determined that everyone should be having a good time before he decides he should have a good time" (3).

26. Online at http://www.channel4learning.com.

Works Cited

Arthurian Animation

Alakazam the Great! (*The Enchanted Monkey, The Magic Land of Alakazam*). Alta Vista/American International Pictures, 1961. Original: *Saiyu-ki*, 1960.

"The Alchemist." *The Real Adventures of Jonny Quest*. Hanna-Barbera, 1996.

Alias the Jester (series). Cosgrove Hall Productions, 1985.

"Alley Oops." *Angry Beavers*. Gunther-Wahl/Nickelodeon, 1998.

"An American Werewolf in America." *Ugly Americans*. Tookie Wilson Productions/Augenblick Studios/Cuppa Coffee Studios, 2010.

"Apocalymon Now." *Digimon: Digital Monsters*. Toei Animation/Saban, 2000.

Arthur! and the Square Knights of the Round Table (series). Air Programs International, 1968. Rereleased in part as *Camelot: An Animated Adventure for Children*. New Pacific Pictures, 1990. Also rereleased in part as *Camelot*. East West Entertainment, 2005.

"Arthur and the Sword." *Fables and Legends: English Folk Heroes*. Donald Thompson & Associates/Milliken Publishing, 1986.

"Avalon." *Gargoyles*. Disney, 1995.

"Baaa-ck in Time!" *Sheep in the Big City*. Curious Pictures, 2000.

"Bango Was His Name, Oh!" *Family Guy*. Fuzzy Door Productions, 2006.

"Bart Gets a Z." *The Simpsons*. Gracie Films, 2009.

"Beach Bummed!" *The Fairly OddParents*. Frederator, 2005.

"Biker Knights of the Round Table." *Biker Mice from Mars*. New World Animation, 1995.

"The Birthday Party." *The Brady Kids*. Filmation, 1972.

The Black Cauldron. Disney, 1985.

"The Black Knight." *The Adventures of Superboy*. Filmation, 1966.

"The Black Knight." *Popeye*. King Features/Jack Kinney Productions, 1960.

Blazing Dragons (series). Nelvana/Ellipse Animation, 1996–98.

"Bosko's Knight-Mare." Warner Bros., 1933.

"Bosko's Parlor Pranks." MGM, 1934.

"Brakstreet: Men in the Band." *The Brak Show*. Wild Hare Studios, 2002.

Bugs Bunny in King Arthur's Court. See *A Connecticut Rabbit in King Arthur's Court*.

Camelot. Burbank Animation Studios [Australia]/Anchor Bay Entertainment, 1997.

Camelot. Golden Films/Sony Wonder, 1997.

Camelot (East West Entertainment). See *Arthur! and the Square Knights of the Round Table*.

Camelot: An Animated Adventure for Children. See *Arthur! and the Square Knights of the Round Table*.

Camelot: The Legend. Tundra Productions/GT Merchandising & Licensing Corp., 1998.

Code Geass: Lelouch of the Rebellion (series). Sunrise, 2006–08.

"A Connecticut Mouse in King Arthur's Cork." *Tom and Jerry Comedy Show*. Filmation/MGM, 1982.

A Connecticut Rabbit in King Arthur's Court. Chuck Jones Enterprises/Warner Bros., 1978. Rereleased as *Bugs Bunny in King Arthur's Court* in 1979.

A Connecticut Yankee in King Arthur's Court. Air Programs International, 1970.

Crusader Rabbit (series). Television Arts Productions/Jerry Fairbanks, 1950–51.

"D & DD." *Dexter's Laboratory*. Hanna-Barbera, 1997.

Daffy Duck & Porky Pig Meet the Groovie Goolies. Filmation, 1972.

"Day for Knight." In "Brave Tales of Real Rabbits." *Steven Spielberg Presents Tiny Toon Adventures*. Warner Bros./Amblin, 1991.

"The Day of the Dark Knight!" *Batman: The Brave and the Bold*. Warner Bros., 2009.

"Dead Putting Society." *The Simpsons*. Gracie Films, 1990.

"A Decepticon Raider in King Arthur's Court." *Transformers*. Sunbow Productions/Hasbro/Marvel Productions, 1985.

Works Cited

"The Demon Within." *Batman. The New Batman/Superman Adventures.* Warner Bros., 1998.

"Diff'rent Braks." See "The Time Machine."

Disney's Adventures of the Gummi Bears (series). Disney, 1985–90.

Dragon and Slippers. See *Sárkány és papucs.*

"E-I-E-I-[Annoyed Grunt]." See "E-I-E-I-D'Oh."

"E-I-E-I-D'Oh" ("E-I-E-I-[Annoyed Grunt]"). *The Simpsons.* Gracie Films, 1999.

"Eggscellent." *Regular Show.* Cartoon Network Studios, 2012.

The Enchanted Money. See *Alakazam the Great!*

Entaku no Kishi Monogatari: Moero Arthur. See *King Arthur and the Knights of the Round Table.*

"Excalibur." *G. I. Joe: A Real American Hero.* Sunbow Productions/Hasbro/Marvel Productions, 1985.

"Excalibur." *ThunderCats.* Pacific Animation/Rankin-Bass, 1985.

"Excalibur Scooby." *The New Scooby-Doo Mysteries.* Hanna-Barbera, 1984.

"Family Scarelooms." *Beetlejuice: The Animated Series.* Nelvana/Geffen/Warner Bros., 1991.

"The Fate of Two Worlds." *Digimon: Digital Monsters.* Toei Animation/Saban, 2000.

Fate/stay night (series). Studio Deen, 2006.

Fate/stay night: Unlimited Blade Works. Studio Deen, 2010.

Fate/zero (series). Ufotable, 2011–12.

"The Fifty-First Dragon." *The Gerald McBoing Boing Show.* UPA, 1957.

"A Fish Called Selma." *The Simpsons.* Gracie Films, 1996.

"Fly by Knight." *Crazy Legs Crane. The All New Pink Panther Show.* DePatie-Freleng, 1978.

The Freedom Force (series). Filmation, 1978–80.

"The Ghost." *The All New Super Friends Hour.* Hanna-Barbera, 1977.

"Gone with the Wand." *The Fonz and the Happy Days Gang.* Hanna-Barbera, 1981.

"Grampa vs. Sexual Inadequacy." *The Simpsons.* Gracie Films, 1994.

"Hamelot." *U. S. Acres* (*Orson's Farm*). *Garfield and Friends.* Wang Film Productions/Lee Mendelson Films, 1989.

"Hedgehog of the 'Hound' Table." *Adventures of Sonic the Hedgehog.* DIC/Bohbot Entertainment, 1993.

"Hexcalibur." *Sabrina, The Animated Series.* Hong Ying Animation/DIC, 1999.

"*Histeria!* Satellite TV." *Histeria!* Wang Film/Warner Bros., 1998.

"Homer Goes to College." *The Simpsons.* Gracie Films, 1993.

"I Married Marge." *The Simpsons.* Gracie Films, 1991.

"I Was a Teenage Thumb." Warner Bros., 1963.

"I'm Only Sleeping." *The Beatles.* King Features, 1967.

"It Hits the Fan." *South Park.* Braniff Productions, 2001.

"Jungle Love." *Family Guy.* Fuzzy Door Productions, 2005.

"Kid Stuff." *Justice League Unlimited.* Warner Bros., 2004.

"King Arthur." *Peabody's Improbable History. Rocky and His Friends.* Jay Ward Productions, 1959.

King Arthur and the Knights of Justice (series). C&D Asia/Golden Films/Bohbot Entertainment, 1992–93.

King Arthur and the Knights of the Round Table (series). Toei Animation, 1981. Original: *Entaku no Kishi Monogatari: Moero Arthur,* 1979.

King Arthur: Prince on a White Horse (series). Toei Animation, c. 1981. Original: *Moero Arthur: Hakuba no Oji,* 1980.

King Arthur's Disasters (series). Zenith Entertainment/Coolabi Production/Neptuno Films, 2005–06.

King Arthur's Knights (unfinished feature film). Hugh Harman Productions, c. 1941.

"King BJ." *Beetlejuice: The Animated Series.* Nelvana/Geffen/Warner Bros., 1991.

"The King Is Dead." *Family Guy.* Fuzzy Door Productions, 2000.

"King Mario of Cramalot." *The Super Mario Brothers Super Show!* Sei Young Animation/DIC, 1989.

"The Knight and the Lady." See *King Arthur's Knights.*

"Knight Must Fall." *Spider-Man.* Grantray-Lawrence Animation/Krantz Films, 1970.

"A Knight of Shadows." *Justice League.* Warner Bros., 2002.

"Knight of the Square Table, or The Joust and the Unjoust." *King Leonardo and His Short Subjects.* Total Television, 1960.

"Knight School." *Huckleberry Hound Show.* Hanna-Barbera, 1960.

"Knight-Mare Hare." Warner Bros., 1955.

"Knights and Demons." *Spider-Man and His Amazing Friends.* Marvel Comics Animation, 1981.

"Knights Must Fall." Warner Bros., 1949.

"Knights of Neverland." *Fox's Peter Pan & the Pirates.* Southern Star Productions/Fox, 1991.

"The Knights of the Round Table" (Hugh Harman Productions). See *King Arthur's Knights.*

Works Cited

"Knighty Knight." *The Fairly OddParents*. Frederator, 2002.

"Knighty Knight Bugs." Warner Bros., 1958.

"Lancelot, chevalier de la chaise longue" ("Sir Lance a Lot, Knight of the Round Coffee Table"). *Patates et dragons (Potatoes and Dragons)*. Alphanim/CINAR, 2003.

"The Land of the Lost." Famous Studios/Paramount, 1948.

"Leafy." *Flint the Time Detective*. Sanrio/Saban Entertainment, 1999.

The Legend of Percival. Gateway Films/Vision Video, 1993.

The Legend of Prince Valiant (series). Sei Young Animation/Hearst Entertainment/King Features/Family Channel, 1991–94.

"A Lighthouse in the Sea of Time." *Gargoyles*. Disney, 1995.

"Lilli und König Artus" ("Lilly and King Arthur"). *Hexe Lilli (Lilly the Witch)*. Trixter Film/Magma Films/Vivatoon, 2007.

"Lilly and King Arthur." See "Lilli und König Artus."

"Lisa the Drama Queen." *The Simpsons*. Gracie Films, 2009.

"The Lost Ball." *Recess*. Beantown/Disney, 1998.

"Love, Springfieldian Style." *The Simpsons*. Gracie Films, 2008.

The Magic Land of Alakazam. See *Alakazam the Great!*

"Marvin, the Magician." *Rocket Robin Hood*. Trillium/Krantz Films, 1967.

"Maximum Homerdrive." *The Simpsons*. Gracie Films, 1999.

"Merlin." *The Centurions*. Ruby-Spears, 1986.

Merlin and the Dragons. Shanghai Animation Film Studio/Lightyear Entertainment, 1990. Broadcast on *Long Ago and Far Away*, 1991.

"Merlin and the Toothless Knights." I. D. T. V., 1970.

"Merlin Brando." *Super Chicken. George of the Jungle*. Jay Ward Productions, 1967.

Merlin the Magic Mouse (theatrical series). Warner Bros., 1967.

"Merlin, the Magician, Jr." *The Reluctant Dragon. The Reluctant Dragon & Mr. Toad Show*. Mushi Studios/Rankin-Bass, 1970.

"Merlin's Lost Book of Magic." *Yogi's Treasure Hunt*. Hanna-Barbera, 1985.

Merlin's Magic Cave. World TV, 1977.

"Merlin's Magic Marbles." *The New Adventures of Superman*. Filmation, 1966.

"Middle Aged Felix." *The Twisted Tales of Felix the Cat*. Rough Draft Studios/Film Roman, 1995.

Mike, Lu & Og (series). Kinofilm/Cartoon Network, 1999–2001.

"Mr. Magoo's King Arthur." *The Famous Adventures of Mr. Magoo*. UPA, 1964.

Monty Python and the Holy Grail [animated segments]. Python Pictures, 1975.

"Natural Born Kissers." *The Simpsons*. Gracie Films, 1998.

"Neptune's Spatula." *SpongeBob SquarePants*. United Plankton Pictures/Nickelodeon, 1999.

"The Night of No Tomorrow." *Dungeons & Dragons*. Toei Animation, 1983.

"Nightmare on Mother Brain's Street." *Captain N: The Game Master*. DIC, 1989.

"No Time for Nuts." Blue Sky Studios/Twentieth Century–Fox Animation, 2006.

"Pain Strikes Underdog." *The Underdog Show*. Total Television/Leonardo Television Productions, 1965.

Patates et dragons (Potatoes and Dragons) (series). Alphanim/CINAR, 2003.

"Paws of the Round Table." *Hello Kitty's Furry Tale Theatre*. DIC, 1987.

"Pendragon." *Gargoyles*. Disney, 1996.

"Penny Antics." King Features/Famous Studios/Paramount, 1955.

"Piedmon's Last Jest." *Digimon: Digital Monsters*. Toei Animation/Saban, 2000.

"The Pig Who Would Be Queen." *Muppet Babies*. Marvel/Jim Henson Productions, 1988.

Potatoes and Dragons. See *Patates et dragons*.

Pound Puppies and the Legend of Big Paw. Wang Film Productions/Cuckoos Nest Studios/Tonka/Family Home Entertainment, 1988.

Princess Gwenevere and the Jewel Riders (Starla and the Jewel Riders) (series). Hong Ying Animation/New Frontier/Enchanted Camelot Productions/Bohbot Entertainment, 1995–96.

Quest for Camelot. Warner Bros. Feature Animation, 1998.

"The Quest for Olwen." *Jackanory*. BBC, 1971.

The Quest for Olwen. Metta and Soyuzmultfilm/S4C and HTV, 1990.

"Quest for the Holy Pail." *Aaahh!!! Real Monsters*. Anivision/Klasky-Csupo/Nickelodeon, 1996.

"Renaissance." *Home Movies*. Burns & Burns Productions/Soup2Nuts, 2002.

"The Return of the King." *Arthur*. CINAR/Cookie Jar, 1999.

"Richie of the Round Table." *The Richie Rich/Scooby-Doo Show — and Scrappy Too!* Hanna-Barbera, 1981.

"Rosebud." *The Simpsons*. Gracie Films, 1993.

Saiyu-ki. See *Alakazam the Great!*

"Sang 'Em High." *Angry Beavers*. Gunther-Wahl/Nickelodeon, 1999.

Sárkány és papucs (*Dragon and Slippers*). Pannónia Filmstúdió, 1989.

"Scared a Lot in Camelot." *Scooby-Doo/Dynomutt Hour*. Hanna-Barbera, 1976.

"Season's Beatings." *American Dad*. Fuzzy Door Productions, 2011.

"Shredder's New Sword." *Teenage Mutant Ninja Turtles*. Fred Wolf Films, 1993.

Shrek the Third. DreamWorks Animation, 2007.

"Sir Galahad, or The Tomorrow Knight." *Fractured Fairy Tales. Rocky and His Friends*. Jay Ward Productions, 1959.

Sir Gawain and the Green Knight. Vinegar Hill/Moving Still/S4C, 2002.

"Sir Gyro de Gearloose." *DuckTales*. Disney, 1987.

"Sir Lance a Lot, Knight of the Round Coffee Table." See "Lancelot, chevalier de la chaise longue."

"Sir Lancelot." *Mel-o-Toons*. New World Productions, 1959.

"Sir Yaksalot." *Animaniacs. Steven Spielberg Presents Animaniacs*. Warner Bros./Amblin, 1993.

"The Smurfs of the Round Table." *Smurfs*. Hanna-Barbera, 1989.

Soul Eater (series). Bones, 2008–09.

"Space Knights of Camelon." *The World's Greatest Super Friends*. Hanna-Barbera, 1979.

"The Spatula and the Stove." See "Neptune's Spatula."

"Spell-Bound." *Pinky and the Brain. Steven Spielberg Presents Animaniacs*. Warner Bros./Amblin, 1993.

"Sports of the Round Table." *Sport Billy*. Filmation, 1982. European first-release c. 1979–80.

Starla and the Jewel Riders. See *Princess Gwenevere and the Jewel Riders*.

"The Super Globetrotters vs. Merlo the Magician." *The Super Globetrotters*. Hanna-Barbera, 1979.

The Sword in the Stone. Disney, 1963.

"The Table Round." *Fables and Legends: English Folk Heroes*. Donald Thompson & Associates/Milliken Publishing, 1986.

"Target." *Superman. The New Batman/Superman Adventures*. Warner Bros., 1997.

Tears to Tiara (series). White Fox/Aquaplus, 2009.

"The Ten-Percent Solution." *The Simpsons*. Gracie Films, 2011.

"The Terrible Time Gun." *Astro Boy*. Mushi Productions, 1963.

"Terror in Time." *Defenders of the Earth*. King Features/Marvel Productions, 1986.

"This Trick Will Kill You." *Rocket Robin Hood*. Trillium/Krantz Films, 1967.

"The Time Machine" ("Diff'rent Braks"). *The Brak Show*. Wild Hare Studios, 2002.

"Time Machine." *The Flintstones*. Hanna-Barbera, 1964.

"The Time Trap." *The Challenge of the Super Friends*. Hanna-Barbera, 1978.

"Tom Thumb." *Fractured Fairy Tales. Rocky and His Friends*. Jay Ward Productions, 1959.

Tom Thumb in King Arthur's Court. Coronet Instructional Films, 1963.

"Tootles and the Dragon." *Fox's Peter Pan & the Pirates*. Southern Star Productions/Fox, 1990.

"Trash of the Titans." *The Simpsons*. Gracie Films, 1998.

Tristan & Iseult: La légende oubliée (*Tristan & Isolde: The Lost Legend*) (series). Arès Films/France 3/Cartoon Express/CNC, 1999.

Tristan & Isolde. See *Tristan et Iseut*.

Tristan & Isolde: The Lost Legend. See *Tristan & Iseult: La légende oubliée*.

Tristan et Iseut (*Tristan & Isolde*). Oniria/Neuroplanet, 2002.

"Twigh School Musical." *MAD*. Warner Bros., 2011.

"What a Knight." *Peter Potamus and His Magic Flying Balloon*. Hanna-Barbera, 1965.

"Where There's a Well, There's a Way." *Danger Mouse*. Cosgrove Hall Productions, 1986.

"Who Do Voo Doo?" *Rocket Robin Hood*. Trillium/Krantz Films, 1967.

"Wife of Bath's Tale." *Geoffrey Chaucer's* The Canterbury Tales. Beryl Productions/Christmas Productions and Right Angle/S4C, 1998.

"The Wizard's Baker." *Home Movies*. Burns & Burns Productions/Soup2Nuts, 2004.

"Wotta Knight." King Features/Famous Studios/Paramount, 1947.

Xcalibur (series). Ellipse Animation (Ellipsanime), 2000–02.

Related Animation

"Bosko the Musketeer." Warner Bros., 1933.

"Croon Crazy." Van Beuren, 1933.

"Daffy Duck in Hollywood." Warner Bros., 1938.

"Dragon Slayer Huck." *Huckleberry Hound Show*. Hanna-Barbera, 1958.

Easy Does It. Hugh Harman Productions, 1946.

Fantasia. Disney, 1940.

"The Good Scout." Ub Iwerks, 1934.

"The Haunted Heist." *The Groovie Goolies and Friends*. Filmation, c. 1978.

"Hollywood Daffy." Warner Bros., 1946.

"Hooray for North Hollywood." *Animaniacs. Steven Spielberg Presents Animaniacs*. Warner Bros./Amblin, 1998.

Works Cited

"I Love a Parade." Warner Bros., 1932.
"I Yam What I Yam." King Features/Fleischer Studios/Paramount, 1933.
"Jokahontas." *Animaniacs. Steven Spielberg Presents Animaniacs*. Warner Bros./Amblin, 1996.
"A Knight for a Day." Disney, 1946.
"Mother Goose Goes Hollywood." Disney, 1938.
"Myron the Magician." *Batfink*. Hal Seeger Productions, 1967.
"Nuts of the Round Table." *Batfink*. Hal Seeger Productions, 1967.
"Oh What a Knight." Winkler Productions/Universal, 1928.
Pinocchio. Disney, 1940.
"Rasslin' Round." Ub Iwerks, 1934.
The Reluctant Dragon. Disney, 1941.
"The Scarlet Pumpernickel." Warner Bros., 1950.
"Scrappy's Party." Columbia, 1933.
"Sir Huckleberry Hound." *Huckleberry Hound Show*. Hanna-Barbera, 1958.
Snow White and the Seven Dwarfs. Disney, 1937.
"The World's Affair." Columbia, 1933.

Print and Online Resources

Adamson, Joe. "Chuck Jones Interviewed." *The American Animated Cartoon: A Critical Anthology*. Ed. Gerald Peary and Danny Peary. New York: Dutton, 1980. 128–41.
Arès Films. 2010. 1 June 2012. http://www.aresfilms.com.
Ashe, Geoffrey. *The Quest for Arthur's Britain*. New York: Praeger, 1968.
Baer, Avi R., and Alexander Neumark. *Zippo: An American Legend*. Philadelphia: Running Press/Compendium, 1999.
Barrier, Michael. *Hollywood Cartoons: American Animation in Its Golden Age*. Oxford: Oxford University Press, 1999.
Beck, Jerry. *The Animated Movie Guide*. Chicago: Chicago Review Press/A Capella Books, 2005.
_____. "FAQ-2." *Jerry Beck's Cartoon Research*. 2003. 1 June 2012. http://www.cartoonresearch.com/faqx.html.
_____, and Will Friedwald. *Looney Tunes and Merrie Melodies: A Complete Illustrated Guide to the Warner Bros. Cartoons*. New York: Henry Holt, 1989.
Bertino, Tom. "Hugh Harman and Rudolf Ising at Warner Brothers." *The American Animated Cartoon: A Critical Anthology*. Ed. Gerald Peary and Danny Peary. New York: Dutton, 1980. 105–09.
Brian, Greg. *Hidden Gags in Looney Tunes and Merrie Melodies Cartoons*. 2000–06. 1 June 2012. http://gregbrian.tripod.com/hidden/hidindx.html.
Broun, Heywood. "The Fifty-first Dragon." [1919.] *Collected Edition of Heywood Hale Broun*. Ed. Broun. New York: Harcourt, Brace, 1941. 27–35.
Chapman, Vera. *The King's Damosel*. London: Collings, 1976.
Ciolek, Todd. "The 10 Most Ridiculous Adaptations of Arthurian Legend." *Topless Robot*. Ed. Rob Bricken. 18 March 2009. 1 June 2012. http://www.toplessrobot.com/2009/03/the_10_most_ridiculous_adaptation_of_arthurian_leg.php.
Ebert, Roger. Rev. of *Quest for Camelot*, dir. Frederik Du Chau. *Chicago Sun-Times* 15 May 1998. 1 June 2012. http://rogerebert.suntimes.com/apps/pbcs.dll/article?AID=/19980515/REVIEWS/805150303/1023.
Erickson, Hal. *Television Cartoon Shows: An Illustrated Encyclopedia, 1949 through 1993*. Jefferson, NC: McFarland, 1995.
"Fate/stay night: 'not the best ending ... SPOILERS.'" Online postings. 24 March 2008–23 February 2010. *Internet Movie Database*. 1 June 2012. http://www.imdb.com/title/tt0774809/board/nest/101275590.
Geoffrey of Monmouth. [*Historia regum Britanniae*.] *The History of the Kings of Britain*. Trans. Lewis Thorpe. Harmondsworth: Penguin, 1966.
Gilbert, Henry. *King Arthur*. Illus. Frances Brundage. Chicago: Saalfield, n.d. [Several editions, c. 1925–35; also as *King Arthur for Boys*.]
_____. *King Arthur's Knights: The Tales Re-told for Boys and Girls*. Illus. Walter Crane. [1st ed.] Edinburgh and London: T. C. and E. C. Jack, 1911. [American imprint, New York: Stokes, 1911.]
_____. *King Arthur's Knights: The Tales Retold for Boys and Girls*. [Illus. Walter Crane and/or T. H. Robinson.] London: Thomas Nelson and Sons, n.d. [Several editions, c. 1925–35.]
Goldmark, Daniel. *Tunes for 'Toons: Music and the Hollywood Cartoon*. Berkeley: Universtiy of California Press, 2005.
Grant, John. *Encyclopedia of Walt Disney's Animated Characters*. 3d ed. New York: Hyperion, 1998.
Green, Thomas. "Tom Thumb and Jack the Giant-Killer: Two Arthurian Fairytales?" *Folklore* 118 (2007): 123–40.
Grellner, Alice. "Two Films that Sparkle: *The Sword in the Stone* and *Camelot*." *Cinema Arthuriana: Twenty Essays*. Ed. Kevin J. Harty. Rev. ed. Jefferson, NC: McFarland, 2002. 118–26.

Works Cited

Hall, Phil. "The Bootleg Files: 'Daffy Duck and Porky Pig Meet the Groovie Goolies.'" *Film Threat.* 3 Sept. 2004. 1 June 2012. http://www.filmthreat.com/features/1196.

[Harman, Hugh, and Robert Edmunds.] "The Knights of the Round Table." Revised Rough Story Line. Typescript. 11 April 1941.

_____. "The Knights of the Round Table." Second Revised Story Line. Typescript. 17 April 1941. [With addenda dated 23 April 1941].

Harty, Kevin J. "Camelot Twice Removed: *Knightriders* and the Film Versions of *A Connecticut Yankee in King Arthur's Court.*" *Cinema Arthuriana: Essays on Arthurian Film.* Ed. Harty. New York: Garland, 1991. 105–20.

_____. "Cinema Arthuriana: A Comprehensive Filmography." *Cinema Arthuriana: Twenty Essays.* Ed. Harty. Rev. ed. Jefferson, NC: McFarland, 2002. 252–301.

_____. "Cinematic American Camelots Lost and Found: The Film Versions of Mark Twain's *A Connecticut Yankee in King Arthur's Court* and George Romero's *Knightriders.*" *Cinema Arthuriana: Twenty Essays.* Ed. Harty. Rev. ed. Jefferson, NC: McFarland, 2002. 96–109.

_____. "Lights! Camelot! Action!—King Arthur on Film." *King Arthur on Film: New Essays on Arthurian Cinema.* Ed. Harty. Jefferson, NC: McFarland, 1999. 5–37.

_____. *The Reel Middle Ages: American, Western and Eastern European, Middle Eastern and Asian Films about Medieval Europe.* Jefferson, NC: McFarland, 1999.

Howey, Ann F., and Stephen R. Reimer. *Bibliography of Modern Arthuriana, 1500–2000.* Cambridge: D. S. Brewer, 2006.

Hugh Harman Productions. "The Knights of the Round Table." Manuscript and typescript working papers, c. 1941–42.

Internet Movie Database. www.imdb.com.

Isola, Zia. "Defending the Domestic: Arthurian Tropes and the American Dream." *King Arthur in Popular Culture.* Ed. Elizabeth S. Sklar and Donald L. Hoffman. Jefferson, NC: McFarland, 2002. 24–35.

Jackson, Kathy Merlock. *Walt Disney: A Bio-bibliography.* Westport, CT: Greenwood, 1993.

Johnson, David. "The Four Faces of Snow." *Animation Artist Magazine.* 2000. 1 June 2012. http://www.animationartist.com/InsideAnimation/DavidJohnson/FourFaces.html.

Jones, Chuck. "What's Up, Down Under? Chuck Jones Talks at The Illusion of Life Conference." *The Illusion of Life: Essays on Animation.* Ed. Alan Cholodenko. Sydney: Power, 1991. 37–66.

Kausler, Mark. E-mail to the author (*King Arthur's Knights*). 1 July 2008.

_____. E-mail to the author (*Tom Thumb in King Arthur's Court*). 18 August 2009.

Klein, Norman M. *7 Minutes: The Life and Death of the American Animated Cartoon.* London: Verso, 1993.

Lacy, Norris J., ed. *The New Arthurian Encyclopedia.* Updated paperback ed. New York: Garland, 1996. [Supplements by Lacy *et al.*, published in *Arthurian Literature* XVIII (2001): 193–255; XXII (2005): 100–75; and XXVI (2009): 171–214.]

_____, Geoffrey Ashe, and Debra N. Mancoff. *The Arthurian Handbook.* 2d ed. New York: Garland Publishing, 1997.

Lenburg, Jeff. *The Encyclopedia of Animated Cartoons.* 3d ed. New York: Facts on File, 2009.

Leydon, Joe. Rev. of *Quest for Camelot*, dir. Frederik Du Chau. *Variety* 10 May 1998. 1 June 2012. http://www.variety.com/review/VE1117912813.

Lowell, James Russell. *The Vision of Sir Launfal.* Cambridge: George Nichols, 1848.

Lupack, Alan C. *The Oxford Guide to Arthurian Literature and Legend.* Oxford: Oxford University Press, 2005.

_____. "Visions of Courageous Achievement: Arthurian Youth Groups in America." *Studies in Medievalism* 6 (1994): 50–68.

_____, and Barbara Tepa Lupack. *King Arthur in America.* Cambridge: D. S. Brewer, 1999.

Lupack, Barbara Tepa. "Introduction." *Adapting the Arthurian Legends for Children: Essays on Arthurian Juvenalia.* Ed. B. Lupack. New York: Palgrave Macmillan, 2004. xiii–xxi.

Malory, Thomas. *Caxton's Malory: A New Edition of Sir Thomas Malory's Le Morte Darthur Based on the Pierpont Morgan Copy of William Caxton's Edition of 1485.* Ed. James W. Spisak. 2 vols. Berkeley: University of California Press, 1983.

Maltin, Leonard. *Of Mice and Magic: A History of American Animated Cartoons.* Rev. ed. New York: New American Library, 1987.

Medved, Harry, and Randy Dreyfuss. *The Fifty Worst Films of All Time (and How They Got that Way).* New York: Popular Library, 1978.

"Merlin and the Toothless Knights." *British Film Institute Film and TV Database.* 2012. 1 June 2012. http://ftvdb.bfi.org.uk/sift/title/280737.

Middleboe, Penelope, and Martin Lamb. *Sir Gawain and the Green Knight.* Script as recorded, 22 April 2002. Tenby: Right Angle, 2001. *Channel 4 Learning.* 1 June 2012. http://www.channel4learning.com/support/programmenotes/netnotes/content/docs/gawainscript.doc.

Works Cited

Nastali, Daniel P. and Phillip C. Boardman. *The Arthurian Annals: The Tradition in English from 1250 to 2000.* 2 vols. Oxford: Oxford University Press, 2004.

Nennius. [*Historia Britonnum.*] *British History* and *The Welsh Annals.* Trans. John Morris. London: Phillimore, 1980.

Noble, James. "Tintagel: The Best of English Twinkie." *King Arthur in Popular Culture.* Ed. Elizabeth S. Sklar and Donald L. Hoffman. Jefferson, NC: McFarland, 2002. 36–43.

Olton, Bert. *Arthurian Legends on Film and Television.* Jefferson, NC: McFarland, 2000.

_____. "Was that in the Vulgate? Arthurian Legend in TV Film and Series Episodes." *King Arthur in Popular Culture.* Ed. Elizabeth S. Sklar and Donald L. Hoffman. Jefferson, NC: McFarland, 2002. 87–100.

Opie, Iona, and Peter. *The Classic Fairy Tales.* New York: Oxford University Press, 1980.

Ortenberg, Veronica. *In Search of the Holy Grail: The Quest for the Middle Ages.* London: Hambledon Continuum, 2006. 225–36.

Price, Brian R. "In the Lists: The Arthurian Influence in Modern Tournaments of Chivalry." *King Arthur in Popular Culture.* Ed. Elizabeth S. Sklar and Donald L. Hoffman. Jefferson, NC: McFarland, 2002. 197–208.

"Princess Gwenevere Homepage." *Amazin! Adventures.* 1996. Online. 26 November 1996. http://www.amazin.com (no longer available).

Quest for Camelot [promotion site]. 1998. 1 June 1998. http://quest4camelot.com (no longer available).

The Quest for Olwen: As Told in Jackanory *by Ray Smith.* [Adapted by Jenny Nimmo.] London: British Broadcasting Company, 1971.

Salda, Michael N. "Arthurian Animation at Century's End." *King Arthur in Popular Culture.* Ed. Elizabeth S. Sklar and Donald L. Hoffman. Jefferson, NC: McFarland, 2002. 111–21.

_____. Rev. of *Quest for Camelot* (Warner Bros. Feature Animation, 1998). *Arthuriana* 8 (1998): 176–78.

_____. Rev. of *Quest for Olwen* (Metta and Soyuzmultfilm/S4C and HTV, 1990). *Arthuriana* 8 (1998): 159–60.

_____. Rev. of *Shrek the Third* (DreamWorks, 2007). *Arthuriana* 17 (2007): 176–78.

_____. "'What's Up, Duke?' A Brief History of Arthurian Animation." *King Arthur on Film: New Essays on Arthurian Cinema.* Ed. Kevin J. Harty. Jefferson, NC: McFarland, 1999. 203–32.

_____. "The Worst Arthurian Cartoon Ever." *Arthuriana* 16 (2006): 54–58.

Sartin, Hank. "From Vaudeville to Hollywood, from Silence to Sound: Warner Bros. Cartoons of the Early Sound Era." *Reading the Rabbit: Explorations in Warner Bros. Animation.* Ed. Kevin S. Sandler. New Brunswick: Rutgers University Press, 1998.

Schneider, Steve. *That's All Folks! The Art of Warner Bros. Animation.* New York: Henry Holt, 1988.

Scott, Keith. *The Moose that Roared: The Story of Jay Ward, Bill Scott, a Flying Squirrel, and a Talking Moose.* New York: St. Martin's, 2000.

ScreenIt: Movie Reviews for Parents. Rev. of *Quest for Camelot*, dir. Frederik Du Chau. 9 May 1998. 1 June 2012. http://www.screenit.com/movies/1998/quest_for_camelot.html.

Shull, Michael S., and David E. Wilt. *Doing Their Bit: Wartime American Animated Short Films, 1939–1945.* 2d ed. Jefferson, NC: McFarland, 2004.

Sklar, Elizabeth S. "The Case of the Disappearing Text: *Connecticut Yankee* for Kids." *Adapting the Arthurian Legends for Children: Essays on Arthurian Juvenalia.* Ed. Barbara Lupack. New York: Palgrave Macmillan, 2004. 73–105.

_____. "Marketing Arthur: The Commodification of the Arthurian Legend." *King Arthur in Popular Culture.* Ed. Sklar and Donald L. Hoffman. Jefferson, NC: McFarland, 2002. 9–23.

Smith, Ken. *Mental Hygiene: Better Living through Classroom Films 1945–1970.* New York: Blast Books, 1999.

Solomon, Charles. E-mail to the author. 15 Sept. 1998.

_____. *Enchanted Drawings: The History of Animation.* Rev. ed. New York: Wings Books/Random House, 1994.

Stanchfield, Steve. E-mail to the author. 21 June 2009.

[_____, as "Steve Stanch."] "Gordon Sheehan's Tom Thumb." Online posting. 11 May 2006. *Golden Age Cartoons Forums.* 15 June 2009. http://www.goldenagecartoons.com/forums/showthread.php?t=6370.

Stewart, Alan. "Camelot in Four Colors: A Survey of the Arthurian Legend in Comics." 2000 (rev. 2008). 1 June 2012. http://www.camelot4colors.com.

[Thiry, Joan, and James Robertson.] *The Legend of Percival Study Guide.* Worcester, PA: Vision Video, c. 1993.

Thomas, Edwin, and Stephen Adams. "A Warrior Bold." n.d. *I Hear America Singing* sheet music

Works Cited

collection, Library of Congress. 1 June 2012. http://lcweb2.loc.gov/cocoon/ihas/loc.natlib.ihas.100004170/full.html.

Thompson, Raymond H. "The Ironic Tradition in Four Arthurian Films." *Cinema Arthuriana: Twenty Essays*. Ed. Harty. Rev. ed. Jefferson, NC: McFarland, 2002. 110–17.

"Title changes." Online posting. 20 September 2006. *SpongeBuddy Mania*. 1 June 2012. http://www.sbmania.net/forums/topic/11295-title-changes.

Tondro, Jason. *Superheroes of the Round Table: Comics Connections to Medieval and Renaissance Literature*. Jefferson, NC: McFarland, 2011.

Twain, Mark. *A Connecticut Yankee in King Arthur's Court*. Ed. Bernard L. Stein. Berkeley: University of California Press, 1984.

"Where I Watch — Fate/Stay Night." Online postings. 21–23 January 2010. *RPG.net*. 1 June 2012. http://forum.rpg.net/showthread.php?489660-Where-I-Watch-Fate-Stay-Night/page46.

White, T. H. *The Once and Future King*. New York: G. P. Putnam's Sons, 1958.

_____. *The Sword in the Stone*. New York: G. P. Putnam's Sons, 1939.

Woolery, George W. *Animated TV Specials: The Complete Directory to the First Twenty-five Years, 1962–1987*. Metuchen, NJ: Scarecrow, 1989.

Zwisohn, Lawrence J. *Bing Crosby: A Lifetime of Music*. Los Angeles: Palm Tree Library, 1978.

Index

Terms denoting royalty or rank are generally omitted, except when these terms bear semantic weight (as in *Sir* Osis of the Liver) or are needed for the sake of clarity (as in *Lady* of the Lake). Page numbers in ***bold italics*** indicate illustrations.

Aaahh!!! Real Monsters 109
ABC 43, 51, 64–66, 69, 73, 76–77, 79–81, 85–86, 95, 108, 119–120, 128–129, 184*n*19
Abdul, Paula 106
Acme 106, 146–148
action figures 103, 149, 176
Adams, Stephen 8, 13
Adamson, Joe 179*n*15
adultery 4, 50, 135–136, 138
Adventure Inc. 186*ch*10*n*1
Adventures of a Teenage Dragonslayer 151
The Adventures of Robin Hood 183*ch*3*n*8
The Adventures of Sir Galahad 37, 40, 181*n*3
Adventures of Sir Lancelot 43
Adventures of Sonic the Hedgehog 117–118
The Adventures of Superboy 69
The Adventures of Timmy the Tooth 176
Aetheling 91
African American 7, 16, 102, 179*n*1
Air Programs International 70
Alakazam 58
Alakazam the Great! 58, 183*n*21
Albion 163
"The Alchemist" 117
alchemy 101, 117
Aleta 91, 102
Alexander, Lloyd 86
Alexander the Great 65, 187*n*13
Alias of Zogma 90
Alias the Jester 90, 104, 158
All in the Family 90
The All New Pink Panther Show 80
The All New Super Friends Hour 79
Allen, Woody 58, 105
"Alley Oops" 111–112
Allfire 104
"Aloha 'Oe" 47
-*alot* 182*ch*3*n*7
Alta Vista 58
Amaranth 90
Amas 58
Amat 58
Amazin! Adventures website 103, 184*ch*8*n*2
Amazon 4
Ambrosius 122, 124; *see also* Merlin Ambrosius
American Dad 163–164
American Greetings 95
American International Pictures 43, 58
"An American Werewolf in America" 163–164
Amo 58
Amulet of First Magic 171–172
Anderson, Alex 40
Anderson, Bob 113
Andromeda 186*ch*10*n*1
Angry Beavers 111–112
Anguish 152, 187*n*2
Animagic 175
Animal (Muppet) 90
Animaniacs see *Steven Spielberg Presents Animaniacs*
animation subtypes: anime ***82***–84, 91, 159–163, 187*n*13; CGI 147, 156; collage 72, 77, 125–126; limited 48–49, 51; Mexican-produced 51, 54; pan-and-zoom style 71–72, 98, 124, 127; pixilation 184*n*19; postwar 36–38, 40–41; stopmotion 175, 177*n*7, 184*n*19
Anne 181*n*24
Annwn 163
The Answer 169
anvil 4, 6, 26, 60, 62, 68–69, 83–84, 107, 112, 122
"Apocalymon Now" 188*n*19
Apostolina, Steve 121
Arawn 163, 188*n*17, 188*n*18
archaeologist 70, 90, 115, 117, 170
Archbishop of Canterbury 83–84, 98
Archie Comics 119
Archimedes 60, 62–63
Archmage 115
Arfur 117–118
Armstrong, Louis (Satchmo) 44
Army of Darkness 100, 186*n*28
Arn 91, 100–101
Arth-Hare 79
Arthur: 1930s 7–16; 1940s 16–42; 1950s 43–54, 57–58; 1960s and 1970s, 47–48, 54–82; 1980s 82–99; 1990s 100–150, 175–176;

2000 and beyond 3–5, 151–176; ***17***, ***82***, ***89***, ***92***, ***95***, ***133***, ***137***, ***140***, ***154***, ***160***, ***166***, ***175***, ***176***; *see also* Allfire; Arfur; Arth-Hare; Arthur VII; Arthur of Houghton Bottoms; Arthus; Artie; Arturia Pendragon; Arturo; Arty; First Warrior; Griffin, Arthur; King, Arthur; Leibowitz, Artie; Saber; Wart; Wimpy
Arthur (CINAR/Cookie Jar series) 129–130
Arthur VII 81
Arthur! and the Square Knights of the Round Table 70, 104, 158, 183*n*14, 185*n*4
"Arthur and the Sword" 98
Arthur of Houghton Bottoms 90
Arthur the King 85
Arthurianimation (defined) 3
Arthur's Quest 100
Arthus 156–157, 187*n*7
Artie 152–***154***, 155
Arturia Pendragon ***160***, 187*n*13; *see also* Saber
Arturo 54
Arty 86
Ashe, Geoffrey 183*n*12
Ashurst, Will 158
Astolat *see* Fair Maid of Astolat
Astro Boy 54–55
"At the Hop" 96
"At the Pound" 96
Autobots 91–92
Avalon 103, 115–116, 136, 138–139, 159–161, 163
"Avalon" (*Gargoyles*) 115–116
Avalon Castle 163
Avalon High 151
"Ave Maria" 48
awards: BAFTA 90, 127, 173; Emmy Award 127, 129; Excalibur Award 118–119; Golden Griffin 129; Humanitas Prize 102; Oscar (Academy Award) 46; Ozzie 76; Peabody Award 129; Silver Angel Award 102; Tony Award 59
Ayden 146–147
Azpiazu, Don 13

Index

"Baa Baa Green Goat" 159
"Baaa-ck in Time!" 163
Babs Bunny 105–106, 185n6
Babylon 5 186ch10n1
Bader, Hilary J. 118
BAFTA 90, 127, 173
Bailey's Comet 87
Baldrick 141
Ban 20, 27, 34, 83–84, 180n17
The Bandit of Sherwood Forest 37
"Bango Was His Name, Oh!" 163–164
"Barbara Ellen" 48
Barrie, J. M. 114
Barrier, Michael 17, 32–33, 62–64, 177n8, 179n2, 180n6, 181ch2n23, 181ch3n1, 182n14
"Bart Gets a Z" 169
Basie, William (Count) 44
Batfink 67
Bath 106
Batman 79, 119, 172–173
Batman 119
Batman: The Brave and the Bold 172–173
BBC 71, 82, 126
BBC1 70–71, 151
BBC2 85
"Beach Bummed!" 163–164
Beagle, Peter S. 136
Beaker 90
Beamish 92
"The Bear Necessities" 159
The Beatles 69–70
Beaumayns (Beaumains) 11, 24–25, 179n8
Beauty and the Beast 142
Beck, Jerry 73, 131, 142, 177n8, 183n21, 184ch5n17, 184ch7n1, 186n2
Bedivere 20, 93, 160
Bedrock World's Fair 65
Beeson, Greg 98
Beetlejuice 108–109, 185n10
Beetlejuice (film) 108
Beetlejuice: The Animated Series 108–109, 111
Beige Knight 106
Bennett, Rodney 82
Bensol, Oscar 69
Benson, Robby 100
Beorht 92
Berkeley, Busby 179n12
Berkowitz, Stan 119
Berserker 187n13
Bertino, Tom 179n15
Big Ben 116, 118
Big Paw 96–97
Big Thumb Gang 52
bigamy 138
Bignell, Ed 158
"Biker Knights of the Round Table" 117
Biker Mice from Mars 116–117
Bildungsroman 59, 152

Billy 39, 56, 88–89
"The Birthday Party" **65**
Bjorklund, Timothy 111, 185n12
Blabber 87
The Black Arrow 37
Black Bart 63
Black Beast of Aaargh 77, 184ch6n1
The Black Cauldron 86
Black Knight 9–10, 12, 20, 23–24, 26, 34, 38–39, 44–47, 50, 55, 66, 69–70, 77–**78**, 81, 83, 89, 91, 99, 118, 178n3, 179n9, 179n13, 185n4, 187n13
The Black Knight (film) 43
"The Black Knight" (*Popeye*) 54–55
"The Black Knight" (*Superboy*) 69
Black Queens 30
The Black Rose 182n1
The Black Shield of Falworth 43
Black Star 161
Black Tuesday 51
Black Witch 126
Blackburn, Norm 179n3
Bladebeak 146, 148–149
Blaisdell, George 179n9
Blaise 186n3
Blake's 7 186ch10n1
Blank, Richard 82
Blaze the Smartly Dressed 104
Blazing Dragons 100, 103–105
Blood, Jason 119, 170, 172; *see also* Etrigan
Bluebeard *see* Gilles de Rais
Bluto **38**–39, 41, 55, 57
B. O. Wulf 108–109
Board from the Bone 108
Boardman, Phillip C. 187n1
Bob the Builder 175
Bohbot Entertainment 102–103
Bohort *see* Bors
Bonanza 102, 186ch10n1
Bone of Scone 96–97
Bonehenge 108
Bonnie Prince Charlie 37
Bono, Sonny 106
Boo Boo 87
Book of Life 157
Booker 88
books read in cartoons 7–8, 10–12, 16, **39**–40, 44–46, 49–50, 53–55, 58, 60–61, 65, 69, 71, 77, 81, 86–88, 90, 106–108, 110–111, 115, 118, 120–121, 157, 161, 168–169
Boorman, John 82, 91, 93, 187n11
Booth, Douglas 91
Bors (Bohort) 155, 159
Bosko 7–**8**, 9–16, 32–33, 35, 46, 177ch1n1, 178n2, 178n4, 178n8, 179n13, 179ch2n1
"Bosko the Musketeer" 32
"Bosko's Holiday" 178n5

"Bosko's Knight-Mare" 7–**8**, 9–16, 20, 32–35, 39, 46, 55, 178n1, 178n2, 178n3, 178n5, 178n6, 179n8, 179n12, 183n8
"Bosko's Parlor Pranks" 16
"Bosko's Picture Show" 179n12
Boss 12–13, 24, 42, 44–46, 70–71, 160
Bouchard, Jacques E. 157
bowdlerizing 5, 98, 104, 127, 178n2, 178n5, 182n14; *see also* censor
Boy Scouts 183ch4n16
Bradley, Marion Zimmer 136, 139
The Brady Kids **65**, 73
Bragan 156–157
Brain 106–107
Brak 165
The Brak Show 163–165
"Brakstreet: Men in the Band" 163–164
branding iron 119
Brando, Marlon 52
Brando, Merlin *see* "Merlin Brando"
Braudis, Bill 167
"Brave Tales of Real Rabbits" 185n5
Bresson, Robert 183n6
Brian, Greg 182n3
British Film Institute Film and Television Database 183n16
British Museum 118
Broadway 59, 64, 85, 185n7
Broceliande 157
Broken Bottom, Quigley 58
Brosnan, Pierce 131, 145
Broun, Heywood 48, 182n14
Brown, Mark 129
Brundage, Frances 178n7, 178n8
Bruno 7–8, 10, 12, 16
"The Brush in the Stone" 175
Brutus 55
Bryant **101**, 102
Buddha 58
Buffy the Vampire Slayer 186ch10n1
Bugs Bunny 4–5, 35, 40–**44**, 45–47, 73, 78–79, 182ch3n8, 182ch4n4
Bugs Bunny in King Arthur's Court see *A Connecticut Rabbit in King Arthur's Court*
Bullwinkle 51
Bunnyvere 89
Buñuel, Luis 183n6
Burbank Animation Studios 139, 141, 186n8
Bureau of Time and Space 121
Burnevere the Overly Educated 104
Burr, Raymond 185n8
Burton, John 44, 182n3
Burton, Tim 108
Buster Bunny 106

198

Index

Butterknife 39–40
Buzz Cola 113

Caesar 65
Caesar and Cleopatra 37
Cafal 96
Caliburn 160
Calloway, Cab 8, 44
Camelhot 104
Camelon 81
Camelost 108
Camelot 3, 12, 23, 27–29, 35, 42, 50, 51, 53, 54–57, 59, 65, 68–69, 77, 79–80, 83–84, 86–87, 89, 91, 99, 100, 102–108, 114, 117–121, 128, 131–***133***, 134–***137***, 138–***140***, 141–***143***, 144–***149***, 150, 152, 158, 161, 163–164, 166–167, 170, 172–173, 175, 176, 182*ch3n*7, 185*n*4, 185*n*21, 186*n*9, 186*n*12, 186*n*13; *see also* Camelhot; Camelon; Camelost; Hamelot; Quackalot
Camelot (1967 film) 59, 64, 107, 132, 136, 138–139, 164
Camelot (1982 film) 85
Camelot (2011 series) 151
Camelot (book Tom reads) 88
Camelot (Burbank Animation) 139–***140***, 141
Camelot (East West Entertainment) *see Arthur! and the Square Knights of the Round Table*
Camelot (Golden Films/Sony Wonder) 136–***137***, 138–139
"Camelot" (song in 1967 *Camelot*) 107, 139
"Camelot" (song in Sony Wonder *Camelot*) 139
Camelot: An Animated Adventure for Children see Arthur! and the Square Knights of the Round Table
Camelot Festival 166–167; *see also* fair, reenactment
Camelot Lanes 111–112
Camelot Room 113
Camelot: The Legend 132–***133***, 134–136, 139
Capone, Al 178*n*2
Captain from Castile 37
Captain Hook 114, 153
Captain N: The Game Master 94–95
Care-a-lot 95
The Care Bears 95, 113
Carlson, Jim 96, 108
Carter, Jimmy 79
Cartoon Network 106, 109, 117, 163–165, 167, 170, 172
Cassidy, Copper-Conk 90
Catnip 89
Cauldron of Revival 188*n*18
Cave of Glass 103

cave paintings 159
Cavendish, Martin *see* Boss
Cavin 85
Caxton, William 6
CBS 43, 48, 64, 69–70, 76, 78, 87–90, 94, 111, 118
Cedric 37–38
Celtic myth 163, 188*n*18
censor 52, 104, 164; *see also* bowdlerizing
Central Park 116
The Challenge of the Super Friends 80
Chalopin, Jean 103
chamber pot 10, 12, 178*n*5
Channel 4 173–174, 188*n*26
Chaplin, Charles 96
Chapman, Vera 131, 141–142, 146, 186*n*10
Charlie's Angels 87
Charmed 186*ch*10*n*1
Charming 153, 155
Chaucer, Geoffrey 126–127, 186*n*26
Chip and Dale 106
Chip the Seal ***89***
"Chirlaxx" 176
Chrétien de Troyes 127–129, 159
Christmas 56, 59, 62, 67, 173
A Christmas Carol 67
Chronicles of Prydain 86
church 62–63, 68, 70, 98–99, 116
Cinderella 36, 61, 153
CinemaScope 5, 43
Ciolek, Todd 103
Citizen Kane 112
CITV 151, 158
Clam-elot Seafood ***169***, 188*n*23
Clapper 135
Clarence 13
Claymation 175
Cleopatra 65
Clinton, Hillary 106
Cobra 92–93
Code Geass: Lelouch of the Rebellion 160–161
Cohen, Dalisa Cooper 144
Cold War 53
colonization 163
Colorland Animation Productions 136, 139
"Colors of the Wind" 139
Colosseum 118, 156
Columbia 181*n*3
comic books 79, 86, 88, 91–92, 105, 117–119, 149, 169, 172, 184*ch*6*n*3, 188*n*24
comics (newspaper) 38, 41, 46, 85–87, 101
"A Connecticut Mouse in King Arthur's Cork" 88
A Connecticut Rabbit in King Arthur's Court 78–79, 81
A Connecticut Yankee (1931 film) 7, 10, 12–13, 45, 179*n*9, 182*n*5

A Connecticut Yankee at King Arthur's Court (1920 film) 13, 179*n*10
A Connecticut Yankee in King Arthur's Court (1949 film) 37–38, 40, 43–45
A Connecticut Yankee in King Arthur's Court (1970 animated film) 70–71, 76
A Connecticut Yankee in King Arthur's Court (1989 film) 85
A Connecticut Yankee in King Arthur's Court (book) *see* Twain, Mark
The Conqueror 43
Corman, Roger 43
Cornwall (character) 142, 144–145, 147–149
Cornwall (place) 104, 134, 138, 152, 158
Coronation Chair 96, 116, 184*ch*7*n*5
Coronet Instructional Films 55–57, 183*n*18, 183*n*19
Cosmo 164, 166
The Court Jester 43
Craddock, Gentleman Jim 79
Crane, Walter 10–***11***, 12, 178*n*7, 178*n*8
Crazy Legs Crane 80–81
"Croon Crazy" 178*n*2
Crosby, Bing 38, 45, 181*n*5
cross-dressing 135
Crown Jewels 118
Crusader Rabbit 5, 35, ***39***–40, 51
crystal ball 19, 22, 27, 31, 91, 120
Crystal Palace 103, 105
Cubby Bear 7, 178*n*2
"Cuddle Up a Little Closer, Lovey Mine" 46
Culhwch and Olwen 71–72, 125–126
Cullen-Harrison Act 178*n*3
Cumference *see* Sir Cumference
Cup of My Blood 151
cyborg 94, 146–147
Cynan 100, 102
Cynthia 139, 141, 186*n*7

"D & DD" 109
Daffy Duck 73–76, 79, 184*ch*5*n*18, 184*ch*6*n*2
Daffy Duck & Porky Pig Meet the Groovie Goolies 73–***75***, 76, 79, 184*n*19
"Daffy Duck in Hollywood" 75
Daggett 112
Damron, Keith 170
damsel-toss 135
Danger Mouse 90–91
Dark Knight 86–87; *see also* Batman
Dating Do's and Don'ts 56
The Da Vinci Code 151, 164

199

Index

Day, Doris 46
"Day for Knight" 105–106
"The Day of the Dark Knight!" 172–173
day residue 13, 46, 88
DC Comics 119, 149, 169, 172, 188*n*24
"Dead Putting Society" 112
Death the Kid 161
Death Weapon Meister Academy 161
de Bourgh, Lady Catherine 20
Decelles, Pierre 96
"A Decepticon Raider in King Arthur's Court" 91–92
Dee Dee 109
deed to kingdom 86, 117
Defenders of the Earth 91
Delfiner, Gary 124–125
DeLuise, Dom 124
DeMatteis, J. M. 172
De Micco, Kirk 141
"The Demon Within" 119, 170
Derevlany, John 111–112
Devon 142, 144–145, 147–149
Dewey 86
Dexter's Laboratory 109
Diarmuid 187*n*13
Dickens, Charles 67
"Diff'rent Braks" *see* "The Time Machine" (*The Brak Show*)
Digalot **95**–97
Digimon: Digital Monsters 188*n*19
direct-to-video 98, 100, 124, 127, 131–132, 141, 150–151, 183*n*5
Dirk 39
"The Dish Ran away with the Spoon" 179*n*12
Disney, Walt 32, 63–64, 178*n*5, 178*n*6
Disney (studio) 3, 5, 16–19, 22, 30–38, 59–64, 76, 81, 85–86, 97, 106, 135, 139, 142, 144, 149–150, 171, 177*n*4, 177*n*8, 181*n*1, 181*n*4, 183*n*3, 183*n*10, 184*ch*7*n*1
Disney Channel 85, 104, 110
Disney's Adventures of the Gummi Bears 85
di Stefano, Dan 92
Dixon, Dianne 102
Djana 157, 187*n*7
Doc Terror 94
Dr. Strangelove 107
Doctor Who 186*ch*10*n*1
Don Quixote 26
Donkey 153, **154**, 187*n*4
Donovan, Tom 82
Dos Santos, Joaquim 170
Dot 107
Double Bubble Bubblegum 51
"Double Double Wizard Trouble" 187*n*8
Douglas, Kirk 107
Drac 73–74
draft 49

dragon 27, 40, 43, 45–51, 53, 65, 69–70, 72–73, 81, 86–87, 89, 92, 94, 97, 104–107, 109, 114, 116, 123, 128, 136, 141–142, 144–145, 147–149, 157–158, 164, 166–168, 172–173, 182*n*14, 185*n*4
Dragon, Henny 107
Dragon and Slippers see Sárkány és papucs
"Dragon Slayer Huck" 48
Dragonheart 100
Dragon's Rock 114
Drake 103
Dread Knight 88
dream 8, 10, 12–13, 15, 46, **50**, **53**, 69–71, 87–88, 99–100, 110–111, 119, 122–**123**, 124, 139, 160, 168, 178*n*6, 178*n*8, 179*n*13
"Dreams of Avalon" 139
DreamWorks Animation 152, 187*n*4
Dreyfuss, Randy 58
Druid 90, 99, 122, 159
Drynwyn 188*n*18
Dubay, Bill 91
Du Chau, Frederik 141
DuckTales 86
"Duke of Earl" 96
Duloc 187*n*4
Dungeons & Dragons 94, 109
Durante, Jimmy 8, 178*n*3
dwarf 20, 22–30, 180*n*8

Earp, Wyatt 65
Eastern characters 8, 91, 117, 157–158, 178*n*2, 181*n*2
Easy Does It 181*n*24
eBay 31, 33, 148, 178*n*1, 181*n*21, 184*n*19
Ebert, Roger 142
Ebony Blade 91
Ector 22, 60–63, 68, 75, 83–84, 98, 183*n*3, 184*n*18
Edens, Michael 108
Edinburgh Castle 184*ch*7*n*5
Edith 90
Edmunds, Robert 19, 22–26, 30–31, 33, 180*n*14, 181*n*18, 181*n*24
education 5, 43, 55–57, 59–63, 67–68, 70–**72**, 73, 78, 81, 88–90, 93–94, 98–99, 113, 115, 118, 122–130, 152, 173–174, 183*n*19, 184*ch*7*n*2, 185*n*18, 186*n*29; *see also* schooling
Edwyn 156–157
"Eggscellent" 164–165
"E-I-E-I-[Annoyed Grunt]" *see* "E-I-E-I-D'Oh"
"E-I-E-I-D'Oh" 113, 185*n*14
18th Amendment 178*n*3
Einstein, Albert 178*n*2
Eisenhower era 52, 182*n*14
Eisenstein, Sergei 96
Eisner, Michael 76

Elaine 99
ElectraWoman and DynaGirl 186*ch*10*n*1
Elefun 55
Elizabeth II 80, 184*ch*7*n*5
Ellington, Edward Kennedy (Duke) 44
Ellipse Animation (Ellipsanime) 156
Elvis 96, 176
"Elvis the King and His Knights of the Round Table" 176
Emmy Award 127, 129
Emrys 122–**123**, 124; *see also* Merlin
The Enchanted Monkey see Alakazam the Great!
Encyclopedia Enchantica 120
Englehardt, Herb 93–94
Entaku no Kishi Monogatari: Moero Arthur see King Arthur and the Knights of the Round Table
environment 78, 114
Equalia **169**
Erickson, Hal 49, 177*n*6, 177*n*8, 182*n*15, 183*n*15, 184*ch*8*n*1
Ermin 163
Erskine, John 10
Esmeralda 37–38
Eternity Stone 91
Ethel Merlin the Magician *see* Merlin the Magician, Ethel
Etrigan 119, 170–172; *see also* Blood, Jason
evangelical 127
Evanier, Mark 94
Evil Queen 31–34
Excaliball 112
Excalibur 4, 30, 66, 68, 70, 82–84, 86–87, **89**, **92**–96, 100, 111–112, 114–116, **118**–121, 126, 128, 136, 139, 141–142, 144–147, 160–164, **166**–167, 170, 172–173, 181*n*19, 183*n*11, 184*ch*6*n*4, 185*n*20, 186*n*9, 187*n*15, 188*n*19; *see also* Board from the Bone; Excalibur Award; Excalibur Swords collection; Excaliburn; Holy Sword; penguin; Shining Blade of Leibowitz; Sword of Justice
Excalibur (1981 film) 82, 85, 91, 93, 184*ch*6*n*4, 187*n*11
Excalibur (book Death the Kid reads) 161
"Excalibur" (*G. I. Joe*) 92–93
"Excalibur" (*ThunderCats*) **92**–93
Excalibur Award **118**–119
Excalibur Casino 164
The Excalibur Kid 100
Excalibur, l'épée magique see Quest for Camelot
"Excalibur Scooby" 86–87

200

Index

Excalibur Swords collection 66
Excaliburn 104
Explorer 47

Fables and Legends: English Folk Heroes 98–99, 127
Fain, David B. 109
fair, reenactment 91, 94, 129–130, 164, 166–167, 188*n*20
Fair Maid of Astolat 118
Fairbanks, Douglas 20
The Fairly OddParents 163–164, **166**–167
fairy 31, 109, 124–125, 161–162, 164, 166
Fallon 103
Family Channel 100–102
Family Guy 163–164
"Family Scarelooms" 108
The Famous Adventures of Mr. Magoo 67
Famous Studios 38–39, 57–58
Fantasia 22, 30–31, 33
Fantasy Island 186*ch*10*n*1
Far Far Away 152–**154**, 155
Farquaad 187*n*4
"The Fate of Two Worlds" 188*n*19
Fate/stay night 159–161, 163, 187*n*12, 187*n*13
Fate/stay night: Unlimited Blade Works 187*n*13
Fate/zero 187*n*13
Faustus 117
Feather, Jacqueline 141
Felix the Cat 111
Fernee, Tim 173–174
Fester, Philo 58
Fields, W. C. 64–65
"The Fifty-First Dragon" 48
Filmation 73, 76, 79, 184*n*19
Fing *see* Sir Fing
Fiona 152–153, 155
Fire and Sword see Tristan und Isolde
Firestar 91
First Knight 100, 132, 135
First Motion Picture Unit (FMPU) 179*n*2, 181*n*1
First Warrior 163
"A Fish Called Selma" 113
Fisher King 187*n*15
The Fisher King 100
Flame 104
The Flame and the Arrow 182*n*1
Flicker 104
Flint the Time Detective 121–122
The Flintstones 65–66
Flip the Frog 7
"Fly by Knight" 80–81
flying carpet 64, 80
Flynn, Errol 41, 182*ch*3*n*8
Foghorn Leghorn 74
The Fonz and the Happy Days Gang 86

Forbidden Forest 145–146
Forest Sauvage 62
Fortier, Jim 165
42nd Street 8–9, 13–14, 20, 179*n*12
"42nd Street" 9, 13, 179*n*12
Foster, Hal 46, 101–102
Foster, Warren 46, 48
foundling 139, 186*n*5; *see also* orphan
"The Fountain of Youth" 159
The Four Diamonds 100
Fox 12–13, 20, 39, 46, 105, 108, 112, 114, 121, 142, 169
Fox's Peter Pan & the Pirates 114–115
Fozzie Bear 90
Fractured Fairy Tales 51–52, **53**–54, 56–57
frame narrative 13, 15, 42, 44, 98, 178*n*6; *see also* Twain, Mark
Frankie 73–74
Fred (Super Chicken's sidekick) 64
Freedman, David 158
The Freedom Force 80
Freleng, Isadore (Friz) 40–42, 46, 79, 182*ch*3*n*8
French Revolution 156
Freud 136
Friedwald, Will 177*n*8
Frost, Sarah 166
Fudd, Elmer 79
Funseyland 171
Furlin the Wise 89
Fuzzalot 90

Gaheris 25
Galahad 4, 40, 51–**53**, 56, 65–67, 69, 77, 79, 99, 114, 128–129, 136, 161, 177*n*2; *see also* Galahad, Sir; Galahot the Proper
Galahad, Harry 52–53
Galahad, Sir 52–**53**
Galahad Glen 40
Galahot the Proper 104
Galron 68
Game Boy 102
games: card 49, 149; role-playing 91, 94, 109, 167; video 4, 91, 94–95, 102–104, 117, 165
Gandhi, Mahatma 8, 178*n*2
Garcia, Greg 136
Gareth 20–30, 33–35, 142, 161, 180*n*8, 180*n*12, 180*n*14, 180*n*15, 180*n*18; *see also* Beaumayns (Beaumains); Garrett; Lucius
Garfield and Friends 87
Gargoyles 115–116, 185*n*22
Garrett 142–**143**, 144, 146–149
Gastar 83–84
Gawain (Gawaine) 20, 23–25, 48, 64–65, 72–73, 84–85, 89–90, 100–102, 114, 161, 173–174, 182*n*14, 188*n*25

Gawain and the Green Knight (1973 film) 64
Gawain and the Green Knight (1991 film) 100
Gawaine le Coeur-Hardy 48, 182*n*14
Gawain's tomb 90
Gem 120
General Dental Council 72
General Specific 164
gentilesse 127
Geoffrey Chaucer's The Canterbury Tales (1998–2000 series) 126–127
Geoffrey de Bouillon 104
Geoffrey of Monmouth 122, 129, 159, 186*n*29
George VI 19
George of the Jungle 64
Georgia Peanut Festival 79
Geraghty, Louise 167
The Gerald McBoing Boing Show 48
Gerdlach 139, 141
Germany 19, 30, 180*n*17
Gery *see* Sir Gery
"The Ghost" 79
G. I. Joe: A Real American Hero 92–93, 184*ch*7*n*2
giant 27, 47, 71–72, 124–126, 159
Gielgud, John 145
Gifford, Kathy Lee 106
Gilbert, Henry 10–**11**, 12, 33, 178*n*7, 179*n*8
Gilbert and Sullivan 9
Gilgamesh 187*n*10, 187*n*13
Gilles de Rais 187*n*13
Gilliam, Terry 184*ch*6*n*1
Gilroy, Henry 170
"Girls Just Want to Have Sums" 185*n*13
Girls Night Out 186*n*26
Glaston Knights 161
Gleason, Jackie 182*n*12
Glenbrook Academy 129–130
Glorianna 86
Glut, Donald P. 91
Gobbo (Oscar) 32, 34–**35**, 181*n*22, 181*n*25
Gobbo, Launcelot 34, 181*n*25
Godzilla, King of the Monsters 107, 185*n*8
Golden Griffin 129
The Golden Horde 182*n*1
Golden Plunger 95
Golden Scrub Brush 109
Goldmark, Daniel 177*n*8, 179*n*11
golem 188*n*18
Góliát 97
Goliath 115–116, 185*n*16
The Goliath Chronicles 115
"Gone with the Wand" 86
Good Knight 128
Good Morning 128
"The Good Scout" 32

Index

Goofy 22, 35, 181n4
Goopy Geer 7
Gordy, Kip 93–94
Gotham City 119, 170
Gournamonde 127
Grail 77, 99, 109, 120, 127, 129, 136, 141–142, 159, 164, 166–167, 187n13; *see also* Hol(e)y Pail
Grail Castle 127
Grail Wars 159–160, 187n10, 187n13
"Grampa vs. Sexual Inadequacy" 113
Grand Magus 157
Grandpa Kitty 89
Grant, John 33, 60, 86, 177n8, 180n5
The Great Dictator 96
Great Hall 187n8
Green, Thomas 182ch4n9
Green Arrow 172–173
Green Knight 84, 173–174
Green Knights of the Round Table 118
Green Knight's wife 174
Green Lantern 80, 171
Greene, Shecky 185n6
Gregor of Dunwyn 85
Grellner, Alice 183n1
Griddle 104
Griff 116
Griffin 146–147, 149
Griffin, Arthur 164
Griffin, Brian 164
Griffin, Peter 164
Grinder the Bulldog 89
Griswald, Gus 110–111
Gromble 109
Groovie Goolies 73–76, 184n19
The Groovie Goolies and Friends 184n19
Grumbong 125
guillotine 156, 171
Guinevere (Guenevere, Guinevra, Gwen, Gwenevere) 4, 20, 23, 47–48, 50, 55–56, 68–70, 74–75, 83–84, 88, 93, 97, 99, 101–103, 105, 108, 114, 117–118, 121, 127, 132–**133**, 134–**137**, 138–139, 153, 155, 158–159, 167, 169, 174, 183n13, 186n4; *see also* Bunnyvere; Whenever
HMS *Guinevere* 47
Guinevere (1994 film) 100
Guinevere Jones 151
Gumby: The Movie 175
Gummi Bears *see Disney's Adventures of the Gummi Bears*
gun 9, 12, 41, 55, 71
GvsE 186ch10n1
gynarchy 136
Gyro 85–86

Hagatha 73–74
hairdryer 44, 46

"Half-Assed Christmas Special" 176
"Half-Decent Proposal" 185n13
Hall, Phil 73, 184n17
Halley's Comet 87
Halloween 149, 170, 174
Hamelot 88, 113
"Hamelot" 87–88
Hamilton, Rollin (Ham) 179n3
Hanna-Barbera 46, 66, 77–81, 86–87, 109, 117
Hannah, Jack 37
Happy Days 86
Hardy, Oliver 8–9
Harlem Globetrotters 80
Harline, Leigh 31
Harman, Hugh 14, 16–22, 25–26, 30–36, 55–57, 179n1, 179n2, 179n3, 179n4, 180n6, 180n14, 181n18, 183n18
Harold the Frog King 152–153, 155
harpy 20, 22, 28–29
Harry Potter and the Prisoner of Azkaban 157
Hartman, Butch 166
Harty, Kevin J. 13, 85, 179n10, 181n5, 181n6, 182n2, 183ch4n16, 184ch6n4
Harvey 120
Harvey Comics 86
"The Haunted Heist" 184n19
Heavenly Creatures 169
Hector 168–169
"Hedgehog of the 'Hound' Table" 117–118
Hefner, Hugh 170
Heinemann, Arthur (Art) 31, 48, 182n13
Hello Kitty's Furry Tale Theatre **89**–90
Henning, Doug 107, 185n7
Hepburn, Katharine 33
Hercules 58, 80
Hercules: The Legendary Journeys 186ch10n1
Herik 157
Herman the Nearsighted 104
Hernádi, Tibor 97
Hero 162
Heston, Charlton 107
Hewson, Isabel Manning 39
"Hexcalibur" 120–121, 185n21
Hexe Lilli 167–169
Hickman, Harv 170
Highway to Heaven 85, 186ch10n1
Hines, Earl 44
Hirsch, Peter K. 129
Histeria! 128
"*Histeria!* Satellite TV" 128–129, 186n29
Historia Britonnum see Nennius
Historia regum Britanniae see Geoffrey of Monmouth
Hitler 181n2

Hol(e)y Pail 87–88, 109
"Hollywood Daffy" 75
Holmes, Sherlock 161
Holy Sword 83, 161–162
Home Movies 163–164, 167
"Homer Goes to College" 112
homework 165
Honey 9–10, 12, 179n13
The Honeymooners 66, 182n12
Hong Ying Animation 139
Honours of Scotland 184ch7n5
"Hooray for North Hollywood" 132
Hotbreath the Not So Proper 104
Hound Table 117
House Un-American Activities Committee 182n14
How Billy Keeps Clean 56
Howard, Max 150
Howey, Ann F. 187n1
HTV 125
Hubley, John 182n14
Huckins, Holly 110
Huckleberry Hound 48–49
Huckleberry Hound Show 48
Huey 86
Hugh Harman Productions 16–**17**, 18–**21**, 22, **25**, 31–**34**, **35**–36, 179n2, 181ch2n24, 181ch3n1, 182n13
Hugh Harman–Rudolf Ising Production 14, 16, 32, 179n2
Hugo III 157–158
Hui, Raman 152
Hultgren, Ken 54
Humanitas Prize 102

"I Love a Parade" 178n2
"I Married Marge" 112
"I Stand Alone" 147
I Was a Teenage Frankenstein 182ch4n10
I Was a Teenage Mummy 182ch4n10
"I Was a Teenage Thumb" 47–48, 52, 56–57
I Was a Teen-age Werewolf 182ch4n10
"I Yam What I Yam" 178n2
Ice Age: The Meltdown 155
Iceman 91
Ickis 109
I. D. T. V. **72**
"If Ever I Would Leave You" 164
Igarashi, Takuya 161
Igrayne 22, 83
"I'm a Puppy, Too" 96
"I'm Only Sleeping" 69–70
Indiana Jones 109, 159, 164
Indiana Jones and the Last Crusade 85, 164
"The Inn" 70
Internet Movie Database 148, 186n14, 187n12
Ireland 82, 152, 187n13

202

Index

Irish myth 187*n*13
Ising, Herman (Sid) 31
Ising, Rudolf (Rudy) 14, 16, 32, 179*n*2, 179*n*3, 179*n*4, 181*n*1
Isis 80
Isola, Zia 177*n*3
"It Hits the Fan" 163–164
It's a Happily Ever After, After All 155
ITV 43
Ivan the Terrible 96
Ivanhoe 182*n*1
"I've Been Working on the Railroad" 41
Iwerks, Ub 32, 178*n*6

Jackanory 71–72, 98, 186*n*25
Jackknife 39–40
Jackson, Kathy Merlock 60
Jackson, Peter 169
Jailhouse Rock 96
Jamelot 132
Janjic, Zoran 70–71, 76, 183*n*14
Janson, Len 73
Japan 54–55, 58, 82, 84, 89, 121, 156, 159, 181*n*2, 183*n*21, 188*n*19
Jedda 91
Jerry 88
Jessica 181*n*25
Jesus 127, 164
Joan of Arc 37
Johnson, David 33–33
"Jokahontas" 142, 144
Jolson, Al 178*n*2
Jones, Ben 172
Jones, Chuck 43–45, 47, 52, 78–79, 81, 179*n*11, 182*ch*3*n*8
Jones, James Earl 122
Jones, Terry 103, 185*n*3
J'onn 170
Joyeuse Garde 138
Juliana 144, 146–148, 186*n*10, 186*n*12
Juliet 169
"Jungle Love" 163–164
Justice League 170
Justice League Unlimited 170–172
juvenile delinquency 52, 56, 183*ch*4*n*16; *see also* social guidance
Juvenile Jungle 52

Kaamelott 151
Kale *see* Lady Kale
Kane, Crystal 93–94
The Karate Kid 168
Kausler, Mark 18, 180*n*6, 181*n*26, 183*n*18
Kay 24–25, 61–63, 68, 83–84, 101–102, 114, 159
Kayley 142–*143*, 144–149, 186*n*12
Keenbeam 86
Keeper of the Bridge of Death 106
Kent, Clark *see* Superboy; Superman

Kermalot of the Lily Pond 90
Kermit 90, 113
Kevin 94
Keys of Truth 103
A Kid in King Arthur's Court 100
"Kid Stuff" 170–172
Kids of the Round Table 100
Killer Rabbit of Caerbannog 126
Kimball, Ward 63–64
King, Arthur 103
The King and I 164
King Arthur *see* Arthur
King Arthur (2004 film) 151
King Arthur (book Gus reads) 110
King Arthur (Gilbert) *see* Gilbert, Henry
"King Arthur" (*Peabody's Improbable History*) 51
King Arthur (stage play) 66
King Arthur and His Knights of the Round Table 73–76
King Arthur and the Knights of Justice 100, 102–103, 105
King Arthur and the Knights of the Round Table **82**–84, 91, 100, 184*ch*6*n*5
King Arthur for Boys see Gilbert, Henry
King Arthur: Prince on a White Horse 84
King Arthur, the Young Warlord 183*n*5
King Arthur's Disasters 158–159
King Arthur's Knights (book Bosko reads) 7–**8**, 10, 12–13, 16, 33, 178*n*8
King Arthur's Knights (Gilbert) *see* Gilbert, Henry
King Arthur's Knights (Hugh Harman Productions) 16–*17*, *18*–*21*, 22–*25*, 26–*34*, *35*–36, 181*n*24
"King BJ" 108–109
King Edward's Chair *see* Coronation Chair
"The King Is Dead" 163–164
King Leonardo and His Short Subjects 54
"King Mario of Cramalot" 95
"The King of Everything" 96
"King of the Moon" 159
King Richard and the Crusaders 43
The King's Damosel see Chapman, Vera
Kinsella, Elaine 173
Kitchen Steward 20, 26–28
Kitty of the Lake of Lost and Found **89**
Klarion 119
Klein, Chuck 109
Klein, Isadore (Izzy) 38, 57
Klein, Norman M. 178*n*5
Kline, Kevin 122

Knife 39–40
"The Knight and the Lady" *see King Arthur's Knights* (Hugh Harman Productions)
"A Knight for a Day" 37–39
"Knight in Armor" (sketch) 32, 34, 181*n*22
A Knight in Camelot 100
"Knight-Mare Hare" 43–**44**, 45–47, 79, 182*n*3
"Knight Must Fall" 66–67
"A Knight of Shadows" 170
Knight of the Spinach 55
"Knight of the Square Table, or The Joust and the Unjoust" 54
"Knight School" 48–49
Knightriders 82, 85
"Knights and Demons" 91
"Knights Must Fall" 40–44, 79, 182*ch*3*n*8, 182*ch*3*n*10
The Knights of Fix-a-Lot 175
"Knights of Neverland" 114–115
Knights of Old 49–50
Knights of Standards and Practices 164
Knights of the Crooked Table 80
Knights of the Round 161
Knights of the Round Table (1953 film) 43, 45
Knights of the Round Table (book Shagworthy reads) 77
Knights of the Round Table (book Sir Galahad reads) 53
"The Knights of the Round Table" (Harman) *see King Arthur's Knights* (Hugh Harman Productions)
Knights of the Round Waller 88
Knights of the Square Table 54, 104, 183*n*16
Knights Who Say "Ni" 106
"Knighty Knight" **166**–167
"Knighty Knight Bugs" 46–49, 57, 105
Knister 167
Knives of the Square Table 39
Knutzy Knights 181*n*3
Kobayashi, Tomoki 163
Koopa 95
Koppel, Ted 128–129
Kowalchuk, William R. 132
Krabappel, Edna 169
Kramden, Ralph 182*n*12
Kramer, Jeremy 111, 185*n*12
Kresel, Lee 58
Kress, Earl 105
Krueger, Freddy 95
Kwodahn 156–157

Lacy, Norris J. 182*ch*4*n*9, 187*n*1
Ladd, Alan 181*n*3
Ladd, Fred 53
Lady Godiva 182*n*1
Lady in the Cake 108
Lady-Jaye 92

Index

Lady Kale 103
Lady M 158–159
Lady of the Lake 30, 68, 88, 92–94, 103, 116, 128, 160, 181*n*19
Lady of the Lanes 112
Lady of the Pond *see* Lady of the Lanes
Laffalot de Puddle 54
Lagrange, Yvan 183*n*6
Lakewood Elementary 129
Lamb, Martin 173–174, 188*n*25
Lana 94
"Lancelot, chevalier de la chaise longue" 157–158
Lancelot du lac 183*n*6
Lancelot: Guardian of Time 100
Land of Lost Stuff 108
Land of the Lost (series) 186*ch*10*n*1
"The Land of the Lost" (cartoon) 39–40
Lane, Lois *118*–119
Lanolin Sheep 88
Las Vegas 164
The Last Legion 151
Laughing Lake 90
Launcelittle 87
Launceloaf 120
Launcelot (Lancelot) 4, 20, 23–25, 27–30, 34, 44–45, 49–50, 56, 65–66, 68, 70, 79, *82*, 84, 87, 97–99, 101, 105, 114, 117, 128–129, *133*–136, 138–139, 153, 155, 157–159, 161, 167–169, 180*n*10, 180*n*14, 180*n*17, 187*n*4, 187*n*13; *see also* Gobbo, Launcelot; Laffalot de Puddle; Launcelittle; Launceloaf; Launcelot (turtle); Launcelot Penguin; Launsilliot; Lies-a-lot; Lostalot; Loungealot; Love-a-lot; Loves-a-lot; Lunchalot
Launcelot (turtle) 164
Launcelot Penguin *89*
Launsilliot 44
Laurel, Stan 9
Lavik of Ruggles 83–84
Lawrence, Peter 93, 117
Leadon, Paul 139
"Leafy" 121–122
Lee, Roddy 139
The Legend of King Arthur 82
The Legend of Percival 127–128, 186*n*27
The Legend of Prince Valiant 100–*101*, 102–103, 105, 185*n*17
Leibowitz, Artie *166*–167
Lenburg, Jeff 76, 177*n*8
Lender, Jay 109
Lennon, John 69–70
Lenore 66
Leodegrance 68, 83–84, 186*n*4
Leonardo da Vinci 65
Leopold, Glenn 120
Lerner, Alan Jay 59

Lessdred 86
"Let's Put Out the Lights and Go to Sleep" 10, 13
Levitow, Abe 67
Leydon, Joe 142
Lies-a-lot 113
lighter 9, 12, 179*n*9
"A Lighthouse in the Sea of Time" 115
"Lilli und König Artus" 167–169
Lillian 153, 155
Lilly 89, 167
"Lilly and King Arthur" *see* "Lilli und König Artus"
Lilly the Witch see Hexe Lilli
Limbo 56–57
Limburger 117
Limwris 163
The Lion King 145
Lionel 144–146, 148, 186*n*11
Lion-O *92*–93
"Lisa the Drama Queen" **169**
Little Bo Peep 33
The Little Mermaid 142
Little Red Riding Hood 36
The Littlest Angel 56
Live-a-lot, Johnny 185*n*13
Ll_r 163
Loch Ness 97
Loewe, Frederick 59
Logun, Elizabeth 132
Loin *see* Sir Loin
Loin of Beef *see* Sir Loin of Beef
Loinsteak *see* Sir Loinsteak
London 67–68, 80, 87, 94, 116, 118, 126, 170
London, Julie 182*ch*4*n*8
Long Ago and Far Away 122
Longinus 84
Looney Tunes 14, 179*n*12, 182*n*3
The Looney Tunes Golden Collection 182*ch*3*n*10
The Lord of the Rings 86
Lorna 156–157
Lorre, Peter 45
"The Lost Ball" 110–111
Lost in Space 186*ch*10*n*1
Lostalot 108
Louie 86
Loungealot 104
Love-a-lot 95
love potion 75, 97–98, 104–105, 135, 152
"Love, Springfieldian Style" 169
Loves-a-lot 113
Lovespell see Tristan and Isolt
Lovy, Alex 48
Lowell, James Russell 109, 184*n*7
Loy, Myrna 12
Lu 163–164
Lucius 142, 146
Luft, Lorna 106
Luigi 95
Lukic, Butch 170
Lunchalot 108

Lupack, Alan C. 181*n*21, 182*ch*4*n*9, 183*ch*4*n*16
Lupack, Barbara Tepa 177*n*3, 184*n*7
Luthor, Lex 64
Lutz, Laverta 112
Lydia 108–109
Lyman, André 167
Lynet (Lynette, Lynett) 20, 23–*25*, 26–30, 32–35, 142, 180*n*12, 180*n*15, 180*n*18, 181*n*22, 181*n*24, 181*n*25, 186*n*10; *see also* Anne; Kayley
Lyonesse (character) 25–26, 180*n*14
Lyonesse (place) 152
Lytener, Edward 118–119

The Mabinogion 10, 71, 125–126
Mabon 126
Macbeth 115–116, 185*n*15
Macbeth 83
MacGyver 85, 186*ch*10*n*1
Machida, Toko 163
MacRae, Gordon 46
MAD 163–164
"Mad Mirror Land" 184*n*19
Madame Tussaud's Wax Museum 87
Magellan 65
Magic Blue Stone 105
The Magic Land of Alakazam see Alakazam the Great!
"The Magic Pony" 81
The Magic Sword: Quest for Camelot see Quest for Camelot
Das magische Schwert: Die Legende von Camelot see Quest for Camelot
Majima, Mitsuru 83
Majutosoland 58
Maldon 102
Malkill 94
Malory, Thomas 3–4, 6, 10, 13, 21–26, 30–31, 33, 50, 60, 67, 69, 74, 76, 82, 84, 89, 93, 96, 98–99, 112, 119, 142, 160, 177*n*4, 177*n*5, 180*n*8, 180*n*12, 180*n*14, 180*n*17, 181*n*19, 183*n*10, 184*ch*5*n*18, 184*ch*7*n*7, 186*n*4, 187*n*10
Malory, Thomas (character) 128–129, 186*n*29
Maltese, Michael 182*ch*3*n*8
Maltin, Leonard 32, 177*n*8, 179*n*3
The Man in the Iron Mask 113
Mandell, Robert 103
manga 55, 117, 121, 161
Marano, Lydia C. 115–116
Marauder's Map 157
Margaret *see* Lady M
Marin, Cheech 113, 185*n*14
Marino, Tony 89

Index

Mario 95
Mark 104, 152
market forces (overview) 3–6
Marlon 65, 164–165
Marmel, Steve 166
Marsales, Frank 14
Martin, Dean 182*ch4n*8
Martin, Hank *see* Boss
Martin, Larry 179*n*3
Martin, Perry 95
Martyn of the East 158–159
Marvin 62
Marvin the Magician 55, 64
"Marvin, the Magician" 64
Marx, Groucho 8, 107
Marx Brothers 8
Marxism 145
Mary Poppins 63
Masefield, John 10
The Mask of Zorro 113
Master 159–160, 187*n*10
"Masterhare Theatre" 185*n*5
matches 12, 45
Matilda 97
"Maximum Homerdrive" 113
Maxtone-Graham, Ian 113
Maxwell, Carmen (Max) 179*n*3
McCallum, Graham 71, 186*n*25
McCann, John P. 106
McClure, Troy 113
McDonnell, Terrence 96, 108
McGuire Sisters 182*ch4n*8
McGuirk 164
McHale, Quentin 106
McKimson, Robert (Bob) 14, 67, 179*n*3, 183*n*8
McKimson, Tom 179*n*3
McNasty, Marvin 97
McSnarl, Herman 58
McSnarl, Vermin 58
medieval fair *see* fair, reenactment
Medieval Knight-Line 128
Medved, Harry 58
Meister 161–162, 187*n*14
Meliagrance 138
Melinda 94
Melissa 83–84
Mel-o-Toons 49
Menville, Chuck 73
The Merchant of Venice 34, 181*n*25
Meredith 90
Merle the Wizard 104
Merlin 4, 12, 19–20, 22–24, 26–31, 45–47, 51–52, 55, 57–58, 60–**65**, 67–**72**, 73–75, 77–**78**, 79–81, 83–87, 89–91, 93–94, 97–103, 106–109, 111, 115–**123**, 124, 128, 132–**133**, 134–**137**, 138–139, 141–142, 145–146, 151, **154**–155, 157–160, 164–**166**, 167–170, 172–173, 175, 179*n*9, 180*n*11, 180*n*18, 183*n*3, 184*ch7n*4, 185*n*7, 185*n*10, 185*n*12, 185*n*19, 185*n*23, 186*n*3, 187*n*8, 188*n*22; *see also* Emrys; Furlin the Wise; Marvin; Marvin the Magician; Merle the Wizard; Merlin Ambrosius; "Merlin Brando"; Merlin of Monroe; Merlin, Ralph K., Jr.; Merlin the Magic Mouse; Merlin the Magician, Ethel; "Merlin, the Magician, Jr."; Merlinus; Merlo the Magician; Merlyn; Merlynx the Magician; Mervin the Magician; Myrddin; "Myron the Magician"; Schmerlin, Merlin
Merlin (1983 Broadway musical) 185*n*7
Merlin (1992 film) 100
Merlin (1998 miniseries) 100
Merlin (2008–12 series) 151
"Merlin" (*Centurions*) 93–94
Merlin, Ralph K., Jr. 47, 182*n*12
Merlin Ambrosius 172–173
Merlin and the Book of Beasts 151
Merlin and the Dragons (book) 185*n*22
Merlin and the Dragons (cartoon) 122–**123**, 124
Merlin and the Sword see Arthur the King
"Merlin and the Toothless Knights" **72**–73, 98, 184*n*16
Merlin and the War of the Dragons 151
"Merlin Brando" 64
Merlin of Monroe 45, 57, 79
Merlin: The Magic Begins see Merlin: The Quest Begins
Merlin the Magic Mouse 64
Merlin the Magician, Ethel 55, 183*n*17
"Merlin, the Magician, Jr." 65
Merlin: The Quest Begins 100
Merlin: The Return 151
Merlin's Apprentice 151
Merlin's Book of Spells 111
"Merlin's Lost Book of Magic" 87
Merlin's Magic Cave 81
"Merlin's Magic Marbles" 64
Merlinus 187*n*17
Merlo the Magician 80
Merlyn 31
Merlynx the Magician 117
Merman, Ethel 183*n*17
Merrie Melodies 14, 179*n*12, 182*n*3
Merrill, Andy 165
Mervin the Magician 95
Métais, Pierre 104–105
Meyer, Carl 38
MGM 7, 16, 32, 43, 45, 178*n*1, 179*n*1, 179*n*2, 179*n*3, 181*n*1
"Middle Aged Felix" 111
Middleboe, Penelope 173–174, 188*n*25
Mike, Lu & Og 163–164
Millennium 186*ch*10*n*1
Miller, Chris 152
Mim 31, 97
"Mine" 134
Ming the Merciless 91
Minton, Tom 105
mirror 64, 94, 184*ch5n*19, 184*ch7n*4
Miss Piggy 90, 113
Mr. Burns 112, 185*n*13
"Mr. Magoo's King Arthur" 67–69
Mr. Wizard 54
The Mists of Avalon (book) *see* Bradley, Marion Zimmer
The Mists of Avalon (film) 151
Mobius 117
Moero Arthur: Hakuba no Oji see King Arthur: Prince on a White Horse
Monsters & Mazes 109
Montegue 117
Monty Python 54, 77, 81, 103–104, 109, 128
Monty Python and the Holy Grail 5, 64, 77, 81–82, 85, 88, 90, 103–104, 106, 126, 151
Monty Python's Flying Circus 70
Moonpie 58
Moor 102, 138
Moppel, Fred 128–129
Mordecai 164–165
Mordred (Modred) 4, 20–**21**, 22–24, 26–30, 32, 34, 54, 65, 74–75, 86, 91, 99, 101–102, 117, 132, 134–135, 138–139, 161, 170–172, 180*n*14, 180*n*18, 181*n*22, 188*n*24; *see also* Lessdred; Mordred of Avalon; Mordred of Herringbone Fleet; Morecash; Moreloon; Morty; Moylin; Murdered
Mordred of Avalon 138–139
Mordred of Herringbone Fleet 47–48
Morecash 86
Moreloon 86
Morgan, Hank *see* Boss
Morgan le Fey (Morgan, Morgana, Morganna) 4, 12, 20, 22–23, 26–**34**, 70, 80–81, 86–87, 94, 99, 101–103, 119–120, 132, 134–136, 159, 163, 170–173, 181*n*22, 187*n*16, 188*n*24; *see also* Morgan le Fur; Sorceress of the Forest
Morgan le Fur 89
Morgause 23, 136, 138
Morholt 105, 152, 187*n*2
Moricoli-Latham, Lisa 132
Le Morte Darthur (1984 film) 85
Le Morte Darthur (Middle English romance) *see* Malory, Thomas

Index

Morty 47
Moss, Francis 118
Mother Brain 94
"Mother Goose Goes Hollywood" 33
motorcycle 52, 67, 71, 82, 116–117
Mountbatten 182*n*12
Moylin 188*n*21
Mulan 149–150
Mumm-Ra **92**–93
Mummy 73
Muppet Babies 90
Muppets 90, 113, 176
The Muppets Go Medieval 113
Muppets Tonight! 176
Murdered 54
Musketeer 32, 37, 113
Mussolini 181*n*2
My Melody the Bunny 89
Myerson, Jonathan 126
Myrddin 187*n*17
"Myron the Magician" 67

Nakada, Masahiko 163
Nakano, Kensyo 83
Nastali, Daniel P. 187*n*1
Native American 178*n*2
The Natural 85
"Natural Born Kissers" 112
NBC 40, 43, 54, 66–67, 76, 80, 85, 87, 91, 94
Neiendorff, John 31
Neitherworld 108
Nennius 96, 122
Neptune 109–**110**
"Neptune's Spatula" 109–**110**, 185*n*11
Nero, Franco 136
The New Adventures of Robin Hood 186*ch*10*n*1
The New Adventures of Superman 64
New Age spirituality 128, 154
The New Batman/Superman Adventures **118**–119
New Dawn 102
New England Knights 103
New Order 101–102
The New Scooby-Doo Mysteries 86
The New Twilight Zone 85, 186*ch*10*n*1
New Year's Day 62, 98, 173–174
New York City 67, 115–116, 164, 183*n*7
Newman, Edwin 106
Nibley, Sloan 67
Nickelodeon 7, 109, 111, 166, 178*n*1
"The Night of No Tomorrow" 94
Nightline 128–129
"Nightmare on Mother Brain's Street" 94–95
Nimmo, Jenny 71, 186*n*25

Nimue 91
Nine Old Men 63
ninja 83, 113, 118
Nintendo 94–95, 102–103
"No Time for Nuts" 155–156
Noble, James 177*n*3
Noble, Maurice 47, 52
Nofziger, Ed 54
Norbert 112
Northern Exposure 186*ch*10*n*1
Norton, Andre 184*ch*7*n*4
Norway 159
Nottingham 121–122
"Nutcracker Suite" 33
"Nuts of the Round Table" 67
Nynyue 30

O of K **44**–45
Octavia 163
October 32nd *see Merlin* (1992 film)
Ogam 163
ogre 49, 66, 147, 152–155, 172
"Oh What a Knight" 178*n*6
Oinkcelot 112
Okouchi, Ichiro 160
Okubo, Atsushi 161
Olive Oyl 38, 55
Oliver, Edna Mae 20
Oliver Twist 37
Olton, Bert 181*n*21, 186*ch*10*n*1
Olwen 71–72, 125–126
The Omen 164
On Moonlight Bay 46
"On My Father's Wings" 144
The Once and Future King see White, T. H.
O'Neil, April 118
Ono, Yoko 106
Opie, Iona 182*ch*4*n*9
Opie, Peter 182*ch*4*n*9
"The Organ Grinder" 179*n*12
orphan 159, 171, 183*n*5; *see also* foundling
Orson Pig 87–88
Orson's Farm see U. S. Acres
Ortenberg, Veronica 177*n*3
Oscar *see* Gobbo (Oscar)
Oscar (Academy Award) 46
Osis of the Liver *see* Sir Osis of the Liver
O'Sullivan, Maureen 12
Oswald the Lucky Rabbit 178*n*6
Otto brothers 112
Overgard, William 114
Ox Ford 161–162
Ozzie Award 76

Pabian, James 31
"Pain Strikes Underdog" 66
Palomides 138
Pan, Peter 114
Pannónia Filmstúdió 97
Pantsalot of Dropseat Manor 41–42

Paramount 38, 43–45
"Parfit, Gentil Knight" 135
Parker, Peter *see* Spider-Man
Parkes, Paul 158
Partner 161–162
Parzival (film) 82
Parzival (medieval German romance) *see* Wolfram von Eschenbach
Patates et dragons 157–158
patriarchy 144
Patten, Fred 183*n*21
"Paws of the Round Table" **89**
PBS 122, 129
Peabody 51
Peabody Award 129
Peabody's Improbable History 51, 54, 120
"The Peanut Vendor" 8, 13
Pedersen, Ted 118
Peet, Bill 37, 59, 62
Peggy 97–98
Pelleas 114
Pelles 99
Pellinore 63, 68
"Pendragon" 116
Penfold 90–91
penguin **89**, 161–163
"Penny Antics" 57
Pent *see* Sir Pent
Pepe le Pew 75
Perceval (Parzival, Percival) 24, 84, 114, 127, 153, 155, 159, 161
Perceval le Gallois see Chrétien de Troyes
Perry Mason 107, 185*n*8
Peter Pan *see* Pan, Peter
Peter Pan & the Pirates see Fox's Peter Pan & the Pirates
Peter Potamus and His Magic Flying Balloon 66
Petra Fina 121
Petunia Pig 74
Phantom of the Flickers 73–76, 184*n*19
Philbin, Regis 106
Phillips, Roz 139
Philomena 55
Philosopher's Stone 117, 170
philter *see* love potion
"Piedmont's Last Jest" 188*n*19
Pierce, Tedd 40–45, 182*ch*3*n*8
"The Pig Who Would Be Queen" 90
Piggy *see* Miss Piggy
pimp cup 164
Pinkley 90
Pinky 107
Pinky and the Brain 105–107, 132
Pinocchio 31
pixilation 184*n*19
PlayStation 104
Plumber's Snake 95
Pocahontas 139, 142
poison 102, 152, 170

Index

The Poke of Zorro 113, 185*n*14
Popeye 5, 35, **38**–39, 41, 54–55, 178*n*2
Popeye 54
Porky Pig 74–75, 79
Porta-Potti 166–167
Potatoes and Dragons see Patates et dragons
Potatoland 157–158
potion 71, 99, 107, 146–148; *see also* love potion
Potter, Harry 153, 157
Pound Puppies and the Legend of Big Paw **95**–97
Pourcel, Didier 156
Powers, Leonard 164
Powys, John Cowper 10
Presto 94
Price, Brian R. 188*n*20
Pride and Prejudice (film) 20
Prince of Foxes 37
The Prince of Thieves 37
Prince Valiant (comic strip) 46, 101–102
Prince Valiant (film) 43, 46
Princess Gwenevere and the Jewel Riders 100, 102–103, 105 184*ch*8*n*2
Prohibition 178*n*3
PSA (public service announcement) 93–94, 184*ch*7*n*2, 185*n*18
psychoanalysis 52, 70, 106, 154–155
Pterry 121
Puck 152
Puppy Power 96–97
Puss in Boots 153–**154**
Putts-a-Lot Merrie Olde Fun Centre *see* Sir Putts-a-Lot Merrie Olde Fun Centre
Pwyll 163, 188*n*17
Pyle, Howard 177*n*4

Quackalot 86
RMS *Queen Elizabeth* 182*n*11
Queen of Faeries 125
Queen of North Galys 30
Queen of the Waste Londes 30
Quentin Durward 43
Quest, Jonny 117
Quest for Camelot 131–132, 141–**143**, 144–**149**, 150–151, 163, 169, 177*n*4, 186*ch*9*n*1, 186*n*2, 186*n*3, 186*n*9, 186*n*10, 186*n*11, 186*n*12, 186*n*13
The Quest for Olwen (1990 animated film) 125–126, 186*n*24
"The Quest for Olwen" (*Jackanory*) 71–72, 186*n*25
The Quest for Olwen (Nimmo) 71–72, 186*n*25
"Quest for the Holy Pail" 109
Quinn, Joanna 126–127, 186*n*26

"Rabbit Hood" 182*ch*3*n*8
"Raging Abe Simpson and His Grumbling Grandson ..." 185*n*13
Ragland T. (Rags) Tiger 40
rape 4, 126–127, 131, 141
Rapunzel 153
"Rasslin' Round" 32
Rathy 163
Read, Arthur 129–130
The Real Adventures of Jonny Quest 117
Reardon, Jim 105
Reaves, Brynne Chandler 115–116
Rebel Without a Cause 52
Recess 110
Red Dwarf 186*ch*10*n*1
Red Knight 127
Reeve, Christopher 131
Regular Show 164
Reimer, Stephen R. 187*n*1
Reitherman, Wolfgang 59, 62–64
Reitho 159
The Reluctant Dragon (Disney film) 18, 36, 106
The Reluctant Dragon (Rankin-Bass series) 65
The Reluctant Dragon & Mr. Toad Show 65
"Renaissance" 167
Renaissance fair *see* fair, reenactment
Renaud, Chris 155
Republican 182*n*14
"The Return of the King" 129–130
R. G. S. *see* Stokes, Robert (R. G. S.)
Riannon 163
Richalot 86
Richard III 43
"Richie of the Round Table" 86
The Richie Rich/Scooby-Doo Show — and Scrappy Too! 86
Riff Raff 66
Rigby 164
Ring of Stones 144
Riot in Juvenile Prison 52
Road Runner 4
Roberts, Rachel 103
Robertson, James 127
Robin 77, 119, 185*n*19
Robin Hood 36, 64, 158, 167, 182*ch*3*n*8
Robinson, Edwin Arlington 10
Robinson, Michael 70–71, 183*n*14
Robinson, T. H. 178*n*7, 178*n*8
Robot Chicken 176
Robotnik 117
Rocket Robin Hood 64
Rockwell, Jake 94
Rocky 51
Rocky and His Friends 51, **53**

Rodgers and Hart 10
Rods of Merlin 79
Roger 164
Roger, Jean-Christophe 157
Rogers, Will 12, 179*n*9, 182*n*5
Rogues of Sherwood Forest 182*n*1
Rohmer, Eric 82
Roman 98, 161–163
Romero, George 82
"Rosebud" 112
Round *see* Sir Round
Rowanne 100–101
Rowlf 90
Roy Rooster 88
Royal Albert Hall 118
Rubbles 65
Ruber 142, 145–149, 186*n*12
Rudish, Paul 109
Ruegger, Tom 128
Rugg, Paul 107
rumba 8, 13
Rumpelstiltskin 153
Rumplesnitz 48, 182*n*14
Runcibel 141
Rup of Figs *see* Sir Rup of Figs
Rusoff, Lou 58
Ryan, Mark 121

S4C 126, 173
Saber 159–**160**, 187*n*10, 187*n*13
Sabrina, The Animated Series 120
Sabrina the Teenage Witch 119–121
Sabrina the Teenage Witch 186*ch*10*n*1
Sacred Sink 95
The Saga of the Viking Women ... 43
Sagramore 12, 24, 55, 71
Saint Joan 182*n*1
Saiyu-ki see Alakazam the Great!
Salda, Michael N. 17–18, 73, 186*n*24, 186*ch*9*n*1, 187*n*3
Salem 120–121
Samurai 80
Sandy 12–13
"Sang 'Em High" 112
Sanrio 89, 121
The Saracen Blade 43
Sarah 121–122
Sárkány és papucs 97–98
Sartin, Hank 179*n*11, 179*n*12
Satan 56–**57**
Sato, Takuya 159
The Saturday Superstar Movie 73, 184*n*19
Saturn 104
Saving Private Ryan 113
Saxon 29–30, 98, 180*n*17
scabbard 160, 187*n*10
"Scared a Lot in Camelot" 77–**78**
Scarlet Pimpernel 113
"The Scarlet Pumpernickel" 75
Schaefer, Bruce 114

Index

Schiel, Thierry 151–152
Schifrin, William 141
Schlesinger, Leon 14, 16, 32, 179*n*15
Schmerlin, Hurlin 120
Schmerlin, Merlin 120
Schneider, Steve 179*n*11, 179*n*15
schooling 48–49, 60–62, 98–99, 103, 109–113, 129–130, 153–155, 161–162, 164–165
Scooby-Doo 77–**78**, 80, 86–87, 177*n*4
Scooby-Doo/Dynomutt Hour 77–**78**
Scotland 92–93, 96, 115, 184*n*5, 185*n*15
Scott, Bill 51–53, 182*n*15, 183*n*16
Scott, Gavin 103, 185*n*3
Scott, Jeffrey 94, 117
Scott, Keith 182*n*15
Scrappy 86–87
"Scrappy's Party" 178*n*2
Scrat 155–156
Scrimshaw 167
Scrolls of Merlin 115
Sea Hag 55, 183*n*17
"Season's Beatings" 163–164
Second Banana 64
The Secret Adventures of Jules Verne 186*ch*10*n*1
"The Secret of Camelot" 141
Sega 104
Seidler, David 141
Servant 159–160, 187*n*10, 187*n*13
"Seventeen Going on Seventy" 70
Shaggy 77–**78**, 86
Shagworthy 77
Shakespeare, William 34, 84, 181*n*25; *see also* Macbeth; Macbeth; *The Merchant of Venice*
"Shave and a Haircut" 8
Shaw, Mel 16, 18, 32, 179*n*4
Sheba 111
Sheehan, Gordon 55–57, 183*n*18
Sheep in the Big City 163–164
Sheldon 88
Sherman 51
Sherman, Richard 59
Sherman, Robert 59
Sherwood 171
Shimizu, Megumi 161
Shining Blade of Leibowitz **166**–167
Shirou 159–160, 187*n*10
Shit 164
Shogi monk 157
Shredder 118
"Shredder's New Sword" 118
Shrek 152–**154**, 155, 187*n*3, 187*n*4
Shrek 187*n*4
Shrek 2 155
Shrek the Third 152–**154**, 155, 187*n*3
Shropshire 49

"Shuffle Off to Buffalo" 179*n*12
Shull, Michael S. 177*n*8, 181*n*1, 181*n*2
Siege of the Saxons 64
Siege Perilous 99, 136
Silver Angel Award 102
Simpson, Abe (Grampa) 185*n*13
Simpson, Bart 112–113
Simpson, Homer 112–113, 169
Simpson, Lisa 113, **169**
Simpson, Marge 112–113, 169
The Simpsons 112–113, **169**, 185*n*13, 185*n*14, 188*n*23
Sinbad 80
Sinestro 80
Singing Sword 46–47, 50–51, 90, 100
Sir Arthur Conan Doyle's The Lost World 186*ch*10*n*1
Sir Cumference 37–38
Sir Fing 108
Sir Gadabout: The Worst Knight in the Land 151
Sir Galahad **39**–40
"Sir Galahad, or The Tomorrow Knight" 52–**53**
Sir Gawain and the Green Knight (2002 animated film) 173–174, 188*n*25
Sir Gawain and the Green Knight (Middle English poem) 23, 84, 173–174, 188*n*25
Sir Gawain and the Green Knight (Middleboe/Lamb script) 188*n*25, 188*n*26
Sir Gery 108
"Sir Gyro de Gearloose" 85–86
"Sir Huckleberry Hound" 48
"Sir Lance a Lot, Knight of the Round Coffee Table" *see* "Lancelot, chevalier de la chaise longue"
"Sir Lancelot" 49–**50**
Sir Loin 108
Sir Loin of Beef 46
Sir Loinsteak 37
Sir Osis of the Liver 44, 46
Sir Pent 108
Sir Putts-a-Lot Merrie Olde Fun Centre 112, 188*n*23
Sir Round 51
Sir Rup of Figs 45
Sir Tifiable 108
"Sir Yaksalot" 105, 107, **175**–**176**
Sirloinalot challenge 113
Skeeter 90
Sklar, Elizabeth S. 177*n*3, 182*ch*3*n*9
Slapczynski, Richard 139
Sleeping Beauty 38–39, 153
Sleeping Beauty 95
Sleeping Beauty's Castle 171
Sliders 186*ch*10*n*1
Slithering Serpent 90
Small, Brendon 167

Smith, Ken 183*n*19
Smith, Pete 165
Smith, Ray 71–72
Smurfs 87
"The Smurfs of the Round Table" 87
Snagglepuss 87
Snooper 87
Snow White 32–33, 153
Snow White and the Seven Dwarfs 19, 22, 31–33, 36
So-So 66
social guidance 56, 93, 183*n*19; *see also* education; juvenile delinquency; toothbrush
Solomon, Charles 16–17, 177*n*8, 179*ch*1*n*15, 179*ch*2*n*4, 181*n*1, 182*n*14
"Sonic Sez" 185*n*18
Sonic the Hedgehog 117–118
Sony Wonder 136, 139, 186*n*6
The Sorcerer's Apprentice 151
Sorceress of the Forest 159
Soul Eater 161–163, 187*n*15
South Cadbury 69–70
South Park 163–164
Space Jam 131–132, 142
"Space Knights of Camelon" 81
The Spaceman and King Arthur see *Unidentified Flying Oddball*
A Spaceman in King Arthur's Court see *Unidentified Flying Oddball*
Spamalot 151
Sparber, Isadore (Izzy) 38–39
"The Spatula and the Stove" *see* "Neptune's Spatula"
"Spell-Bound" 105–107, 175
Spenser, Edmund 184*ch*7*n*4
Spider-Man 66–67, 91
Spider-Man 66
Spider-Man and His Amazing Friends 91
Spielberg, Steven 105, **175**–**176**
Spindle 68
SpongeBob SquarePants 4, 109–**110**, 185*n*11
SpongeBuddy Mania 185*n*11
Sport Billy 88–89
sports: auto racing 37; baseball 37, 41; billiards 41; boxing 37, 39, 41, 54; commentator 37, 39, 41; football 37, 41–42, 103, 111; horse racing 37, 39; referee 38, 42, 54; soccer 88–89
"Sports of the Round Table" 88–89
Springfield 112–113, 188*n*23
Sputnik 47
Square Heads of the Round Table 181*n*3
square table 39, 51, 54, 104, 183*ch*4*n*16
Stab-a-Lot: The Itchy and Scratchy Musical 185*n*13

Index

stage production 9–10, 59, 64–68, 85, 89, 105–107, 151, 155, 161, 164, 167, 183*n*11, 185*n*7, 185*n*13
Stalin 181*n*2
Stanchfield, Steve 183*n*18
Star Wars 81, 85, 126, 168
Starla and the Jewel Riders see *Princess Gwenevere and the Jewel Riders*
Steven Spielberg Presents Animaniacs 105–107, 111, 132, 142, **175–176**, 185*n*8
Steven Spielberg Presents Tiny Toon Adventures 105–106, 132, 185*n*5
Stewart, Alan 184*ch*6*n*3
Stokely Van Camp 181*n*24
Stokes, Jack 69
Stokes, Robert (R. G. S.) 14, **17**, **21**, **25**, 32–33, **34–35**, 179*n*3, 181*n*23, 181*n*24, 183*n*8
Stone of Destiny 116
Stone of Scone 96, 116, 184*ch*7*n*5
Stone of Silence 90
Stonehenge 87, 90–92, 94, 122, 139, 141, 159; see also Bonehenge; Ring of Stones
Sunstar 103
Super Chicken 64
Super Friends 79–81
The Super Globetrotters 80
"The Super Globetrotters vs. Merlo the Magician" 80
The Super Mario Brothers Super Show! 95
Super Samurai 80
Superboy 69, 73; see also Superman
Superman 64, 69, 79–81, **118**–119, 171
Superman Adventures **118**–119
Sutherland, Hal 73
Swamp of Silliness 90
The Sword and the Rose 182*n*1
The Sword in the Stone (book) see White, T. H.
The Sword in the Stone (film) 5, 35, 59–65, 73, 76, 86, 112, 132, 136, 139, 151, 177*n*4, 183*n*10
Sword of Justice 156–157
Sword of Lancelot 64, 68
Sword of Omens **92–93**
Sword of the Valiant 85
sylph 156
Sylvester 74
syndication 40, 49, 54, 64, 66–67, 70, 81–82, 84, 87–88, 91–95, 102, 104–105, 115–116, 156–157, 159, 168, 184*n*19

"The Table Round" 98–99
Tales of Knighthood and Gallantry 44
Taliesin 163
Tamara 103
Taniguchi, Goro 160
Tantris 152; see also Tristan (Tristram)
Tara 157
"Target" **118**–119
Tartakovsky, Genndy 109
taxes 68, 74, 81
Tazewell, Charles 56
TBS 117
Tears to Tiara 163, 187*n*16, 187*n*17, 188*n*18
Technician 161
Technicolor 16
Teenage Bad Girl 182*ch*4*n*10
Teenage Caveman 182*ch*4*n*10
Teenage Crime Wave 182*ch*4*n*10
Teenage Monster 182*ch*4*n*10
Teenage Mutant Ninja Turtles 118
The Teenage Psycho Meets Bloody Mary 182*ch*4*n*10
Teenage Tramp 182*ch*4*n*10
Teenagers from Outer Space 182*ch*4*n*10
teeth 9, 35, 48, **72**–73, 97, 109, 147, 176
Tekwar 186*ch*10*n*1
Tempo 55
"The Ten-Percent Solution" 169
Tennyson 4, 76, 142, 177*n*4
"The Terrible Time Gun" 54–55
"Terror in Time" 91
Tetsuwan Atomu see *Astro Boy*
Thames 116
Thames Television 90
Thanksgiving 70, 76, 78
"There Will Always Be an England" 19, 30
Thiry, Joan 127
"This Trick Will Kill You" 64
Thomas, Edwin 8, 13
Thomas, Gwyn 125–126
Thomas, Jack 166
Thompson, Raymond H. 60
Thorpe, Richard 96
Threadbare 104
The Three Musketeers 37
Three Stooges 181*n*3
"The Three Wishes" 81
Thule 100
Thumb, George Ebenezer 47–48
Thumb, Prunhilda 47–48
Thumb, Tom see Tom Thumb
"Thumbelina" 81
Thumbus of Thumbatten 47
ThunderCats **92–93**
Thurmeier, Michael 155
Tifiable see Sir Tifiable
Till Death Do Us Part 90
Tim the Enchanter 77, 126
"Time Machine" (*The Flintstones*) 65–66
"The Time Machine" (*The Brak Show*) 165
"The Time Trap" 80

time travel 8–10, 12, 15, 42, 44, 46, 51, 54–55, 62, 64–67, 69, 71, 80, 86–92, 95, 103, 108, 111, 115–118, 120–122, 155–156, 160, 163–170, 185*n*15; see also dream; Twain, Mark
The Time Tunnel 186*ch*10*n*1
Timmy 69, 166–167, 176
Tinker Bell 114
Tiny Toons see *Steven Spielberg Presents Tiny Toon Adventures*
"Tips to Remember When Submitting Gags" 178*n*5
Titanic 156
TNT 117
Toadstool 95
Tobias the Dragon 65
Toei Animation 58, 82, 84, 94, 100, 188*n*19
Tolkien, J. R. R. 86
Tom (*Gargoyles*) 115
Tom (*Tom and Jerry*) 88
Tom and Jerry Comedy Show 88
Tom Thumb 47, 51–53, 55–**57**, 124–125, 182*ch*4*n*9, 183*n*18
Tom Thumb (Delfiner cartoon) 124–125
"Tom Thumb" (*Fractured Fairy Tales*) 51–52, 56–57
Tom Thumb in King Arthur's Court 55–**57**, 183*n*18
Tondro, Jason 184*ch*6*n*3
Tony 121
Tony Award 59
Tooter Turtle 54
toothbrush **72**–73, 109, 175–176
"Tootles and the Dragon" 114
Topsy, Prakash 104
Total Television 54
Tower of Excalibur 172
Tower of London 118
toys 3–4, 85, 91, 95, 103, 105, 113, **149**, 187*n*6; see also action figures; games; trading cards
Tracy, Dick 41
trading cards 103, 149
The Tragedy of King Arthur and Robin Hood 167
Transformers 91–92
"Trash of the Titans" 113
Travis, Merle 182*ch*4*n*8
treasury **57**, 67, 77, 80, 111–112, 125, 167
Tristan (Tristram) 20, **82**, 84, 104–105, 114, 151–152, 161, 187*n*2
Tristan + Isolde 151
Tristan & Isolde see *Tristan et Iseut*
Tristan & Isolde: The Lost Legend see *Tristan & Iseult: La légende oubliée*
Tristan and Isolt 82
Tristan et Iseult (1972 film) 183*n*6

209

Index

Tristan & Iseult: La légende oubliée 100, 104–105, 152
Tristan et Iseut 151–152
Tristan und Isolde 82
Tristana 183n6
Tron 95
Trueman, Brian 90
Tube 118
Tufts, Sonny 106
Tundra Productions 132, 139
Tuxedo Sam **89**
Twain, Mark 7, 12–13, 15, 24, 39–40, 42–46, 55, 70–71, 78–79, 81, 86, 91, 112, 160, 181n6, 182ch3n9
Tweety 74–75, 184n18
21st Amendment 178n3
"Twigh School Musical" 163–164
Twin Peaks 186ch10n1
The Twisted Tales of Felix the Cat 111
Twrch Trwyth 96, 126
Tyme 48
Type-Moon 159, 187n13

Ugarov, Valeri 125–126
Ugly Americans 163–164
The Unconquered 37
The Undead 43
The Underdog Show 66
Ungar, Rick 116
Unidentified Flying Oddball 81–82
"United We Stand" 145
UPA 48, 67, 182n14, 183n10
Upright Citizens Brigade 186ch10n1
U. S. Acres 87
Uther 22, 60, 67–68, 74–75, 83–84, 98, 124, 156, 183n3, 183n9

The Vagabond King 43
Valiant 91, 100–***101***, 102
Vallee, Rudy 13
Van Rijsselberge, Jan 157
Vanda 88–89
Vanguard 47
vaudeville 9, 45, 64–65, 81, 105, 107
Velma 77
Venger 94
Videoland 94
Viking 101–102, 159, 185n16
"The Viking Venture" 159
The Vikings 43
V. I. P. 186ch10n1
Viper 103
The Vision of Sir Launfal see Lowell, James Russell
visual novel 159, 163, 187n13
Vita Merlini 186n29
Viviane 136, 138
von Fürstenberg, Veith 82
von Kiss-a-lot 185n13
Vortigern 122–***123***, 124

WABAC 51, 55
Wade Duck 88
Wagner, Robert 46
Wakko 107
Wales 71–72, 100, 122, 125–127, 129, 159, 173
Wanda 164
Wanda the Wise 187n8
Ward, Jay 40, 51–54, 183n15, 183n16
WarGames 107
Warlock 91
Warner, Jack 75
Warmer Brothers 75
Warner Bros. 3, 7–8, 13–14, 16, 20, 32, 41–44, 46–48, 56, 64, 73, 75, 78–79, 105–108, 128, 131–132, 141–142, 144, 146, 148, 150, 177Intro-n8, 177ch1n1, 179ch1n12, 179ch1n15, 179ch2n1, 182ch3n8, 182ch3n10, 182ch4n3, 186n9
"A Warrior Bold" 8, 13–14, 179n14
Wart 59–63, 183n2, 183n4
Watos 163
Watson, Richard Jesse 124–125
Wayne, Bruce *see* Batman
WB 105, 128, 132, 142
WDR 168
Weisman, Greg 115
Wendy 114
Wendy's **149**
West, Mae 178n2
Westminster Abbey 96, 116
"What a Knight" 66
What's Up, Tiger Lily? 58
Wheelmen 151
Whenever 108
"Where There's a Well, There's a Way" 90–91
Whispering Forest 90
"Whistler's Mother-in-Law" 67
White, T. H. 31, 59–62, 76, 86, 136, 177n4, 183n3
White Spirits 163, 188n17, 188n18
"Who Do Voo Doo?" 64
Whopper 96–97
Why We Respect the Law 56
wiccan 136
Wicked Witch 31, 153
"Wife of Bath's Tale" (Quinn) 126–127, 186n26
Wigend 91
Wilbur 16
The Wild One 52
Wile E. Coyote 61, 75
"Will the Real King Arthur Please Stand Up" 70
Williams, Charles 10
Willie McBean and His Magic Machine 175
Willie Whopper 32
Willowmarsh 65

Willy 89
Wilma 65–66
Wilt, David E. 177n8, 181n1, 181n2
Wimpy 55, 57
Winchester 187n8
Winters, Jonathan 183n20
Witch beyond the Waterfall 121–122
The Wizard of Oz 31
"The Wizard's Baker" 163–164
Wolfie 73
Wolfram von Eschenbach 127
Wonder Woman 79, 81, 170–171
Wonderful World of Disney 76
Woodyard, Dennis J. 115, 122, 185n22
Woolery, George W. 78, 177n8
Worcestershire Academy 153–155
World Cup 89
world war 65
World War II 5, 16–17, 19, 30, 32, 35–38, 40–41, 113, 177n8, 179n2, 180n17, 181n1, 181n2
"The World's Affair" 178n2
World's Fair 65, 178n2, 183n7
The World's Greatest Super Friends 81
World's Oldest Woman 128
"Wotta Knight" ***38***–41, 55–58
WottaSnozzle 54–55
Wulf, B. O. *see* B. O. Wulf
Wynn, Ed 8

Xcalibur 156–157, 187n6
Xena: Warrior Princess 186ch10n1

Yakko 107
Yamaguchi, Yuji 159
Yamatoya, Akatumi 161
Yellow Submarine 69
Yihong, Hu 122
Ymadawiad Arthur 100
"The Yodelling Dolphin of Kirkwall" 158
Yogi Bear 87
Yogi's Treasure Hunt 87
Yolen, Jane 122, 185n22
Yosemite Sam 46–47, 74–75, 79
"Young and Healthy" 8, 13, 179n10
A Young Connecticut Yankee in King Arthur's Court 100
Ysbaddaden 71–72, 125–126

Zaslove, Mark 85
Zelda 120–121
Zimbalist, Efrem, Jr. 185n17
Zippo lighter 179n9
Zorak 165
Zorro 113
Zwisohn, Lawrence J. 181n5

www.ingramcontent.com/pod-product-compliance
Ingram Content Group UK Ltd.
Pitfield, Milton Keynes, MK11 3LW, UK
UKHW050527150426
5217IPUK00026B/1834